American Ethnic Writers

MAGILL'S CHOICE

American Ethnic Writers

Volume 3

Gordon Parks, Sr.—Al Young

Appendixes

Indexes

Editors, Revised Edition

The Editors of Salem Press

Editor, First Edition

David Peck

California State University, Long Beach

SALEM PRESS, INC.

Pasadena, California   Hackensack, New Jersey

Cover image: © Ejla/Dreamstime.com

These essays originally appeared in *Issues and Identities in Literature* (1997), edited by David Peck; *Critical Survey of Drama, Second Revised Edition* (2003); *Critical Survey of Long Fiction, Second Revised Edition* (2000); *Critical Survey of Poetry, Second Revised Edition* (2002); *Cyclopedia of World Authors, Fourth Revised Edition* (2003); *Magill Book Reviews* (online); *Magill's Survey of American Literature* (2006); *Masterplots II, African American Literature Series* (1994); *Masterplots II, Women's Literature Series* (1995); *Notable African American Writers* (2006); and *Notable Latino Writers* (2005). New material has been added.

∞ The paper used in these volumes conforms to the American National Standard for Permanence of Paper for Printed Library Materials, Z39.48-1992 (R1997).

Library of Congress Cataloging-in-Publication Data

American ethnic writers / editors, the editors of Salem Press. — Rev. ed.
p. cm. — (Magill's choice)
Includes bibliographical references and index.
ISBN 978-1-58765-462-6 (set : alk. paper) — ISBN 978-1-58765-463-3 (vol. 1 : alk. paper) — ISBN 978-1-58765-464-0 (vol. 2 : alk. paper) — ISBN 978-1-58765-465-7 (vol. 3 : alk. paper) 1. American literature—Minority authors—Bio-bibliography—Dictionaries. 2. Minority authors—United States—Biography—Dictionaries. 3. Ethnic groups in literature—Dictionaries. 4. Minorities in literature—Dictionaries. I. Salem Press.
PS153.M56A414 2008
810.9′920693—dc22

2008018357

First Printing

PRINTED IN CANADA

Contents

Pronunciation Guide

Many of the names of personages covered in *American Ethnic Writers* may be unfamiliar to students and general readers. For these unfamiliar names, guides to pronunciation have been provided upon first mention of the names in the text. These guidelines do not purport to achieve the subtleties of the languages in question but will offer readers a rough equivalent of how English speakers may approximate the proper pronunciation.

Vowel Sounds

Symbol	*Spelled (Pronounced)*
a	answer (AN-suhr), laugh (laf), sample (SAM-puhl), that (that)
ah	father (FAH-thur), hospital (HAHS-pih-tuhl)
aw	awful (AW-fuhl), caught (kawt)
ay	blaze (blayz), fade (fayd), waiter (WAYT-ur), weigh (way)
eh	bed (behd), head (hehd), said (sehd)
ee	believe (bee-LEEV), cedar (SEE-dur), leader (LEED-ur), liter (LEE-tur)
ew	boot (bewt), lose (lewz)
i	buy (bi), height (hit), lie (li), surprise (sur-PRIZ)
ih	bitter (BIH-tur), pill (pihl)
o	cotton (KO-tuhn), hot (hot)
oh	below (bee-LOH), coat (koht), note (noht), wholesome (HOHL-suhm)
oo	good (good), look (look)
ow	couch (kowch), how (how)
oy	boy (boy), coin (koyn)
uh	about (uh-BOWT), butter (BUH-tuhr), enough (ee-NUHF), other (UH-thur)

Consonant Sounds

Symbol	*Spelled (Pronounced)*
ch	beach (beech), chimp (chihmp)
g	beg (behg), disguise (dihs-GIZ), get (geht)
j	digit (DIH-juht), edge (ehj), jet (jeht)
k	cat (kat), kitten (KIH-tuhn), hex (hehks)
s	cellar (SEHL-ur), save (sayv), scent (sehnt)
sh	champagne (sham-PAYN), issue (IH-shew), shop (shop)
ur	birth (burth), disturb (dihs-TURB), earth (urth), letter (LEH-tur)
y	useful (YEWS-fuhl), young (yuhng)
z	business (BIHZ-nehs), zest (zehst)
zh	vision (VIH-zhuhn)

Complete List of Contents

Volume 1

Volume 2

Volume 3

American Ethnic Writers

Gordon Parks, Sr.

Born: Fort Scott, Kansas; November 30, 1912
Died: New York, New York; March 7, 2006

African American

A writer, photographer, musician, composer, and filmmaker, Parks was a highly accomplished African American artist widely regarded as a renaissance man.

Principal works

LONG FICTION: *The Learning Tree*, 1964; *Shannon*, 1981; *Sun Stalker*, 2003; *Eyes with Winged Thoughts*, 2005

POETRY: *Gordon Parks: A Poet and His Camera*, 1968 (poetry and photographs); *Gordon Parks: Whispers of Intimate Things*, 1971 (poetry and photographs); *In Love*, 1971; *Moments Without Proper Names*, 1975 (poetry and photographs); *Arias in Silence*, 1994 (poetry and photographs); *Glimpses Toward Infinity*, 1996 (poetry and photographs); *A Star for Noon: A Homage to Women in Images, Poetry, and Music*, 2000 (poetry, music, and photographs)

SCREENPLAY: *The Learning Tree*, 1969 (adaptation of his novel)

NONFICTION: *Flash Photography*, 1947; *Camera Portraits: The Techniques and Principles of Documentary Portraiture*, 1948; *A Choice of Weapons*, 1966; *Born Black*, 1971; *Flavio*, 1978; *To Smile in Autumn: A Memoir*, 1979; *Voices in the Mirror: An Autobiography*, 1990; *Half Past Autumn: A Retrospective*, 1997; *A Hungry Heart*, 2005

The youngest of fifteen children, Gordon Parks was born on a farm to Sarah Ross Parks and Andrew Jackson Parks. His mother died when he was sixteen, and he was sent to St. Paul, Minnesota, to live with a married sister and her husband. Parks clashed with his brother-in-law, and, within a few weeks of his arrival, he was forced out of the home. With no money or place to live, Parks was on his own in St. Paul, far from familiar territory in Kansas. He tried to continue with his high school classes, but it was difficult: He could only find refuge during the day in the school building or hanging out in a neighborhood pool hall. He finally found work in various jobs, such as hotel busboy, piano playing in a brothel, playing semiprofessional basketball, and even touring with a jazz band.

In 1933, at the age of twenty-one, he joined the Civilian Conservation Corps (CCC) and married Sally Alvis. This marriage, the first of three, produced three children. He continued to work at various jobs, and it was while working as a railroad porter and bar car waiter that he discovered he had a talent for photography. He

Gordon Parks, Sr. (AP/Wide World Photos)

bought a cheap camera and taught himself the basics of photography, practicing by shooting pictures in the poor black neighborhoods of Minneapolis. A series of pictures of ordinary African Americans and their lives in black ghettos that he shot in Chicago received considerable attention and won for him a Julius Rosenwald Fellowship in 1941. He moved to Washington, D.C., where he worked at the Farm Security Administration. Later he became a correspondent for the Office of War Information but never received an overseas assignment.

Between 1944 and 1948, he was part of a team at Standard Oil of New Jersey that made documentaries. In 1948 he became the first African American photographer on staff for *Life* magazine. Between 1949 and 1951, he lived in Paris, France, enjoying the comparatively racially neutral climate there. The Civil Rights movement, however, was getting under way in the United States, and he returned to the States because he wanted to be a part of the struggle. During the 1950's he became involved with film and television production. These experiences made it easier for him to become the first black film director of a major motion picture: He directed the commercially successful *Shaft* in 1971 and *Shaft's Big Score* in 1972.

He had already published a couple of books by 1966, when his autobiographical work *A Choice of Weapons* came out. Between 1966 and 1975, other works, including photographic exhibits, poem collections, essay collections, films, and documentaries were produced. In 1975, at age sixty-three, he married his third wife, Genevieve Young, and published a book of photographs, *Moments Without Proper Names*. His second autobiographical volume, *To Smile in Autumn: A Memoir*, was published in 1979.

Over the years, Parks won wide recognition for his work. Some of the most prestigious honors include a Julius Rosenwald Fellowship in 1941 for his photography, a Notable Book Award from the American Library Association for his autobiographical work *A Choice of Weapons*, the Spingarn Award in 1972, the National Medal of the Arts in 1988, the 2002 induction into the International Photography Hall of Fame and Museum, more than forty honorary degrees, and, in 2002, the Jackie Robinson Foundation Lifetime Achievement Award. In 1995, after years of productive, creative activity, Parks donated his films, photographs, writings, and memorabilia to the United States Library of Congress, where he felt they would be respectfully stored and preserved. In October, 2004, his hometown, Fort Scott, Kansas, honored him with the first Gordon Parks Celebration of Culture and Diversity, a four-day event celebrating Parks's amazing contribution to American culture. In the same year, the Art Institute of Boston awarded him an honorary doctorate of humane letters.

Parks died at age ninety-three from cancer. He was considered a renaissance man, one who truly exemplified his own goal of "not allowing anyone to set boundaries, cutting loose the imagination and then making the new horizons." He will above all be remembered for his photographs for *Life* and other publications, including the iconic "American Gothic," of a black cleaning woman standing in front of an American flag and flanked by a broom and a mop—an ironic commentary on American ideals. He will also be remembered for the film *Shaft*, but his accomplishments extend far beyond these to encompass musical compositions, poetry, journalism, and novels, including *The Learning Tree*, about an adolescent boy from an African American family in a small Kansas town who must deal with racism in the 1920's, and *Shannon*, his first attempt at an adult novel, the story of a New York family and its tragic rise to prominence during the World War I era. He wrote several volumes of poetry, often accompanied by photographs; a collection of essays; a commentary accompanying a traveling exhibit of his photographs; and two technical books on photography.

A Choice of Weapons

Type of work: Autobiography
First published: 1966

A Choice of Weapons is the first of three nonfiction autobiographical works. The other two continue his life through his prominent career as a photographer and filmmaker. This one starts when he is sixteen years old and his mother has died, essentially the point at which his autobiographical novel *The Learning Tree* ends. In *A Choice of Weapons*, he details the clash with his brother-in-law that causes the man to throw him out of the house and describes the nearly destitute life he is forced to live for weeks as a homeless, penniless teenager. Parks goes to school or to a pool hall during the day and rides streetcars at night because he has no place else to spend the nights. He finds a job playing jazz piano at a brothel, which in one way is fortunate: After he hones his skill as a piano player, a white bandleader hears him play and offers him a job touring with his band. Before this opportunity comes along, though, he works at other jobs, as a busboy and a flophouse cleaner. Sometimes he has no work and no money. One such time he actually fights a hungry dog for a pigeon. He wins, plucks the bird, cooks it on an open fire, and eats it. Another time, he has no money and has been stranded in New York City by the very bandleader who recruited him for his piano playing. This time he is forced to make ends meet by working for a drug dealer, delivering dope.

Occasions arise when he is tempted to take the path that is easier and handier, to do something that is immediately profitable but is also either illegal or immoral. Once, when he was still riding the streetcars as a way to spend his homeless nights, he was accosted by a streetcar conductor and he pulled a knife on the man. These tribulations serve to show Parks the limited options available to a young black man in the early 1930's. He could have gone a violent, criminal route; he chose instead to join the Civilian Conservation Corps, get married, become a father, and seek personal as well as financial fulfillment through a career in photography.

His introduction to photography comes about quite implausibly. Working as a railroad porter on a run between St. Paul and Seattle, he becomes fascinated with the photo stories in the *Life* magazines left behind by departing passengers. The work of the Depression-era photographers leads him to decide he can document in pictures the same kinds of things, and, with that in mind, he buys his first camera at a pawnshop in Seattle, Washington. He leaves his film for developing at Eastman Kodak in Minneapolis, and when he picks them up is complimented for their quality and offered his own show if his work continues to improve.

It does, of course, and he soon gets his own exhibit in Chicago and a subsequent chance to work with Roy Stryker at the Farm Security Administration in Washington, D.C. His most famous photograph, "American Gothic," a stark portrait of a black charwoman holding a mop and broom in front of the American flag, is one result of this experience. He goes on to work at *Life* magazine, becoming the first African American to join the staff of a major American magazine. Some of his most striking photojournalistic work is done during this period in his life.

All is not smooth sailing for him, however. He faces prejudice and even violence in the pursuit of his career. Once he is nearly assaulted by three Texans who object to his being kissed on the cheek in public by a white colleague. Then, when Malcolm X is assassinated, the Federal Bureau of Investigation fears Parks and his family might be targeted because of his friendship with Malcolm, and he is persuaded to take his family abroad for safety.

The memoir's title, *A Choice of Weapons*, suggests he is aware of his options and makes a conscious decision to follow his mother's teachings to make his life worthwhile. He chooses not to follow the readily expedient route so often taken by those who are disadvantaged. When he chooses a camera instead of a gun as his weapon against poverty and racism, he has already seen and experienced the side of life that drove other African American men to desperate measures. When he uses his camera to document and display those who have not escaped despair and hopelessness, he begins an odyssey of creative achievement unparalleled by any other African American man of his time.

Voices in the Mirror

Type of work: Autobiography
First published: 1990

Voices in the Mirror takes up Parks's story from where he left off in *To Smile in Autumn*, the second memoir, which opens in 1944, when his career as a photographer blossoms, and ends at the height of his artistry in the late 1970's. *Voices in the Mirror* covers Parks's career from 1978, when he worked as a photographer of the rich and famous and—more significantly for him as an artist—as a photographer of the poor, the downtrodden, and the desperate. The memoir covers several decades of his life as he develops his craft. He works in the world of fashion, taking pictures for *Vogue* magazine, but he also works as a photojournalist at *Life* magazine taking pictures of life in black America and in other parts of the world. One of his more memorable stories captured in photographs is of an impoverished Brazilian boy, Flavio. The photo-essay had such an impact that thousands of dollars were donated to help the boy, who was close to dying, enabling Parks to bring the youth to the United States for treatment and eventual cure.

Parks's encounters with famous people are recorded in some of his best-received portraits. He photographs activists such as Malcolm X and Elijah Muhammed, music and film legends including Duke Ellington, Louis Armstrong, Ingrid Bergman, and Roberto Rossellini, prominent athletes such as Muhammad Ali, artists such as Marcel Duchamp and Alexander Calder, and celebrities such as Gloria Vanderbilt. He conveys the glamour of Paris as well as the often-overlooked misery of Rio de Janeiro and the well-known but ignored, downtrodden, and newly militant section of New York's Harlem. His tales of encounters with the many different segments of national and international society communicate his intent to call attention to their often-undetected or unappreciated significance.

This volume not only records Parks's life during a significant time in his evolution as an artist but also provides insight into an important period of American history. The recounting of the harshness of African American existence during the Civil Rights movement is both informative and fascinating, and it reveals the paradoxes inherent in the oddly distorted African American dream.

Suggested Readings

Berry, Skip. *Gordon Parks*. New York: Chelsea House, 1991.

Donloe, Darlene. *Gordon Parks*. Los Angeles, Calif.: Melrose Square, 1993.

Harnan, Terry. *Gordon Parks: Black Photographer and Film Maker*. Champaign, Ill.: Garrard, 1972.

Home Box Office. *Half Past Autumn: The Life and Works of Gordon Parks*. Videorecording. New York: Author, 2006.

Lamb, Yvonne Shinhoster. "*Life* Photographer and *Shaft* Director Broke Color Barriers." *The Washington Post*, March 8, 2006.

Moore, Deedee. "Shooting Straight: The Many Worlds of Gordon Parks." *Smithsonian* 20 (April, 1989): 66-77.
Parks, Gordon, Sr. "How It Feels to Be Black." *Life*, August 16, 1963.
Turk, Midge. *Gordon Parks*. New York: Crowell, 1971.

Contributor: Jane L. Ball

Suzan-Lori Parks

BORN: Fort Knox, Kentucky; May 10, 1963

AFRICAN AMERICAN

The first African American woman to receive the Pulitzer Prize in drama, Parks regarded the achievement as more than personal: "And anytime America recognizes a member of a certain group for excellence . . . it's a great moment for American culture."

PRINCIPAL WORKS

DRAMA: *The Sinner's Place*, pr. 1984, pb. 1995; *Betting on the Dust Commander*, pr. 1987, pb. 1995; *Imperceptible Mutabilities in the Third Kingdom*, pr. 1989, pb. 1995; *The Death of the Last Black Man in the Whole Entire World*, pr. 1990, pb. 1995; *Devotees in the Garden of Love*, pr. 1991, pb. 1995; *The America Play*, pr. 1993, pb. 1995; *The America Play, and Other Works*, pb. 1995; *Venus*, pr. 1996, pb. 1997; *In the Blood*, pr. 1999, pb. 2000; *Fucking A*, pr. 2000, pb. 2001; *The Red Letter Plays*, pb. 2001 (includes *In the Blood* and *Fucking A*); *Topdog/Underdog*, pr., pb. 2001

LONG FICTION: *Getting Mother's Body*, 2003

RADIO PLAYS: *Pickling*, 1990; *The Third Kingdom*, 1990; *Locomotive*, 1991

SCREENPLAYS: *Anemone Me*, 1990; *Girl 6*, 1996

Suzan-Lori Parks was born in Fort Knox, Kentucky, in 1963, the daughter of a career army officer. She spent her early childhood in several cities across the United States and lived in Germany, where she attended high school. She began writing short stories as a third grader and continued to focus on prose writing until her undergraduate years at Mount Holyoke College in Massachusetts. There, she met the distinguished author and essayist James Baldwin, who recognized her gift for dialogue and suggested that she explore drama.

Parks wrote her first play, *The Sinner's Place*, in 1984 as a student at Mount Holyoke. Though she earned an honors citation for her work, the college's theater department refused to stage the play. Parks graduated with honors in 1985 and moved to London for a year to study acting. *Betting on the Dust Commander*, her first play to be produced in New York City, debuted in 1987. Two years later, Parks received an Obie Award for *Imperceptible Mutabilities in the Third Kingdom*, and *The New York Times* named Parks the most promising playwright of 1989.

Following the successful production of *The Death of the Last Black Man in the Whole Entire World* at the Brooklyn Arts Council's BACA Downtown Theatre in

Suzan-Lori Parks (AP/Wide World Photos)

1990, Parks produced her next two plays, *Devotees in the Garden of Love* and *The America Play* on smaller stages in Lexington, Kentucky, and Dallas, Texas, respectively. *The America Play* later opened Off-Broadway at the Joseph Papp Public Theater in New York City in 1994. Parks earned a second Obie Award in 1996, for her play *Venus*, which also debuted at the Joseph Papp Public Theater. Also in 1996, Parks wrote the screenplay for director Spike Lee's film *Girl 6*.

The productions of *In the Blood*, which was nominated for the Pulitzer Prize in drama in 2000, and *Fucking A*, both of which draw on elements in Nathaniel Hawthorne's classic novel, *The Scarlet Letter* (1850), continued to earn for Parks wide critical acclaim. She received the prestigious Guggenheim Fellowship in 2000 and the MacArthur Fellowship in 2001. Parks's growing reputation as a brilliant young playwright reached new heights in 2001 with the production of *Topdog/Underdog*. The play opened on July 22, 2001, at the Joseph Papp Public Theater in New York City to rave reviews and earned for Parks the Pulitzer Prize in drama in 2002, garnering her the further distinction of being the first African American woman to win that honor. *Topdog/Underdog* opened on Broadway in April of 2002, the first Broadway opening for an African American woman since Ntozake Shange, whose *for colored girls who have considered suicide/ when the rainbow is enuf* opened in 1976.

"I think it's a great moment for all African-American women writers," Parks has explained about becoming the first African American woman to receive the

Pulitzer Prize in drama. "And anytime America recognizes a member of a certain group for excellence—one that has not traditionally been recognized—it's a great moment for American culture." Parks married Paul Oscher, a blues musician, in 2001, and joined the faculty of the California Institute of the Arts in Valencia, California, as the director of the Audrey Skirball-Kenis Theatre Projects Writing for Performance program.

Imperceptible Mutabilities in the Third Kingdom

TYPE OF WORK: Drama
FIRST PRODUCED: 1989, pb. 1995

Rather than separating her first major play into traditional acts, Parks created four separate stories to provide a nonlinear and sometimes surreal look at aspects of the African American experience in her *Imperceptible Mutabilities in the Third Kingdom*.

"Snails," the first section of the play, looks at a contemporary group of women who possess two names, one they have chosen and another that has been imposed on them. The second section, "Third Kingdom," re-creates the tragic Middle Passage, through which enslaved Africans journeyed on their way to America, and the details of which are narrated by characters such as Kin-Seer, Us-Seer, and Over-Seer. "Open House," the third section, depicts the life of Aretha Saxon, a black servant/slave in the household of the white Saxon family. Aretha's departure from the family is occasioned by the removal with pliers of all of her teeth. The play's final section, "Greeks," is a modern interpretation of Homer's *Odyssey* (c. 750 B.C.E.; English translation, 1614), with Mr. Seargant Smith in the role of Odysseus. Hoping to earn "his Distinction" in the army, Seargant Smith spends most of his life away from his family, who await his return and the honor he hopes to bring back with him.

The four stories in *Imperceptible Mutabilities in the Third Kingdom* depict characters whose identity and culture are marginalized by others. From the three women in "Snails," whose identities are studied and inevitably altered by the invasive Lutsky, to Miss Faith's extraction of Aretha Saxon's teeth in an act that functions metaphorically as a means of extracting Aretha from the Saxon family history, Parks dramatizes the struggle of African Americans against cultural, historical, and linguistic sabotage. A critical and popular success, *Imperceptible Mutabilities in the Third Kingdom* earned for Parks her first Obie Award for best new American play. *The New York Times* also named her 1989's most promising young playwright.

Venus

Type of work: Drama
First produced: 1996, pb. 1997

Venus received mixed reviews for its portrayal of an African woman whose unconventional physiognomy becomes the basis for her exhibition in a traveling sideshow in Europe. Parks based her play on a historical character, Saartjie Baartman, a South African woman whose body was displayed publicly in London and Paris in the early nineteenth century. Dubbed the Hottentot Venus, Baartman became a popular spectacle for white audiences who were fascinated and revolted by her appearance. After her death, Baartman's sexual organs and buttocks were preserved and housed in the Musée de l'Homme in Paris until the late twentieth century.

As the play opens, Venus is a popular attraction in Mother Showman's traveling show of Nine Human Wonders in London. Because slavery has been outlawed in England, Mother Showman's captivity of Venus sparks a debate about whether such exhibitions constitute slavery. Venus eventually escapes to Paris, where she falls under the influence of the Baron Docteur, who falls in love with Venus but also assures his colleagues that he intends to make her the object of scientific study. A twisted custody battle ensues as Mother Showman and Baron Docteur fight over who has the right to exhibit Venus.

In the character of Venus, Parks explores the objectification of human beings, and particularly African Americans, whose humanity was denied in the nineteenth century (and beyond) on the basis of pseudoscientific theories that reinforced prejudices against physical and cultural difference. Venus, a woman who desires to be treated with love and respect, becomes an oddity in a circus sideshow, reduced to little more in the public consciousness than her "great heathen buttocks."

In the Blood

Type of work: Drama
First produced: 1999, pb. 2000

A modern interpretation of Nathaniel Hawthorne's novel *The Scarlet Letter*, *In the Blood* depicts a homeless woman's struggle to care for herself and her family. Hester, La Negrita, and her five children, all from different fathers, live under a bridge, making what little money they have from collecting cans. Hester spends much of her time practicing her writing (she knows only the letter *A*). As her health declines, Hester appeals for assistance to a street doctor, her welfare caseworker, a former lover and father of her first child, and eventually a local reverend, who is the father of her youngest child.

The actors who portray Hester's five children also double as adult characters. In a series of stage confessions that resemble the chorus of a Greek tragedy, these characters (Amiga Gringa, Chilli, The Doctor, The Welfare Lady, and Reverend D) explain the ways in which they have taken advantage of Hester, who has been sexually exploited by almost everyone whom she knows.

In the Blood is a hopeless tale of a woman undone by poverty and a social system that cannot meet her needs. Individuals in a position to help Hester can think only of how to use her. The word "slut," scrawled on the wall of Hester's makeshift home under the bridge in the play's opening scene, serves a purpose similar to Hawthorne's scarlet letter on Hester Prynne's chest. Both Hesters are defined almost exclusively by what their societies perceive as aberrant sexuality. When every means of salvation is exhausted, Hester is left, in the final scene of the play, with the word "slut," this time on the lips of her oldest child. Hester's murder of her son Jabber at the end of the play functions as an attempt to efface the word, and the identification, both of which have followed her throughout the play. A critical and popular success, *In the Blood* was named a finalist for the 2000 Pulitzer Prize in drama.

Topdog/Underdog

Type of work: Drama
First produced: 2001, pb. 2001

Departing from the unorthodox staging and characterization of her previous plays, Parks presented what appears on the surface to be a traditional tale of sibling rivalry in *Topdog/Underdog*, which opened at the Joseph Papp Public Theater on July 22, 2001, and opened on Broadway at the Ambassador Theater in New York less than a year later. However, Parks links the struggle of her two characters, named Lincoln and Booth, to more complex and historical struggles of race, family, and identity.

The two brothers, Lincoln and Booth, share a seedy urban apartment. Lincoln, a former street hustler whose skill at the card game three-card monte is legendary, now works at an arcade where he impersonates Abraham Lincoln for patrons who pay money to reenact his assassination. Booth, who aspires to his brother's greatness at three-card monte, relies on Lincoln's paychecks and whatever he can steal to make ends meet.

As Lincoln and Booth, so named as a joke by their father, try to plan for their future, they confront the realities of the past: their abandonment by their parents and the buried animosities toward each other. In the play's final scene, Booth flies into a rage when Lincoln bests him at three-card monte, thereby winning the family legacy (five hundred dollars rolled in a stocking) left to each son when their parents fled. Lincoln's violent end is foreshadowed by his job at the arcade and by his and Booth's names. How each brother accepts and realizes the roles imposed by family history, circumstance, and the inherent opposition of their names, however, makes the play a deeply compelling one. In 2002, shortly after its debut on Broadway, *Topdog/Underdog* earned for Parks the Pulitzer Prize in drama.

Suggested Readings

Brown-Gillory, Elizabeth. "Reconfiguring History: Migration, Memory, and (Re)Membering in Suzan-Lori Parks's Plays." In *Southern Women Playwrights: New Essays in Literary History and Criticism*, edited by Robert L. McDonald and Linda Rohrer Paige. Tuscaloosa: University of Alabama Press, 2002.

Frieze, James. "*Imperceptible Mutabilities in the Third Kingdom*: Suzan-Lori Parks and the Shared Struggle to Perceive." *Modern Drama* 41, no. 4 (Winter, 1998): 523.

Garrett, Shawn-Marie. "The Possession of Suzan-Lori Parks." *American Theatre* 17, no. 8 (October, 2000): 22.

Parks, Suzan-Lori. "Interview with Suzan-Lori Parks." Interview by Shelby Jiggetts. *Callaloo* 19, no. 2 (1996): 309-317.

Pochoda, Elizabeth. "I See Thuh Black Card . . . ?" *Nation* 274, no. 20 (May 27, 2002): 36.

Wilmer, S. E. "Restaging the Nation: The Work of Suzan-Lori Parks." *Modern Drama* 43, no. 3 (Fall, 2000): 442-452.

Contributor: Philip Bader

Ann Petry

Born: Old Saybrook, Connecticut; October 12, 1908
Died: Old Saybrook, Connecticut; April 28, 1997

African American

Petry was the first African American woman to sell over a million copies of a novel and the first African American woman to publish a collection of short stories.

Principal works

CHILDREN'S LITERATURE: *The Drugstore Cat*, 1949; *Harriet Tubman: Conductor on the Underground Railroad*, 1955; *Tituba of Salem Village*, 1964; *Legends of the Saints*, 1970

LONG FICTION: *The Street*, 1946; *Country Place*, 1947; *The Narrows*, 1953

SHORT FICTION: *Miss Muriel, and Other Stories*, 1971

Ann Lane Petry (PEH-tree) was born in Old Saybrook, Connecticut, to one of the town's two African American families. Her father owned the village drugstore. A 1931 graduate of the University of Connecticut College of Pharmacy, for a time Petry operated the pharmacy in Old Lyme, one of two family-owned pharmacies. Petry grew up listening to stories of the African American experience told by family, visiting friends, and relatives.

In 1938 Ann Lane was married to George Petry; they moved to New York City. Petry left the pharmacy to follow a family tradition of storytelling. She worked for two Harlem newspapers, the *Amsterdam News* and *People's Voice*. Petry's first published work, "Marie of the Cabin Club," a tale of romance and suspense, appeared under the pseudonym Arnold Petri in a Baltimore weekly newspaper.

In 1943, "On Saturday the Siren Sounds at Noon," appeared in *Crisis*, a magazine founded by W. E. B. Du Bois. This story brought her to the attention of a book editor, who encouraged Petry to apply for the Houghton Mifflin Literary Fellowship. In 1945, Petry entered and won the award. Her entry would become the first chapters of the novel *The Street*.

Petry returned to Old Saybrook in 1947, the debut year of her second novel, *Country Place*. In 1949, Petry launched a career as a children's and young adults' writer with *The Drugstore Cat*. Other works for children and young adults include *Harriet Tubman, Conductor on the Underground Railroad*, *Tituba of Salem Village*, and *Legends of the Saints*.

Although in the later part of her life Petry left the ivory-tower life of university and publishing centers, she continued to write short stories while she published novels and juvenile literature. Most of these stories were first published in African American journals. With one previously unpublished story, "Mother Africa," these stories were collected in *Miss Muriel, and Other Stories*. The core themes of her writing include racial identity, racism in America, and the experience of the African American woman. She did return to universities occasionally, holding a visiting professorship at the University of Hawaii in 1974-1975, and in 1977 she was awarded a grant from the National Endowment for the Arts. Boston's Suffolk University awarded her a D.Litt. degree in 1983. She died in a convalescent home.

The Street

Type of work: Novel
First published: 1946

The Street portrays the economic plight of African Americans in northern cities. Themes of the novel include the problem of latchkey children, single parenting, and sexual oppression. This novel is perhaps the first written by an African American woman that probes the triple threat to African American women of race, gender, and class.

Much of the action of *The Street* takes place on 116th Street in Harlem in 1944. The central character, Lutie Johnson, leaves an unemployed womanizing husband and a nice frame house in Jamaica, New York. She moves to Harlem with her eight-year-old son, Bub. Lutie moves to the city to realize a comfortable life. Instead of an independent and prosperous life in New York City, Lutie finds herself living in a tenement. The janitor, William Jones, is a sociopath who lusts after Lutie. A major presence on the street is Mrs. Hedges, who runs a whorehouse. Qualified for clerical or secretarial employment, Lutie can find only menial work in a laundry. Instead of ownership of a piece of the American Dream, Lutie finds herself trapped in a nightmare.

Lutie becomes fair game for males. William makes advances and tries to molest Lutie. Junto, the white business partner of Mrs. Hedges, tries to seduce Lutie. Boots Smith, a musician in a bar that Junto owns, charms Lutie with visions of a better life with him. Boots lures her to his apartment, where he attempts to rape her. In an effort to ward off Boots's rape, Lutie kills him. Vowing revenge on Lutie, William tricks Bub into stealing and gets him in trouble with the law. Disillusioned and defeated, Lutie abandons Bub and runs away to Chicago.

Sexual politics drive the novel and rest on a concept that African American women are sexual prey. Negative sexual imagery of Lutie and by extension of all African American women is held by black and white males and by white females. A mixture of race and gender politics pushes Lutie over the edge. Lutie represents all the walking wounded of 116th Street and all of Harlem's downtrodden residents. *The Street* is not merely a graphic portrayal of what it means to be female and to be poor; it is also a story of protest and defeat. *The Street* presents the African American woman as the center of the family and the community. She shoulders the moral responsibilities of the race.

Miss Muriel, and Other Stories

Type of work: Short fiction
First published: 1971

While Petry's reputation rests primarily on her novels, she saw herself quite differently at the start of her career:

> I set out to be a writer of short stories and somehow ended up as a novelist—possibly because there simply wasn't room enough within the framework of the short story to do the sort of thing I wanted to do.

Yet the pieces in *Miss Muriel, and Other Stories*, written over the course of several decades, provide a compact and provocative introduction to her imaginative concerns, chief among them her sensitivity to racism's psychological as well as material consequences.

"Like a Winding Sheet"

Type of work: Short fiction
First published: 1971, in *Miss Muriel, and Other Stories*

In the prize-winning story "Like a Winding Sheet," she depicts the physical and mental toll exacted by the nature of work in an industrial society where laborers are treated as interchangeable machines. The story dramatizes how the corrosive humiliations of prejudice, when added to work stresses, can trigger blind and catastrophic violence. A husband's inability to challenge the string of racist assaults on his dignity delivered both during and after his exhausting night shift at a World War II defense plant not only make him incapable of imagining benign white behavior (even in the face of apologies) but also cause him to respond to his wife's affectionate teasing with the beating he is forbidden to direct at his real oppressors. While racism provides the context for his rage, however (her unwitting use of the word "nigger" echoing the hostile epithet regularly used against him by the outside world), his reaction exposes the starkness of the struggle between male and female in Petry's world and the sobering betrayals it can provoke. The title image begins as the bedsheet in which he has tossed and turned all day in a futile effort to sleep, but his wife jokingly casts it as a burial linen—a reference ironically appropriate to his sense of himself as the walking dead. By story's end, that reference has assumed sinister dimensions as he feels trapped by the violence he is committing but cannot control, "and he thought it was like being enmeshed in a winding sheet."

"In Darkness and Confusion"

Type of work: Short fiction
First published: 1971, in *Miss Muriel, and Other Stories*

"In Darkness and Confusion" fictionalizes the Harlem riot of 1943, an event sparked by the wounding of a black soldier whose uniform provided scant protection on his own home front. The story's protagonist, William Jones, a drugstore porter who, despite endless humiliations, has worked hard all of his life to secure a better world for his son Sam, suddenly loses that son to the wartime draft and the dangers of a Jim Crow world at the southern training camp to which he is sent. When Sam, who once aspired to college and his share of the American Dream, protests an order to move to the back of the bus and then shoots the aggressive military police officer who gave it, he is court-martialed and sentenced to twenty years of hard labor.

As Jones broods over this news in a Harlem bar, he watches as another uniformed black G.I., this one standing in the supposedly more egalitarian north, tries to help a black woman being beaten by a white policeman, punches the lawman, runs, and is summarily gunned down. Jones erupts into a violence ignited by grief and rage and becomes the leader of a mob. When his churchgoing wife learns of their son's fate, she, too, turns to retributive action with an explosive passion that kills her: Her religion proves unable to provide her with the strength to resume her burden and go on with her life. Nor is the mob's looting of local merchants legitimized, for it is produced by the intoxicating siren song of white capitalist materialism, with which the culture regularly deflects attention from matters of real social justice. The riot leaves Jones more completely bereft than he had been before, for it literally costs him his heart and soul, even as it finally allows him to understand the anomie of his disaffected teenage niece, who has baldly scorned his lifetime of exhausting effort for the whites, who in the end allow them "only the nigger end of things."

"The New Mirror"

Type of work: Short fiction
First published: 1971, in *Miss Muriel, and Other Stories*

Petry as skillfully evokes the impact of racism on the black bourgeoisie as she does on the proletariat, and in several tales she demonstrates how a lifetime of belittlement and intimidation can erode one's ability to act ethically in the world. In "Miss Muriel" and "The New Mirror," Petry creates a black family much like her own—the Layens are professionals who own the pharmacy in a small New England town. The adolescent girl who narrates these tales speaks of "the training in issues of race" she has received over the years, not only through the casual bigotries she has witnessed but also through the painful self-consciousness of respectable people

Ann Petry (AP/Wide World Photos)

like her parents, whose behavior is a continual exercise in refuting cultural stereotypes while carefully preserving proudly held racial loyalties. In "The New Mirror" the ironies are more overt, cleaner. Mr. Layen's decision to take a day off to outfit himself with a new pair of false teeth leads his unknowing wife to an excruciating encounter with police, from whom she withholds her fear that the absent Layen may have become another black man who deserts his family as a delayed response to a lifetime of indignities within the white patriarchal social order. Layen's surprising secrecy leads his daughter to realize that even securing a new set of teeth subjects a black male to humiliation, in this case taking the form of the grinning Sambos and toothless Uncle Toms he fears his dental problems will call to mind. The child learns to use the codes by which the black middle class shields itself from white contempt—just as she shoulders her own share of the burden of always acting with an eye on the reputation of "the Race": She thus learns why "all of us people with this dark skin must help hold the black island inviolate."

"The Necessary Knocking on the Door"

Type of work: Short fiction
First published: 1971, in *Miss Muriel, and Other Stories*

In "The Necessary Knocking on the Door" a similar loss of agency is made bitingly ironic by the context in which Alice Knight's dilemma unfolds: A participant at a conference about the role of Christianity in the modern world, she finds herself unable to master her dislike for a white woman dying in the hotel room across the hall from hers—a woman who had earlier in the day refused to be seated next to a "nigger" and had thus awakened in Alice the bitterness that a lifetime of such indignities has nurtured. Her hardened heart is jolted the next day by news of the woman's death during the night—and her own guilty knowledge that she alone had heard the woman's distress but had let the hated epithet reduce her to that "animal," "outcast," "obscene" state it implies—not because it had been leveled at her but because she had let it rob her of her Christian commitment to do good to those who harm her. Even her own dreams indict Alice: "The octopus moonlight" pitilessly asserts, "Yours is the greater crime. A crime. A very great crime. It was a crime. And we were the witnesses." Like other African American writers before and since, Petry warns that prejudice delivers its most sinister harm when it saps its victims' capacity for decency and compassion and enlists them in the service of a gospel of irreparable division. In these stories Petry vividly captures the spiritual anguish of discovering that one's own grievances can weaken rather than deepen one's moral courage.

"The Bones of Louella Brown"

Type of work: Short fiction
First published: 1971, in *Miss Muriel, and Other Stories*

Her handling of white perspectives on racism is more unyielding. The absurdities into which segregationist practices lead multiracial societies (including the pseudosciences hunting frantically for physical evidence of racial "difference") are lampooned in "The Bones of Louella Brown." The most prestigious family in Massachusetts, the Bedfords, find their plans to build a chapel for its deceased members compromised when an undertaker's assistant confuses the bones of an African American maid with the sole noblewoman in their clan and, because of the "shocking" similarities of hair, teeth, height, and bone mass between the two skeletons, cannot differentiate the two. That alone is newsworthy enough to attract a Boston reporter sniffing for scandal, but the story gets juicier when it becomes clear there is every likelihood that the segregation that has been a hallmark of the cemetery in question will be permanently breached once it can no longer guarantee that "black" bones will not commingle in the same park with "white" bones. After Mrs. Brown makes a series of ghostly visitations to principals in the story, they decide to acknowledge the truth with an epitaph explaining that either woman (or both) may lie in the crypt, along with the admission of their common humanity: "They both wore the breastplate of faith and love, and for a helmet, the hope of salvation." Here, too, Petry moves her reader beyond social contexts and into metaphysical ones by reminding readers that this story of dry bones (an unmistakable homage to a favorite trope of black oral tradition) is also a meditation on mortality itself, which exposes such preoccupation with earthly pecking orders for the consummate folly it is.

"The Migraine Workers"

Type of work: Short fiction
First published: 1971, in *Miss Muriel, and Other Stories*

"The Migraine Workers" offers another example of white protagonists brought up short in the knowledge of their moral blindness in following the unquestioned attitudes of a lifetime. Pedro Gonzalez, proud owner of a successful truckstop, suddenly finds himself staring into a trailer full of migrant laborers exuding a human misery more palpable than anything he has ever encountered. Outraged by the black driver, who blithely explains how he usually hides such scenes from public scrutiny, Pedro feeds the people with the surplus food left on his premises by other haulers. When he later discovers that an elderly man from the crew has hidden himself in the area and is living off what he can scavenge from the truckstop, his first impulse is to have the man removed by the police. It is only when his longtime assistant challenges his callousness and points to the resources they could easily spare for the man's upkeep that Pedro realizes how his own fleshy body indicts him of complicity in a system of polarized haves and have-nots: migraine-producing epiphanies indeed in the land of equal opportunity.

"Mother Africa"

Type of work: Short fiction
First published: 1971, in *Miss Muriel, and Other Stories*

Other stories in the collection evoke the mysterious private centers of grief hidden in the human heart: "Olaf and His Girl Friend" and "Solo on the Drums" show Petry's interest in African American music as an exquisite, untranslatable evocation of that pain. "Mother Africa" introduces Emanuel Turner, another of Petry's junk men, whose business indicts the acquisitive mandate of American consumer culture. Years earlier, the loss of his wife and baby in childbirth had robbed him of any further desire for self-improvement; as a junk dealer he is free from anxious adherence to other people's standards of worth or accomplishment, and because he is his own man, he is a welcome figure to those around him. All that changes when a friend blesses him with the huge sculpture of a female nude being discarded by a wealthy white woman. The statue seduces Turner back into a realm of self-conscious striving as he tries to live up to its grandeur; in the process he loses his liberty and the easy rapport he has had with his neighbors. Convinced that she is a mythic evocation of Africa itself, he resents the prudish efforts of others to clothe her as missionaries had once done to his ancestors. Thus he is stunned to learn that this dark madonna is not a black woman at all but a white woman—the oxidized metal had misled him.

By parodying the assumed black male obsession with white women in this way, Petry implies that the real hunger at work is for authentic enunciation of the African

American experience, a hunger left unsatisfied when Turner hurriedly rushes to sell the piece for scrap. In succumbing to the desire to make a world fit for his queenly companion, Turner submits himself for the first time in twenty-five years to the pressures of conformity and material acquisition. Is it love that so compromises him, or are the statue's racial associations Petry's warnings against the lure of cultural standards derived from the spiritually bankrupt spheres of white consumer capitalism?

Suggested Readings

Bell, Bernard. "Ann Petry's Demythologizing of American Culture and Afro-American Character." In *Conjuring: Black Women, Fiction, and Literary Tradition*, edited by Marjorie Pryse and Hortense J. Spillers. Bloomington: Indiana University Press, 1985.

Clark, Keith. "A Distaff Dream Deferred? Ann Petry and the Art of Subversion." *African-American Review* 26 (Fall, 1992): 495-505.

Ervin, Hazel Arnett, and Hilary Holladay, eds. *Ann Petry's Short Fiction: Critical Essays*. Westport, Conn.: Praeger, 2004.

Gross, Theodore. "Ann Petry: The Novelist as Social Critic." In *Black Fiction: New Studies in the Afro-American Novel Since 1945*, edited by A. Robert Lee. New York: Barnes and Noble, 1980.

Hernton, Calvin. "The Significance of Ann Petry." In *The Sexual Mountain and Black Women Writers*. New York: Doubleday, 1987.

Washington, Gladys. "A World Made Cunningly: A Closer Look at Ann Petry's Short Fiction." *CLA Journal* 30 (September, 1986): 14-29.

Wilson, Mark. "A *MELUS* Interview: Ann Petry—The New England Connection." *MELUS* 15 (Summer, 1988): 71-84.

Contributors: Muriel W. Brailey and Barbara Kitt Seidman

Marge Piercy

Born: Detroit, Michigan; March 31, 1936

Jewish

Piercy is known for her political, feminist novels, which often feature women protagonists and occasionally draw on her Jewish roots.

Principal works

DRAMA: *The Last White Class: A Play About Neighborhood Terror*, pr. 1978 (with Ira Wood)

LONG FICTION: *Going Down Fast*, 1969; *Dance the Eagle to Sleep*, 1970; *Small Changes*, 1973; *Woman on the Edge of Time*, 1976; *The High Cost of Living*, 1978; *Vida*, 1980; *Braided Lives*, 1982; *Fly Away Home*, 1984; *Gone to Soldiers*, 1987; *Summer People*, 1989; *He, She, and It*, 1991 (also known as *Body of Glass*, 1992); *The Longings of Women*, 1994; *City of Darkness, City of Light*, 1996; *Storm Tide*, 1998 (with Ira Wood); *Three Women*, 1999; *The Third Child*, 2003; *Sex Wars: A Novel of the Turbulent Post-Civil War Period*, 2005

POETRY: *Breaking Camp*, 1968; *Hard Loving*, 1969; *Four-Telling*, 1971 (with Bob Hershon, Emmett Jarrett, and Dick Lourie); *To Be of Use*, 1973; *Living in the Open*, 1976; *The Twelve-Spoked Wheel Flashing*, 1978; *The Moon Is Always Female*, 1980; *Circles on the Water: Selected Poems of Marge Piercy*, 1982; *Stone, Paper, Knife*, 1983; *My Mother's Body*, 1985; *Available Light*, 1988; *Mars and Her Children*, 1992; *Eight Chambers of the Heart*, 1995; *What Are Big Girls Made Of? Poems*, 1997; *The Art of Blessing the Day: Poems with a Jewish Theme*, 1999; *Early Grrrl*, 1999 (also known as *Written in Bone: The Early Poems of Marge Piercy*, 1998); *Colors Passing Through Us*, 2003

NONFICTION: *Parti-Colored Blocks for a Quilt: Poets on Poetry*, 1982; *The Earth Shines Secretly: A Book of Days*, 1990; *So You Want to Write: How to Master the Craft of Writing Fiction and the Personal Narrative*, 2001 (with Ira Wood); *Sleeping with Cats: A Memoir*, 2002; *Pesach for the Rest of Us: Making the Passover Seder Your Own*, 2007

EDITED TEXT: *Early Ripening: American Women's Poetry Now*, 1987

Marge Piercy (PEER-see), a daughter of the Jewish millwright Robert Piercy and his wife, Bert Bunnin Piercy, grew up in a primarily African American, working-class Detroit neighborhood. Coming from a poor white family, she early realized that she was a minority member of her community, and this sense of minority status remained with her, in various forms, throughout her life. As a child Piercy learned to escape feelings of loneliness through reading. She was the first member of her family to go to college. More important, she broke from the pattern most of her friends followed, that of marrying young and often unwisely, having too many children, being dependent and docile, and living life as housewives who, as Piercy says in some of her poems, are property, like dogs with tags.

Piercy was an outstanding student who during her undergraduate career at the University of Michigan won the coveted Hopgood Prize in writing several times. After receiving a bachelor's degree in 1957 she continued her studies at Northwestern University, where she received a master's degree in 1958. Piercy realized early that her future was in writing, but it took a decade before she was able to support herself as a writer.

After completing her education Piercy supported herself as well as she could with odd jobs that left time for writing. During this period of great social unrest in the United States, particularly in Detroit, her hometown, she was an organizer for the radical Students for a Democratic Society (SDS) and active in the Civil Rights movement that was developing its own strong rhetoric. As the decade advanced, however, Piercy came to realize that SDS and the Civil Rights movement were both based on a paradigm of male supremacy that she could not accept. By the end of the decade she had become a committed feminist. Because of her work in this arena many critics came to view her writing almost exclusively in its political rather than its artistic context.

Her first six novels, each with feminist protagonists, were rejected by every publisher to whom she sent them, mostly because of the strident note of feminism. In 1968, however, *Breaking Camp*, her first collection of poems, appeared, in which she makes statements similar to those in the rejected novels. About the same time the novel *Going Down Fast*, too, found a publisher, partly because Piercy was beginning to establish a reputation, but partly because this novel has a male protagonist and lacks the earlier "militant" tone.

Marge Piercy (AP/Wide World Photos)

In 1973 two of Piercy's most significant books were published. In the novel *Small Changes*, which focuses on Beth, a working-class woman, and Miriam, a middle-class Jewish intellectual, who are both oppressed and exploited by a male-dominated culture, she demonstrates how sexism pervades every social sphere. A pivotal book in Piercy's development,

Small Changes irritated even some feminist critics because it did not contain a single male character with any redeeming qualities. In *Woman on the Edge of Time* and *He, She, and It* Piercy's feminist commitment develops an important ecological dimension. Locked away in a mental institution, Connie Ramos, the protagonist of *Woman on the Edge of Time*, fantasizes about two potential future worlds, one communal, the other militaristic and death-driven. Set in the year 2059, *He, She, and It* depicts an Earth ill-suited to sustain human life. Even these utopian novels are skillful examples of what Piercy calls "character-centered fiction," works whose plot arises out of the development of characters.

In *To Be of Use*, a collection of poems, Piercy expresses what she wants all her work to be: something of use to women, a reference point as their consciousness is raised about their place in society. The poems in *Available Light*, whose title suggests enlightenment, are less strident and focus mostly on her early life, on her Jewishness, and on her relationship with her father. *Available Light* seems a book of reconciliation rather than of protest. Her poetry of the 1990's was continuously well received; *What Are Big Girls Made Of?* received a Library Association Notable Book Award, and *The Art of Blessing the Day* received the Paterson Poetry Prize.

Piercy has also continued writing novels. *The Longings of Women* are for a safe, secure place to call home. The three protagonists—Mary, a recently divorced, homeless house cleaner; Leila, an unhappily married professor who is one of Mary's clients; and Becky, a young woman accused of conspiring to murder her husband—are all dealing with problematic relationships with men. The *Three Women* of Piercy's 1999 novel are three generations of independent Jewish women whose bonds become ever closer over the course of the narrative.

Piercy's work has received numerous honors, including a National Endowment for the Arts award, the Carolyn Kizer Poetry Prize, and the Arthur C. Clarke Award.

Gone to Soldiers

Type of work: Novel
First published: 1987

More than sixty years after the conclusion of World War II, the conflict still exert a tremendous hold on the imaginations of many Americans. Its villains remain the ultimate measure of evil, its major battles landmarks of heroism, its consequence the shape of the modern world. Marge Piercy's *Gone to Soldiers* is a novel, consciously epic in scope, that follows the linked lives of ten central characters who are designed to reflect the range of human experience during the war.

Piercy, an accomplished novelist and poet, intends to retell the honored legends of courage and valor for the generation that lived through the war and to introduce a contemporary audience to the politics, social movements, and fierce battles of the struggle. Effectively intertwining extensive research, personal family experience, and a very powerful imagination, the novel is structured around several Jewish families of widely varying social backgrounds whose lives are drawn together by their work for the Office of Strategic Services (OSS), the army's intelligence organization. Piercy's poetic skills enable her to produce battlefield scenes of harrowing intensity, but her primary focus is an intelligence agency because she wishes to demonstrate that the mind is the most fascinating weapon of human combat.

Although the multicharacter narrative is sometimes distracting when abrupt shifts undercut the momentum of the story, and although not all of the characters are imagined or developed with equal interest or insight, the wide range of the book gives it the panoramic power of the great novels of the nineteenth century. While Piercy is equally capable of rendering male or female perspectives on reality, her special concentration on the sensibility of several especially interesting women offers another view of a war which has generally been covered by male writers such as James Jones or Herman Wouk.

The action sequences, an obvious necessity in a work set directly in the tradition of VANITY FAIR and FROM HERE TO ETERNITY, are equal to the descriptions of Piercy's predecessors, but the novel is also informed by a very strong sense of social justice and human decency. Piercy's design is to combine the romance and adventure of the commercially popular novel with the sociological realism of the best historical journalism and to thread an argument for progressive democratic values throughout the book. Scenes such as the siege of Guadalcanal, the infamous Detroit race riot, and the horrifying Polish death march are complemented by subtle examinations of the motives and desires of individuals caught in the turmoil of a global cataclysm. The realm of the novel has been made as real as the world to which the reader returns at its conclusion.

Suggested Readings

Cooperman, Jeanette. *The Broom Closet: Secret Meanings of Domesticity in Postfeminist Novels by Louise Erdrich, Mary Gordon, Toni Morrison, Marge Piercy, Jane Smiley, and Amy Tan*. New York: P. Lang, 1999.

Michael, Magali Cornier. *Feminism and the Postmodern Impulse: Post-World War II Fiction*. Albany: State University of New York Press, 1996.

Rodden, John. "A Harsh Day's Light: An Interview with Marge Piercy." *The Kenyon Review* 20, no. 2 (1998): 132-143.

Shand, Kerstin. *The Repair of the World: The Novels of Marge Piercy*. Westport, Conn.: Greenwood Press, 1994.

Walker, Sue, and Eugenia Hamner, eds. *Ways of Knowing: Essays on Marge Piercy*. Mobile, Ala.: Negative Capability Press, 1992.

Contributors: R. Baird Shuman and Trey Strecker

Darryl Pinckney

Born: Indianapolis, Indiana; 1953

African American

Known initially as a literary critic, Pinckney in 1992 brought out High Cotton, *a humorous yet often painful examination of America's black middle class.*

Principal works

LONG FICTION: *High Cotton*, 1992
NONFICTION: *Out There: Mavericks of Black Literature*, 2002

Born in Indianapolis, Darryl Pinckney (PIHNK-nee) had a comfortable middle-class childhood. The idealism of the 1950's flavored his midwestern youth, which he later said he found unspectacular until he traveled from his native Indiana and discovered his blackness. Meanwhile, he attended high school in the suburbs and developed a love for English history and literature, fantasizing about the day he would get to go to England.

Pinckney was a member of the fourth generation of his family to be college-educated. He attended Columbia University, later commenting on his time there that he found himself surrounded by intellectual "weirdness." Nevertheless, he developed confidence and style in his writing classes. Pinckney tinkered with radical thoughts and attended a few black militant gatherings, but his interest in militancy was short-lived. He went on to graduate study at Princeton University. After leaving the academic environment, he took a number of jobs, eventually attaching himself to writer Djuna Barnes, performing odd jobs and relishing the experience of living around the reclusive author of *Nightwood* (1937). Pinckney whimsically submitted a book review of Gayle Jones's *Corrigidora* (1975). Published, the review opened doors for further work, and *The New York Review of Books* began to publish his writing. Eventually his freelance status evolved into a staff position.

He lived in Europe for a time, drifting between London, Paris, and Germany, finally settling in Berlin, where he collaborated with an Eastern German playwright, Heiner Müller, writing texts for the theater. Pinckney had grown tired of the commercialism of the United States, and he enjoyed the separation from his homeland. He participated in the culture of students and intellectuals who moderated the pace of Berlin. Pinckney likened his self-imposed European exile to that of James Baldwin. Pinckney's isolation allowed him, perhaps for the first time, to consider his African American roots. Before the publication of *High Cotton* in 1992 he had written for such publications as *Granta*, *Vogue*, *The New Yorker*, and *The New York*

Times Book Review as well as *The New York Review of Books*, establishing himself as a new, independent voice in African American critical writing. His essays discussed authors including Jean Toomer, Alice Walker, Zora Neale Hurston, and Langston Hughes. He received Guggenheim and Ingram Merrill grants to pursue his writing, and he was given the Whiting Writers Award in 1986.

Pinckney has taught at Columbia and been a visiting lecturer at Harvard. In 1995 *The New York Review of Books* published three long critical essays by Pinckney on autobiographies by African Americans: "Promissory Notes," focusing on nineteenth and twentieth century accounts of growing up black, "The Professionals," on black journalists, and "Black Aristocrats," on works portraying the lives and culture of people in the black middle class. In 2002 he published *Out There*, based on a series of lectures given at Harvard which assess the literary contributions of three black writers, Vincent O. Carter, J. A. Rogers, and Caryl Phillips.

High Cotton

Type of work: Novel
First published: 1992

High Cotton contains strongly autobiographical elements, and parts seem as much memoir as novel; Pinckney once hinted that he was born with the subject matter he addresses in the book and had long intended to write about the generational differences in African American life using relatives' stories and personal histories. The novel is a sometimes humorous and many times painful examination of America's black middle class. These are the descendants of W. E. B. DuBois's "Talented Tenth," fourth-generation college graduates. However, navigation of America's social and cultural waters proves precarious for Pinckney's narrator. The novel traces the narrator's progress from his urban childhood in the 1960's through his suburban adolescence to college and young adulthood. What Pinckney reveals is that for African Americans, the status and success inherent in the American Dream come at the sacrifice of family, racial identity, and self-knowledge.

Among the novel's characters is Uncle Castor, expatriate jazz musician from Paris, who tells the unnamed narrator tales of adventure while engaging in such idiosyncratic behaviors as drinking coffee sucked through a sugar cube perched on his lips. Grandfather Eustace, a Harvard-educated, strict Congregationalist minister, is one of the central figures; unrelenting and misunderstood, he periodically antagonizes the young narrator by making him question his view of the world. Upon Eustace's death, the narrator travels down south to take care of the family farm in Georgia. He finds no bucolic homeland but rather shopping malls and business strips—and racism. The youth's nostalgic dreams and visions of the Deep South fade. The term "high cotton" refers to ease of living: If one is chopping high cotton, life is easier than stooped picking. In this case, it is the black middle class—including the novel's narrator and Pinckney himself—that flourishes in taller crops.

In *High Cotton*, Pinckney re-creates the America experienced by those who benefited from the Civil Rights movement without having to enter the fray directly. As the narrator observes, "someone was seeing to things and had been ever since my great-grandfather's grandmother stepped on the auction block." The future had been secured for this generation by those who had gone before, paving the way for homes in the white suburbs of Indianapolis, for college educations at prestigious universities such as Columbia (allowing the narrator to visit Harlem without having to live there), for trips to Europe, and for marginal employment supplemented by parents' checks from home. The narrator, however, comes to realize that integration into the larger white society comes at a price: a sense of belonging nowhere. Only when he goes South to his grandfather's Georgia birthplace and reconnects with his personal and racial past can he fill that emotional vacuum.

Suggested Readings

Als, Hilton. "Word!" *The Nation*, May 18, 1992, pp. 667-670.

Bell, Pearl K. "Fiction Chronicle." *Partisan Review* 59, no. 2 (1992): 288-291.

Carroll, Rebecca, comp. *Swing Low: Black Men Writing*. New York: Carol Southern Books, 1995.

Moore, Lorrie. "The Long Voyage Home." *The New York Review of Books*, October 10, 2002, pp. 33-35.

White, Edmund, and Nora Kerr. Reviews of *High Cotton*, by Darryl Pinckney. *The New York Times Book Review*, February 2, 1992, p. 3.

Contributor: Craig Gilbert

Miguel Piñero

BORN: Gurabo, Puerto Rico; December 19, 1946
DIED: New York, New York; June 17, 1988

PUERTO RICAN

Piñero was a member of the Nuyorican (New York and Puerto Rican) literary and political movement that crystallized in the late 1960's and early 1970's in New York City.

PRINCIPAL WORKS

DRAMA: *Short Eyes*, pr. 1974; *The Sun Always Shines for the Cool*, pr. 1976; *Eulogy for a Small-Time Thief*, pr. 1977; *A Midnight Moon at the Greasy Spoon*, pr. 1981; *Outrageous: One-Act Plays*, pb. 1986
DRAMA (SCREENPLAY): *Short Eyes*, 1977 (adaptation of his play)
DRAMA (TELEPLAY): "Smuggler's Blues," 1984 (episode of *Miami Vice*)
POETRY: *La Bodega Sold Dreams*, 1980
EDITED TEXT: *Nuyorican Poetry: An Anthology of Puerto Rican Words and Feelings*, 1975

Miguel Piñero (mih-GEHL peen-YEHR-oh) is an important member of the Nuyorican (New York and Puerto Rican) literary and political movement that crystallized in the late 1960's and early 1970's in New York City. Born in Puerto Rico, Piñero moved to New York City with his parents when he was four. His father, Miguel Angel Piñero, abandoned the family four years later, and Piñero subsequently experienced the poverty, marginalization, and crime of New York's lower East Side. Piñero remained devoted to his mother, Adelina, as his poems and opening dedication to *Short Eyes* ("El Cumpleaños de Adelina" by Miguel Algarín) reveal.

At an early age, Piñero fell victim to his harsh environment: He began "hustling" and taking drugs and soon entered the world of petty crime that was to shape his future. A truant, shoplifter, and drug addict by his teenage years, Piñero never graduated from junior high. He was convicted of armed robbery at age twenty-four and was sent to Sing Sing, the notorious New York prison. Ironically, it was in prison that Piñero experienced his literary awakening, thanks to a theater workshop established at Sing Sing by Clay Stevenson. Like that of most Nuyorican authors, Piñero's experience as a marginalized Puerto Rican in America was to become the source for much of his literary output.

Through Stevenson's prison workshop, Piñero began his first and most recognized play, *Short Eyes*. In addition, while still in prison he came into contact with Marvin Felix Camillo, actor and activist, who had formed The Family, an acting troupe of former inmates, and who encouraged Piñero's writing and acting. Out of prison, Piñero worked with Camillo and The Family to develop *Short Eyes* for performance. The play moved from its opening in the Riverside Church to Off-Broadway, to the Public Theater with the help of producer Joseph Papp, and finally to the Vivian Beaumont Theater. Piñero received an Obie Award and the New York Drama Critics Circle Award for best American play.

Piñero's success in playwriting put him in contact with the thriving Puerto Rican literary and political community. In the mid-1970's, as a member of the Nuyorican artistic community, Piñero cofounded the Nuyorican Poets Café with Miguel Algarín and edited a volume of Nuyorican poetry with Algarín as well. After a return to Puerto Rico, Piñero in his work also reflected the displacement of the Puerto Rican experience in America: He and his fellow artists felt accepted neither in their native land nor in their land of adoption, and such alienation is a major tenet of Nuyorican literature. Like the dialogue of his characters, his poetry—and the poetry of the Nuyorican Poets Café—was characterized by oral performances of it, as poets performed their works in an apparently improvisational style, reflecting the influence of the Beat poets, of Puerto Rican street culture, and of the emerging African American rap and hip-hop styles. Piñero continued to write and see his plays performed, but none were to have the success of *Short Eyes*.

In 1977 Piñero wrote the screenplay and performed in the film version of his play *Short Eyes*. From the early 1970's into the 1980's, he began a long series of guest-starring appearances in television and cinema. Most notably, he played a series of drug smugglers and ne'er-do-wells in such television series as *Miami Vice* (1984), *The Equalizer* (1985), and *Kojak* (1973). On film, he appeared in *Breathless* (1983), *Exposed* (1983), and *Fort Apache, The Bronx* (1981).

In addition to working in Hollywood, Piñero also taught writing at Rutgers University and received a Guggenheim Fellowship for playwriting in 1982. Such activity and influence in his ethnic and literary community could not help in his battle against addiction, however, and Piñero continued to struggle with drugs and alcohol. Never married, Piñero had a series of serious relationships with both women and men, and an intense, although nonsexual, relationship with fellow Nuyorican poet Algarín. Piñero died in 1988 of cirrhosis of the liver.

Piñero's *Short Eyes* remains his most successful and enduring contribution to American playwriting and reveals his primary concerns with ethnic and racial alienation in the United States, the all-controlling power of violence, and the hope of individual triumph against such terror. In addition, it offers a window onto the language—a mixture of Spanish, English, street language, and profanity—that in many ways embodies the world of New York's lower East Side, where Nuyorican literature developed and thrived. His later works, although virtually ignored by literary critics, reveal Piñero's continued focus on the language, alienation, and perseverance of his community. Despite his close dealings with the New York and Hollywood elite, Piñero remained rooted in his lower East Side, Nuyorican experiences.

In December, 2001, *Piñero*, a film of the author's life directed by Leon Ichaso, opened in limited release and prompted renewed interest in the author and actor, particularly in his poetic performances. The film had the support and cooperation of Piñero's friends and family. Actor Benjamin Bratt's performance as Piñero, particularly in his "performance" of Piñero's poems at the Nuyorican Poets Café, suggests the intensity and immediacy of his poetry as performance that mere readings of Piñero's work cannot impart.

Short Eyes

Type of work: Drama
First produced: 1974

Short Eyes was Miguel Piñero's first and most famous play. After its debut, critics hailed the author as the first Puerto Rican playwright to enter theater's mainstream.

The play begins with a group of prisoners—mostly African American and Latino—struggling to maintain a sense of dignity under deplorable conditions. Early action focuses on Clark Davis, one of only two white members of the group, who is from a socioeconomic background different from that of most of the other inmates. Davis has been accused of child molestation, a crime that the other inmates consider especially shameful, and makes his situation worse by refusing to adapt to the prison's customs. Through the play's second act he is harassed constantly, and is ultimately murdered. The guilty prisoners are not punished—the guards look the other way—but must come to terms with their guilt and responsibility.

Only one of the inmates, an elderly Puerto Rican man named Juan, refused to participate in the murder. Paradoxically, he is the only one who knows that Davis is guilty. Critics have argued whether Juan abstained from the murder because of its immorality or because it was in the interest of his self-preservation to do so; perhaps both are true. Juan does not allow himself to take another's life, but neither does he make any attempt to relieve Davis's murderers of their guilt (the other prisoners have been told by a guard that Davis had been mistakenly identified and was innocent).

Miguel Piñero wrote *Short Eyes* after serving a jail sentence (his third) for armed robbery at Sing Sing prison. It draws heavily from his knowledge of life in jail, depicting the violence of prison life from the inmates' perspectives. In fact, the play's title comes from a slang term for pornography, "short heist." Piñero explained many Puerto Ricans had difficulty pronouncing the *h* in "heist," so the word sounded more like "eyes."

Suggested Readings

Camillo, Marvin Felix. Introduction to *Short Eyes*, by Miguel Piñero. New York: Hill & Wang, 1975.

Maffi, Mario. "The Nuyorican Experience in the Plays of Pedro Pietri and Miguel Piñero." In *Cross-Cultural Studies; American, Canadian and European Literatures: 1945-1985*, edited by Mirko Jurak. Bled, Slovenia: Symposium on Contemporary Literatures and Cultures of the United States of America and Canada, 1988.

Piñero, Miguel. "An Interview with Miguel Piñero." Interview by Norma McKesson Alarcon. *Revista Chicano-Riqueña* 2, no. 4 (1974): 55-57.

_______. "Miguel Piñero: 'I Wanted to Survive.'" Interview by Nat Hentoff. *The New York Times*, May 5, 1974, pp. 1, 8.

Saldivar, José David. "Miguel Piñero." In *Biographical Dictionary of Hispanic Literature in the United States: The Literature of Puerto Ricans, Cuban Americans, and Other Hispanic Writers*, edited by Nicolás Kanellos. New York: Greenwood Press, 1989.

Contributors: Cami D. Agan and Anna A. Moore

Mary Helen Ponce

Born: Pacoima, California; January 24, 1938

Mexican American

Ponce's writing resides in the matrix of identities (Mexican, Mexican American, Anglo-American, Spanish language, English language) and issues (the socialization of men and women, the church, school) that concern many Latinos today.

Principal works

LONG FICTION: *The Wedding*, 1989

SHORT FICTION: *Recuerdo: Short Stories of the Barrio*, 1983; *Taking Control*, 1987

NONFICTION: *Hoyt Street: An Autobiography*, 1993 (reprinted in 1995 in English as *Hoyt Street: Memories of a Chicana Childhood* and in Spanish as *Calle Hoyt: Memorias de una juventud chicana*)

A prolific author of Chicano prose, Mary Helen Ponce (POHN-say) was born and raised in the San Fernando Valley of Southern California. The youngest of ten children (seven girls and three boys), Ponce grew up in the security of her barrio (neighborhood) community, a blend of Mexicans and Mexican Americans for whom the family, the Catholic church, the school, and the little local grocery store provided stable landmarks for a world moving between languages and cultures. Writing in English and Spanish, or in English with brief shifts to Spanish, Ponce conjures the experiences of her childhood and youth in a bilingual and bicultural context, addressing the female experience in particular.

Ponce attended California State University at Northridge, earning a B.A. and an M.A. in Mexican American studies. She earned a second M.A. from the University of California at Los Angeles in history, minoring in anthropology and women's studies. She pursued course work toward a doctorate in American studies at the University of New Mexico, combining her twin interests in history and literature, receiving her Ph.D. in 1995.

The mother of four children, Ponce delayed the start of her writing career until she was in her forties, beginning to publish short stories in Spanish in the early 1980's. She soon wrote stories in English and translated some of her Spanish stories into English. She has published nonfiction essays on Latino topics ("Latinas and Breast Cancer," for example) and interviews of Latino figures ("Profile of Dr. Shirlene Soto: Vice Provost, CSU Northridge"). She has also given presentations on such topics as Spanish American pioneer women in California, Chicana literature, and oral history. She has read her fiction at college campuses and conferences in the United States and El Colegio de Mexico in Mexico City and has published in the largest Spanish-language newspaper in Southern California, *La Opinión*.

Recuerdo: Short Stories of the Barrio gathers a number of Ponce's earliest pieces, some of which begin with the Spanish word "Recuerdo," which may be translated as "I recall," "I remember," or simply "memory," suggesting the autobiographical element typical of Ponce's writing. Her early narratives are first-person, allowing Ponce to describe the experiences of Mexican women with an intimate tone. Later some of Ponce's stories would employ third-person narration.

Taking Control contains several short narratives. Though the characters of these stories are often subject to difficult circumstances, Ponce's title reflects her decision to emphasize the positive outcomes of even the most negative circumstances. Both *Recuerdo* and *Taking Control* are firmly anchored in the Mexican American experience, particularly as lived by women.

Ponce's novel *The Wedding* is set in a fictional small-town neighborhood near Los Angeles. It depicts the San Fernando Valley in the 1940's and 1950's while exploring women's place in Mexican American society of the time. Blanca is planning the wedding of her dreams, although the marriage is not necessarily to the man of her dreams. She has to work Saturdays plucking turkeys in order to pay for the fancy gown she wants, despite its reduced, factory-seconds price. Her fiancé is a *pachuco*, or zoot-suit-wearing member of a 1950's gang. Blanca does have her fancy wedding—but she also has a miscarriage and has to leave the party in an ambulance as two rival gangs fight in the background. Like many of Ponce's other works, *The Wedding* examines the stereotypes that seem to circumscribe the lives of Mexican American women, who are subject to their husband's whims, who endure multiple pregnancies, and who must rise to the social expectations inculcated in them by their families and the Catholic church. Nonetheless, Blanca, like other Ponce characters, is strong, tough, and essentially optimistic. A panorama of Mexican American life is presented in the book: the gangs; the hardworking women; the swaggering men; the influences of family, friends, and church; the financial struggle; and the changing culture.

Ponce's 1993 nonfiction work *Hoyt Street: An Autobiography* returns to the San Fernando Valley of the 1940's. (The book was reprinted in 1995 simultaneously in Spanish and English editions: *Hoyt Street: Memories of a Chicana Childhood* and *Calle Hoyt: Memorias de una juventud chicana*.) *Hoyt Street* leaves fiction behind to tell Ponce's own story of growing up Chicana in a bilingual, bicultural neighborhood whose population is gradually acculturating to the dominant Anglo culture. The book begins with Ponce as a preschooler and ends at the beginning of puberty, depicting the neighborhood and introducing friends and family as it goes. Though her memories are mostly happy ones, Ponce comments: "It seems that we Mexican-Americans, as we were called, had so many things wrong with us that I wondered why it was we were happy." The voice is Ponce's, but the vision is split between her own childhood recollections and the implied critique by Anglos. It is in this matrix of identities (Mexican, Mexican American, Anglo-American, Spanish language,

English language) and issues (the socialization of men and women, the church, school) that Ponce positions all of her writing. It has been remarked that minority writers usually begin their careers by writing their autobiography and only then move toward less personalized fictions. Ponce's fiction, however, has always had autobiographical elements, and she moved through fictional representation to the nonfiction autobiography itself.

The Wedding

Type of work: Novel
First published: 1989

The Wedding is dedicated to "the chicks and guys from the barrios who remember the big, fun weddings . . . and fights." The book follows the life of Blanca Munoz, who lives in Taconos, a poor Chicano neighborhood not far from Los Angeles. Like many of her peers, Blanca lives in a single-parent home and drops out of school to look for work. She is young, uneducated, and without skills, and finally has to take a job at a turkey-processing plant, picking the feathers off turkeys while she imagines a better life.

She meets Cricket, the twenty-two-year-old leader of the local gang, the Tacones. Although she calls him honey, their relationship seems based more on proximity than on love. Blanca and Cricket focus much more on the impending wedding as a social symbol than as the symbol of their union. Each wants a splendid wedding for different reasons: Cricket wants to raise his status among the gang members with a wedding that "would outclass all others"; Blanca wants to salvage the family's pride, increase its social status and, consequently, please her mother.

Father Ranger, the parish priest, reluctantly agrees to perform the wedding, which will fulfill Blanca's destiny as yet another woman subject to the double standard. "Married men come and go at will," says Father Ranger. "They are free to find other women, abandon wives and children at whim, then return to claim their rights." Blanca constantly acquiesces to Cricket. She hopes for a single night of honeymoon at a hotel, but Cricket refuses, explaining that first he has to take care of the dance. On the way to the dance, as his new bride leans against him, Cricket admonishes her not to wrinkle his clothes. He knows he will be facing the rival gang and must look his best.

As the novel closes, Cricket is carried to the hospital in an ambulance after the rumble, and Blanca is taken to the hospital suffering a miscarriage. She still has hopes for a good future with Cricket. Her last words before passing out are "the best wedding, in all of Taconos."

Suggested Readings

McCracken, Ellen. "Subculture, Parody, and the Carnivalesque: A Bakhtinian Reading of Mary Helen Ponce's *The Wedding*." *MELUS* 23, no. 1 (Spring, 1998): 117-132.

Rochy, John. "A Pacoima Childhood." Review of *Hoyt Street*, by Mary Helen Ponce. *Los Angeles Times*, October 3, 1993.

Sanchez, Beverly. Review of *Hoyt Street*, by Mary Helen Ponce. *Hispanic* 8, no. 5 (July, 1995): 1.

Veyna, Angelina F. "Mary Helen Ponce." In *Chicano Writers, Second Series*, edited by Francisco A. Lomeli. Vol. 122 in *Dictionary of Literary Biography*. Detroit: Gale Group, 1992.

Contributor: Linda Ledford-Miller

Chaim Potok

Born: New York, New York; February 17, 1929
Died: Merion, Pennsylvania; July 23, 2002

Jewish

Potok has presented issues and concerns in Jewish (especially Hasidic) identity to a large reading audience.

Principal works

children's literature: *The Tree of Here*, 1993; *The Sky of Now*, 1995

long fiction: *The Chosen*, 1967; *The Promise*, 1969; *My Name Is Asher Lev*, 1972; *In the Beginning*, 1975; *The Book of Lights*, 1981; *Davita's Harp*, 1985; *The Gift of Asher Lev*, 1990; *I Am the Clay*, 1992; *Old Men at Midnight*, 2001 (3 novellas)

nonfiction: *Wanderings: Chaim Potok's History of the Jews*, 1978; *Tobiasse: Artist in Exile*, 1986; *The Gates of November: Chronicles of the Slepak Family*, 1996; *My First Seventy-nine Years*, 1999 (with Isaac Stern); *Conversations with Chaim Potok*, 2001 (Daniel Walden, editor)

Chaim Potok (ki-EEM POH-tok) was born and reared in New York City. His writings reveal a wealth of learning, due in part to his impressive academic credentials; he was a rabbi who held a doctorate from the University of Pennsylvania. His eight novels, various plays, one nonfiction historical text, and two children's books are concerned with Jewish (often Hasidic) characters who are challenged by the conflicting identities of their cultures as Americans, Jews, Hasids, family members, and post-World War II citizens of the world.

Ordained as a Conservative rabbi in 1954, Potok became national director for the Conservative youth organization, the Leaders Training Fellowship. In 1955, as a chaplain in the United States Army, he served in Korea during the Korean War. His overseas experience proved to be formative for his writing career. In *Wanderings: Chaim Potok's History of the Jews*, his nonfiction account of Jewish history, Potok explains:

> My early decades had prepared me for everything—except the two encounters I in fact experienced: a meeting with a vast complex of cultures perfectly at ease without Jews and Judaism, and a confrontation with the beautiful and the horrible in the world of oriental human beings. . . . Jewish history began in a world of pagans: my own Judaism was transformed in another such world.

Though his first novel, based on his Korean experiences, was repeatedly rejected, a second novel, *The Chosen* (1967), became a popular success. In the intervening years, Potok had married a psychiatric social worker, Adena Mosevitzky (their daughter Rena was born in 1962, Naama in 1965, and son, Akiva, in 1968), and had become managing editor of the New York-based *Conservative Judaism*.

Chaim Potok (© Jerry Bauer)

In 1965, Potok received the doctorate in philosophy from the University of Pennsylvania and became associate editor of the Jewish Publication Society of America. A year later, he was named editor in chief and appointed to the society's Bible Translation Committee. *The Promise*, a sequel to *The Chosen*, followed in 1969; *My Name Is Asher Lev* was published in 1972. After living for some four years in Jerusalem in the mid-1970's, Potok and his family settled in Pennsylvania, where he taught courses in the philosophy of literature at the University of Pennsylvania. He also taught occasionally at Bryn Mawr College and at the Johns Hopkins University. Diagnosed with cancer in 2000, Potok remained as active as his health permitted. He was coeditor with David Lieber and Harold Kushner of *Etz Hayim*, a new commentary on the Torah aimed at Conservative Jews that was published in 2001. He finally succumbed to his cancer on July 23, 2002, at the age of seventy-three

The Chosen and its sequel, *The Promise*, confront issues of value and identity. The novels examine the tensions between Orthodox and Hasidic Jews. An injury in a baseball game initiates a friendship between Reuven Malter, pitcher on the Orthodox team whose father is a fervent Zionist, and Danny Saunders, batter on the Hasid team who is heir to the rebbe position of his father. *The Chosen* has an ironic conclusion; Reuven Malter decides to become an Orthodox rabbi, but Danny Saunders decides, after much family pain, to become a secular psychologist, a "tzaddik for the world," as his father finally understands.

Potok's most critically acclaimed novel, *My Name Is Asher Lev*, details the struggle for personal identity of a young Hasidic boy who struggles between his love for family and religion and his obligation as an artist to study and create. The sequel to this novel, *The Gift of Asher Lev*, did not appear until nearly two decades later. It tells of an adult Asher Lev, married and with children, who must confront again his unresolved status in the Brooklyn Hasidic community when the death of a family member requires his return.

In the early and mid-1990's, Potok moved beyond the genre of the novel to write four plays, which were locally produced in Philadelphia, and two works of children's literature (*The Tree of Here* and *The Sky of Now*), which enjoyed critical acclaim.

My Name Is Asher Lev

Type of work: Novel
First published: 1972

My Name Is Asher Lev, perhaps Potok's greatest novel, is an excellent example of the *Künstlerroman*, which is a novel about an artist's development. It confronts issues of Jewish and family identity in the post-Holocaust world. Asher Lev is a child prodigy artist, the only child of a Hasidic Jewish couple that lives in the Crown Heights section of Brooklyn. Aryeh Lev, Asher's father, serves as a personal emissary for the *rebbe* or tzaddik, the "righteous one" or religious leader of the Hasidic community.

The Orthodox Hasidic Jewish culture into which Asher is born approves of creativity only in the context of interpretation of Talmudic passages. Asher finds it difficult, and at times embarrassing, to follow his muse; he finds it natural to draw and to create pictures. Rivkeh Lev, Aryeh's mother, initially supports Asher's desire to draw, but she soon sides with her husband, who believes that drawing and the fine arts are products of a gentile culture. In the years during and immediately following World War II, Aryeh Lev travels the world to minister to Hasidic Jews who have been displaced by the Nazi Holocaust. Since Hasids believe that the Jewish state will be re-created in Israel only with the coming of the Messiah, who has not yet arrived, Hasidic Jews generally did not support the creation of the state of Israel in 1948. Aryeh travels about the world for the tzaddik, defending himself and his spiritual leader from the arguments of Zionist Jews and gentiles and attempting to do good works. He returns to a household in Brooklyn where his son is neglecting study of the Talmud because of his personal obsession with art and aesthetics.

The tzaddik, however, is wise enough to allow Asher to follow his destiny and to mediate between his conflicting identities. The tzaddik arranges for Jacob Kahn, an expatriate from the Hasidic community and a world-renowned sculptor, to serve as Asher's artistic mentor. Asher's apprenticeship as an artist culminates with a midtown New York showing of his work. Central to the showing is a pair of paintings, *Brooklyn Crucifixion I* and *Brooklyn Crucifixion II*, which show his mother, crucified in the venetian blinds of their apartment, her face split into "Picassoid" thirds, looking to the father, the son, and the street. The works assure Asher's reputation as a great artist but also assure, because of their religious content, that he will have to leave his Hasidic community in Brooklyn, as he does at the end of the novel. With the tzaddik's blessing, he goes to Paris to board with a Hasidic family and to continue to worship and define himself as a Hasidic Jew artist.

Davita's Harp

Type of work: Novel
First published: 1985

Potok has written several highly acclaimed novels about American-Jewish life, but he enters new territory when he explores the milieu of areligious Jewish radicals in *Davita's Harp*. This is also his first novel in which a young girl is the protagonist. Ilana Davita Chandal's life has been filled with uncertainty as well as with the love of her radically idealistic parents. Her journalist father Michael has been disowned by his patrician family for both his politics and his marriage to a Jewish woman. Her mother Channah bears the scars of a brutal pogrom and the senseless tragedies of World War I. The horrors of the twentieth century become Ilana's when Michael is killed during the bombing of Guernica while covering the Spanish Civil War. Then Channah's closest friend, Jacob Daw, because of his previous membership in the Communist Party, is deported to Adolf Hitler's Europe, where he dies.

Although she does not abandon her parents' idealism, Ilana needs something more. She first finds comfort in her Aunt Sarah's Christianity. Later, however, she is attracted to the Orthodox Judaism of her mother's youth. Channah's remarriage to a religious cousin completes the family's return to the Jewish world. In focusing on Ilana, Potok was able to explore the role of women in traditional Judaism. He gives no easy answers. Ilana may be the school valedictorian, but because of her sex she is denied her school's top prize. Nor does Potok allow the shelter of Judaism to eradicate the pain of Ilana's tragedies. Through Ilana's struggle to understand the world and make it a better place, Potok affirms his faith in the ultimate decency of human beings in a novel that is moving in its humanity.

Suggested Readings

Abramson, Edward A. *Chaim Potok*. Boston: Twayne, 1986.

Bloom, Harold, ed. *Chaim Potok's "The Chosen."* Philadelphia: Chelsea House, 2005.

Shaked, Gershon. "Shadows of Identity: A Comparative Study of German Jewish and American Jewish Literature." In *What Is Jewish Literature?*, edited by Hana Wirth-Nesher. Philadelphia: Jewish Publication Society, 1994.

Sternlicht, Sanford. *Chaim Potok: A Critical Companion*. Westport, Conn.: Greenwood Press, 2000.

Studies in American Jewish Literature 4 (1985).

Walden, Daniel, ed. *Conversations with Chaim Potok*. Jackson: University Press of Mississippi, 2001.

Contributors: Richard Sax and Dan Barnett

Dudley Randall

Born: Washington, D.C.; January 14, 1914
Died: Southfield, Michigan; August 5, 2000

African American

Beyond his own poetry, it was as an editor and publisher that Dudley Randall's literary talents were most significant.

Principal works

POETRY: *Poem Counterpoem*, 1966 (with Margaret Danner); *Cities Burning*, 1968; *Love You*, 1970; *More to Remember: Poems of Four Decades*, 1971; *After the Killing*, 1973; *A Litany of Friends: New and Selected Poems*, 1981, revised 1983

NONFICTION: *Broadside Memories: Poets I Have Known*, 1975

EDITED TEXTS: *For Malcolm: Poems on the Life and Death of Malcolm X*, 1967 (with Margaret G. Burroughs); *Black Poetry: A Supplement to Anthologies Which Exclude Black Poets*, 1969; *The Black Poets*, 1971; *Homage to Hoyt Fuller*, 1984

Dudley Randall was one of the most influential black publishers of his time: His refusal to place commercial interests ahead of literary education helped to inform a whole generation of the richness and diversity of black poetic traditions. In doing so, he introduced new African American writers, and he fostered an awareness of the reciprocity between black writers in the United States and Africa.

Born in 1914 to Arthur and Ada Randall, Dudley Felker Randall spent his childhood in Washington, D.C., his birthplace, and in East St. Louis. His father was responsible for the young Randall's awareness of political commitment; he frequently campaigned for blacks seeking political office, and he took Randall with him to hear such speakers as James Weldon Johnson and W. E. B. Du Bois (although Randall reports that at the time he "preferred playing baseball"). Randall's public education continued when his family moved to Detroit. By this time, he was conscious not only of the political process, but also of black literature. Having first begun to write poetry at the early age of thirteen, Randall purchased a copy of Jean Toomer's *Cane* (1923) when he was sixteen; he was so impressed by Toomer's precise images and powerful symbolism that Toomer became—and remains—his favorite black poet. By 1930, the time of his graduation from the public school system, also at sixteen, Randall was well read in the major writers of the Harlem Renaissance.

After graduation in the midst of the Great Depression, Randall eventually found work as a foundry worker for the Ford Motor Company from 1932 to 1937. Sometime in 1933, he met the poet Robert Hayden, also living in Detroit, with whom he shared his poetry and discussed the major poets of the time. Their exchange of poems and ideas was to help him sharpen his skills and was to remain a mutually enriching friendship for many years. By 1938, Randall had taken a job with the U.S. Post Office as a letter carrier, work he was to continue until 1951, except for his service in the United States Army during World War II as a member of the signal corps in the South Pacific (1942-1946). After returning from military duty, Randall attended Wayne State University and graduated in 1949. While still working for the post office, Randall also managed to complete work for a master's degree in library science from the University of Michigan in 1951.

Degree in hand, Randall began his career as a librarian by accepting an appointment with Lincoln University in Jefferson City, Missouri, where he remained until 1954. He was promoted to associate librarian when he moved to Baltimore to work for Morgan State College for the next two years. In 1956, he returned to Detroit, where he was to work for the Wayne County Federated Library System until 1969, first as a branch librarian and then as head of the reference and interloan department (1963-1969). Randall's introduction to several relatively unknown black poets from Detroit at a planning meeting for a special issue of *Negro History Bulletin* in 1962 led to his determination to see more work by new black poets become available; thus, he became the founding editor of the Broadside Press in 1965. His collaboration with Margaret Danner, who had founded Boone House, a Detroit cultural center, produced his first published book of poems, *Poem Counterpoem* from Broadside Press (its first publication as well).

With the publication of Randall's second book, *Cities Burning*, his reputation as a poet and publisher grew, and he doubled as poet-in-residence and reference librarian for the University of Detroit from 1969 to 1975. During this time, he also taught courses in black literature at the university, gave a number of readings, and was involved in conferences and seminars throughout the country. In 1966, Randall, with a delegation of black artists, visited Paris, Prague, and the Soviet Union, where he read his translations and his own poems to Russian audiences. In 1970, Randall visited West Africa, touring Ghana, Togo, and Dahomey, and meeting with African writers.

In 1969, aware that many current anthologies excluded or gave only limited representation to black poets, Randall edited and published *Black Poetry: A Supplement to Anthologies Which Exclude Black Poets*, which brought such omissions to the attention of larger publishing houses in the country. By 1971, a number of anthologies of African American poetry were in circulation, but many of them were seriously flawed by too-narrow criteria for selection. Randall's *The Black Poets* enjoyed wide distribution in an inexpensive paperback format and corrected many of the deficiencies of previous black poetry anthologies. Presenting a full range of African American poetry from folklore and spirituals to the Black Nationalist poets of the late 1960's, the anthology offered a substantial selection from each of its contributors and stressed the continuity of a rich oral tradition while delineating various periods in the history of black American poetry. It quickly became one of the most widely read and influential anthologies of its kind.

In his critical writings, Randall came to be known as a moderating voice, maintaining respect for poets of earlier periods while accepting the new directions of black poetry since the 1960's. One important article, "The Black Aesthetic in the Thirties, Forties, and Fifties" (*The Black Aesthetic*, 1971), clearly establishes the vital role of such poets as Sterling Brown, Margaret Walker, Melvin B. Tolson, Robert Hayden, and Gwendolyn Brooks, among others who wrote in the wake of the Harlem Renaissance. In providing an essential chapter in black literary history, Randall, here and in other essays, countered eloquently the tendency for young black poets in the 1960's to dismiss gifted, significant writers because they seemed too accommodationist. On the other hand, Randall's productive generosity in publishing and reviewing introduced a great variety of young black poets to literary America and provided an unparalleled availability of black poetry, in general, not only to the black community but also to the mainstream reading public.

Two additional literary forms must be mentioned in assessing Randall's career: interviews and translations. His insights into literary history, political developments, and his own methods of composition can be found in published interviews. While such interviews are frequently useful in understanding his own work, they are also immensely instructional in the field of African American poetry. Randall's translations from Russian, Latin, and French are also worthy of note. He published translations from major figures influential on his own poetic sensibilities, from Alexander Pushkin to K. M. Simonov. Translating from the Latin, he has mastered the classical lyricism of Catullus. From Paul Verlaine, Randall assimilated the influence of the French Symbolists.

Randall's work garnered a number of honors. Beginning in 1962, he received the Tompkins Award from Wayne State University for both poetry and fiction, and in 1966, he received the same award for poetry. In recognition of his contributions to black literature, he received the Kuumba Liberation Award in 1973. He was awarded National Endowment for the Humanities Fellowships in 1981 and 1986, and was named the first poet laureate of the city of Detroit in 1981. In 1996, Randall received a Lifetime Achievement Award from the National Endowment for the Arts.

After his retirement in 1975, Randall continued his involvement in writing conferences and readings, but he devoted the majority of his time to the Broadside Press and his own writing. Melba Boyd's well-received documentary film on Randall's life and work, *Black Unicorn*, was released in 1996. Randall died of congestive heart failure on August 5, 2000.

Poem Counterpoem

Type of work: Poetry
First published: 1966

The polarities of tension in Randall's poetry seem to be the necessity of personal love and social change. These themes underlie most of his poems, which sometimes focus on the one value while faintly suggesting the other but more often than not are characteristic of a tension between the two. In one early poem from his first book, *Poem Counterpoem*, Randall reflects on his youthful experience as a foundry worker while he visits an ailing coworker many years later in a hospital. In "George," the speaker recalls "the monstrous, lumpish cylinder blocks" that too often "clotted the line and plunged to the floor/ With force enough to tear your foot in two." George's response to the industrial hazards of the assembly line was to step calmly aside; working side by side with the older man in his younger days, the speaker looked to George as an example of quiet endurance, even though George, "goggled, with mask on [his] mouth and shoulders bright with sweat," was not particularly articulate in his guidance of the young Randall. George's "highest accolade," in fact, following the clean-up of "blocks clogged up" which came "thundering down like an avalanche," was the gnomic folk expression: "'You're not afraid of sweat. You're strong as a mule.'" As the speaker visits George in a "ward where old men wait to die," he realizes that George "cannot read the books" brought to him while he sits "among the senile wrecks,/ The psychopaths, the incontinent." In the transition from the first stanza (set in the past) to the second (set in the present), the long lines of the first (which suggest the rhythm of the assembly line) give way to a shorter line that underscores George's confinement. When George falls from his chair in the course of the visit, his visitor lifts him back into it "like a cylinder block" and assures him: "'You'll be here/ A long time yet, because you're strong as a mule.'"

While the poem relates little more than the memory of assembly line comradeship and the subsequent visit many years later, it suggests a great deal more than that. The sheer physical drudgery of the foundry site is apparent in both imagery and rhythm; George's quiet but resolute determination to survive the toll of accidents is also implicit, but he survives only to find himself relegated to little more than a warehouse for the aged. Juxtaposed, however, with the dismal irony of George's fate is Randall's emphasis on the personal bond of mutual respect between the two men. Just as George encouraged him, the younger man now offers the aging George the same encouragement that he once offered the young worker. George's persistence in overcoming his fear of death, however, is not enough to restore his dignity. The social conditions must change as well, and that will necessitate formal education; this, too, as Randall's own biography might suggest, has been an inadvertent gift from the older man. In stressing the personal bond between them and yet not losing sight of their common experience in the workplace, Randall celebrates the endurance of friendship while condemning the dehumanizing factors of the assembly line and the hospital. That all of this is expressed in one brief mirrored, metaphorical aphorism suggests that the simple eloquence of the poem itself is, like George, rich beneath its surface.

Cities Burning

Type of work: Poetry
First published: 1968

Randall's second book, *Cities Burning*, focuses on the disintegrating cities during the urban riots and civil struggles of the 1960's. His observations on social change are not, however, solely the result of the 1960's, for several of these poems were written much earlier. "Roses and Revolution," for example, was written in 1948 and attests to Randall's exploration of the dual themes of personal love and social change long before that tumultuous decade. Hauntingly prophetic, Randall's apocalyptic poem speaks of "the lighted cities" that "were like tapers in the night." He sees "the Negro lying in the swamp with his face blown off" and "in northern cities with his manhood maligned." Men work but take "no joy in their work." As a result of the inner turmoil caused by prejudice and oppression, love becomes severely distorted; they greet "the hard-eyed whore with joyless excitement" and sleep "with wives and virgins in impotence." While the poem's speaker searches for meaningful value "in darkness/ and felt the pain of millions," he sees "dawn upon them like the sun," a vision of peace and beauty in which weapons are buried "at the bottom of the ocean/ like the bones of dinosaurs buried under the shale of eras." Here people "create for others the house, the poem, the game of athletic beauty." Having described the misery in the first stanza and the vision of deliverance in the second stanza, Randall proceeds to analyze its meaning in the third: "Its radiance would grow and be nourished suddenly/ burst into terrible and splendid bloom/ the blood-red flower of revolution."

As it is for many of the poems in this volume, the title of the collection is somewhat misleading with respect to "Roses and Revolution," for the city in *Cities Burning* is humankind and the fires are transforming agents. While acknowledging the violence and destruction as literal events, Randall also sees revolution occurring within the heart of man as well. The real revolution is "not for power or the accumulation of paper," greed for money, but for a blossoming of love that can occur when the black American no longer feels "the writhing/ of his viscera like that of the hare hunted down or the bear at bay." The symbolic rose no longer holds its power for transformation unless it is "blood-red" in its "terrible and splendid bloom," for Randall does not sentimentalize love at the expense of the political process.

In "Ballad of Birmingham," for example, Randall dramatically presents a dialogue between a black mother, who fears for her daughter's safety and forbids her to "march the streets of Birmingham/ to make our country free," and the girl herself, who is willing to risk the "clubs and hoses, guns and jails" in order to assert her rights. Obeying her mother, the daughter goes "to church instead" to "sing in the children's choir" rather than join the other children in the freedom march. The historical event on which the ballad is based was the bombing of a black church in Birmingham on September 15, 1963, when four teenage girls were murdered in a dynamite explosion while they were attending a Bible class. When the mother hears the explosion, she rushes to the scene of the violence; although she claws "through bits of glass and brick," she finds only a shoe: "O, here's the shoe my baby wore,/ but, baby, where are you?" Her protective reluctance to become involved in the Civil Rights struggle, although understandable, has failed to preserve her loving security for her daughter or even her daughter herself. Despite the elegiac ballad form, Randall's dramatic irony here is politically and personally potent: Love cannot hide from death in the pursuit of freedom; it must risk it.

Randall, however, is unwilling to endorse violence for its own sake—in revolution or in literature. In "The Rite" and in "Black Poet, White Critic," he addresses, respectively, both the young militant black poet who would annihilate the pioneers of the black literary tradition and the white critic who would deny that such a tradition even existed. The young poet in "The Rite" murders an older poet, whom he views as reactionary, but in sacrificing him to the new revolutionary program, the young poet ritually "drank his blood and ate his heart," thus drawing his revolutionary sustenance from his forebears without conscious knowledge of doing so. That the older writer provides continuing life for the younger one—and is conscious of that fact—not only endorses the persistence of the political struggle, but also establishes a political context for black literature that reaches back to protest elements in the slave songs. The struggle is nothing new to Randall's generation, or to those generations before him; yet the older poet is quite willing to offer his life in order to broaden the continuity of that protest. On the other hand, Randall challenges—in "Black Poet, White Critic"—the establishment critic who "advises/ not to write on controversial subjects/ like freedom or murder" to reexamine his own critical premises. The critic suggests "universal themes/ and timeless symbols/ like the white unicorn," to which Randall responds: "A *white* unicorn?" Refusing to deny his own heritage and experience as a black man, he realizes that the argument is bogus in any context: The timeless drama of Sophocles or William Shakespeare can hardly be said to ignore freedom and murder. Randall, then, implies that the critic who so blatantly misreads his own literary tradition fears not so much a lack of quality on the part of black poets as the fulfillment of that advice on "universal themes" and "timeless symbols" that would indict the critic's own racism and shoddy intellect as a result of that racism. Black poets might, indeed, write *too well.*

Suggested Readings

Boyd, Melba Joyce. *Wrestling with the Muse: Dudley Randall and the Broadside Press.* New York: Columbia University Press, 2003.

Melhem, D. H. "Dudley Randall: A Humanist View." *Black American Literature Forum* 17 (1983).

Randall, Dudley. "The Message Is in the Melody: An Interview with Dudley Randall." Interview by Leana Ampadu. *Callaloo* 22, no. 2 (Spring, 1999): 438-445.

Thompson, Julius Eric. *Dudley Randall, Broadside Press, and the Black Arts Movement in Detroit, 1960-1995*. Jefferson, N.C.: McFarland, 1999.

Waters, Mark V. "Dudley Randall and the Liberation Aesthetic: Confronting the Politics of 'Blackness.'" *CLA Journal* 44, no. 1 (September, 2000).

Contributors: Michael Loudon and Leslie Ellen Jones

John Rechy

Born: El Paso, Texas; March 10, 1934

Mexican American

Rechy explores the intersection of Chicano, gay, and Roman Catholic identities in his autobiographical fiction.

Principal works

DRAMA: *Momma as She Became—Not as She Was*, pr. 1978; *Tigers Wild*, pr. 1986

LONG FICTION: *City of Night*, 1963; *Numbers*, 1967; *This Day's Death*, 1970; *The Vampires*, 1971; *The Fourth Angel*, 1972; *Rushes*, 1979; *Bodies and Souls*, 1983; *Marilyn's Daughter*, 1988; *The Miraculous Day of Amalia Gómez*, 1991; *Our Lady of Babylon*, 1996; *The Coming of the Night*, 1999; *The Life and Adventures of Lyle Clemens*, 2003

NONFICTION: *Beneath the Skin: The Collected Essays of John Rechy*, 2005; *About My Life and the Kept Woman: An Autobiographical Memoir*, 2008

MISCELLANEOUS: *The Sexual Outlaw: A Documentary, a Non-fiction Account, with Commentaries, of Three Days and Nights in the Sexual Underground*, 1977, revised 1985

With the publication of his first novel, *City of Night*, John Rechy (REH-chee) commenced a lifelong process of self-analysis. "My life," Rechy stated, "is so intertwined with my writing that I almost live it as if it were a novel." In particular, Rechy examines the ways in which gay sexuality, Chicano and European American heritages, and the strictures of the Roman Catholic Church struggle and sometimes harmonize with one another despite incompatibilities. Rechy writes what he calls "autobiography as fiction" in order to construct parables of spiritual salvation and damnation. Alternately remote from or near to God, family, and human connection, Rechy's protagonists struggle against self-absorption and the fear of death.

Rechy's parents immigrated to the southwestern United States during the Mexican Revolution. Rechy grew up torn between his father's stern sense of defeat in the face of anti-Mexican discrimination and his mother's intense protection of her son. The combination of his father's Scottish heritage and his mother's traditional Mexican background made Rechy intensely aware of his status as a person of mixed ancestry in the El Paso of his youth.

Conflicts and pressures at home caused him to move into a narcissistic remoteness that found comfort in the emotional distance of purchased sex. Wandering the country after high school, Rechy worked as a male prostitute in New York, Los Angeles, San Francisco, Chicago, and New Orleans. These experiences as a hustler became the material for *City of Night*. This first-person narrative of sexual and spiritual salvation combines an unapologetic depiction of the sexual underground. The work features a sympathetic protagonist's search for ultimate connection and caring.

Set against either the urban indifference of Los Angeles or the unforgiving landscape of the desert Southwest, Rechy's novels explore the thematic connections between sex, soul, and self. In subsequent works—in particular, *This Day's Death* and *The Miraculous Day of Amalia Gómez*—Rechy has extended his explorations of the spirit to the particulars of Chicano family and culture.

Rechy's autobiographical fictions chart the intersections of ethnic, sexual, regional, and religious identities. He journeys across the Southwestern landscape, through sex and spirit, along the night streets of Los Angeles, and through his own memories of growing up in El Paso.

City of Night

Type of work: Novel
First published: 1963

Based on the author's experiences, *City of Night* explores sexuality and spirituality as they develop during the protagonist's quest for salvation. Combining Chicano heritage, autobiographical material, and a poetic rendering of the restless loneliness of America's sexual underground, *City of Night*—Rechy's first and best-known novel—investigates difficulties and rewards of an individual's search to claim the many identities that intersect in a single life.

The unnamed protagonist's "journey through nightcities and nightlives—looking for . . . some substitute for salvation" begins with his childhood in El Paso, Texas. Rechy draws on stark, lonely imagery (the fiercely unforgiving wind, the father's inexplicable hatred of his son, the mother's hungry love) to portray a childhood and adolescence denied any sense of connection and certainty. Disconnected and detached from his home, the protagonist stands before the mirror confusing identity with isolation. He asserts a narcissistic removal from the world ("I have only me!") that his quest at first confirms, then refutes.

The first-person narrative chronicles the protagonist's wanderings through New York City, Los Angeles, Hollywood, San Francisco, Chicago, and New Orleans. For Rechy, these various urban settings are "one vast City of Night" fused into the "unmistakable shape of loneliness." Working as a male prostitute, the protagonist navigates this landscape, portraying the types of sexual and spiritual desperation he encounters along the way. His journey is a pilgrimage first away from home and then back to it, as he accepts the possibility that he might come to terms with his family, his childhood, and himself.

City of Night interweaves chapters that describe the geographies of the cities the protagonist passes through with chapters that portray people condemned to these dark cities. Sometimes humorous, sometimes bitter, sometimes indifferent, these portraits of people trapped in the loneliness and cruelty of the cities mirror the protagonist's quest. He is like and unlike the denizens of this world.

In New Orleans during Mardi Gras, the protagonist encounters and rejects his first sincere invitation to love: the "undiscovered country which may not even exist and which I was too frightened even to attempt to discover." This invitation nevertheless triggers the narrator's search for redemption and salvation. The memory of his rejection of Jeremy's love haunts him. Caught up in the festivity of the carnival, surrounded by masked revelers and cathedrals, the protagonist affirms the possibility for change.

He returns to El Paso. Exposed to the West Texas wind, "an echo of angry childhood," the protagonist acknowledges uncertainty, the need for hope, and renewal. Rechy leaves the culmination of this search unresolved, a matter of existential self-definition. Combining ethnic, sexual, and spiritual identities, *City of Night* establishes important themes that Rechy explores in greater depth in later works. *City of Night* represents a pioneering look at the interdependency of multiple identities in an individual's search for meaning.

This Day's Death

Type of work: Novel
First published: 1970

This Day's Death, Rechy's third novel, explores Chicano identity and gay sexuality. Unlike other novels by Rechy, however, *This Day's Death* does not initially embody the two identities in one complex character. Instead, the novel shuttles—like its protagonist—between two identities (Chicano and gay) in two separate and yet interdependent situations (El Paso and Los Angeles). Known for acknowledging the autobiographical origins of his fiction, Rechy skillfully illustrates how identities develop, sometimes demanding a person's attention despite that person's effort of will to ignore or deny a given identity.

West Texas and Los Angeles are two poles of identity for Rechy; the one is bound up with his Chicano upbringing and his family, the other with sexual freedom and discovery. As the novel opens, Jim Girard is not gay. He has a fiancée and a promising career in law. His arrest on a lewd conduct charge is a mistake. He keeps his ongoing prosecution on that charge a secret from his mother, who is ill in El Paso. In the course of the novel, Jim recalls his Chicano upbringing. Jim also acknowledges and acts on previously unacknowledged desires for other men. Thus, he gradually becomes gay and Chicano, an embodiment of a complex intersection of identities and an opportunity for Rechy to explore the intertwined roots of self.

Bound up with guilt, pretense, and hypochondria, Girard's "terrible love" for his mother ties him to a childhood and a life that he recognizes as familiar but loathes. He knows that "she will brand each such day with memories he will carry like deep cuts forever." Like other mother-son relationships in Rechy's fiction, the relationship between Girard and his mother is an intense, stifling entanglement of need and rejection. Rechy utilizes the West Texas landscape (the wind, the sky, the desert) to impart a sense of loneliness and austerity that surrounds and amplifies Girard's life with his mother. This love-hate relationship becomes the foundation of the novel, ironically suggesting that identity is inextricably connected to relationship rather than to the isolation that Girard maintains at the beginning of the novel.

This Day's Death is an ironic coming-out story in which circumstances collude to reveal a gay man to himself. Found guilty of the crime, and therefore unable to pursue his career, Jim returns to the park where he was arrested and finds himself accepting, even celebrating desires he never before acknowledged. On one level, the novel advocates social reform, depicting an innocent man convicted of a crime that is not really criminal. On another level, *This Day's Death* is an analysis of the personal and bittersweet complex of experiences from which identities arise. *This Day's Death* acknowledges identities and their complexity. To be Chicano and gay is a burdensome and miraculous combination. Girard's relationship with his mother and whatever relationships he develops from his newly accepted desires will be tinged with joy and sadness, liberation and obligation. "The terrible love left empty" once his mother dies will be a necessary, affirming fact of having cared for his mother.

The Life and Adventures of Lyle Clemens

Type of work: Novel
First published: 2003

There is always more than a touch of the picaresque in Rechy's novels. *City of Night* and *Numbers* are episodic romps through an erotic underworld many readers had never experienced in legitimate fiction before. Certainly the subject matter is arresting (the graphic depictions of homosexual encounters and the dubious terrain of male prostitution); but it really was the pace of if all that created the energy, that driving, obsessive pull of sex reflected in the rush of events, the parade of characters, the breathless narrative. That same energy characterizes Rechy's *The Life and Adventures of Lyle Clemens*, another characteristic account of a young man's journey in search of love and identity.

Readers will surely be tempted to compare Henry Fielding's *Tom Jones* (1749)—an understandable, even irresistible temptation, because *The Life and Adventures of Lyle Clemens* consciously harks back to that "rollicking" eighteenth century narrative of a bastard who takes to the road, fighting past the obstacles of a society stacked against him to emerge his own man. It is the perennial story of the outsider, the innocent eye through which the hypocrisy and affectation of contemporary society are registered and exposed. Like Fielding, Rechy embraces this traditional material with gusto and great invention. In this new version there is Lyle Clemens, the beautiful if troubled Texas youth "who would grow up to become the Mystery Cowboy who appeared naked along Hollywood Boulevard." Before that quintessentially Californian apotheosis, however, he must flee his mother, a bundle of mysteries and madness who schemes to turn her son into the cowboy father he never knew. He must flee the rapacious Texas fundamentalists who scheme to turn him into the Lord's Cowboy, exploiting him to beef up their evangelical network. And he must flee the aging actress, Tara Worth, who schemes to turn him into her own fantasy cowboy and the vehicle of her Hollywood comeback. Lyle escapes them all, though not in a way readers might expect. As was Tom Jones, he has been the instrument for unmasking hypocrisy and unleashing love, and in the process he has found himself.

Rechy tells the tale with his patented raw honesty, the tawdry urban landscapes of Las Vegas and Los Angeles neatly skewered in language that is at once powerful and funny. It is this comic touch that seems new; targets are punctured and charlatans exposed with wonderful ferocity, but there is a hilarity to the book that comes down firmly on the side of life in spite of all its deception and double-dealing. It is as if Rechy has resurrected not only Fielding's elaborate plot but his ebullient good humor as well.

Suggested Readings

Bredbeck, Gregory W. "John Rechy." In *Contemporary Gay American Novelists: A Bio-Bibliographical Critical Sourcebook*, edited by Emmanuel S. Nelson. Westport, Conn.: Greenwood Press, 1993.

Casillo, Charles. *Outlaw: The Lives and Careers of John Rechy*. Los Angeles: Advocate Books, 2002.

Minority Voices 3 (Fall, 1979).

Nelson, E. S. "John Rechy, James Baldwin, and the American Double Minority Literature." *Journal of American Culture* 6 (Summer, 1983).

Ortiz, Ricardo. "L.A. Women: Jim Morrison with John Rechy." *Literature and Psychology* 44 (1998).

_______. "Sexuality Degree Zero." *Journal of Homosexuality* 26 (August/September, 1993).

Rechy, John. Interview by Debra Castillo. *Diacritics* 25 (Spring, 1995).

Steuervogel, T. "Contemporary Homosexual Fiction and the Gay Rights Movement." *Journal of Popular Culture* 20 (Winter, 1986).

Contributor: Daniel M. Scott III

Ishmael Reed

Born: Chattanooga, Tennessee; February 22, 1938

African American, Native American

Reed has created a rich, unique literary synthesis from such diverse elements as African folktales, Caribbean ritual, and European culture.

Principal works

LONG FICTION: *The Free-Lance Pallbearers*, 1967; *Yellow Back Radio Broke-Down*, 1969; *Mumbo Jumbo*, 1972; *The Last Days of Louisiana Red*, 1974; *Flight to Canada*, 1976; *The Terrible Twos*, 1982; *Reckless Eyeballing*, 1986; *The Terrible Threes*, 1989; *Japanese by Spring*, 1993

POETRY: *Catechism of D Neoamerican Hoodoo Church*, 1970; *Conjure: Selected Poems, 1963-1970*, 1972; *Chattanooga*, 1973; *A Secretary to the Spirits*, 1977; *Cab Calloway Stands in for the Moon*, 1986; *New and Collected Poems*, 1988

NONFICTION: *Shrovetide in Old New Orleans*, 1978; *God Made Alaska for the Indians*, 1982; *Writin' Is Fightin': Thirty-seven Years of Boxing on Paper*, 1988; *Airing Dirty Laundry*, 1993; *Conversations with Ishmael Reed*, 1995; *Another Day at the Front: Dispatches from the Race War*, 2002 (essays); *Blues City: A Walk in Oakland*, 2003

EDITED TEXTS: *Nineteen Necromancers from Now*, 1970; *Yardbird Lives!*, 1978 (with Al Young); *Calafia: The California Poetry*, 1979 (with Young and Shawn Hsu Wong); *The Before Columbus Foundation Fiction Anthology: Selections from the American Book Awards, 1980-1990*, 1992 (with Kathryn Trueblood and Wong); *MultiAmerica: Essays on Cultural Wars and Cultural Peace*, 1997; *From Totems to Hip-Hop*, 2003

MISCELLANEOUS: *The Reed Reader*, 2000

The writing of Ishmael Reed (IHSH-may-ehl reed) can be said to mirror his own multiethnic descent, which includes African American, Native American, and Irish. His stepfather, Bennie Stephen Reed (an autoworker), later adopted him. He married Priscilla Rose in 1960; they were divorced in 1970. Reed has two children—Timothy and Brett—from his first marriage and a daughter, Tennessee Maria, from his second.

Early in his life his family moved to Buffalo, New York. He attended the State University of New York at Buffalo from 1956 to 1960 but was not graduated. He has published books of essays and poetry, but he is primarily known as a novelist. He has edited two multicultural anthologies: *Nineteen Necromancers from*

Now (1970) and *Calafia* (1979). He moved to Berkeley, California, where he taught at the University of California, and he served as a visiting professor or writer-in-residence at many other schools.

Reed's first novel, *The Free-Lance Pallbearers*, shows most of the elements for which his writing is known. It is the wildly picaresque and often scatological tale of the adventures of an African American, Bukka Doopeyduk, in Harry Sam, a city that reflects and exaggerates the most repressive aspects of Christian, European culture.

Reed's best-known novel, *Mumbo Jumbo*, uses the conventions of the detective story. PaPa LaBas—whose name, typically for Reed, refers to the Voodoo god Papa Legba and French writer Joris-Karl Huysmans's decadent novel *Là-Bas* (1891; *Down There*, 1924)—investigates an alleged plague called Jes Grew, which turns out to be spontaneous joy, opposed to the grim power structure of monotheistic European culture.

Reed is widely praised for his style, his imaginative story construction, and his masterly use of elements from many cultural backgrounds, but he is often attacked by African American and feminist critics. He has continually satirized other African Americans, especially in *The Last Days of Louisiana Red*, in which he refers to many of them as "Moochers." His criticisms of feminism, most notably in *Reckless Eyeballing*, are widely considered to be misogynistic. *Japanese by Spring* satirizes the politics of the university.

The Free-Lance Pallbearers

Type of work: Novel
First published: 1967

Reed's first novel, *The Free-Lance Pallbearers*, takes place in a futuristic America called Harry Sam: "a big not-to-be-believed out-of-sight, sometimes referred to as O-BOP-SHE-BANG or KLANG-A-LANG-A-DING-DONG." This crumbling and corrupt world is tyrannized by Sam himself, a vulgar fat man who lives in Sam's Motel on Sam's Island in the middle of the lethally polluted Black Bay that borders Harry Sam. Sam, doomed by some terrifying gastrointestinal disorder, spends all of his time on the toilet, his filth pouring into the bay from several large statues of Rutherford B. Hayes.

The bulk of the novel, although framed and periodically informed by a jiving narrative voice, is narrated by Bukka Doopeyduk in a restrained, proper English that identifies his passive faith in the establishment. Doopeyduk is a dedicated adherent to the Nazarene Code, an orderly in a psychiatric hospital, a student at Harry Sam College, and a hapless victim. His comically futile efforts to play by the rules are defeated by the cynics, who manipulate the unjust system to their own advantage. In the end, Doopeyduk is disillusioned: He leads a successful attack on Sam's Island, uncovers the conspiracy that protects Sam's cannibalism, briefly dreams of becoming the black Sam, and is finally crucified.

Ishmael Reed (AP/Wide World Photos)

The Free-Lance Pallbearers is a parody of the African American tradition of first-person, confessional narratives, a book the narrator describes as "growing up in soulsville first of three installments—or what it means to be a backstage darky." Reed's novel challenges the viability of this African American version of the bildungsroman, in which a young protagonist undergoes a painful initiation into the darkness of the white world, a formula exemplified by Richard Wright's *Black Boy* and James Baldwin's *Go Tell It on the Mountain* (1953). In fact, the novel suggests that African American authors' use of this European form is as disabling as Doopeyduk's adherence to the dictates of the Nazarene Code.

The novel is an unrestrained attack on U.S. politics in the 1960's. Harry Sam, alternately referred to as "Nowhere" or "Now Here," is a dualistic vision of a United States that celebrates vacuous contemporaneity. The novel, an inversion of the Horatio Alger myth in the manner of Nathanael West, mercilessly displays American racism, but its focus is the corruptive potential of power. Sam is a grotesque version of President Lyndon B. Johnson, famous for his bathroom interviews, and Sam's cannibalistic taste for children is an attack on Johnson's Vietnam War policy. With *The Free-Lance Pallbearers*, Reed destroys the presumptions of his society, but it is not until his later novels that he attempts to construct an alternative.

Yellow Back Radio Broke-Down

Type of work: Novel
First published: 1969

Yellow Back Radio Broke-Down is set in a fantastic version of the Wild West of popular literature. Reed's protagonist, the Loop Garoo Kid, is a proponent of artistic freedom and an accomplished Voodoo *houngan* who is in marked contrast to the continually victimized Doopeyduk. Armed with supernatural "connaissance" and aided by a white python and the hip, helicopter-flying Chief Showcase, the Kid battles the forces of realistic mimesis and political corruption. His villainous opponent is Drag Gibson, a degenerate cattle baron given to murdering his wives, who is called upon by the citizens of Yellow Back Radio to crush their rebellious children's effort "to create [their] own fictions."

Although *Yellow Back Radio Broke-Down* satirizes Americans' eagerness to suspend civil rights in response to student protests against the Vietnam War, its focus is literature, specifically the dialogue between realism and modernism. The Loop Garoo Kid matches Reed's description of the African American artist in *Nineteen Necromancers from Now*: "a conjurer who works JuJu upon his oppressors; a witch doctor who frees his fellow victims from the psychic attack launched by demons." Through the Loop Garoo Kid, Reed takes a stand for imagination, intelligence, and fantasy against rhetoric, violence, and sentimentality. This theme is made explicit in a debate with Bo Shmo, a "neo-social realist" who maintains that "all art must be for the end of liberating the masses," for the Kid says that a novel "can be anything it wants to be, a vaudeville show, the six o'clock news, the mumblings of wild men saddled by demons."

Reed exhibits his antirealist theory of fiction in *Yellow Back Radio Broke-Down* through his free use of time, characters, and language. The novel ranges from the eighteenth century to the 1960's, combining historical events and cowboy myths with modern technology and cultural detritus. Reed's primary characters are comically exaggerated racial types: Drag Gibson represents the whites' depraved materialism, Chief Showcase represents the American Indians' spirituality, and the Loop Garoo Kid represents the African Americans' artistic soul. Reed explains the novel's title by suggesting that his book is the "dismantling of a genre done in an oral way like radio." "Yellow back" refers to the popular dime novels; "radio" refers to the novel's oral, discontinuous form; and "broke-down" is a dismantling. Thus, Reed's first two novels assault America in an attempt to "dismantle" its cultural structure.

Mumbo Jumbo

Type of work: Novel
First published: 1972

In *Mumbo Jumbo*, Reed expands on the neo-hoodooism of the Loop Garoo Kid in order to create and define an African American aesthetic based on Voodoo, Egyptian mythology, and improvisational musical forms, an aesthetic to challenge the Judeo-Christian tradition, rationalism, and technology. Set in Harlem during the 1920's, *Mumbo Jumbo* is a tragicomical analysis of the Harlem Renaissance's failure to sustain its artistic promise. Reed's protagonist is PaPa LaBas, an aging hoodoo detective and cultural diagnostician, and LaBas's name, meaning "over there" in French, reveals that his purpose is to reconnect African Americans with their cultural heritage by reunifying the Text of Jes Grew, literally the Egyptian Book of Thoth. Reed takes the phrase Jes Grew from Harriet Beecher Stowe's Topsy and

James Weldon Johnson's description of African American music's unascribed development, but in the novel, Jes Grew is a contagion, connected with the improvisational spirit of ragtime and jazz, that begins to spread across America in the 1920's. Jes Grew is an irrational force that threatens to overwhelm the dominant, repressive traditions of established culture. LaBas's efforts to unify and direct this unpredictable force are opposed by the Wallflower Order of the Knights Templar, an organization dedicated to neutralizing the power of Jes Grew in order to protect its privileged status. LaBas fails to reunify the text, a parallel to the dissipation of the Harlem Renaissance's artistic potential, but the failure is seen as temporary; the novel's indeterminate conclusion looks forward to a time when these artistic energies can be reignited.

The novel's title is double-edged. "Mumbo jumbo" is a racist, colonialist phrase used to describe the misunderstood customs and language of dark-skinned people, an approximation of some critics' description of Reed's unorthodox fictional method. Yet "mumbo jumbo" also refers to the power of imagination, the cultural alternative that can free African Americans. A text of and about texts, *Mumbo Jumbo* combines the formulas of detective fiction with the documentary paraphernalia of scholarship: footnotes, illustrations, and a bibliography. Thus, in the disclosure scene required of any good detective story, LaBas, acting the part of interlocutor, provides a lengthy and erudite explication of the development of Jes Grew that begins with a reinterpretation of the myth of Osiris. The parodic scholarship of *Mumbo Jumbo* undercuts the assumed primacy of the European tradition and implicitly argues that African American artists should attempt to discover their distinct cultural heritage.

The Last Days of Louisiana Red

Type of work: Novel
First published: 1974

In *The Last Days of Louisiana Red*, LaBas returns as Reed's protagonist, but the novel abandons the parodic scholarship and high stylization of *Mumbo Jumbo*. Although LaBas again functions as a connection with a non-European tradition of history and myth, *The Last Days of Louisiana Red* is more traditionally structured than its predecessor. In the novel, LaBas solves the murder of Ed Yellings, the founder of the Solid Gumbo Works. Yellings's business is dedicated to combating the effects of Louisiana Red, literally a popular hot sauce but figuratively an evil state of mind that divides African Americans. Yelling's gumbo, like Reed's fiction, is a mixture of disparate elements, and it has a powerful curative effect. In fact, LaBas discovers that Yellings is murdered when he gets close to developing a gumbo that will cure heroin addiction.

In *The Last Days of Louisiana Red*, Reed is examining the self-destructive forces that divide the African American community so that its members fight one another "while above their heads . . . billionaires flew in custom-made jet planes."

Reed shows how individuals' avarice leads them to conspire with the establishment, and he suggests that some of the most vocal and militant leaders are motivated by their egotistical need for power rather than by true concern for oppressed people. Set in Berkeley, California, *The Last Days of Louisiana Red* attacks the credibility of the black revolutionary movements that sprang up in the late 1960's and early 1970's.

Flight to Canada

Type of work: Novel
First published: 1976

Flight to Canada, Reed's fifth novel, is set in an imaginatively redrawn Civil War South, and it describes the relationship between Arthur Swille, a tremendously wealthy Virginia planter who practices necrophilia, and an assortment of sociologically stereotyped slaves. The novel is presented as the slave narrative of Uncle Robin, the most loyal of Swille's possessions. Uncle Robin repeatedly tells Swille that the plantation is his idea of heaven, and he assures his master that he does not believe that Canada exists. Raven Quickskill, "the first one of Swille's slaves to read, the first to write, and the first to run away," is the author of Uncle Robin's story.

Like much of Reed's work, *Flight to Canada* is about the liberating power of art, but in *Flight to Canada*, Reed concentrates on the question of authorial control. All the characters struggle to maintain control of their stories. After escaping from the plantation, Quickskill writes a poem, "Flight to Canada," and his comical verse denunciation of Swille completes his liberation. In complaining of Quickskill's betrayal to Abraham Lincoln, Swille laments that his former bookkeeper uses literacy "like that old Voodoo." In a final assertion of authorial control and the power of the pen, Uncle Robin refuses to sell his story to Harriet Beecher Stowe, gives the rights to Quickskill, rewrites Swille's will, and inherits the plantation.

God Made Alaska for the Indians

Type of work: Essays
First published: 1982

God Made Alaska for the Indians, a collection of essays, manages to pack into its 130 pages many of the widely varied interests of one of the most interesting multicultural figures on the American literary scene. Reed is primarily thought of as an African American writer, but he is also very aware of his Native American ancestry. This dual viewpoint informs the title essay, a lengthy account of political and legal conflicts over the use of Alaskan lands. Reed sympathizes with the Sitka Tlingit Indians, but he realizes that the question is complicated, with other tribes opposing them. As always, Reed is critical of the white establishment, and he demonstrates that supposedly benign conservationist forces such as the Sierra Club can be as uncaring of the interests and customs of the indigenous population as any profit-maddened capitalist corporation. An afterword informs the reader that the Sitka Tlingits finally won.

"The Fourth Ali" covers the second fight between Muhammad Ali and Leon Spinks, late in Ali's career. There is little description of the actual fight, and one learns little more than that Ali won. Reed emphasizes the fight as spectacle, describing the followers, the hangers-on, and Ali's near-mythic role. In the brief "How Not to Get the Infidel to Talk the King's Talk," Reed demolishes the theory that the supposed linguistic flaws of black English keep African Americans from social advancement by pointing to the success of such verbally challenged European Americans as Gerald R. Ford and Nelson A. Rockefeller. "Black Macho, White Macho" attacks some of the male-supremacist views Reed has been accused of holding, pointing out that such views are particularly dangerous in those with access to atomic weapons. "Race War in America?" makes some strong points about racial attitudes in the United States, in the then-pressing context of worry about the minority government in South Africa. In "Black Irishman" Reed, who has always refused to consider himself anything but an African American, looks at his Irish ancestry.

Perhaps the most interesting essay in the book is the last, "American Poetry: Is There a Center?" Reed recounts the controversies over a poetry center set up in Colorado by an Asian religious leader. The center's supporters made claims that it represented a focal point of all that is good in American poetry. Reed replies with his uncompromising view that the genius of American art can be found in the works of all races and cultures.

The Terrible Twos

Type of work: Novel
First published: 1982

In *The Terrible Twos*, Reed uses a contemporary setting to attack Ronald Reagan's administration and the exploitative nature of the American economic system. In the novel, President Dean Clift, a former model, is a mindless figurehead manipulated by an oil cartel that has supplanted the real Santa Claus. Nance Saturday, another of Reed's African American detectives, sets out to discover Saint Nicholas's place of exile. The novel's title suggests that, in its second century, the United States is acting as selfishly and irrationally as the proverbial two-year-old. The central theme is the manner in which a few avaricious people seek vast wealth at the expense of the majority of Americans.

Reckless Eyeballing

Type of work: Novel
First published: 1986

Reckless Eyeballing takes place in the 1980's, and Reed employs a string of comically distorted characters to present the idea that the American literary environment is dominated by New York women and Jews. Although *Reckless Eyeballing* has been called sexist and anti-Semitic by some, Reed's target is a cultural establishment that creates and strengthens racial stereotypes, in particular the view of African American men as savage rapists. To make his point, however, he lampoons feminists, using the character Tremonisha Smarts, a female African American author who has written a novel of violence against women. Reed's satire is probably intended to remind readers of Alice Walker's *The Color Purple* (1982).

Because the novel's central subject is art and the limitations that society places on an artist, it is appropriate that Reed once again employs the technique of a story-within-a-story. Ian Ball, an unsuccessful African American playwright, is the novel's protagonist. In the novel, Ball tries to succeed by shamelessly placating the feminists in power. He writes "Reckless Eyeballing," a play in which a lynched man is posthumously tried for "raping" a woman with lecherous stares, but Ball, who often seems to speak for Reed, maintains his private, chauvinistic views throughout.

New and Collected Poems

Type of work: Poetry
First published: 1988

Reed is primarily known as a novelist. Most critical works about him deal with his fiction, and the leading books about contemporary African American poetry mention him only in passing. His poetry, however, repays reading and study—for the light it casts on his novels, for its treatment of the Hoodoo religion, and for the same verbal facility and breadth of reference that is praised in his fiction. *New and Collected Poems* includes the earlier works *Conjure* (1972), *Chattanooga* (1973), and *A Secretary to the Spirits* (1977). *Conjure*, Reed's first and longest book of poems, is a mixed bag. Filled with typographical tricks that Reed later all but abandoned, it also has moments of striking wit, such as the comparison of the poet to a fading city in "Man or Butterfly" or the two views of "history" in "Dualism: In Ralph Ellison's *Invisible Man*."

Conjure largely deals with the Hoodoo religion, Reed's idiosyncratic combination of ancient Egyptian and contemporary North American elements with the Caribbean religion of vodun, or Voodoo, itself a mix of Yoruba and Christian elements. In "The Neo-HooDoo Manifesto," Reed invokes American musicians, from jazz and blues greats to white rock and rollers, as exemplars of a religious approach based on creativity and bodily pleasure. Hoodoo is polytheistic, excluding only those gods who claim hegemony over the others. Reed's main disagreement with vodun springs from its acceptance of the "dangerous paranoid pain in the neck . . . cop-god from the git-go, Jeho-vah." The history of Hoodoo is outlined in Reed's novel *Mumbo Jumbo* (1972). Its view of all time as synchronous informs the setting of *Flight to Canada* (1976), in which airplanes coexist with plantation slavery, but the fullest expression of Hoodoo's spirit and aesthetic is given in *Conjure*.

Chattanooga is named for Reed's hometown, and the title poem is a paean to the area where Reed grew up and its multicultural heritage. "Railroad Bill, a Conjure Man" is a charming account of how the hero of an old-fashioned trickster tale deals with Hollywood. *A Secretary to the Spirits* is a short book with a few impressive works in it, notably, the first poem, "Pocodonia," expanding what seems to have been a traditional blues song into something far more complex and strange.

The work since *A Secretary to the Spirits* appears in the last section of *New and Collected Poems*, "Points of View." The quality is mixed, but the outrage and the wit that characterize so much of Reed's work can be found in this last section, as in "I'm Running for the Office of Love."

The Terrible Threes

Type of work: Novel
First published: 1989

The Terrible Threes, a sequel to *The Terrible Twos*, continues Reed's satirical attack on the contemporary capitalist system, which, he argues, puts the greatest economic burden on the least privileged. (Reed was also planning a third book in the series, *The Terrible Fours*.) In the first book, there appears a character named Black Peter—an assistant to St. Nicholas in European legend. This Black Peter is an imposter, however, a Rastafarian who studied and appropriated the legend for himself. In *The Terrible Threes*, the true Black Peter emerges to battle the false Peter but is distracted from his mission by the need to do good deeds. Black Peter becomes wildly popular because of these deeds, but a jealous St. Nick and concerned toy companies find a way to put Santa Claus back on top. Capitalism wins again.

Japanese by Spring

Type of work: Novel
First published: 1993

Japanese by Spring is postmodern satire. Like much of Reed's imaginative work, the book mixes fictional characters with "fictionalized" ones. Reed himself is a character in the book, with his own name. The protagonist of *Japanese by Spring* is Benjamin "Chappie" Puttbutt, a teacher of English and literature at Oakland's Jack London College. Chappie dabbled in activist politics in the mid-1960's, but his only concern in the 1990's is receiving tenure and the perks that accompany it. He will put up with virtually anything, including racist insults from students, to avoid hurting his chances at tenure. As in many of Reed's books, Chappie is passive in the face of power at the beginning of his story. He is a middle-class black conservative, but only because the climate at Jack London demands it. Chappie is a chameleon who always matches his behavior to the ideology of his environment. However, when he is denied tenure and is about to be replaced by a feminist poet who is more flash than substance, Chappie's hidden anger begins to surface. Chappie has also been studying Japanese with a tutor named Dr. Yamato. This proves fortuitous when the Japanese buy Jack London and Dr. Yamato becomes the college president. Chappie suddenly finds himself in a position of power and gloats over those who denied him tenure. He soon finds, however, that his new bosses are the same as the old ones. Dr. Yamato is a tyrant and is eventually arrested by a group that includes Chappie's father, a two-star Air Force general. Dr. Yamato is released, though, and a surprised Chappie learns that there is an "invisible government" that truly controls the United States. Chappie has pierced some of his illusions, but there are others that he never penetrates, such as his blindness to his own opportunism.

The novel's conclusion moves away from Chappie's point of view to that of a fictionalized Reed. This Reed skewers political correctness but also shows that the people who complain the most about it are often its greatest purveyors. Reed also lampoons American xenophobia, particularly toward Japan, but he does so in a balanced manner that does not gloss over Japanese faults. Ultimately, though, Reed uses *Japanese by Spring* as he used other novels before, to explore art and politics and the contradictions of America and race.

Suggested Readings

Boyer, Jay. *Ishmael Reed.* Boise, Idaho: Boise State University Press, 1993.

Dick, Bruce, and Amritjit Singh, eds. *Conversations with Ishmael Reed.* Jackson: University Press of Mississippi, 1995.

Dick, Bruce, and Pavel Zemliansky, eds. *The Critical Response to Ishmael Reed.* Westport, Conn.: Greenwood Press, 1999.

Fox, Robert Elliot. *Conscientious Sorcerers: The Black Post-Modern Fiction of LeRoi Jones/Amiri Baraka, Ishmael Reed, and Samuel R. Delaney.* New York: Greenwood Press, 1987.

Gates, Henry Louis, Jr. *The Signifying Monkey: A Theory of Afro-American Literary Criticism.* New York: Oxford University Press, 1988.

McGee, Patrick. *Ishmael Reed and the Ends of Race.* New York: St. Martin's Press, 1997.

Reed, Ishmael. *Conversations with Ishmael Reed.* Edited by Bruce Dick and Amritjit Singh. Jackson: University Press of Mississippi, 1995.

Weisenburger, Steven. *Fables of Subversion: Satire and the American Novel, 1930-1980.* Athens: University of Georgia Press, 1995.

Contributors: Arthur D. Hlavaty, Carl Brucker, and Charles A. Gramlich

Adrienne Rich

Born: Baltimore, Maryland; May 16, 1929

Jewish

Rich is an articulate, conscious, and critical explorer of such subjects as feminism and lesbianism.

Principal works

POETRY: *A Change of World*, 1951; *The Diamond Cutters, and Other Poems*, 1955; *Snapshots of a Daughter-in-Law*, 1963; *Necessities of Life*, 1966; *Selected Poems*, 1967; *Leaflets*, 1969; *The Will to Change*, 1971; *Diving into the Wreck*, 1973; *Poems: Selected and New, 1950-1974*, 1975; *Twenty-one Love Poems*, 1976; *The Dream of a Common Language*, 1978; *A Wild Patience Has Taken Me This Far: Poems, 1978-1981*, 1981; *Sources*, 1983; *The Fact of a Doorframe: Poems Selected and New, 1950-1984*, 1984; *Your Native Land, Your Life*, 1986; *Time's Power: Poems, 1985-1988*, 1989; *An Atlas of the Difficult World: Poems, 1988-1991*, 1991; *Collected Early Poems, 1950-1970*, 1993; *Dark Fields of the Republic: Poems, 1991-1995*, 1995; *Selected Poems, 1950-1995*, 1996; *Midnight Salvage: Poems, 1995-1998*, 1999; *Fox: Poems, 1998-2000*, 2001; *The School Among the Ruins: Poems, 2000-2004*, 2004; *Telephone Ringing in the Labyrinth: Poems, 2004-2006*, 2007

NONFICTION: *Of Woman Born: Motherhood as Experience and Institution*, 1976; *On Lies, Secrets, and Silence: Selected Prose, 1966-1978*, 1979; *Blood, Bread, and Poetry: Selected Prose, 1979-1985*, 1986; *What Is Found There: Notebooks on Poetry and Politics*, 1993; *Arts of the Possible: Essays and Conversations*, 2001; *Poetry and Commitment: An Essay*, 2007

EDITED TEXTS: *The Best American Poetry, 1996*, 1996; *Selected Poems/Muriel Rukeyser*, 2004

MISCELLANEOUS: *Adrienne Rich's Poetry and Prose: Poems, Prose, Reviews, and Criticism*, 1993 (Barbara Chartesworth Gelpi and Albert Gelpi, editors)

As a child, Adrienne Rich was encouraged to write poetry by her father. At Radcliffe College, she continued to study the formal craft of poetry as practiced and taught by male teachers. In 1951, Rich's first volume of poetry, *A Change of World*, was selected for the Yale Series of Younger Poets. Rich was praised as a fine poet and as a modest young woman who respected her elders. The poems in her first two collections are traditional in form, modeled on the male poets Rich studied.

At twenty-four, Rich married a Harvard professor. She had three children by the time she was thirty. The conflict between the traditional roles of mother and wife and her professional accomplishments left her frustrated. *Snapshots of a Daughter-in-Law* begins to express a woman's point of view. Rich moved to New York City in 1966 and became involved in civil rights and antiwar campaigns. In 1969, she separated from her husband, who committed suicide in 1970. During the 1970's, Rich became a radical feminist, active in the women's rights movement. The collections published during these years express these political themes.

Rich came out as a lesbian in 1976, and her collection *The Dream of a Common Language* includes explicitly lesbian poems. In the early 1980's, she moved to western Massachusetts with her companion, Michelle Cliff. Her essays and poetry with political themes were sometimes criticized as more didactic than artful. Rich continued to evolve politically and artistically. She moved to California, writing and teaching at Stanford University. Her books published in the 1990's confront the relationship of poetry and politics and issues of contemporary American life.

Rich's life and work have sought to balance the conflicting demands of poetry, which is her vocation, with the ideology of engagement that her life has brought to her art. Most critics have characterized her work as an artistic expression of feminist politics. Some critics feel that the politics overwhelm the lyricism of her art. It is generally accepted, however, that she is an important voice in political and artistic issues, and perhaps the most important poetic voice of twentieth century feminism.

Poetry

Rich's poetry traces the growth of a conscious woman in the second half of the twentieth century. Her first two books, *A Change of World* and *The Diamond Cutters* (1955), contain verses of finely crafted, imitative forms, strongly influenced by the modernist poets. *Snapshots of a Daughter-in-Law* is a transitional work in which Rich begins to express a woman's concerns. Her form loosens as well; she begins to experiment with free verse.

Adrienne Rich (Library of Congress)

The collections *Necessities of Life* (1966), *Leaflets* (1969), and *The Will to Change* (1971) openly reject patriarchal culture and language. Experiments with form continue as she juxtaposes poetry and prose and uses multiple voices. With *Diving into the Wreck* Rich's poetry becomes clearly identified with radical feminism and lesbian separatism. A theme of the title poem is the need for women to define themselves in their own terms and create an alternative female language. *The Dream of a Common Language* was published after Rich came out as a lesbian and includes the explicitly sexual "Twenty-one Love Poems."

By the time of the publication of *A Wild Patience Has Taken Me This Far* (1981), the influence of Rich's poetry extended beyond art and into politics. As a woman in a patriarchal society, Rich expresses a fundamental conflict between poetry and politics, which occupies her poetic voice. The collections *Your Native Land, Your Life* (1986), *Time's Power* (1989), and *An Atlas of the Difficult World* address new issues while continuing to develop Rich's feminist concerns. The long poem "Sources" addresses Rich's Jewish heritage and the Holocaust. "Living Memory" addresses issues of aging. In *Dark Fields of the Republic*, Rich continues to develop her preoccupations with the relationship of poetry and politics and grapples with issues of contemporary American society.

An Atlas of the Difficult World

Type of work: Poetry
First published: 1991

In *An Atlas of the Difficult World*, Rich offers twenty-five poems written between 1988 and 1991. Visionary in content, elegiac in tone, and Whitmanesque in scope, the poems divide into two principal sections. The first consists of the thirteen-part title poem, which maps the physical and spiritual landscape of the United States, crisscrossing the country to capture its divergent elements and forge a link between the author's personal past and the country's current social and moral state. Much of the material focuses on the death of innocence and the emergence of violence in American culture. The second section of the book consists of twelve poems, several in multiple parts. It opens with five separate poems portraying women in various manifestations, then moves to a ten-part poem entitled "Eastern War Time," a powerful piece evoking the experiences of Jews in America and in Europe primarily during World War II. The section concludes with poems on art, friendship, and transformation.

Characteristically, Rich uses free forms for most of the poems in this collection. The notable departure is the five-part poem, "Through Corrolitos Under Rolls of Cloud," where each section consists of twelve lines, often with interlocking end rhymes reminiscent of the formalism of Rich's poetry prior to *Snapshots of a Daughter-in-Law*. Drawing her images from domestic life, the countryside and landscape of California and New England, personal memory, and history, Rich writes about love, sacrifice, friendship, art, violence, and death—much broader themes than the women's issues that dominate her other collections. Women are still prominent in *An Atlas of the Difficult World*, for much of the text is written clearly from a female perspective. However, Rich has moved beyond the purely feminist to larger concerns facing America. Rejecting the often deliberate obscurity of modernism, she presents a powerful work in accessible language, a book deserving of the National Book Award nomination it garnered.

Suggested Readings

Cooper, Jane Roberta, ed. *Reading Adrienne Rich: Review and Re-Visions, 1951-1981*. Ann Arbor: University of Michigan Press, 1984.

Dickie, Margaret. *Stein, Bishop, and Rich: Lyrics of Love, War, and Place*. Chapel Hill: University of North Carolina Press, 1997.

Gelpi, Barbara Charlesworth, and Albert Gelpi, eds. *Adrienne Rich's Poetry and Prose*. New York: W. W. Norton, 1993.

Keyes, Claire. *The Aesthetics of Power: The Poetry of Adrienne Rich*. Athens: University of Georgia Press, 1986.

Langdell, Cheri Colby. *Adrienne Rich: The Moment of Change*. Westport, Conn.: Praeger, 2004.

Ratcliffe, Krista. *Anglo-American Feminist Challenges to the Rhetorical Traditions: Virginia Woolf, Mary Daly, Adrienne Rich*. Carbondale: Southern Illinois University Press, 1996.

Sickels, Amy. *Adrienne Rich*. Philadelphia: Chelsea House, 2005.

Templeton, Alice. *The Dream and the Dialogue: Adrienne Rich's Feminist Poetics*. Knoxville: University of Tennessee Press, 1994.

Wadden, Paul. *The Rhetoric of Self in Robert Bly and Adrienne Rich: Doubling and the Holotropic Urge*. New York: Peter Lang, 2003.

Yorke, Liz. *Adrienne Rich: Passion, Politics, and the Body*. Newbury Park, Calif.: Sage, 1998.

Contributor: Susan Butterworth

Mordecai Richler

Born: Montreal, Quebec, Canada; January 27, 1931
Died: Montreal, Quebec, Canada; July 3, 2001

Jewish

Challenging the myths of his culture, Richler exposes the rottenness at the heart of the human condition.

Principal works

CHILDREN'S LITERATURE: *Jacob Two-Two Meets the Hooded Fang*, 1975; *Jacob Two-Two and the Dinosaur*, 1987; *Jacob Two-Two's First Spy Case*, 1997

LONG FICTION: *The Acrobats*, 1954 (alsp pb. as *Wicked We Love*); *Son of a Smaller Hero*, 1955; *A Choice of Enemies*, 1957; *The Apprenticeship of Duddy Kravitz*, 1959; *The Incomparable Atuk*, 1963 (also pb. as *Stick Your Neck Out*); *Cocksure: A Novel*, 1968; *St. Urbain's Horseman*, 1971; *Joshua Then and Now*, 1980; *Solomon Gursky Was Here*, 1989; *Barney's Version*, 1997

SCREENPLAYS: *No Love for Johnnie*, 1961 (with Nicholas Phipps); *Young and Willing*, 1964 (with Phipps); *Life at the Top*, 1965; *The Apprenticeship of Duddy Kravitz*, 1974 (adaptation of his novel); *Joshua Then and Now*, 1985 (adaptation of his novel)

SHORT FICTION: *The Street: Stories*, 1969

NONFICTION: *Hunting Tigers Under Glass: Essays and Reports*, 1968; *Shovelling Trouble*, 1972; *Notes on an Endangered Species and Others*, 1974; *The Great Comic Book Heroes, and Other Essays*, 1978; *Home Sweet Home*, 1984; *Broadsides: Reviews and Opinions*, 1990; *Oh Canada! Oh Quebec! Requiem for a Divided Country*, 1992; *This Year in Jerusalem*, 1994; *Belling the Cat: Essays, Reports and Opinions*, 1998; *Dispatches from the Sporting Life*, 2001; *On Snooker: The Game and the Characters Who Play It*, 2001

EDITED TEXTS: *Canadian Writing Today*, 1970; *Writers on World War II: An Anthology*, 1991

Mordecai Richler (MOHR-deh-ki RIHK-lur) was born in a Jewish section of Montreal. His education at Jewish parochial schools reinforced his Jewish identity, and the French language that he spoke identified him as French Canadian. Richler would embrace neither identity comfortably.

He began writing seriously when he was fourteen. At about the same time, he rejected the family expectation that he become a rabbi and ceased his religious training. After high school, Richler attended Sir George Williams University in Montreal for two years, then grew restive and left for Paris in 1951 to join such other aspiring writers as Mavis Gallant and Terry Southern. The separation from his beginnings helped to sharpen the perspective on his heritage. He knew that escape from the past is impossible and even undesirable. After two years, an invitation to become writer-in-residence at his alma mater attracted him back to Montreal.

The Acrobats introduced concerns that would recur in much of Richler's later fiction: the place of Jews in contemporary society, the need for values, and the exercise of personal responsibility. Deciding that he would make his living solely by writing, Richler moved to England, where his next six novels were published. Most of these novels revealed their author as a severe, often shocking critic of the Jewish ghetto (*Son of a Smaller Hero*), of Jewish greed and ruthlessness (*The Apprenticeship of Duddy Kravitz*), of Canadian nationalism (*The Incomparable Atuk*), and of the North American entertainment industry (*Cocksure*). The writing often reflects a certain degree of ambivalence about the author's ethnic identity, with the need to reject dominating the inclination to affirm.

When Richler returned to Canada—to "the roots of his discontent"—in 1972, his many years of "exile" in Europe had heightened his own sense of self as a Jewish Canadian writer. Richler did not always see himself as others saw him: abrasive, arrogant, and perverse. He has been described as an anti-Canadian Canadian and an anti-Semitic Jew. Richler saw himself, however, as a moralist who wrote out of a sense of "disgust with things as they are," who debunked the bankrupt values that characterized his culture and his ethnic community. His later works established him as a more evenhanded critic of Jewish and Canadian identity, one who affirmed the need for the bonds of family and community in an unstable, corrupt world. He died in Montreal in 2001 after a long battle with cancer, lionized as one of Canada's first internationally recognized writers.

Son of a Smaller Hero

Type of work: Novel
First published: 1955

Son of a Smaller Hero is the story of an angry young man's confused search for his identity. In what is generally regarded as an apprentice work, Richler presents a fairly realistic story of a rebellious and rather self-centered hero who struggles to escape the restrictive identity that his ethnic community and his society would place on him.

Noah Adler is a second-generation Canadian, born and raised in the Montreal Jewish ghetto. His family's strife and the religious and social strictures of his milieu, which he finds stifling, impel him to leave in search of freedom and selfhood in the gentile world. That world, too, fails to fulfill the hero's quest. Through a literature class, Noah meets Professor Theo Hall, who befriends him and takes him into his home. Soon, Hall's wife, Miriam, does more than befriend their boarder and eventually leaves her husband to live with Noah. The romance, so passionately pursued by Noah at first, fades rather quickly when he discovers that the posses-

Mordecai Richler (Christopher Morris)

sive love of and responsibility for a woman can turn into its own kind of ghetto.

In addition, the ghetto of his upbringing still has its hold on him. When his father dies in a fire, Noah abandons Miriam and returns to his family, no longer the adolescent rebel that he was. Neither has he become a quiescent conformist. When the Jewish community attempts to raise his feckless father to sainthood, he demurs. When his rich Uncle Max greedily tries to exploit the dead father's new status, Noah resists. When Noah discovers his grandfather's secret, repressed, lifelong love for a gentile woman he met years before in Europe, this clarifies Noah's own predicament. The ways of his family and of his ghetto community cannot be his. When Noah's ambitious mother becomes increasingly emotionally demanding, Noah knows that he cannot stay.

The story ends as it began: Noah leaves home, this time for Europe. He turns his back on his ailing, grasping mother and on his lonely, isolated grandfather. He turns his back on his restrictive ethnic community. The search for self continues, but it is a search permeated with ambivalence. Noah has found that he cannot affirm his identity apart from community, family, and place. His confusion and torment stem from his problem that he can neither embrace nor finally reject community, family, or place. He chooses to escape them for the time being, but his search for an independent identity leads finally to a sense of futility.

The Apprenticeship of Duddy Kravitz

Type of work: Novel
First published: 1959

There is so much comic energy in *The Apprenticeship of Duddy Kravitz* that the reader can easily underestimate the social and moral implications of the work. Richler stated that to a certain extent the reader should sympathize with Duddy, who must rise above the poverty of the St. Urbain ghetto to challenge and defeat powerful manipulators such as Jerry Dingleman, the Boy Wonder. The ambiguity of Duddy's character creates a problem of moral focus, however, in that some of his victories are at the expense of truly kindhearted people, such as Virgil Roseboro and Yvette.

There are certainly many reasons for Duddy's aggressive, almost amoral behavior. His mother died when Duddy was very young, leaving him without the female stability he needed at the time. His father, Max the Hack, who drives a Montreal cab and pimps on the side, lets Duddy fend for himself, as most of his affection and attention went to the older son, Lenny. Duddy remembers that his father wrote many letters to Lenny when he worked at a resort, but Max refuses to write to Duddy. Max also encourages Lenny to go to medical school and is proud of his achievements; he makes it obvious that he expects little from Duddy and does not perceive the extent of Duddy's ambition nor his loyalty to his family. Duddy is also often humiliated by the affluent university students with whom he works as a waiter at the Hotel Lac des Sables. Irwin Shubert, for instance, considers Duddy a social inferior and, using a rigged roulette wheel, cheats him out of three hundred dollars.

Although eliciting sympathy by explaining Duddy's situation, Richler undercuts a completely sympathetic attitude toward Duddy by detailing the results of his actions. His exploitation of the other students of Fletcher's Field High School leads even his friend Jake Hersh to believe that he makes everything dirty. Duddy's schemes to make money are clever enough; he works out a system to steal hockey sticks from the Montreal Canadians, but he does not realize that the blame rests on the stick boy, who is trying to earn money through honest, hard work. More seriously, Duddy, through a cruel practical joke, is responsible for the death of Mrs. Macpherson, the wife of one of his teachers. Later, as he tries to make his dream of owning land come true, Duddy rejects his lover Yvette, causes the paralysis of his friend Virgil, from whom he also steals money, and alienates his grandfather, Simcha, who cares for him more than anyone else.

Duddy's relationship with Simcha provides both the moral tone and the narrative drive of the novel. Simcha, a man trusted but not loved by the elders of the St. Urbain ghetto for his quiet, patient integrity, is loved by his favorite, Duddy. Like many others of his generation, Simcha feels the weight of the immigrant's fear of failure and instills Duddy with the idea that a man without land is a nobody. For Simcha, this cliché is a more complex concept associated with the traditional struggles of the Jews and presupposes a sense of responsibility. Duddy misinterprets the implications of his grandfather's advice and perceives it as being a practical imperative to be gained at any cost, involving himself in many schemes—from importing illegal pinball machines to filming bar mitzvahs with a bizarre, alcoholic documentary director—in order to purchase land for commercial development.

For a short time, Duddy's plans misfire; he goes bankrupt and is unable to pay for the land he wants so badly. Upon hearing that the Boy Wonder, the ghetto "miracle" who has escaped his environment by drug peddling and other corrupt means, covets the same land, Duddy forges checks in Virgil's name to get enough money to make the purchase. In a closing scene, Duddy brings his family to see his property. By coincidence, the Boy Wonder arrives, and Duddy drives him away with verbal abuse. His father is more impressed with this act of defiance than with Duddy's achievement, and later, among his circle of friends, Max begins to create a legend about Duddy in much the same way as he created the legend of the Boy Wonder. Although his victory has been effected by deceit and victimization, Duddy's behavior seems vindicated; he smiles in triumph, unaware that he continues only under the spell of a shared illusion. The reader is left elated to a certain extent at the defeat of the Boy Wonder, yet sobered by the figure of Simcha, crying in the car, after having been informed by Yvette of Duddy's method of acquiring the land.

Suggested Readings

Brenner, Rachel Feldhay. *Assimilation and Assertion: The Response to the Holocaust in Mordecai Richler's Writings*. New York: P. Lang, 1989.

Craniford, Ada. *Fiction and Fact in Mordecai Richler's Novels*. Lewiston, N.Y.: E. Mellen, 1992.

Darling, Michael, ed. *Perspectives on Mordecai Richler*. Toronto: ECW Press, 1986.

Ramraj, Victor J. *Mordecai Richler*. Boston: Twayne, 1983.

Richler, Jacob. "My Old Man." *Gentlemen's Quarterly* 65 (May, 1995).

Richler, Mordecai. Interview by Sybil S. Steinberg. *Publishers Weekly* 237 (April 27, 1990): 45-46.

Sheps, G. David, ed. *Mordecai Richler*. Toronto: McGraw-Hill Ryerson, 1971.

Woodcock, George. *Mordecai Richler*. Toronto: McClelland and Stewart, 1970.

Contributors: Henry J. Baron and James C. MacDonald

Alberto Ríos

Born: Nogales, Arizona; September 18, 1952

Mexican American

Ríos's writings have placed increasing importance on such means of bridging the gulfs that divide people.

Principal works

POETRY: *Elk Heads on the Wall*, 1979; *Whispering to Fool the Wind*, 1982; *Five Indiscretions*, 1985; *The Lime Orchard Woman*, 1988; *The Warrington Poems*, 1989; *Teodoro Luna's Two Kisses*, 1990; *The Smallest Muscle in the Human Body*, 2002; *The Theater of Night*, 2005

SHORT FICTION: *The Iguana Killer: Twelve Stories of the Heart*, 1984; *Pig Cookies, and Other Stories*, 1995; *The Curtain of Trees: Stories*, 1999

NONFICTION: *Capirotada: A Nogales Memoir*, 1999

Both in fact and in spirit, Alberto Ríos (al-BEHR-toh REE-ohs) is a native of the Southwest. He was born to a Mexican father, Alberto Alvaro Ríos, a justice of the peace, and an English mother, Agnes Fogg Ríos, a nurse. Early in his life he was nicknamed Tito, a diminutive of Albertito, that is, "Little Albert." The nickname referred to his small physical frame and differentiated him from his father. In 1975 the future author earned a bachelor of arts degree, with a major in psychology, from the University of Arizona. He then entered the university's law school, only to find that poetry rather than the law was to be his calling. After one year of legal training he switched to the graduate program in creative writing, taking a master of fine arts degree in 1979. He joined the faculty of Arizona State University in 1982 and became Regents' Professor of English there in 1994.

Ríos grew up on the Mexican American border, and the work that first brought him widespread attention, *Whispering to Fool the Wind*, addressed most of all the splay of his roots. This volume won for Ríos the prestigious Walt Whitman Award from the National Academy of American Poets in 1981. His first collection of short fiction, *The Iguana Killer*, winner of the Western States Book Award for fiction some two years later, dealt with similar concerns. Taken together, these works identified Ríos as a first-generation American artist chronicling an ethnic experience that had too long gone unexplored in American letters. After their publication, Ríos was warmly praised and widely anthologized, often embraced for this subject matter.

Ríos's work extended beyond the provincial with the publication of the collection of poems *Teodoro Luna's Two Kisses* and his second short-fiction collection,

Pig Cookies, and Other Stories. These works still spoke of a culture in transition, but they also displayed an evolving artistic vision, one having as much to do with the human condition as it has to do with an ethnic experience per se. Ríos's writing began to manifest something beyond the tangible. A man spits on the pavement in order to rid himself of an intolerable thought. A priest's soul leaves his body, with animal-like instinct. A fat man's body is proof of a weight within him having nothing to do with scales or the flesh. A number of critics noted Ríos's ability to make the commonplace seem strange—as well as his capacity to make the familiar seem magical—and aligned him in this regard with the Latin Magical Realists, such as Gabriel García Márquez.

Ríos's vision is important in its own right, however. In an early short story, "The Birthday of Mrs. Pineda," a character brings a cup of coffee to his face only to discover the aroma pulling his head toward the lip of the cup. A short story published a decade later brings this conceit to fruition. "The Great Gardens of Lamberto Diaz" begins with these words:

> A person did not come to these gardens . . . to admire them or simply to breathe them in. No. One was breathed in by them, and something more. In this place a person was drawn up as if to the breast of the gardens, as if one were a child again, and being drawn up was all that mattered and meant everything.

Often in his interviews Ríos speaks of "situational physics," of "emotional science." Readers are asked in reading Ríos not simply to revise their suppositions about natural law but to relocate themselves, to reconsider their relationship to all that is tangible. People must reconfirm their presence on the planet, and then reconfirm this presence to one another; the process must begin by listening to language.

Ríos is bilingual, and from the beginning he has called on the idioms and syntax of both English and Spanish in his work. He has also concerned himself with what he calls "a third language," a language that people's bodies speak to one another with or without their conscious knowledge—the wink, the nod, the small and still smaller gesture. The reader encounters this type of language even in such early poems as "Nani," in which a small boy speaks English, his grandmother, only Spanish. She serves him lunch each week, and the old woman and the boy discover a shared understanding, bringing them closer than words ever could.

Ríos has placed increasing importance on such means of bridging the gulfs that divide people. In the title poem of *Teodoro Luna's Two Kisses*, aged Teodoro Luna and his equally aged wife know an intimacy that the young are denied—a glance from one to the other, an eyebrow raised that turns a public event into a private experience between them. Kissing is the single act that most occupies Ríos's attention. It illustrates both the enormity of human desire and the inability of people to express themselves in commensurate proportions. It stands for all that divides people and all that might bring them together. Ríos is often at his best when he is exploring how people turn public events into private experience and what they must dare in order to show themselves to the world. Certainly this is the case in several of the stories in *Pig Cookies*. Lazaro, the small boy in the title story, is so consumed with love for a neighbor girl that his very being is shaken, his baker's hands overcome. To put this love of her into words is a much different matter, as the story's ending reminds the reader: "The most difficult act in the world, he thought with his stomach, was this first saying of *hello*. This first daring to call, without permission, Desire by its first name."

In 1999 Ríos published a memoir, *Capirotada*, named for a Mexican bread pudding made (like his life, as Ríos notes) from "a mysterious mixture of prunes, peanuts, white bread, raisins, *quesadilla* cheese, butter, cinnamon and cloves . . . and things people will not tell you." It won the Latino Literary Hall of Fame Award. In 2002 he published *The Smallest Muscle in the Human Body*, in which poems honed from fable, parable, and family legend use the "intense and supple imagination of childhood to find and preserve history beyond facts"; this collection was a finalist for the National Book Award. In addition to winning these honors, Ríos is the recipient of the Arizona Governor's Arts Award, fellowships from the Guggenheim Foundation and the National Endowment for the Arts, the Walt Whitman Award, the Western States Book Award for Fiction, and six Pushcart Prizes in both poetry and fiction. In 2002, he won the Western Literature Association's Distinguished Achievement Award, the group's highest distinction for authors whose work has defined and influenced the literature and study of the West.

"The Purpose of Altar Boys"

Type of work: Poetry
First published: 1982, in *Whispering to Fool the Wind*

In "The Purpose of Altar Boys" the adult Alberto Ríos assumes the voice of a mischievous altar boy who "knew about . . . things." For example, when he assisted the priest at Communion on Sundays, he believed he had his own mission. On some Sundays, he says, his mission was to remind people of the night before. Holding the metal plate beneath a communicant's chin, he would drag his feet on the carpet, stirring up static electricity. He would wait for the right moment, then touch the plate to the person's chin, delivering his "Holy Electric Shock" of retribution.

The sense of ease and speed in the poem's narration is facilitated by the poet's use of a relatively short poetic line, usually containing six or seven syllables. Although the lines are short, the sentences are long. The combination of short lines and long sentences creates a sense not only of speed but also of breathlessness—these features express the altar boy's excitement as he tells his story of good and evil, judgment and temptation. His excitement is also conveyed by repetition. For example, the boy's repeated use of the pronoun "I" reflects his self-assertion and reveals the pride he takes in fulfilling his mission.

The altar boy is a comic character, a prankster whose mischief is essentially harmless. What is harmless in a child, however, may be evil in an adult. A voyeur is not an attractive person. Far worse are people who commit murder and claim that God told them to do it. The altar boy is merely flirting with the sin of pride when he takes upon himself the authority to judge and punish others. Thus, it is important that the poem is written in the past tense. The adult narrator has experience that he lacked as a boy, and his concepts of good and evil are no longer naïve.

Suggested Readings

Logue, Mary. Review of *Whispering to Fool the Wind*, by Alberto Ríos. *Village Voice Literary Supplement*, October, 1982.

Ríos, Alberto. "Words like the Wind: An Interview with Alberto Ríos." Interview by William Barillas. *Américas Review* 24 (Fall/Winter, 1996).

Ullman, L. "Solitaries and Storytellers, Magicians and Pagans: Five Poets in the World." *Kenyon Review* 13 (Spring, 1991).

Wild, Peter. *Alberto Ríos*. Boise, Idaho: Boise State University Press, 1998.

Contributors: Jay Boyer and James Green

Tomás Rivera

BORN: Crystal City, Texas; December 22, 1935
DIED: Fontana, California; May 16, 1984

MEXICAN AMERICAN

Rivera's writings sparked an explosion of work about the Chicano identity and focused attention on the experiences of migrant workers.

PRINCIPAL WORKS

LONG FICTION: *. . . y no se lo tragó la tierra/. . . and the earth did not part*, 1971 (also pb. as *This Migrant Earth*, 1985; *. . . and the earth did not devour him*, 1987)
POETRY: *Always, and Other Poems*, 1973; *The Searchers: Collected Poetry*, 1990
SHORT FICTION: *The Harvest: Short Stories*, 1989 (bilingual)
MISCELLANEOUS: *Tomás Rivera: The Complete Works*, 1991

Tomás Rivera (toh-MAHS ree-VAY-rah) was the first winner of the Quinto Sol literary prize for the best Chicano work. His death cut short a life full of achievements and promise. Rivera was born to a family of migrant farmworkers in south Texas, and much of his writing is derived from his childhood experiences in a poor, Spanish-speaking, nomadic subculture.

Rivera began college in 1954, with concerns for his people motivating him to become a teacher. He earned his bachelor's degree in 1958 and two master's degrees, in 1964 and 1969, from Southwest Texas State University. He received his doctorate in romance literatures in 1969 from the University of Oklahoma. His career as a college teacher and administrator included appointments in Texas at Sam Houston State University, Trinity University, and the University of Texas at San Antonio and at El Paso.

In 1979, Rivera became the youngest person and the first member of a minority group to be appointed chancellor of a campus of the University of California. Rivera spent his last five years at the helm of the University of California, Riverside. He died at the young age of forty-eight, of a heart attack. His devotion to and achievements in education for Latino youth were honored with the naming of the main University of California, Riverside library after him, and the establishment of the Tomás Rivera Center (later the Tomás Rivera Policy Institute) at Claremont, California.

Rivera's poems and short stories are included in many anthologies of Chicano or Latino literature. He is recognized as one of the first to give voice to the silent Latino underclass of the American Southwest. His works explore the difficulties of growing up, of sorting truth from myth, and of finding one's identity and self-esteem in the midst of oppressive poverty. The struggle to overcome internal and external difficulties is portrayed vividly in his novel *and the earth did not part* and in such stories as "Eva and Daniel," "The Harvest," and "Zoo Island."

. . . and the earth did not part

TYPE OF WORK: Novel
FIRST PUBLISHED: *. . . y no se lo tragó la tierra/and the earth did not part*, 1971

Rivera's only published novel exerted a great influence on the blossoming of Chicano literature. The book explores the psychological and external circumstances of a boy who is coming of age in a Mexican American migrant family. The novel is a collection of disjointed narratives, including twelve stories and thirteen vignettes, told with various voices. This unusual structure evokes impressions of a lifestyle in which the continuity of existence is repeatedly broken by forced migration, in which conflicting values tug at the emerging self, and in which poverty creates a deadening sameness that erases time.

The story begins with "The Lost Year," which indicates the boy has lost touch with his identity and with the reality of events. Several sections portray the dismal, oppressed condition of migrant farmworkers. "Hand in His Pocket" tells of a wicked couple—immigrants who prey on their own people. In "A Silvery Night," the boy first calls the devil, then decides that the devil does not exist. Religious awakening continues in the title chapter, in which the boy curses God and is not punished—the earth remains solid.

The nature of sin, the mystery of sex, and the injustices and tragedies visited upon his people are all confusing to the boy. Brief moments of beauty are eclipsed by injuries and horrible deaths. A mother struggles to buy a few Christmas presents for her children and is thwarted by the disturbing confusion and noise of the town. In a swindle, a family loses their only photograph of a son killed in the Korean War. Bouncing from place to place in rickety trucks, the workers lose all sense of continuity. The boy becomes a man, hiding under his house. The final scene offers a glimmer of hope, as he climbs a tree and imagines that someone in another tree can see him.

The simple language and humble settings make the book accessible, but the novel's unique structure and symbolism present challenges to the reader. *and the earth did not part* has been reprinted several times, and a retelling in English (*This Migrant Earth*, 1985) was published by Rolando Hinojosa. A film version, *and the earth did not swallow him*, was released in 1994.

Suggested Readings

Grajeda, Ralph F. "Tomás Rivera's Appropriation of the Chicano Past." In *Modern Chicano Writers: A Collection of Critical Essays*, edited by Joseph Sommers and Tomás Ibarra-Frausto. Englewood Cliffs, N.J.: Prentice-Hall, 1979.

Kanellos, Nicolás, ed. *Short Fiction by Hispanic Writers of the United States*. Houston, Tex.: Arte Público, 1993.

_______. "Tomás Rivera." *The Hispanic Literary Companion*. Detroit: Visible Ink, 1996.

Saldívar, Ramón. "Tomas Rivera." In *Heath Anthology of American Literature*. Vol. 1. Lexington, Mass.: D. C. Heath, 1994.

Stavans, Ilan. *Art and Anger: Essays on Politics and the Imagination*. Albuquerque: University of New Mexico Press, 1996.

Contributor: Laura L. Klure

Abraham Rodriguez, Jr.

Born: Bronx, New York; 1961

Puerto Rican

Although citizens of the United States, mainland Puerto Ricans are rooted in a culture, race, and class that have been recategorized by the American establishment. These categories often conflict with their family and traditional beliefs. Rodriguez gives voice to that experience.

Principal works

LONG FICTION: *Spidertown*, 1993; *The Buddha Book*, 2001
SHORT FICTION: *The Boy Without a Flag: Tales of the South Bronx*, 1992

Abraham Rodriguez (roh-DREE-gehs), Jr., is a Puerto Rican writer. Having been raised in the Bronx, he writes stories that depict the experiences of "Nuyoricans." The concept of Nuyorican varies from generation to generation; Puerto Ricans living in New York during the 1950's experienced life in that city differently than do members of today's Nuyorican population. However, the struggle of Puerto Ricans, whether on the island of Puerto Rico or on the American mainland, continues to involve issues of culture and identity not easily revealed in the literature of social sciences, fiction, or elsewhere. The issues are generally complex, and work that tells the stories of the Puerto Ricans living in New York is of value both to the community in New York and to the communities of Puerto Rican people on Puerto Rico and throughout the mainland.

Colonization of Borinquén (Puerto Rico's indigenous name) resulted in cultural conflicts for those whose parents migrated to New York in several waves. Puerto Ricans, although citizens of the United States, find their identities in terms of culture, race, and class re-categorized by the establishment in the United States. These categories often conflict with their family and traditional beliefs—hence the conflicts and problems with their sense of self-identification and how to express their identification with two countries. Rodriguez gives voice to that experience.

In *The Boy Without a Flag*, Rodriguez retells the stories he has heard from his father about American imperialism, specifically the conquest of Puerto Rico in 1898. Conscious of this history, the narrator refuses to salute the American flag. In other stories, Rodriguez depicts violence and poverty in barrio life. He uses the language of the streets and the rhythms of the island from which his family comes. Drugs, promiscuity, and other social issues are addressed in his other works. They reveal the intimate knowledge of a man born and raised in New York's South Bronx. This area is home to people from various ethnic groups, where they live often in poverty but never in a culturally poor environment. Salsa, guns, and early death are all part of Rodriguez's milieu, and his writing evokes passion underlying the story lines.

In the novel *Spidertown*, Rodriguez portrays the life of a young man, Miguel, who works as a drug runner for his friend and "mentor," Spider. He seems satisfied with the world he lives in until he becomes involved with a beautiful, practical-minded young woman. He then he sees the lack of substance to his life and realizes he must make some choices. Comments about this work praise Rodriguez's use of language, the pacing of the story, and the realism of the lives portrayed. It is a portrait of poor, urban Puerto Rican lives.

In 1993 Rodriguez earned *The New York Times* Notable Book of the Year award for *The Boy Without a Flag*. He also won the 1995 American Book Award for *Spidertown*, which was also published in British, Dutch, German, and Spanish editions. In conjunction with Scan/LaGuardia and the National Book Foundation's donation of copies of *The Boy Without a Flag*, Rodriguez conducted a workshop for youths and others at Scan/LaGuardia Memorial House in East Harlem, New York, in the spring of 2001. His works have appeared in anthologies and literary magazines including *Boricuas*, *Growing up Puerto Rican*, *Story*, *Best Stories from New Writers*, *The Chattahoochee Review*, and *Alternative Fiction and Poetry*.

Rodriguez received a grant from the New York Foundation for the Arts in 2000, and he served as a literary panel member on the New York State Council of the Arts. His involvement with both the literary foundation and the Scan/LaGuardia Memorial House demonstrates his commitment to his community and to his art. In 2001, he wrote the narration for a film called *Chenrezi Vision* and started an East Coast small press named Art Bridge.

The Boy Without a Flag

Type of work: Short fiction
First published: 1992

The Boy Without a Flag: Tales of the South Bronx was the first book of fiction from Rodriguez. These stories, Rodriguez himself has declared, are "about the rancid underbelly of the American Dream. These are the kids no one likes to talk about. I want to show them as they are, not as society wishes them to be."

The narrator of the title story is a precocious eleven-year-old schoolboy who refuses to stand up to salute the American flag during a school assembly, an act of defiance that, he hopes, will impress his father, a frustrated poet and Puerto Rican nationalist who has planted the seeds of rebellion in his young son's malleable mind. As it turns out, though, the plan backfires, and the boy's father, when summoned to the school, is nothing but meekly apologetic and self-critical for his son's "crazy" behavior. The boy is left alone to come to terms with his father's betrayal, which triggers a preadolescent passage into disillusion. Later, though, he comes to the understanding that his father has, in fact, provided him with a most valuable lesson.

He has learned that he must break away from his father's sphere of influence and must find his own means of independence. In the process of assimilating into that cauldron known as the melting pot, ethnicity, the salt-and-pepper seasoning of identity, is lost, washed away into a tasteless, watered-down broth. The narrator works his way up from this epiphany, and it is clear that he has pledged allegiance to no one but himself, "away from the bondage of obedience."

The successes of this book—Rodriguez's portrayal of the South Bronx, a place that inhabits his characters, brought to life with an affection, a sympathy that is in no way sentimental—cancel out its scattering of stylistic shortcomings. Rodriguez's depictions of lost childhoods are true and brutal, and he is a writer driven by the impulse to tell the stories belonging to those who are voiceless. Their stories deserve to be heard.

Suggested Readings

Flores, Juan. *From Bomba to Hip-Hop: Puerto Rican Culture and the Latino Identity*. New York: Columbia University Press, 2000.

Hernandez, Carmen Dolores. *Puerto Rican Voices in English: Interviews with Writers*. Westport, Conn.: Praeger, 1997.

Shreve, Susan Richards, and Porter Shreve, eds. *Tales Out of School: Contemporary Writers on Their Student Years*. Boston: Beacon Press, 2000.

Contributors: Louise Connal Rodriguez and Peter Markus

Richard Rodriguez

Born: San Francisco, California; July 31, 1944

Mexican American

Rodriguez's autobiography explores the identity of one whose roots can be traced to two cultures.

Principal works

NONFICTION: *Hunger of Memory: The Education of Richard Rodriguez*, 1982; *Days of Obligation: An Argument with My Mexican Father*, 1992; *Brown: The Last Discovery of America*, 2002

During the 1980's, Richard Rodriguez (roh-DREE-gehs) became well known as a broadcast essayist whose work was often aired by the Public Broadcasting Service. His *Hunger of Memory* is a collection of essays tracing his alienation from his Mexican heritage. The son of Mexican immigrants, Rodriguez was not able to speak English when he began school in Sacramento, California. The Catholic nuns who taught him asked that his parents speak English to him at home so that he could hear English spoken all the time. When his parents complied, Rodriguez experienced his first rupture between his original culture and his newly acquired culture. That initial experience compelled him to see the difference between "public" language—English—and "private" language—Spanish. To succeed in a world controlled by those who spoke English, to succeed in the public arena, Rodriguez learned that he had to choose public language over the private language spoken within his home. Hence he opted for alienation from his Mexican heritage and roots, a choice that he viewed with resignation and regret.

His educational journey continued as he proceeded to earn a master's degree and then to become a Fulbright scholar studying English Renaissance literature in London. At that time, he decided to leave academic life, believing that it provided an advantage to Mexican Americans at the expense of those who did not possess this hyphenated background.

Rodriguez proceeded to become an opponent of affirmative action and details his opposition to this policy in *Hunger of Memory*. Another policy to which he voices his opposition is bilingual education. Believing that "public educators in a public schoolroom have an obligation to teach a public language," Rodriguez has used various opportunities—interviews, his autobiography, television appearances—to emphasize his view of the relationship between a person's identity in a majority culture and his or her need to learn the language of that culture.

Another component of Rodriguez's identity that he has explored through various means is his relationship with the Roman Catholic Church. Having been raised in a traditional Catholic home, he was accustomed to the symbols and language of the Catholic Church as they were before the changes that resulted from the Second Vatican Council, which convened in 1962. After this council, the rituals of the Church were dramatically simplified, and the liturgy was changed from Latin to vulgar tongues, such as English. According to Rodriguez, these changes in the Roman Catholic Church challenged the identity of people whose early sense of self was shaped by traditional Catholicism.

A thoughtful and articulate writer regarding the tensions experienced by Mexican Americans growing up in America and by a Catholic struggling with the changes in the Catholic Church, Richard Rodriguez has given voice to the frequently unspoken difficulties of possessing a complex identity.

Hunger of Memory

Type of work: Memoir
First published: 1982

Hunger of Memory: The Education of Richard Rodriguez is a memoir that explores Rodriguez's coming-of-age in an America that challenges him to understand what it is to be a Mexican American and what it is to be a Catholic in America. At the heart of this autobiography is Rodriguez's recognition that his is a position of alienation, a position that he accepts with resignation and regret. As the title of this collection of autobiographical pieces suggests, he remembers his early childhood with nostalgia, while acknowledging that his coming-of-age has resulted in his displacement from that simple, secure life.

The most critical aspect of his education and his development of an adult self is language. He explores his first recollection of language in the opening essay, which describes his hearing his name spoken in English for the first time when he attends a Catholic elementary school in Sacramento, California. He is startled by the recognition that the impersonality and public quality of this announcement herald his own adoption of public language—English—at the expense of his private language—Spanish. Rodriguez has begun to be educated as a public person with a public language.

This education, as he recalls it, occurred before the advent of bilingual education, an event that Rodriguez soundly criticizes. In his view bilingual education prevents children from learning the public language that will be their passport to success in the public world, and he uses his own experience—being a bilingual child who was educated without bilingual education as it was introduced into the American school system in the 1960's—as an example.

Rodriguez offers himself as another example in criticizing affirmative action programs. Turning down offers to teach at various postsecondary educational institutions that he believed wanted to hire him simply because he was Latino, Rodriguez began what has been his persistent criticism of affirmative action policies in America.

Still another object of his criticism in *Hunger of Memory* is the Roman Catholic Church and its changed liturgy, language, and rituals. Recalling the religious institution that had shaped his identity, he regrets the changes that he believes have simplified and therefore diminished the mystery and majesty that he associates with the traditional Catholic Church. He is nostalgic about what has been lost while accepting the reality of the present.

In providing an account of his education, Rodriguez also provides an account of his profession: writing. From his early choice of a public language to his later choice to write about this decision, he paints a self-portrait of a man whose love of words and ideas compels him to explore his past. Rodriguez accepts the adult who writes in English and who writes about the person whose identity is defined by his struggle to find his own voice.

Days of Obligation

Type of work: Essays
First published: 1992

In *Days of Obligation*, Richard Rodriguez pushes the poetic style of his much acclaimed *Hunger of Memory* to even more ambitious literary and cultural limits. In the earlier book, Rodriguez dramatized how his successful academic education as a "scholarship boy" painfully but inevitably alienated him from his Mexican American parents, and he surprisingly argued against affirmative action and bilingual education. In contrast, *Days of Obligation* presents a much wider range of personal experience and cultural issues: historical, religious, educational, and racial.

Though he subtitles the book as an "argument," Rodriguez pursues neither a single consistent argument nor an unbroken autobiographical line. Rather, he plays numerous variations on the contrasts he derives from an argument he once had with his father: "Life is harder then you think, boy." "You're thinking of Mexico, Papa." "You'll see." For Rodriguez, the contrast between Mexican and Californian sensibilities symbolizes the tensions in himself and in American life between Catholicism and Protestantism, communalism and individualism, cynicism and optimism, past and future, age and youth—in his own life and in history—to which he and the reader must attend.

Ultimately, however, Rodriguez is more committed to the truth as he discovers it than to any political orthodoxy or agenda. Though deeply conditioned by Mexican and Catholic values, Rodriguez dramatizes how alien he feels when he actually travels in Mexico; and he asserts that "we are all bandits," for if the United States stole California from Mexicans, the Mexicans had stolen it from Spaniards, who had originally stolen it from the Indians.

Written in a boldly mercurial and allusive style, *Days of Obligation* provides both a brilliant reexamination of multicultural issues and an exhilarating reading experience.

Brown

Type of work: Short fiction
First published: 2002

Hunger of Memory and *Days of Obligation* were the first two installments of "a trilogy on American public life and my private life" that *Brown* completes. Though it is doubtful that Rodriguez has identified "the last discovery of America," as his book's subtitle claims, in *Brown* he musters considerable evidence to support his thesis that brown—not the red, white, and blue of the Stars and Stripes—is the quintessential American color.

Rodriguez believes that "America is browning" and that this process is unavoidable; increasingly, Americans are unable to clearly define where they come from, no matter how detailed their family trees may be. This process continues even—often especially—when Americans oppose it, and they may fail to see the passion of "browning" because of their individualism. Overlooking how profoundly "the 'we' is a precondition for saying 'I,'" Americans underplay the very impurity that enriches both the American "I" and "we," a theme that Rodriguez calls his most important. Thus, making the identification his "mestizo boast," Rodriguez gladly describes himself as "a queer Catholic Indian Spaniard at home in a temperate Chinese city in a fading blond state in a post-Protestant nation." Rodriguez makes no mistake in linking the personal to the public and political. The roots of individual American identities, often oppressed and oppressing, are increasingly entangled, so much so that "righteousness should not come easily to any of us."

Rodriguez's parents emigrated from their native Mexico to California, where Richard, the third of their four children, was born. Although American census classifications have dubbed him "Hispanic," a category he attacks, Rodriguez sometimes underscores the complexity of American identity by contending that he is "Irish," because of the formative influence of Irish nuns who taught him English. In its "brown" form, English becomes a language best called "American," and it is to the multiple expressions of that tongue that Rodriguez owes much of his hard-earned optimism.

Suggested Readings

Christopher, Renny. "Rags to Riches to Suicide: Unhappy Narratives of Upward Mobility—*Martin Eden*, *Bread Givers*, *Delia's Song*, and *Hunger of Memory*." *College Literature* 29 (Fall, 2002).

Collado, Alfredo Villanueva. "Growing up Hispanic: Discourse and Ideology in *Hunger of Memory* and *Family Installments*." *The Americas Review* 16, nos. 3/4 (Fall/Winter, 1988).

Danahay, Martin A. "Richard Rodriguez's Poetics of Manhood." In *Fictions of Masculinity: Crossing Cultures, Crossing Sexualities*, edited by Peter F. Murphy. New York: New York University Press, 1994.

De Castro, Juan E. "Richard Rodriguez in 'Borderland': The Ambiguity of Hybridity." *Aztlan* 26 (Spring, 2001).

Guajardo, Paul. *Chicano Controversy: Oscar Acosta and Richard Rodriguez.* New York: Peter Lang, 2002.

Rodriguez, Richard. "A View from the Melting Pot: An Interview with Richard Rodriguez." Interview by Scott London. In *The Writer's Presence*, edited by Donald McQuade and Robert Atwan. New York: Bedford/St. Martin's Press, 2000.

_______. "Violating the Boundaries: An Interview with Richard Rodriguez." Interview by Timothy Sedore. *Michigan Quarterly Review* 38 (Summer, 1999).

Romer, Rolando J. "Spanish and English: The Question of Literacy in *Hunger of Memory.*" *Confluencia* 6, no. 2 (Spring, 1991).

Contributors: Marjorie Smelstor and John K. Roth

Ninotchka Rosca

Born: Manila, Philippines; 1946

Filipino American

Rosca was the first Filipina to publish a serious political novel in the United States.

Principal works

LONG FICTION: *State of War*, 1988; *Twice Blessed*, 1992
SHORT FICTION: *The Monsoon Collection*, 1983
NONFICTION: *Endgame: The Fall of Marcos*, 1987; *Jose Maria Sison: At Home in the World, Portrait of a Revolutionary*, 2004

Ninotchka Rosca (nih-TAHSH-kah ROH-shah) accepted as her pen name that of the Russian radical played in an American film by Greta Garbo. Rosca thought of herself as a militant liberal among the students at the University of the Philippines. Her columns as associate editor of *Graphic* magazine after 1968 reinforced her image as a controversial figure. Her first fiction complained about the political passivity of the educated elite, and she remained a friend of those former classmates who joined the New People's Army against the rule-by-decree of President Ferdinand Marcos. In 1973, shortly after Marcos declared martial law, she was arrested and placed for several months in Camp Crame Detention Center. She used her experience there to provide realistic detail for nine stories about parallels between military detention and a nation run under rules of "constitutional authoritarianism." *The Monsoon Collection* was published in Australia in order to safeguard its author.

Rosca found her role as a nationalist difficult when loyalty was defined as adhering to Marcos's rule. By 1977, Rosca had gone into political self-exile among relatives connected with the University of Hawaii at Manoa, where she taught. Later she moved to New York City to be closer to opportunities within the publishing industry, despite her misgivings that several American presidents had sponsored Marcos's rise to power on the premise that he was anti-Communist. After his forced flight from the Philippines in February, 1986, she returned briefly to Manila and later, with *Endgame*, contributed to reportage on Marcos's final days.

Although Rosca remained in the United States, her focus on the Philippines did not falter. She became the U.S. representative of GABRIELA, an organization named after Gabriela Silang, an eighteenth century warrior who continued the revolt against Spain after her husband's death. GABRIELA in America protects overseas workers from various kinds of abuse. She has also maintained a column of commentary in *Filipinas*, a popular magazine on the West Coast. Since the late 1980's Rosca has written novels describing the militant role of youth organizations in the Philippines.

State of War

Type of work: Novel
First published: 1988

State of War's dominant story line portrays a failed attempt by young radicals to assassinate Philippines dictator Ferdinand Marcos (referred to only as The Commander). The book's larger concern is with the effect of centuries of colonialism on the Filipino people's search for national identity. Portions of the novel try to reconstruct the ancestry of the principal characters during centuries of Spanish rule and fifty years of American occupation. Even after independence is achieved in 1946, freedom still is withheld from the people by troops serving The Commander. "Internal colonialism," controlled by the Filipinos' own countryman, merely replaces the tyranny that formerly came from outside. Ninotchka Rosca describes a nation forever being betrayed and, therefore, forever just beginning to find itself.

The seriousness of the assassination attempt is masked by the resplendent color and the joyful sounds of the festival that surround the attempt. Annually, in the Ati-Atihan celebration, Filipinos celebrate the clash between the Spanish and the native islanders. Anna Villaverde, who during martial law once was detained by military authorities because of her closeness to Manolo Montreal, a radical oppositionist who is assumed dead, becomes aware that Colonel Urbano Amor, her original torturer, is securing the area for The Commander's visit. Anna is protected from exposure by Adrian, a young member of the elite class. Then he is captured, and under the influence of drugs he is forced to reveal parts of the plot. Trying to compensate for this betrayal by warning Anna, he becomes crippled when the bomb intended for The Commander explodes prematurely. As for Manolo Montreal, he is not dead after all but has joined forces with his previous captors. He is prepared to betray the plans of the young conspirators, but Anna manages to kill him. What begins as a festival of song and dance ends in a bloody melee with The Commander still alive and in charge.

The only hope for social change, the novel suggests, lies in Anna and Adrian's son, who will have to become a historian of the people and storyteller of collective memories and democratic ideals. He will be expected to serve as a reminder of the recurring frustration of Filipino hopes for self-definition during centuries of foreign rule. The novel's story line is filled with intrigue from all sides, continuously defeating the examples of reform and of resistance that, historically, only relatively few rebellious nationalists have courageously provided. A persistent "state of war," Rosca implies, has long existed, and true independence has yet to be achieved. Anna's dream of a different future among peasants, who want only a right to the land that they till, is a declaration of faith rather than of hope. Romantic as Anna's expectations of democracy might seem to be under the circumstances, the only alternative is to surrender hope for a free society. It is not in her nature to give up the beliefs that make her life worth living; and in the author, she has found an ally.

Twice Blessed

Type of work: Novel
First published: 1992

Twice Blessed is a comic parable. It shares with Rosca's more dramatic *State of War* a lasting concern for "a nation struggling to be born." Its method is less confrontational than Rosca's earlier work, but it goes beyond mockery of President Ferdinand Marcos and First Lady Imelda Marcos who, on the novel's publication date, were already in exile in Hawaii. The basic satire exposes a phenomenon in Filipino culture larger than the behavior of a single ruling couple: instincts of the wealthy to preserve their power through arranged marriages. This hoarding of power, Rosca has long argued as a journalist, is the source not only of vast class differences but also of elitist willingness to collaborate with foreign enemies in order to survive. Through comic irony and despite the novel's farcical features, Rosca suggests that the greed responsible for putting dynastic wealth before the welfare of the people eventually can be self-destructive.

The sibling rule of Katerina and Hector Basbas in a tropical Pacific country is reminiscent of what several commentators have called the "conjugal dictatorship" of the Marcoses. Katerina's attempts to forget her humble beginnings resemble Imelda's well-publicized delusions of grandeur, and the collapse of a heavy crane on the roof of the inaugural structure seems inspired by the fatal collapse of the Manila International Film Festival building in 1983 because of haste in its construction. In addition, Imelda not only was actually considered Ferdinand's replacement if his health failed but also ran (unsuccessfully) as a presidential candidate in 1992. These are just a few of the historical parallels borrowed by Rosca to provide realistic dimensions to a tale that otherwise might seem far-fetched. Reality can be much more outlandish than fiction.

Rosca's fictional account portrays what might have resulted had Hector crashed in his airplane, been lost, and been considered dead. His twin sister, Katerina, seems less to grieve his possible loss than suddenly to imagine herself as his replacement. Trying to forget her lowly origins, Katerina's ambition has only been whetted by her marriage to aristocratic Armand Gloriosa. Once dreams of individual glory have been placed before the nation's needs, corruption spreads even to such opponents to oppressive government as Teresa Tikloptihod. She is the headstrong daughter of a provincial governor who at first resisted strenuously collaboration with the tyranny of Hector. Her independent thinking washes away like sand when she allies herself with Katerina. The military, in the person of Captain de Naval, also decides to grasp this unforeseen opportunity for its own advancement. Those events recall Marcos's secretary of defense, Ponce Enrile, who, having fallen out with Marcos, tried to ensure Marcos's defeat in the 1986 election. Enrile backed Corazon Aquino, although with the intent of establishing a government run by a military junta. Even with Hector's return, coups, countercoups (such as those suffered by Aquino during her rule), and the fortification of the presidential palace follow.

If this farce were to be taken at face value, the prospects for the Philippines would be grim. Rosca's witty, colorful style, however, makes the novel seem closer to light opera. Its "music" is very different from the gongs and drums of her novel about the attempted assassination of Marcos, *State of War*. The source of Rosca's implied hope in *Twice Blessed* seems to be that when greed becomes so deeply embedded in a small class of people, alliances among even the most powerful can turn to bitter rivalry, and the system of social oppression can self-destruct.

Suggested Readings

Casper, Leonard. *In Burning Ambush: Essays, 1985-1990*. Quezon City, Philippines: New Day, 1991.

Davis, Rocio G. "Postcolonial Visions and Immigrant Longings: Ninotchka Rosca's Versions of the Philippines." *World Literature Today* 73, no. 1 (Winter, 1999): 62ff.

_______. *Sunsurfers Seen from Afar: Critical Essays, 1991-1996*. Pasig City, Philippines: Anvil, 1996.

Manuel, Dolores de. "Decolonizing Bodies, Reinscribing Souls in the Fiction of Ninotchka Rosca and Linda Ty-Casper." *MELUS* 29, no. 1 (Spring, 2004): 99ff.

Contributor: Leonard Casper

Henry Roth

Born: Tysmenica, Galicia, Austro-Hungarian Empire (now in Ukraine); February 8, 1906
Died: Albuquerque, New Mexico; October 13, 1995

Jewish

Rediscovered in 1964, thirty years after it was written, Roth's breakthrough novel Call It Sleep *evokes the childhood traumas of a sensitive Jewish immigrant boy in a New York ghetto.*

Principal works

LONG FICTION: *Call It Sleep*, 1934; *Mercy of a Rude Stream*, 1994-1996 (includes *A Star Shines over Mt. Morris Park*, 1994; *A Diving Rock on the Hudson*, 1995; *From Bondage*, 1996; and *Requiem for Harlem*, 1998)

SHORT FICTION: "Broker," 1938; "Somebody Always Grabs the Purple," 1940; "Petey and Yorsee and Mario," 1956; "At Times in Flight," 1959 (parable); "The Dun Dakotas," 1960 (parable)

MISCELLANEOUS: *Shifting Landscape: A Composite, 1925-1987*, 1987 (Mario Materassi, editor)

Henry Roth, born in Austria-Hungary in 1906, wrote his first novel in the early 1930's. Published in 1934 and rediscovered in 1964, *Call It Sleep* vividly evokes the childhood traumas of a sensitive Jewish immigrant boy in the hostile—and sometimes gentle—New York ghetto. Though not strictly autobiographical, the novel derives much from Roth's own boyhood in turbulent New York City, as do most of his short pieces published in *The New Yorker*.

Roth began writing at City College, where he majored in English and graduated in 1928. His chief mentor was Eda Lou Walton of New York University, whose encouragement and support enabled him to devote almost four years to completing *Call It Sleep*. Published in 1934, the novel drew reviewers' praise but made little impact on the public or on most literary scholars. Its subject and style reminded critics of the works of James T. Farrell, James Joyce, and Theodore Dreiser. Psychologically truthful and unified by skillfully handled themes and motifs, the book demonstrated Roth's considerable skill in the art of fiction.

Between the late 1930's and the mid-1960's, Roth largely abandoned writing for a variety of other occupations: high school teacher in the Bronx, precision metal grinder, teacher in a one-room school in Maine, orderly and supervisor in a mental hospital, breeder of ducks and geese, tutor in Latin and mathematics.

In 1964 *Call It Sleep* was reissued to considerable critical fanfare. Interviewers who sought out Roth found him a sensitive and thoughtful man who had gone his own way, living on a Maine farm after the fashion of Henry David Thoreau. Roth expressed his admiration for the poet Robinson Jeffers and discussed his personal rejection of the notion that the world is absurd. In 1965 he was recognized with an award from the National Institute of Arts and Letters.

After *Call It Sleep*, Roth published memoirs, short stories, autobiographical sketches, and other miscellaneous pieces, many of which were collected in *Shifting Landscape*. In 1979 he began work on *Mercy of a Rude Stream*, a multivolume work that in a sense continues *Call It Sleep*, since it, too, is loosely based on Roth's life. In 1994, *A Star Shines over Mt. Morris Park*, the first volume of *Mercy of a Rude Stream* and Roth's second novel, appeared. The second volume, *A Diving Rock on the Hudson*, appeared in 1995, the same year in which Roth died. Posthumously published volumes were *From Bondage*, which appeared in 1996, and *Requiem for Harlem*, in 1998.

Call It Sleep

Type of work: Novel
First published: 1934

In retrospect, *Call It Sleep* seems so unequivocally a major artistic achievement that it is difficult to understand why it was neglected for thirty years. However, in 1934 American culture lacked a category for American Jewish literature. By 1964, Roth fulfilled the need to anoint a worthy ancestor to Saul Bellow, Bernard Malamud, and Philip Roth, to legitimate a newly canonized tradition. It was only after ethnicity became a crucial issue in American society that Roth's novel could be appreciated for its pioneering embodiment of multiculturalism and multilingualism.

Call It Sleep begins in May, 1907, with the arrival by ship from Europe of two-year-old David Schearl and his mother, Genya. They are met at Ellis Island by David's father, Albert, a surly, abusive man who is embittered by disappointment. Albert is forever falling out with fellow workers and forced to seek new employment, as a printer and then as a milkman. The family moves from modest lodgings in Brooklyn's Brownsville neighborhood to a crowded tenement on the lower East Side of Manhattan. Roth's book focuses on young David's troubling experiences during the years 1911-1913, as a stranger in a strange land. *Call It Sleep* is a coming-of-age novel about a hypersensitive Jewish boy who is forced to cope alone with the mysteries of sex, religion, and love.

After a brief prologue recounting David's arrival in America, Roth organizes his story into four sections, each defined by a dominant image: "The Cellar," "The Picture," "The Coal," and "The Rail." What might otherwise seem casual details are magnified by refraction through the mind of an anxious child. Roth's use of stream of consciousness intensifies the sense of an unformed mind trying to assimilate the varied sensations that assault it. The family apartment is a haven for David, as long as his father, who even doubts his paternity of the boy, is not home and his doting mother can lavish her affections on him. When David ventures out into the clamorous streets, he encounters threats, from both rats and humans.

At the cheder, the drab religious school where Jewish boys are given rote instruction in a Hebrew Bible they cannot understand, David is confused and inspired by Isaiah's account of the angel with a burning coal. Eavesdropping on a conversation between his mother and her sister Bertha, he misconstrues an explanation for why Genya, disgraced after being jilted by a Gentile, married Albert. When Leo, an older Polish boy, persuades David to introduce him to his cousin Esther, David is overwhelmed by incredulity and guilt over the sexual liberties that Leo takes. Fleeing his brutal father, David is shocked into unconsciouness after touching the live rail of a street car. Faced, like the reader, with sensory overload, David might as well call it sleep, embracing temporary oblivion as restoration after a long, disorienting day.

To explore the tensions among Albert, Genya, and David, a clanging family triangle rife with resentments and recriminations, Roth appropriates the theories of Sigmund Freud, particularly in describing the powerful Oedipal bond between mother and son as well as the almost patricidal strife between Albert and David. The authority of James Joyce asserts itself, not only in the fact that Roth's account of David Schearl, a surrogate for the author himself, is in effect another portrait of the artist as a young man but also in his lavish use of stream of consciousness and his meticulous deployment of recurrent imagery.

During the two decades surrounding the turn of the twentieth century, massive, unprecedented migration from eastern and southern Europe was radically reshaping American society, and, more effectively than any other novel, *Call It Sleep* records the traumas experienced when the Old World met the New. Many of Roth's immigrants are inspired by the American Dream of enlarged opportunity, while others are repulsed by an urban nightmare. Call it, too, sleep. Though the Schearls are Polish Jews, the eclectic slum in which they live also serves as home to immigrants and natives from many other backgrounds. Not the least of Roth's accomplishments is his success at rendering the diversity of David's environs. Yiddish is the first language of the Schearls, but English, German, Hebrew, Italian, and Polish are also spoken, in varying registers, by characters in the story. In a novel designed for an anglophonic reader, it would be misleading and demeaning to put fractured English into the mouths or minds of fluent Yiddish speakers when they are assumed to be using their native language. Instead, Roth fashions English prose supple enough to represent the varying speech and thoughts of those who speak and think in other tongues.

Call It Sleep is significant for reflecting a momentous phenomenon that transformed the United States but was ignored by many of Roth's literary contemporaries. In its vivid rendition of a child's-eye view, its dramatic exposure of family tensions, and its creation of a rich linguistic texture, Roth's first novel is an artistic triumph.

Mercy of a Rude Stream

Type of work: Novel
First published: *A Star Shines over Mt. Morris Park*, 1994; *A Diving Rock on the Hudson*, 1995; *From Bondage*, 1996; *Requiem for Harlem*, 1998

Though they were published separately and can be read independently and autonomously, the four novels that constitute *Mercy of a Rude Stream* are best understood together, as a single narrative sequence. The entire tetralogy follows the coming of age of Ira Stigman, a Jewish emigrant to New York, from 1914, when he is eight years old, until 1927, when he is twenty-one and a senior at City College. Despite the change in names and the addition of a younger sister, Minnie, Ira seems largely an extension of David Schearl from *Call It Sleep*. He is also a thinly disguised version of Roth himself. The autobiographical basis of the books is made even more apparent by interpolated sections in which an older Ira, an ailing octogenarian author living in Albuquerque, addresses his word processor, calling it "Ecclesias." He comments on his own renewed, belated efforts at writing fiction. Ira as author poses the question that most readers will raise about Roth himself—why, approaching death, does he struggle to record such lacerating memories?

In narrating his story, Ira forces himself to revisit an unhappy childhood and adolescence, in which he and his mother, Leah, are terrorized by his psychotic father, Chaim. When the family moves from the lower East Side to a largely Irish neighborhood in East Harlem, Ira feels rudely wrenched out of an organic, nurturing Jewish community. He recalls the painful details of broken friendships and of his public disgrace when he was expelled from high school for stealing fountain pens. The most agonizing recollections—and the element that has drawn the most attention to Roth's final books—concern Ira's sexual transgressions. The second volume, *A Diving Rock on the Hudson*, offers the startling revelation that, beginning when he was sixteen and she was fourteen, Ira regularly, furtively committed incest with his sister, Minnie. He also maintained covert sexual relations with his younger cousin Stella. Recollections of incest continue through volumes 3 and 4 and fuel the author's suicidal self-loathing. The older Ira longs to die but feels compelled to tell his story first, as though narration might bring purgation and even redemption.

Unlike the bravura *Call It Sleep*, much of *Mercy of a Rude Stream* is written in undistinguished prose that is at best serviceable in evoking working-class, urban life during and after World War I. Ira offers details of jobs he held, including stock boy in an upscale food store, soda peddler at Yankee Stadium and the Polo Grounds, and salesman in a candy shop. His sentimental education is very much connected to his intellectual one, and, though his grades are mediocre, Ira thrives in college. Publication of a short story in the student magazine awakens literary ambitions; his friendship with affluent Larry Gordon enlarges Ira's life beyond his own squalid situation. He begins to acquire social graces and to strike on ideas. Ira becomes inebriated with reading, particularly after Edith Welles, the professor who was Larry's lover, becomes Ira's mentor and lover. Edith, who is modeled after Roth's own Eda Lou Walton, introduces Ira to the most influential books and people of New York's bohemian culture. In the final pages of the cycle's final book, *Requiem for Harlem*, Ira bids farewell to his dysfunctional, debilitating family and his loathsome sexual compulsions by moving down to Greenwich Village to live with Edith. The apprentice artist is finally ready to write a novel very much like *Call It Sleep*. Finally, after disburdening himself of excruciating secrets, the eighty-nine-year-old Roth finished writing and prepared at last to call it sleep.

Suggested Readings

Adams, Stephen J. "'The Noisiest Novel Ever Written': The Soundscape of Henry Roth's *Call It Sleep*." *Twentieth Century Literature* 35 (Spring, 1989).

Buelens, Gert. "The Multi-Voiced Basis of Henry Roth's Literary Success in *Call It Sleep*." In *Cultural Difference and the Literary Text: Pluralism and the Limits of Authenticity in North American Literatures*, edited by Winfried Siemerling and Katrin Schwenk. Iowa City: University of Iowa Press, 1996.

Halkin, Hillel. "Henry Roth's Secret." *Commentary* 97 (May, 1994).

Kellman, Steven G. *Redemption: The Life of Henry Roth*. New York: W. W. Norton, 2005.

Lyons, Bonnie. *Henry Roth: The Man and His Work*. New York: Cooper Square, 1976.

Sokoloff, Naomi B. *Imagining the Child in Modern Jewish Fiction*. Baltimore: The Johns Hopkins University Press, 1992.

Walden, Daniel, ed. *Studies in American Jewish Literature* 5, no. 1 (Spring, 1979).

Wirth-Nesher, Hana, ed. *New Essays on "Call It Sleep."* New York: Cambridge University Press, 1996.

Contributors: Richard Tuerk and Steven G. Kellman

Philip Roth

Born: Newark, New Jersey; March 19, 1933

Jewish

Roth's comic fiction has consistently challenged definitions of Jewish identity in late twentieth century America.

Principal works

LONG FICTION: *Letting Go*, 1962; *When She Was Good*, 1967; *Portnoy's Complaint*, 1969; *Our Gang (Starring Tricky and His Friends)*, 1971; *The Breast*, 1972, revised 1980; *The Great American Novel*, 1973; *My Life as a Man*, 1974; *The Professor of Desire*, 1977; *The Ghost Writer*, 1979; *Zuckerman Unbound*, 1981; *The Anatomy Lesson*, 1983; *Zuckerman Bound*, 1985 (includes *The Ghost Writer*, *Zuckerman Unbound*, *The Anatomy Lesson*, and *Epilogue: The Prague Orgy*); *The Counterlife*, 1986; *Deception*, 1990; *Operation Shylock: A Confession*, 1993; *Sabbath's Theater*, 1995; *American Pastoral*, 1997; *I Married a Communist*, 1998; *The Human Stain*, 2000; *The Dying Animal*, 2001; *The Plot Against America*, 2004; *Everyman*, 2006; *Exit Ghost*, 2007

SHORT FICTION: *Goodbye, Columbus, and Five Short Stories*, 1959; "Novotny's Pain," 1962, revised 1980; "The Psychoanalytic Special," 1963; "On the Air," 1970; "'I Always Wanted You to Admire My Fasting': Or, Looking at Kafka," 1973

NONFICTION: *Reading Myself and Others*, 1975, expanded 1985; *The Facts: A Novelist's Autobiography*, 1988; *Patrimony: A True Story*, 1991; *Shop Talk: A Writer and His Colleagues and Their Work*, 2001

Philip Roth's youth in a largely Jewish neighborhood of Newark, New Jersey, established his first subject: the ambivalence felt by American Jews on facing assimilation into American culture, which entails the loss of much, possibly all, of their distinctive Jewishness. Roth grew up in a middle-class home where, he writes, "the Jewish family was an inviolate haven against every form of menace, from personal isolation to gentile hostility." Roth has been unwilling, however, simply to depict the Jewish family as a haven. His inclination to challenge Jewish American propriety and his extravagant comic imagination have won for him a controversial place in American letters. After an education at Bucknell University and the University of Chicago, Roth earned with the publication of *Goodbye, Columbus, and Five Short Stories* the National Book Award and condemnation as an anti-Semite by some Jewish leaders.

Roth's tendency to use details from his life in his fiction has invited misinterpretations of his work as autobiography. An unhappy and short-lived marriage to Margaret Martinson, for example, was translated by Roth into *My Life as a Man*, in which Margaret's fictional surrogate attracts and devastates the protagonist in part because she is not Jewish. Roth's second wife, the Jewish actress Claire Bloom, may have provided in her English background a context for Roth's alter ego, the writer Nathan Zuckerman, to explore his identity as a Jew in *The Counterlife*, in which Zuckerman becomes involved with a Christian Englishwoman. A suicidal breakdown in 1987, caused by medication prescribed for Roth after minor surgery, appears undisguised in *Operation Shylock: A Confession*, a probing quest for cultural and personal identity.

Roth's writing can be seen in stages, from the early realist fiction to the discovery of his comic voice in *Portnoy's Complaint* to the mid-career novels featuring Jewish writer-protagonists to the works of the late 1980's and 1990's that either overtly recount Roth's past or collapse the distinction between fiction and reality. Throughout, however, the thread that weaves the work together is Roth's interest in exploring and exposing the Jewish American self.

Goodbye, Columbus, and Five Short Stories

Type of work: Novella and short fiction
First published: 1959

Roth's first published volume, *Goodbye, Columbus, and Five Short Stories*, won for the young writer not only the National Book Award in 1960 but also accusations, as a result of the book's comically piercing portraits of middle-class American Jews, of Roth's harboring self-hatred. The ambivalent exploration of Jewish American life in *Goodbye, Columbus*, and its mixed reception among Jewish readers who were sensitive to the public image of Jews established two of the central themes of Roth's fiction: a frank and often ironic look at Jewish American identity, and an intense but playful examination of the relationship between art and life.

In the novella *Goodbye, Columbus*, Neil Klugman's confrontation with his Jewish American identity is represented by his love affair with Brenda Patimkin. Brenda signifies the American Dream, her parents' suburban prosperity symbolized by a refrigerator in the basement overflowing with fresh fruit. Neil's ambivalence toward the Patimkins' conspicuous consumption and their eager assimilation into American culture is expressed by the guilt he feels when he helps himself to fruit from the refrigerator. Although Neil finally rejects Brenda, the novella closes without offering Neil a clear sense of where he might belong.

Roth poses other choices in the book's subsequent stories. Ozzie Freedman in "The Conversion of the Jews" believes he must choose between Jewish authority and the American notion of personal freedom. In outrage at his rabbi's denial that an omnipotent God could indeed have caused Mary to conceive without intercourse, Ozzie threatens to leap from the roof of the synagogue, and demands that the rabbi, his mother, and the assembled crowd kneel and affirm belief that God can do anything he wants, with the clear implication that God could have created Jesus in the manner that Christians believe. When Ozzie experiences the power of self-definition at this ironic climax, Roth suggests that Judaism, personified by the rabbi, must confront the shaping forces of the American context if it is not to lose its adherents.

Philip Roth (© Nancy Crampton)

In "Defender of the Faith," Sergeant Nathan Marx questions whether Jews are obligated to define themselves in relation to other Jews. After a Jewish recruit repeatedly manipulates Nathan for favors during basic training, he realizes that his greater responsibility to his fellow Jews lies in refusing to let them be different, despite the dangers that assimilation poses. As if Roth is in dialogue with himself, however, the final story in the collection reverses Nathan's decision. Eli of "Eli, the Fanatic" dons, as a challenge to his "progressive suburban community," the stale black clothes of a recent Jewish immigrant, and, with them, an identity that refuses assimilation into American life. *Goodbye, Columbus, and Five Short Stories*, then, represents Roth's first and notable attempt to explore the problem of Jewish American identity from a variety of angles and without resolution.

Portnoy's Complaint

Type of work: Novel
First published: 1969

Philip Roth's third novel, *Portnoy's Complaint*, takes the form of an outrageous, comic rant by Alexander Portnoy to his psychoanalyst, whose help Portnoy seeks because he feels that his life has come to be a "Jewish joke." Portnoy's impassioned, self-absorbed monologues explore his childhood and his erotic relationships. He wishes to locate the source of his pain, composed of guilt, shame, desire, and emotional paralysis, and to free himself from his past. The best-selling novel shocked readers with its obscenity, graphic sexual descriptions, and exaggerations of Jewish stereotypes.

Portnoy's early memories include his mother's intense overprotectiveness and warnings against pleasure, his father's emasculation by the gentile firm for which he works, and his own efforts to loosen the chains that bind him by breaking taboos, especially by frequent, ill-timed sexual escapades. His furious attempts at "self-loving" can be seen as symbolic expressions of self-loathing, intricately related to his position as a Jew in America. The satiric presentation of Portnoy as a figure of excess who wants to put the "id back in Yid" and the "*oy* back in *goy*," provided Roth with a way to inquire into the complacency and neuroses of assimilated Jews in gentile America.

In the postwar years, the Holocaust—the "saga of the suffering Jews"—defined Jewish American identity and encouraged Jews to assimilate inconspicuously. Portnoy's ambivalence toward this Jewish response is represented in his adolescence and adulthood by his relationships with a series of gentile women. Portnoy desires simultaneously to flaunt and to reject himself as a Jew. In each case, he uses women to transgress religious and sexual taboos, imagining that his wild and occasionally abusive relationships with them will allow him to "discover America. *Conquer* America." Yet each of these relationships results for him in intense guilt. His acknowledgement that his self-hatred makes him unable to love causes him to flail against his guilt with further transgressions, ending in more guilt, trapping him in a vicious circle.

The novel ends with Portnoy's primal scream, expressing his recognition that he cannot spring himself "from the settling of scores! the pursuit of dreams! from this hopeless, senseless loyalty to the long ago!" Portnoy, Roth's Jewish American Everyman, cannot escape his past. He struggles to discover who he is, as a Jew and as a human being.

Suggested Readings

Baumgarten, Murray, and Barbara Gottfried. *Understanding Philip Roth*. Columbia: University of South Carolina Press, 1990.

Bloom, Harold, ed. *Philip Roth*. New York: Chelsea House, 1986.

Cooper, Alan. *Philip Roth and the Jews*. Albany: State University of New York Press, 1996.

Halio, Jay L. *Philip Roth Revisited*. New York: Twayne, 1992.

Kahn-Paycha, Danièle. *Popular Jewish Literature and Its Role in the Making of an Identity*. Lewiston, N.Y.: Edwin Mellen Press, 2000.

Milowitz, Steven. *Philip Roth Considered: The Concentrationary Universe of the American Writer*. New York: Taylor & Francis, 2000.

Omer-Sherman, Ranen. *Diaspora and Zionism in Jewish American literature: Lazarus, Syrkin, Reznikoff, and Roth*. Hanover, N.H.: University Press of New England, 2002.

Parrish, Timothy, ed. *The Cambridge Companion to Philip Roth*. New York: Cambridge University Press, 2007.

Rand, Naomi R. *Silko, Morrison, and Roth: Studies in Survival*. New York: Peter Lang, 1999.

Roth, Philip. *Conversations with Philip Roth*. Edited by George J. Searles. Jackson: University Press of Mississippi, 1992.

Wade, Stephen. *The Imagination in Transit: The Fiction of Philip Roth*. Sheffield: Sheffield Academic Press, 1996.

Contributor: Debra Shostak

Muriel Rukeyser

Born: New York, New York; December 15, 1913
Died: New York, New York; February 12, 1980

Jewish

Rukeyser's poems gave voice to social consciousness, embracing all ethnic identities that she saw being treated unjustly.

Principal works

CHILDREN'S LITERATURE: *Come Back, Paul*, 1955; *I Go Out*, 1961; *Bubbles*, 1967; *Mayes*, 1970; *More Night*, 1981

DRAMA: *The Colors of the Day: A Celebration for the Vassar Centennial, June 10, 1961*, pr. 1961; *Houdini*, pr. 1973, pb. 2002

LONG FICTION: *The Orgy*, 1965

POETRY: *Theory of Flight*, 1935; *Mediterranean*, 1938; *U.S. 1*, 1938; *A Turning Wind: Poems*, 1939; *The Soul and Body of John Brown*, 1940; *Wake Island*, 1942; *Beast in View*, 1944; *The Green Wave*, 1948; *Elegies*, 1949; *Orpheus*, 1949; *Selected Poems*, 1951; *Body of Waking*, 1958; *Waterlily Fire: Poems, 1935-1962*, 1962; *The Outer Banks*, 1967; *The Speed of Darkness*, 1968; *Twenty-nine Poems*, 1972; *Breaking Open: New Poems*, 1973; *The Gates: Poems*, 1976; *The Collected Poems of Muriel Rukeyser*, 1978; *Out of Silence: Selected Poems*, 1992; *The Collected Poems of Muriel Rukeyser*, 2005 (Janet E. Kaufman and Anne F. Herzog, editors)

TRANSLATIONS: *Selected Poems*, 1963 (of Octavio Paz's poems); *Sun Stone*, 1963 (of Paz's poems); *Selected Poems*, 1967 (of Gunnar Ekelöf's poems; with Leif Sjoberg); *Three Poems*, 1967 (of Ekelöf's poems); *Early Poems, 1935-1955*, 1973 (of Paz's poems); *Uncle Eddie's Moustache*, 1974; *A Mölna Elegy*, 1984 (of Ekelöf's poem)

NONFICTION: *Willard Gibbs*, 1942; *The Life of Poetry*, 1949; *One Life*, 1957; *Poetry and the Unverifiable Fact: The Clark Lectures*, 1968; *The Traces of Thomas Hariot*, 1971

MISCELLANEOUS: *A Muriel Rukeyser Reader*, 1994

The literary career of Muriel Rukeyser (REW-ki-zur) began early with the publication of *Theory of Flight* in the Yale Series of Younger Poets in 1935. Her poetry reflected her intense personal passion, her call to freedom, and her search for justice. Readers may detect the influence of Walt Whitman in her sense of American identity as something all-embracing.

Muriel Rukeyser (Library of Congress)

Rukeyser's sense of personal responsibility and social protest may have been forged by her political experience. Two years before her first book of poetry was published, while covering the Scottsboro trials for Vassar College's leftist *Student Review*, Rukeyser was arrested—and caught typhoid fever while in jail. This event ignited her social awareness as evidenced in her writing and subsequent actions. This particular event is recalled as "The Trial" in *Theory of Flight*.

Wherever Rukeyser saw oppression, she became involved. To an extent, the social and political history of the United States, as distilled through the reactions of a female Jewish intellectual activist, may be read through Rukeyser's poems. She supported the Loyalists during the Spanish Civil War. Later, she was jailed while protesting the Vietnam War. She rallied in South Korea against the death sentence of the poet Kim Chi-ha. The event then became the focus of her poem "The Gates."

Bringing the perspective of her Jewish upbringing to her poetry, Rukeyser wrote about the horrors of World War II. Though her concern about the oppression of the Jews may have stemmed personally from her religion, she had already demonstrated her global concern about fascism.

Rukeyser's early marriage did not last; later she became the single parent of a son. Although motherhood became a subject in her poetry and she wrote about women from a feminist perspective, Rukeyser was never as singly feminist in her poetry as others of her generation. Still, her influence as a woman writer on those who followed her was acknowledged by Anne Sexton, who named her "Muriel, mother of everyone," and who kept Rukeyser's *The Speed of Darkness* on her desk.

"Ajanta"

Type of work: Poetry
First published: 1944, in *Beast in View*

"Ajanta" is a long poem written in five subtitled parts: "The Journey," "The Cave," "Les Tendresses Bestiales," "Black Blood," and "The Broken World." The poem, written in free verse, is given form by the progression of the journey it describes, in which the poet goes into herself in search of a sense of the unity of life. It is an exploration of her spirit, mind, and body.

"Ajanta" is named for the great painted caves in India, famous for their magnificent religious frescoes painted by Buddhist monks. Rukeyser uses this setting in her poem to suggest the sacredness of her own interior places, her Ajanta, both psychic and physical. The figures of gods, men, and animals in the poem are accurate descriptions of the caves' artwork.

"Ajanta" opens *Beast in View*, Rukeyser's fourth book of poems. The "beast" she hunts on her spiritual voyage is not always in view—in "Ajanta" it remains hidden from her until her final reconciliation in the cave to which it has led her. The beast is her innermost self, what makes her who she is, what is vital to her being. The thematic energy of "Ajanta" is devoted to capturing the beast—herself in her own myth of herself—so that she can be a whole person again. Because the poem is about transformation, and adapting to changes in life and the world, the beast in "Ajanta" often appears in disguises. All these masks are part of the poet's personality and her changes. She seeks to unify them and accept them all.

The search for self-identity in "Ajanta," however, is not an end in itself. Beginning with descriptions of war atrocities, the poem reminds readers that to know oneself is vital also for the sake of the world in which one lives. The poet seeks the strong armor of self-knowledge, rather than the armor of rage, in order to know better how to aid the struggles of those who have been betrayed or who are suffering loss. The "world of the shadowed and alone" is a place in which the conscientious must fight for those in need and confront "the struggles of the moon." In "Letter to the Front" (also from *Beast in View*), Rukeyser praises the healing power that women can offer the world, especially in time of war. She envisioned female sensibilities transforming traditional man, or the traditional masculine ideal. This vision laid a path for later women poets, such as Adrienne Rich, who continue to explore similar themes.

The cave is a symbol for female sensibility, mystery, and strength. It is a dark interior, a place of hiding or hibernation, a place of meditation, a vault from which one emerges reborn, as did Jesus. It is also a source of life: Its watery, quiet space nurtures, like a womb. Its interior can be mysterious yet comforting, black and frightening, or cool and beckoning. "Ajanta," said Kenneth Rexroth (1905-1982), is "an exploration . . . of her own interior—in every sense." That is, as a poet and a woman, Rukeyser is interested in her mind and in her body's flesh and form and how they shape her quest for fulfillment. The beauty, complexity, and energy of "Ajanta" has made it one of her most famous and powerful poems.

"Eyes of Night-Time"

Type of work: Poetry
First published: 1948, in *The Green Wave*

"Eyes of Night-Time" is a full-throated song about the beauty of night and darkness. This short poem in free verse expresses the poet's awe over nature's beauty at night. The first stanza describes with passionate wonder the creatures that see in the dark. In the second stanza, the poet considers what human beings may see in the darkness, or what the darkness may reveal to them.

For Rukeyser, "night-time" has strong metaphorical connections to the human spirit's darkness or hidden truths. The poem, while offering minute observations on nature at night, also deals with self-examination and attempts to comment on human nature in general.

In many of her poems, Rukeyser relies on a fabric woven of imagery and rhythm to provide formal unity. *The Green Wave* (1948), in which "Eyes of Night-Time" first appeared, contains other poems in which she experimented with her powers of observation and concentrated on new rhythms. Rukeyser preferred not to use traditional forms or patterns of fixed rhyme and meter. She wanted a poetry in which the material would generate its own form. Therefore, rhythm—the cadence, pace, and momentum of the line—was important to her. The music of the poem ought to allow it to echo and suggest—perhaps reproduce—the natural rhythms of the world she was attempting to describe.

In the poem, images of light and dark intertwine; points of light continually pierce the darkness. These emerging lights represent, as images of light often do in poetry, possible revelations of truth. The play between dark and light, shadow and eye shine, gives the poem both tension and balance. Dark things bear light: "the illumined shadow sea" and "the light of wood" are two examples.

Images of darkness inhabit every corner of "Eyes of Night-Time." The poet has studied night, and nighttime is this poem's territory. The earth's night and the human spirit's darkness, metaphorical counterparts in the poem, are fertile places the poet considers with full respect. The soul's darkest, most threatening realizations, she knows, will reveal the light (self-knowledge) that is needed to free the "prisoners in the forest . . . in the almost total dark."

Rukeyser's poem offers her ecstatic awareness of the healing power of darkness: If one goes deeply enough into one's own darkness, one finds, paradoxically, the light of truth that heals dark sufferings and misgivings. This light is the "glitter" she recognizes in the last line as "gifts" given, really, by all those people who have gone before her and all those who are alive now.

The poem is about examining oneself and one's spirit. It is also a statement on the need for human unity. "And in our bodies the eyes of the dead and the living" is a powerful way of saying that human beings inhabit not only the earth but also one another. Like the creatures of nighttime—the cat, moth, fly, beetle, and toad—humans are interdependent and must rely on one another to survive.

Suggested Readings

Gardinier, Suzanne. "A World That Will Hold All People: On Muriel Rukeyser." *Kenyon Review* 14 (Summer, 1992): 88-105.

Herzog, Anne F., and Janet E. Kaufman, eds. *How Shall We Tell Each Other of the Poet? The Life and Writing of Muriel Rukeyser*. New York: St. Martin's Press, 1999.

Kertesz, Louise. *The Poetic Vision of Muriel Rukeyser*. Baton Rouge: Louisiana State University Press, 1980.
Rosenthal, M. L. "Muriel Rukeyser: The Longer Poems." In *New Directions in Prose and Poetry* 14, edited by James Laughlin. New York: New Directions Books, 1953.
Untermeyer, Louis. "The Language of Muriel Rukeyser." *Saturday Review* (August 10, 1940): 11-13.
Ware, Michele S. "Opening 'The Gates': Muriel Rukeyser and the Poetry of Witness." *Women's Studies* 22 (June, 1993): 297-308.

Contributors: Holly Dworken Cooley and JoAnn Balingit

Luis Rafael Sánchez

Born: Humacao, Puerto Rico; November 17, 1936

Puerto Rican

Sánchez focuses on the new urban Puerto Rico that emerged after World War II and postwar industrialization and Americanization.

Principal works

DRAMA: "Cuento de cucarachita viudita," wr. 1959; *La espera*, pr. 1959; *Farsa del amor compradito*, pb. 1960; *Los ángeles se han fatigado*, pb. 1960 (*The Angels Are Exhausted*, 1964); *La hiel nuestra de cada día*, pr. 1962, pb. 1976 (*Our Daily Bitterness*, 1964); *Casi el alma: Auto da fe en tres actos*, pr. 1964, pb. 1966 (*A Miracle for Maggie*, 1974); *La pasión según Antígona Pérez*, pr., pb. 1968 (*The Passion According to Antígona Pérez*, 1968; also known as *The Passion of Antígona Pérez*, 1971); *Teatro de Luis Rafael Sánchez*, pb. 1976 (includes *Los ángeles se han fatigado*, *Farsa del amor compradito*, and *La hiel nuestra de cada día*); *Quíntuples*, pr. 1984, pb. 1985 (*Quintuplets*, 1984)

LONG FICTION: *La guaracha del Macho Camacho*, 1976 (*Macho Camacho's Beat*, 1980); *La importancia de llamarse Daniel Santos*, 1988

SHORT FICTION: *En cuerpo de camisa*, 1965, revised 1971

NONFICTION: *Fabulación e ideología en la cuentística de Emilio S. Belaval*, 1979; *No llores por nosotros, Puerto Rico*, 1997

The success of his 1976 novel *Macho Camacho's Beat* catapulted the Puerto Rican playwright, short-story writer, and essayist Luis Rafael Sánchez (lwees rah-FYEHL SAHN-chehz) to international fame. Sánchez was born to a working-class family in a small coastal town in Puerto Rico. He went to San Juan to study theater at the University of Puerto Rico. For a time he moved back and forth between his native land and New York City. Sánchez spent a year at Columbia University, where he studied theater and creative writing. Later he returned to New York to pursue a master's degree in Spanish literature at New York University. He began but did not complete his doctoral studies at Columbia University; he would receive his Ph.D. in 1973 from the University of Madrid. He went on to teach Latin American and Spanish literature at the University of Puerto Rico, occasionally traveling and living abroad.

Sánchez began his writing career as a playwright. While there is some low-key experimentalism in his drama, typical of the Latin American scene of the 1960's, the thrust of his works lies in social criticism, with heavy moralizing, rhetoric, and transparent allegories. His political stance is that of an *independentista* (represented by the left-wing intellectual elite proposing independence for his native island), which in the Puerto Rico of the late twentieth century had become inextricably entangled with upholding Fidel Castro's Cuban Revolution of 1959 as the model for such independence.

The mastery of language and the hyperbolism employed in *Farsa del amor compradito* recall Ramón María del Valle-Inclán's farcical *esperpentos* from the early twentieth century. This quality continues through the short stories *En cuerpo de camisa* and reaches a high point in *Macho Camacho's Beat*. Sánchez turns his back on the romantic icon of Puerto Rican cultural identity, the mainly white, peasant *jíbaro*. Instead, he focuses on the new Puerto Rico that emerged, after postwar industrialization and Americanization, in the cities. In these early works Sánchez starts learning to "write in this new Puerto Rican," developing a neobaroque language that celebrates popular urban culture, discourse, music, and humor.

The Passion According to Antígona Pérez is generally considered one of the highlights of the first period of Sánchez's work. However, the tragic moral dilemma of the Sophoclean Antigone is considerably weakened in this version, and the story is transformed into a predictable political allegory that criticizes stale stereotypes and situations in Latin America (such as the mutual support of church and state). Read decades later, the drama does not seem to have withstood the ravages of time, history, and failed master ideologies. Indeed, the dictatorship in Sánchez's apocryphal Latin American "banana republic" bears a striking, if unintentional and ironic, resemblance to Castro's regime in Cuba.

Macho Camacho's Beat

Type of work: Drama
First published: *La guaracha del Macho Camacho*, 1976 (English translation, 1980)

Macho Camacho's Beat, published originally in Argentina, was an instant success. In this novel Sánchez blends the language of an apocryphal popular hit song, real-life commercial hype, and contemporary urban mass-media culture into a masterful stream of radio advertisement babble that unmasks commercialism, superficial journalism, and popular hyperreal lifestyles propagated by commercial radio, all while criticizing some more serious aspects of Puerto Rican political life, such as all-pervasive corruption.

The entire plot occurs within the few minutes before, at, and just after five o'clock on a steamy Wednesday afternoon. As an immense traffic jam paralyzes San Juan, the novel's characters are depicted in the act of waiting. With the accumulative fragments of sounds, images, thoughts, and experience, the reader is able to piece together a composite picture of Puerto Rican culture.

Sánchez's prose is rich with the colorful and often obscene language of the streets, loaded with the language of consumerism, and abundant in references to the lifestyles of the rich and famous, fictional and otherwise. The fragmented, baroque surface of Sánchez's highly allusive prose is a brilliant reflection of the kaleidoscopic confusion caused by the indiscriminate acceptance of the material values espoused by a profit-oriented consumerist society. Language defines thought, and in this novel, language is the product of a largely American-controlled mass media. The resulting inability to communicate on an intimate, personal level creates in the reader a sense of the moral and spiritual poverty of Sánchez's characters.

Macho Camacho's Beat clearly calls for a radical reformation of Puerto Rican society and of the ways in which individuals perceive themselves. The political push to Americanize Puerto Rico and the corruption of government officials is exemplified in the character of Reinosa. The moral decay of the population is sardonically expressed in the Mother's prostitution and Benny's love affair with his Ferrari, which supersedes his affection for any human being. Even the personal physical reality of the people is being transformed, Americanized, foreignized. This is clearly expressed in Graciela's obsession with makeup, hair, and fashion, in her social life, and in her absurd proposed design for typical Puerto Rican dress: a tailored suit in spotted calfskin.

The key metaphor of the monstrous traffic jam symbolizes the stagnation of a Puerto Rican society that constantly denies its own seedy reality as it becomes obsessed with the fleeting distractions offered by a sensationalist media and subscribes to the seductive but clearly false philosophy of the seductive *guaracha*. No element of Puerto Rican society is immune from Sánchez's irreverent and biting sense of humor. The sins of elitism, racial discrimination, and denial of self are laid bare before the grotesque feet and obtuse minds of the sinners. Just as the Kid is forced to confront his ugly and deformed reality reflected in the surface of a fragmented mirror, Sánchez compels his fellow Puerto Ricans to confront themselves in the fragmented and glittering surface of *Macho Camacho's Beat*.

Quintuplets

Type of work: Drama
First produced: 1984, pb. 1985 (English translation, 1984)

In 1984 Sánchez's play *Quintuplets* was staged, to critical acclaim, in San Juan, New York, Buenos Aires, Santo Domingo, and Oporto. The play consists of monologues by the five children of the actor The Great Mandrake; criticizing patriarchy, it also deals with the nature of acting and writing. In 1985 Sánchez received a grant from the German academic exchange board and spent that year in Berlin. In 1988 he published *La importancia de llamarse Daniel Santos*, a fictionalized biography of Daniel Santos, a real-life Puerto Rican singer of boleros from the 1940's and 1950's who was both a pop-culture idol and a fervent believer in the island's independence. The text is a hybrid work, a mosaic of essay, fiction, and (pseudo) documentary narrative spiced with fragments of Santos's best-known romantic and sentimental bolero songs.

Quintuplets is written for two performers, each of who plays several roles. Critics have said that it is necessary to consult one's playbill to make sure that only two performers are involved because each one acts so convincingly in the variety of roles undertaken. Sánchez has called the play a parody of suspense comedy. It is played as a family vaudeville act that, in the course of its unfolding, comments sociopolitically and philosophically on what it means to act and what it means to produce drama.

The play is acted out before the delegates at a Conference on Family Affairs. The participants, the Morrison Quintuplets and their father, each occupy one of the play's six acts, presenting a monologue that details his or her perceptions of what it is to be a member of the Morrison family. Among the Morrisons, Dafne is cast as a bombshell, radiant in a provocative red dress. She rejects traditional femininity but adopts the mask of femininity. In contrast is Bianca, whose sexual identity is not clearly revealed, although it is suggested that she has lesbian tendencies. All three Morrison boys are named Ifigenio, so they adopt names that distinguish them from each other: Baby and Mandrake are particularly telling among these assumed names.

The father, Papá Morrison, referred to as El Gran Semental (the great stud), is viewed quite differently by each of the quintuplets. For Dafne, he represents perfection and is to be emulated. For Mandrake, he is the competition as a performer but also in an Oedipal sense. Bianca considers him a controlling, domineering patriarchal archetype. Baby, the least secure of the quintuplets, sees his father as someone whose example he can never live up to no matter how hard he tries.

According to Sánchez's directions, each member of the family improvises his or her part in a vaudevillian style. The play comments stingingly on patriarchy and, indirectly, on the paternalism of the United States toward Puerto Rico, a topic that Sánchez injects into most of his writing. The play's lengthy stage directions also comment on the meaning of acting and drama; hence, on different levels, *Quintuplets* is rewarding both to see in performance and to read.

Suggested Readings

Flores, Angel, ed. *Spanish American Writers: The Twentieth Century*. New York: H. W. Wilson, 1992.

Guinness, Gerald. "Is *Macho Camacho's Beat* a Good Translation of *La guaracha del Macho Camacho*?" In *Images and Identities: The Puerto Rican in Two World Contexts*, edited by Asela Rodriguez de Laguna. New Brunswick, N.J.: Transaction Books, 1987.

Luis, William. *Dance Between Two Cultures: Latino Caribbean Literature Written in the United States*. Nashville: Vanderbilt University Press, 1997.

Melendez, Priscilla. "Towards a Characterization of Latin American Farce." *Siglo XX* 11 (1993).

Perivolaris, John Dimitri. *Puerto Rican Cultural Identity and the Work of Luis Rafael Sánchez*. Chapel Hill: University of North Carolina Press, 2000.

Quintana, Hilda E. "Myth and Reality in Luis Rafael Sánchez's *La pasión según Antígona Pérez*." *Revista/Review interamericana* 19, nos. 3/4 (1989).
Zamora, Lois Parkinson. "Clichés and Defamiliarization in the Fiction of Manuel Puig and Luis Rafael Sánchez." *Journal of Aesthetics & Art Criticism* 41, no. 4 (June, 1983): 421.

Contributors: Emil Volek and R. Baird Shuman

Sonia Sanchez

(Wilsonia Benita Driver)

Born: Birmingham, Alabama; September 9, 1934

African American

Among the black poets who emerged during the 1960's, Sanchez has stood out for her activism.

Principal works

children's literature: *It's a New Day: Poems for Young Brothas and Sistuhs*, 1971; *The Adventures of Fat Head, Small Head, and Square Head*, 1973; *A Sound Investment, and Other Stories*, 1979

drama: *The Bronx Is Next*, pb. 1968, pr. 1971; *Sister Son/ji*, pb. 1969, pr. 1972; *Uh, Huh; But How Do It Free Us?*, pb. 1974, pr. 1975; *Malcolm Man/Don't Live Here No Mo'*, pr. 1979; *I'm Black When I'm Singing, I'm Blue When I Ain't*, pr. 1982; *Black Cats Back and Uneasy Landings*, pr. 1995

poetry: *Homecoming*, 1969; *We a BaddDDD People*, 1970; *A Blues Book for Blue Black Magical Women*, 1973; *Love Poems*, 1973; *I've Been a Woman: New and Selected Poems*, 1978; *Homegirls and Handgrenades*, 1984; *Under a Soprano Sky*, 1987; *Wounded in the House of a Friend*, 1995; *Does Your House Have Lions?*, 1997; *Like the Singing Coming Off the Drums: Love Poems*, 1998; *Shake Loose My Skin: New and Selected Poems*, 1999

nonfiction: *Crisis in Culture: Two Speeches by Sonia Sanchez*, 1983; *Conversations with Sonia Sanchez*, 2007 (Joyce A. Joyce, editor)

edited text: *We Be Word Sorcerers: Twenty-five Stories by Black Americans*, 1973

Sonia Sanchez (SOH-nyah SAHN-chehz) emerged as a writer and political activist in the 1960's, marking the beginning of her career of a poet, playwright, and cultural worker. She became known as a black activist committed to the belief that the role of the artist is functional. Sanchez's political interpretation of the situation of African Americans informs the creative forms she produces. The activist spirit would remain a constant in her work.

Sonia Sanchez's mother died when Sanchez was one year old. Her father, Wilson Driver, Jr., a jazz musician, moved the family to New York when Sanchez was nine years old; she was thrust into the jazz world of her father. She entered Hunter College and received her bachelor's degree in political science in 1955. As a graduate student, Sanchez studied with Louise Bogan at New York University. Bogan, a poet and literary critic, wrote restrained, concise, and deeply intellectual poetry, often compared to that of the English metaphysical poets. Bogan's influence upon Sanchez is most evident in the conciseness of her lyrical poetry; Bogan's encouragement caused Sanchez to pursue the life of a poet. Sanchez formed a writers' workshop and soon began reading poetry around New York City.

Sanchez's early works were published in little magazines; later they were published in black journals. *Homecoming*, Sanchez's first anthology of poetry, placed her among poets who espoused a philosophy of functional art. Functional art is characterized by a sense of social purpose, information, instruction, and inspiration. Sanchez's improvisational style combines strategies common to black speech. This is particularly evident in her early poetry. Indirection, or signifying, is a key element of this poetic style. Another key element of Sanchez's style is her oral delivery, reminiscent of improvisation in jazz. Her creative vision is also expressed in her inventive poetic forms. Sanchez's speechlike, versatile style is evident in all of her poetry.

Although Sanchez's literary reputation rests primarily on her poetry, she sees her plays as an extension of her poetic art, saying that their longer form gives her more room to express her ideas. She has also written short stories, children's books, essays, literary criticism, and social commentary. She has an impressive record as a university teacher and political activist and as a driving force behind the movement to include writings by African American authors in the college curriculum. She frequently gives public readings, performances that are noted for their dramatic power and include music, drum beats, and chanting. Some of her best-known works were inspired by the Black Arts movement of the 1960's, and her later writings have continued to focus on African American themes.

The Bronx Is Next

Type of work: Drama
First published: 1968, pr. 1971

Sanchez's first brief play, *The Bronx Is Next*, was, she says, a condemnation of what Harlem was becoming in the 1960's. Once the site of the great outpouring of creativity called the Harlem Renaissance, the area was being destroyed by drugs and violence. The play's two major characters are Old Sister, representing the past oppression of African Americans in the Old South, and Black Bitch, a sexually promiscuous woman accused by the black male characters of sleeping with a white police officer and failing to support the revolution. When Black Bitch accuses the black male leader of abusing women, he brutally rapes her. The black male revolutionaries force both women back into the burning buildings to die. Sanchez's language is explicitly sexual and violent in this play. Although some critics believe the work contains one of the first examples of strong black women characters in drama, others find the message disturbing, with the playwright seeming to blame the women characters for not supporting the revolution.

Sister Son/ji

Type of work: Drama
First published: 1969, pr. 1972

The narrator in this one-act play is an African American woman in her fifties recalling important episodes of her history as a revolutionary. By changing her makeup and costumes, she recalls her early college days, her first sexual experience, her black consciousness awakening through the speeches of Malcolm X, an episode of near insanity when she loses control of her life, and the death of her teenage son in the revolution. Sanchez portrays the conflicted relationship between black men and women, with the men exploiting their power and expecting the women to take a subservient role in the movement. Sister Son/ji pleads with black men to admit women as equals and respect love and family life rather than a false idea of manhood.

By tracing Sister Son/ji's experiences, Sanchez explores themes that dominate all her work: the exploitation of black women by black men, the destructive power of drugs and violence, the urgent need for African American men and women to work together to combat racism. The play concludes with a statement of Sister Son/ji's strength and survival skills:

> Death is a five o-clock door forever changing time. And wars end. Sometimes too late. i am here. still in mississippi. Near the graves of my past. We are at peace . . . but I have my memories. . . . i have my sweet/astringent memories becuz we dared to pick up the day and shake its tail until it became evening. A time for us. blk/ness. blk/people.

We a BaddDDD People

Type of work: Poetry
First published: 1970

In the 1970 collection *We a BaddDDD People*, Sanchez's political voice protesting the injustice of growing up in a country that did not "tell me about black history" and "ma[d]e me feel so inferior." These poems function to answer those questions for herself. The discovery is thematically addressed in the poem "Questions" and in the section titled "Survival." Depicting the political unrest of the period of the late 1960's, the collection has been criticized for being unoriginal in its political diatribe. However, the importance of the work in posing the political and personal questions of black existence for the poet and her readers is articulated in the following lines from "Questions": "we suicidal/ or something/ or are we all bugalooers/ of death:/ our own???" and "why they closing down/ prisons as they close off/ our blk/ minds."

The structure of the poems often represents the urgency of the poetic voice. For example, lines are fractured and split off by slashes and spaces. In "right on: wite america," the first stanza uses virgules and abbreviations:

starting july 4th is
bring in yr/guns/down/to
yr/nearest/po/lice/station

The troubled tone of the collection, reinforcing the structure, is loud and vociferous, as in "words for our children (from their many parents)":

we are the
screeeeeamers/
seaaaarcherrrs/
weepeeers

Although the tone is often soul-searching, the thrust of the poetry strives metaphorically to force change.

More than featuring poems of political dissent, the collection reaffirms the need for poetry, the desire to chant or even shout out one's thoughts, as exhibited in "a/coltrane/poem":

stretchen the mind
till it bursts past the con/fines of
solo/en melodies

and concluding with the need to listen:

showen us life/
liven.
a love supreme.
for each
other
if we just
lissssssSSSTEN.

Uh, Huh; But How Do It Free Us?

Type of work: Drama
First published: 1974, pr. 1975

This play is experimental in form, with three unrelated scenes connected by dance sequences. In the first scene, three characters (Malik, Waleesha, and Nefertia) represent the black male's need to dominate women to assure his manhood. Both women are pregnant and enemies of each other, rather than sisters, as they try to hold on to Malik's love.

The next scene is a surreal dramatization of male cocaine addicts, four black and one white, riding horses that represent their drug-induced fantasies. Two prostitutes, one white and one black, are whipping them and providing drugs. At the end of this scene, the white man dresses in drag, proclaiming himself the "real queen." Sanchez represents black men as superior to white men, but sees women, both black and white, as subordinate to the degenerate needs of men of both races.

The final scene portrays a black male revolutionary called Brother in relationships with both a black woman and a white woman. The white woman functions as a symbol of the white man's property. She supports him financially and makes him feel powerful. Sister, the black woman, is conflicted in her role as angry lover demeaned by Brother's betrayal with the "devil/woman" and her hopes that he will reform himself and return to his true responsibility as a man committed to his role in the black community. Sanchez stops short of supporting the sisterhood of black women, emphasizing Sister's individual strength and ability to survive both racism and her oppression by the black male.

I've Been a Woman

Type of work: Poetry
First published: 1978

I've Been a Woman: New and Selected Poems is a compilation of selections from Sanchez's major works up to 1978. This collection offers a cross section of the themes that characterize Sonia Sanchez's poetic vision. Sanchez's work balances the private and the public. The private, or introspective, poems are intensely personal. The public poems cover a number of concerns. Selections from *Homecoming* (1969), *We a BaddDDD People* (1970), *Love Poems* (1973), *A Blues Book for Blue Black Magical Women* (1973), and *Generations: Selected Poetry 1969-1985* (1986) make up *I've Been a Woman.*

Themes include issues of identity among African Americans. Sanchez's work is characterized by her ability to offer clear-eyed commentary on African American conditions while offering poetry of destiny and self-determination. For example, one of Sanchez's ongoing concerns is drug addiction among African Americans. In works such as *Wounded in the House of a Friend* (1995), she focuses this concern on the devastating effects of addiction to crack cocaine.

This intermingling of themes is found in poems such as "Summary." This poem represents an example of Sanchez's technique. She combines personal and public concerns. Within this poem, Sanchez does not allow the narrator to move inward and remain there. She seems to assume an introspective position as a momentary restful pose. In this energizing space, the narrator is renewed and arrives at a political solution to problems noted in the poems.

The poems included in these sections are examples of Sanchez's virtuosity as a poet. Section 5 is devoted exclusively to Sanchez's "Haikus/Tankas & Other Love Syllables." Use of forms offers an example of the poet's technique. This collection offers an excellent example of Sanchez's range as an artist. In the various sections of *I've Been a Woman*, the speaker of Sanchez's poetry is revealed as a quester for identity and resolution. Distinguished from male quest epics, Sanchez's quest focuses on the desire to embark on a quest not only for herself but also for other women. The knowledge that the quester seeks is assumed to be available in the person of an Earth Mother who can help the quester understand the relationship between past and present. Such a figure can also help the quester learn to have faith in the future.

Homegirls and Handgrenades

Type of work: Poetry
First published: 1984

Critically acclaimed, Sanchez's *Homegirls and Handgrenades* is divided into four sections: "The Power of Love," "Blues Is Bullets," "Beyond the Fallout," and "Grenades Are Not Free." The thematic opposites of rage and love, cynicism and compassion, and pain and joy coalesce in this volume.

The varying rhythmic style of the poems reflects the forms language takes in articulating diverse, sometimes conflicting, views. For example, the language of the street often labeled by Sanchez as "black English," spoken by her stepmother and her beloved grandmother, is used to describe "Poems Written After Reading Wright's 'American Hunger'": "such a simple need/ amid yo/easy desire."

In four of the poems she uses haiku, a Japanese lyric form that represents a single, concentrated image in seventeen syllables and arranged in three unrhymed lines of, traditionally, five, seven, and five syllables. Aptly named "Haiku," each poem conveys a single impression of a scene in motion: "your love was a port/ of call where many ships docked/ until morning came." In the section "Beyond the Fallout," the haiku exhibits raw anger: "I see you blackboy/ bent toward destruction watching/ for death with tight eyes."

The visionary quality of Sanchez's poem is articulated in poetic language that projects versatility because American life cannot be reflected in one homogenous voice. Sanchez uses the English vernacular to apprehend the complexity of human existence, as she states in a 1985 interview with Herbert Leibowitz: "Playing with words, as I used to, was like going outside and running and jumping over walls." As she explains further in the same interview, "A lot of my poetry expresses what it means to let people taste and feel sweetness and power running together, hate and love running together, beauty and ugliness also running together."

Does Your House Have Lions?

Type of work: Poetry
First published: 1997

Does Your House Have Lions? is a book-length poem memorializing the life and death of Sanchez's brother, a young black man who died of AIDS after a

Sonia Sanchez (AP/Wide World Photos)

brief, furious exploration of the gay subculture in New York City. The title, *Does Your House Have Lions?*, comes from an interview with jazz great Rahsaan Roland Kirk and in this context speaks of a household's need to face life with courage. Sanchez's poem is a record of how one family found the courage of lions.

The poem is written in four parts, "sister's voice," "brother's voice," "father's voice," and "family voices/ ancestors' voices." The first three sections, and most of the fourth section, use a modified terza rima rhyme scheme; each individual unit poem has a rhyme scheme of *ababbcc*. This tight structure suggests the emotional confinement her brother is rebelling against. The first section, "sister's voice," presents the most detached, assured poetry, as the sister (a persona representing Sanchez herself) describes her brother's immersion into the New York gay subculture as "a migration unlike/ the 1900s of black men and women/ coming north for jobs." To repay his father's desertion, he sold his body as a prostitute, auctioning off "his legs. eyes./ heart. in rooms of specific pain." By contrast, the second section, "brother's voice," is written with the emotional directness of pain. He begins by saying, "father. i despise you for abandoning me," and tells of trying to make a new life on the New York streets, "a country of men/ where dollars pump their veins." "Father's voice" tells poignantly of a father's neglect and is remarkably alive with the rhythms of the music the father plays professionally; "i come to collapse the past/ while bonfires burn up your orphan's mask," the father sings about trying to reconcile with a son approaching death.

The last section is the most magisterial. Most of these poems represent the voices of the family, but several represent "the ancestor" and have a distinct African folk quality to them. Together, they chart the family's attempt to heal even as one of them is dying. The cumulative effect is both wrenching and uplifting. This is poetry that demands performance; a reader almost has to imagine the poetry being staged to fully appreciate it.

Suggested Readings

Brown-Guillory, Elizabeth, ed. Introduction to *Sister Son/ji*, by Sonia Sanchez. In *Wines in the Wilderness: Plays by African American Women from the Harlem Renaissance to the Present*. New York: Praeger, 1990.

De Lancey, Frenzella Elaine. "Refusing to Be Boxed In: Sonia Sanchez's Transformation of the Haiku Form." In *Language and Literature in the African American Imagination*, edited by Carol Aisha Blackshire-Belay. Westport, Conn.: Greenwood Press, 1992.

Jennings, Regina B. "The Blue/Black Poetics of Sonia Sanchez." In *Language and Literature in the African American Imagination*, edited by Carol Aisha Blackshire-Belay. Westport, Conn.: Greenwood Press, 1992.

Joyce, Joyce A. *Ijala: Sonia Sanchez and the African Poetic Tradition*. Chicago: Third World Press, 1996.

Sanchez, Sonia. "As Poets, as Activists." Interview by David Reich. *World*, May/June, 1999, 1-11.

_______. "Disciple and Craft: An Interview with Sonia Sanchez." Interview by Susan Kelly. *African American Review* 34, no. 4 (Winter, 2000): 679-687.

_______. "Exploding Myths: An Interview with Sonia Sanchez." Interview by Herbert Leibowitz. *Parnassus*, Spring/Summer/Fall/Winter, 1985, 357-368.

Contributors: Frenzella Elaine De Lancey, Cynthia S. Becerra, and Marjorie Podolsky

Thomas Sanchez

Born: Oakland, California; February 26, 1944

Spanish American

Sanchez's novels portray the diverse, multiethnic experience of twentieth century American life.

Principal works

LONG FICTION: *Rabbit Boss*, 1973; *Zoot Suit Murders*, 1978; *Mile Zero*, 1989; *Day of the Bees*, 2000; *King Bongo: A Novel of Havana*, 2003

NONFICTION: *Four Visions of America: Henry Miller, Thomas Sanchez, Erica Jong, Kay Boyle*, 1977 (with others); *Native Notes from the Land of Earthquake and Fire*, 1979 (also known as *Angels Burning: Native Notes from the Land of Earthquake and Fire*, 1987)

Descended from Spanish and Portuguese ancestors and growing up in a poor family, Thomas Sanchez (SAHN-chehz) was sent to a Catholic boarding school in Northern California after his mother became ill. There he developed his interest in Native American subjects, which informs his fiction. An outspoken advocate for human rights, Sanchez was a member of the Congress for Racial Equality, the United Farm Workers, and the Student Nonviolent Coordinating Committee during the 1960's. Sanchez participated in the Sacramento Valley grape strikes and the Vietnam antiwar movement. As a radio correspondent in 1973, he reported on the American Indian Movement's takeover of the Wounded Knee Reservation in South Dakota—a protest that prompted a Senate investigation into the conditions of Indian life.

In 1969, Sanchez left the United States to visit Spain, where he wrote his first novel. *Rabbit Boss* chronicles four generations of the Washo Indian tribe. The tribe's leader, the Rabbit Boss, encounters the Donner party, a group of white settlers who became snowbound in the mountains and resorted to cannibalism. A Washo legend that whites are cannibals originates from this 1846 encounter. The cannibalism overturns the civilized white man-savage Indian dichotomy. Cultures clash again in Sanchez's next novel, *Zoot-Suit Murders*, a mystery set in a Los Angeles barrio of the 1940's. The story concerns the murder of two Federal Bureau of Investigation agents in a rioting neighborhood where the local zoot-suiters are regularly terrorized by sailors.

A Guggenheim Fellowship and the proceeds from the sale of his house allowed Sanchez to move to Key West, Florida, where he wrote *Mile Zero*. *Rabbit Boss* describes the beginning of an American campaign against indigenous people that culminated in the destructive logic of the Vietnam War. *Mile Zero* is Sanchez's attempt to connect with the post-Vietnam generation. For Sanchez, the tide of refugees fleeing Haiti and the increasing cocaine traffic through Florida stem from the same folly that fueled the United States' involvement in Vietnam. The novel's brilliant evocation of Key West and its political vision elicited favorable comparisons with the work of John Steinbeck and Robert Stone.

Sanchez writes novels infused with the richness of America's cultural heritage, so his work is difficult to categorize. His fiction has received laudatory reviews and other critical accolades, but it has yet to attract the scholarly attention it deserves. Nevertheless, Sanchez is an important critic of the United States' destructive desire for "progress" at the expense of others.

Mile Zero

Type of work: Novel
First published: 1989

Mile Zero, Sanchez's sweeping vision of Key West, Florida, brilliantly evokes the rich history and lyrical passion of the island. Key West is the southernmost point of the continental United States, where "Mile Zero," the last highway sign before the Atlantic Ocean, symbolizes the end of the American road. While Key West represents the end for the downtrodden Americans who gravitate there, the island promises hope for refugees fleeing Haiti's poverty across shark-ridden waters. Sanchez traces the island's shifting economy from a hub of the cigar industry to "a marijuana republic," then to "a mere cocaine principality." Sanchez laments how the drug trade has corrupted the American Dream.

Mile Zero's main character, St. Cloud, a former antiwar activist, drowns his self-doubt in Haitian rum and ponders his inability to sacrifice himself for his beliefs. He feels a strange kinship with MK, once a soldier in Vietnam and now a dangerous smuggler who has fled Key West for South America. MK's mysterious presence and the shadow of Vietnam permeate the book. St. Cloud imagines that his pacificism and MK's violence are two sides of the same coin. After Vietnam, returning soldiers and protesters both found themselves cast out of society.

When a Coast Guard cutter tows a refugee boat from Haiti into the harbor, Justo Tamarindo, a Cuban American police officer, drafts St. Cloud to help him prevent the deportation of the sole survivor, a boy named Voltaire. Voltaire's sad story reveals how America thrives at the expense of developing nations. Late in the novel, Voltaire escapes from the detention center where he is waiting to be deported. The young, malnourished boy dreams he has reached a heavenly land of plenty at a garish shopping mall before he dies a tragic death.

Meanwhile, Justo pursues Zobop, an enigmatic killer, who is roaming the island and leaving Voodoo-inspired clues everywhere. After Zobop is killed, Justo learns that the murderer sought purification by destruction. Like El Finito, a powerful, apocalyptic hurricane that threatens to destroy the island, Zobop believes everything must be wiped out before it can be renewed.

In *Mile Zero*, Sanchez signals the necessity of cultural change. Vietnam is over, Justo thinks, but the bodies of the dead refugees augur the arrival of a new devil. America is doomed if it does not change. The novel's ambiguous ending, in which Justo, who may have contracted AIDS, pulls St. Cloud out of the ocean, brings its readers to mile zero, a place that can be either an ending or a beginning.

Suggested Readings

Kirkus Reviews. Review of *King Bongo*, by Thomas Sanchez. 71, no. 1 (March 15, 2003): 425.

Marovitz, Sanford E. "The Entropic World of the Washo: Fatality and Self-Deception in *Rabbit Boss*." *Western American Literature* 19 (Fall, 1984).

Rieff, D. "The Affirmative Action Novel." *The New Republic* 202, no. 14 (April 2, 1990).

Sanchez, Thomas. "An Interview with Thomas Sanchez." Interview by Kay Bonetti. *The Missouri Review* 14, no. 2 (1991).

_______. "The Visionary Imagination." *MELUS* 3, no. 2 (1976).

Contributor: Trey Strecker

George S. Schuyler

Born: Providence, Rhode Island; February 25, 1895
Died: New York, New York; August 31, 1977

African American

Schuyler, whose specialty was ridiculing bigotry, was one of the leading satirists of the Harlem Renaissance era.

Principal works

LONG FICTION: *Slaves Today: A Story of Liberia*, 1931
SHORT FICTION: *Black No More: Being an Account of the Strange and Wonderful Workings of Science in the Land of the Free, A.D. 1933-1940*, 1931; *Ethiopian Stories*, 1994
NONFICTION: *Fifty Years of Progress in Negro Journalism*, 1950; *Black and Conservative: The Autobiography of George S. Schuyler*, 1966

Born in Rhode Island and raised in Syracuse, New York, George S. Schuyler (SHI-lur) dropped out of high school to join the Army. There, as a member of the famous Twenty-fifth U.S. Infantry regiment, he served seven years before being discharged as a first lieutenant in 1919. After several odd jobs in New York City, Schuyler returned home and joined the Socialist Party, for which he held several offices.

Schuyler was later involved with Marcus Garvey's Universal Negro Improvement Association but became disillusioned with Garvey's plan to return to Africa. Schuyler often spoke publicly on political and cultural issues, and by the 1920's, he had joined a black socialist group, Friends of Negro Freedom, and had accepted a job on the staff of the organization's official magazine, *The Messenger*. He also wrote as the New York correspondent for an African American weekly newspaper, *The Pittsburgh Courier*. He continued to live in New York and write for *The Pittsburgh Courier* until 1966.

Schuyler's literary identity evolves from his career as a journalist and from his deep respect for his mother's ideas and values. The product of a middle-class family, Schuyler comments in his autobiography, *Black and Conservative*, that his mother taught him to consider all sides of a question and to establish and stand by principles of personal conduct whether others agreed or not. True to his mother's teaching, Schuyler seldom opted for the popular road. His public actions and political views were often regarded as extremely conservative and iconoclastic.

His cynical view of race in America led to razor-sharp attacks upon racial patriots (black leaders he perceived as self-interested and bigoted) and upon white supremacists, who, he believed, exploited racism for economic reasons. In his autobiography he asserts that blacks never thought themselves inferior to whites; rather, blacks "are simply aware that their socio-economic position is inferior, which is a different thing." In chiding race organizations as perpetuating the problems of racism, Schuyler contended that ridding the United States of racial hatred would absolutely disrupt the national economy.

His irreverent attacks on the traditional values and cherished beliefs of black and white society earned him much notoriety during his forty-year career, which spanned from the Harlem Renaissance to the 1960's.

Black No More

Type of work: Novel
First published: 1931

Schuyler's *Black No More: Being an Account of the Strange and Wonderful Workings of Science in the Land of the Free, A.D. 1933-1940* offers a bitingly satirical attack upon America's color phobia. His targets included bigoted whites who see the perpetuation of racism as a matter of economic and political interest, black leaders who waffle between appealing to white financial backers and appeasing their black constituents, and all who cloak their ignorance and hatred in racial rhetoric.

George S. Schuyler (Arkent Archives)

The plot of *Black No More* centers upon Schuyler's speculation of what might happen if America were to find a means to rid itself of the "Negro problem." In an effort to uplift his race, Dr. Junius Crookman, a respected black physician, invents a process by which black people can inexpensively turn themselves permanently white. The success of his process leads him to open up numerous Black No More clinics across America to handle the throngs of hopeful clients.

His first and most eager customer is Max Disher, who sees "chromatic enhancement" initially as a chance to get a white woman and eventually to run various fund-raising shams under the auspices of the Knights of Nordica, led by the Imperial Grand Wizard Reverend Givens. As a white man, Max takes a new name, Matthew Fisher. He soon is proving his talents as a brilliant organizer, political manipulator, and white supremacist working for "the cause." Ironically, the woman of his Harlem dreams and eventual wife, Helen, turns out to be the daughter of Reverend Givens.

Matthew's schemes initially are simply quick-money ploys that amusingly take advantage of the Knights of Nordica's ignorance and obsession for racial supremacy. As the plot moves along, however, Matthew begins to sound too sincere in his racist rhetoric and becomes obsessed with earning money and political power. An old friend, Bunny Brown, arrives to keep Matthew in line. With the numbers of blacks steadily dwindling, thanks to Crookman's clinics, Matthew and Bunny plot to expose and destroy the institution of racism in America, along with its vested leaders.

The novel concludes in a calamity as the national presidential race becomes a matter of reciprocated political tricks. The former blacks are whiter than whites, the two most notorious bigots in the book go up in flames, and Matthew's wife gives birth to a mulatto child.

Schuyler, through frequent barbs and sarcastic commentaries, exposes the hypocrisy of both white and black leaders. There are numerous thinly disguised caricatures of the black leaders of the time of the novel: W. E. B. Du Bois, Marcus Garvey, C. J. Walker, James Weldon Johnson, and many others. Schuyler's satire contends that blacks are motivated by the same economic and political interests as whites and, once given the opportunity, will resort to the same means to preserve those interests.

Suggested Readings

Davis, Arthur P. "George Schuyler." In *From the Dark Tower*. Washington, D.C.: Howard University Press, 1974.

Ferguson, Jeffrey B. *The Sage of Sugar Hill: George S. Schuyler and the Harlem Renaissance*. New Haven, Conn.: Yale University Press, 2005.

Schuyler, George. *Black and Conservative: The Autobiography of George S. Schuyler*. New Rochelle, N.Y.: Arlington House, 1966.

Contributor: Betty L. Hart

Delmore Schwartz

Born: Brooklyn, New York; December 8, 1913
Died: New York, New York; July 11, 1966

Jewish

Schwartz's work affirms the power of the independent mind against materialism.

Principal works

CHILDREN'S LITERATURE: *"I Am Cherry Alive," the Little Girl Sang*, 1958

DRAMA: *Shenandoah*, pb. 1941

POETRY: *In Dreams Begin Responsibilities*, 1938 (includes poetry and prose); *Genesis, Book I*, 1943; *Vaudeville for a Princess, and Other Poems*, 1950; *Summer Knowledge*, 1959; *Last and Lost Poems of Delmore Schwartz*, 1979 (Robert Phillips, editor)

SHORT FICTION: *The World Is a Wedding*, 1948; *Successful Love, and Other Stories*, 1961

NONFICTION: *Selected Essays of Delmore Schwartz*, 1970; *Letters of Delmore Schwartz*, 1984; *The Ego Is Always at the Wheel: Bagatelles*, 1986; *Portrait of Delmore: Journals and Notes of Delmore Schwartz, 1939-1959*, 1986

The life of Delmore Schwartz (DEHL-mohr shwohrts) reflects the Jewish American experience of the 1930's. Schwartz was the son of Romanian immigrants, and his career unfolded against the backdrop of political and social tensions of the Depression. Thus, much of his writing articulates the drama of alienation; poetic realism and psychological intensity are common characteristics. The shadow of Fyodor Dostoevski looms over Schwartz's literary figures—human archetypes of internalized chaos and ritualistic narcissism. Schwartz is often associated with the confessional school of his generation; the school includes John Berryman, Randall Jarrell, Theodore Roethke, Anne Sexton, and Robert Lowell. He fits squarely into the Jewish intellectual milieu of the post-World War I era, which produced many luminaries.

Schwartz grew up in Brooklyn, New York, and attended New York University. In 1935, he entered Harvard University to study philosophy and, despite impressive achievements, left after two years, without receiving an advanced degree. Throughout his life he held numerous university and college teaching positions but was reluctant to commit himself to an academic career. His writings suggest a bohemian strain in his personality that drove him toward self-discovery instead of the regularity of a permanent job.

The publication of *In Dreams Begin Responsibilities* galvanized Schwartz's career. Within several years, he was recognized as a seminal figure. In 1943, he became an editor of the Partisan Review. The publication of *The World Is a Wedding*, a collection of semiautobiographical stories, and *Summer Knowledge* led to numerous awards and several distinguished lectureships.

Schwartz's volatile personality is apparent in the disenchanted loneliness of his artistic imagery, vividly depicted by Saul Bellow in *Humboldt's Gift* (1975), in which Von Humboldt Fleisher's self-destruction is modeled after Schwartz's pathetic decline. He often hurt those who loved him best, and this led to the dissolution of two marriages, insomnia, acute paranoia, heavy drinking, drug abuse, and failing health. From 1962 to 1965, he was a visiting professor of English at Syracuse University. He was popular with students, but his poetic talents had clearly deteriorated. Many of his later works seem like old pictures reframed, although he retained the brilliant flashes of a virtuoso. He died isolated and alone.

In Dreams Begin Responsibilities

Type of work: Poetry, short fiction, and drama
First published: 1938

The short story "In Dreams Begin Responsibilities," which lends its title to this collection of prose, poetry, and drama, was apparently written over a weekend in July, 1935. Vladimir Nabokov recognized its merit and recommended it as the lead piece in the *Partisan Review*. Schwartz's literary career was launched. The enigmatic title suggests that destiny is located in dreams, what Schwartz would later call in his fictional autobiography *Genesis* (1943) "a fixed hallucination." The attempt to realize dreams in poetry and to acknowledge the past as prologue to the future draws its inspiration from the artistic context established by William Butler Yeats and T. S. Eliot—perhaps the most powerful forces to influence Schwartz's writing.

The narrator witnesses the events leading up to his father's marriage proposal. The narrator watches a series of six film episodes depicting Sunday afternoon, June 12, 1909, in Coney Island, New York. The climactic moment when his mother accepts proves unbearable to the eventual offspring of this union and, in the darkened, womblike theater, he screams in protest against his future birth. An authoritative usher, representing the narrator's superego, reminds him that he has no control over his birth, and hence the outburst is futile. The scene closes when a fortune-teller predicts an unhappy marriage, ending in divorce.

The theme of the anguished child continues in the five-act-long poem "Coriolanus and His Mother," in which the protagonist shifts his allegiance from Rome to a barbarian cause. Based on William Shakespeare's play, the drama unfolds before a boy, the poet's alter ego, and five ghosts: Karl Marx, Sigmund Freud, Ludwig van Beethoven, Aristotle, and a small anonymous presence, perhaps Franz

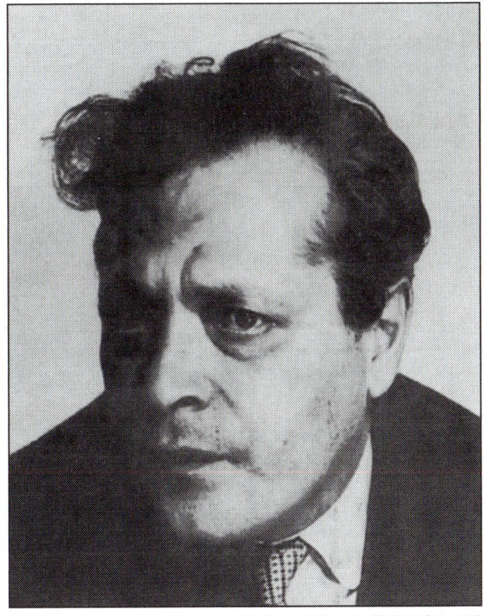

Delmore Schwartz (© Jane Lougee)

Kafka, chronicler of the absurd. This "dream of knowledge" play is a parable about self-destructive tendencies—anger, insolence, pride.

The management of identity is a theme carried through many of the thirty-five poems collected under the heading "Experimentation and Imitation." For example, rebel spirits such as Hart Crane, Robinson Crusoe, Wolfgang Amadeus Mozart, and Charlie Chaplin inhabit the vaudevillian circus atmosphere of the poetry, captured in the phrases "the octopus in love with God" ("Prothalamion"), "Now I float will-less in despair's dead sea ("Faust in Old Age"), and "the radiant soda of the seashore fashions" ("Far Rockaway").

"Dr. Bergen's Belief," a short play, is a lamentation on the death by suicide of the doctor's daughter. After meditating on the promise of an afterlife and God's providence—"the dream behind the dream, the Santa Claus of the obsessed obscene heart," the doctor and a second daughter leap to their deaths. Schwartz's lurid inventiveness and capricious style conjure a world of comic shame and imminent dread. *In Dreams Begin Responsibilities* represents an attempt to mold commonplace happenings into mystical shapes.

Suggested Readings

Ashbery, John. *The Heavy Bear: Delmore Schwartz's Life Versus His Poetry—A Lecture Delivered at the Sixty-seventh General Meeting of the English Literary Society of Japan on 21st May 1995*. Tokyo: English Literary Society of Japan, 1996.

Atlas, James. *Delmore Schwartz: The Life of an American Poet*. San Diego, Calif.: Harcourt Brace Jovanovich, 2000.

Bawer, Bruce. *The Middle Generation: The Lives and Poetry of Delmore Schwartz, Randall Jarrell, John Berryman, Robert Lowell*. Hamden, Conn.: Archon Books, 1986.

Goldman, Mark. "Reflections in a Mirror: On Two Stories by Delmore Schwartz." *Studies in American Jewish Literature* 2 (1982): 86-97.

Howe, Irving. Foreword to *In Dreams Begin Responsibilities*. New York: New Directions, 1978.

McDougall, Richard. *Delmore Schwartz*. New York: Twayne, 1974.

Malin, Irving. *Jews and Americans*. Carbondale: Southern Illinois University Press, 1965.

New, Elisa. "Reconsidering Delmore Schwartz." *Prooftexts: A Journal of Jewish Literary History* 5, no. 3 (September, 1985): 245-262.

Schwartz, Delmore. *Delmore Schwartz and James Laughlin: Selected Letters*. Edited by Robert Phillips. New York: W. W. Norton, 1993.

Waldhorn, Arthur, and Hilda K. Waldhorn, eds. *The Rite of Becoming: Stories and Studies of Adolescence*. Cleveland, Ohio: World, 1977.

Contributor: Robert Frail

Ntozake Shange
(Paulette Williams)

Born: Trenton, New Jersey; October 18, 1948

African American

Shange's novels, plays, and poems speak for African American girls and women.

Principal works

children's literature: *Whitewash*, 1997; *Muhammad Ali: The Man Who Could Float Like a Butterfly and Sting Like a Bee*, 2002; *Daddy Says*, 2003; *Ellington Was Not a Street*, 2004

drama: *for colored girls who have considered suicide/ when the rainbow is enuf*, pr., pb. 1975; *A Photograph: Still Life with Shadows; A Photograph: A Study in Cruelty*, pr. 1977, revised pr. 1979, pb. 1981 (as *A Photograph: Lovers in Motion*); *Where the Mississippi Meets the Amazon*, pr. 1977 (with Thulani Nkabinde and Jessica Hagedorn); *From Okra to Greens: A Different Kinda Love Story*, pr. 1978, pb. 1985; *Boogie Woogie Landscapes*, pr. 1979, pb. 1981; *Spell # 7: Geechee Jibara Quik Magic Trance Manual for Technologically Stressed Third World People*, pr. 1979, pb. 1981; *Mother Courage and Her Children*, pr. 1980 (adaptation of Bertolt Brecht's play); *Three Pieces*, pb. 1981; *Betsey Brown*, pr. 1989 (adaptation of her novel); *The Love Space Demands: A Continuing Saga*, pb. 1991, pr. 1992; *Plays: One*, pb. 1992; *Three Pieces*, pb. 1992

long fiction: *Sassafras: A Novella*, 1976; *Sassafras, Cypress, and Indigo*, 1982; *Betsey Brown*, 1985; *Liliane: Resurrection of the Daughter*, 1994

poetry: *Nappy Edges*, 1978; *Natural Disasters and Other Festive Occasions*, 1979; *A Daughter's Geography*, 1983, 1991; *From Okra to Greens: Poems*, 1984; *Ridin' the Moon in Texas: Word Paintings*, 1987; *I Live in Music*, 1994; *The Sweet Breath of Life: A Poetic Narrative of the African American Family*, 2004 (photographs by the Kamoinge Workshop; photos edited by Frank Stewart)

nonfiction: *See No Evil: Prefaces, Essays, and Accounts, 1976-1983*, 1984; *If I Can Cook, You Know God Can*, 1998

edited texts: *The Beacon Best of 1999: Creative Writing by Women and Men of All Colors*, 2000

Ntozake Shange (N-toh-zah-keh SHAHN-geh), born Paulette Williams, was raised in an African American middle-class family in Trenton, New Jersey. Her mother was a social worker, and her father was a surgeon—the same occupations held by the parents in Shange's novel *Betsey Brown.* Also like Betsey, young Paulette was encouraged to get an education and was introduced to leading figures of African American music and literature. Unlike Betsey, however, the writer remembers herself as always obedient and "nice."

Not until she was in her thirties did she allow herself to express the anger always lurking beneath her polite surface. Depressed over a failed marriage, and frustrated over the roadblocks of racism and sexism she encountered as she attempted to establish a career, she began to explore anew her own identity as an African American woman. She took the African name Ntozake Shange, which means "she who comes with her own things" and "she who walks like a lion."

Her first major piece of writing remains her most important. The play *for colored girls who have considered suicide/ when the rainbow is enuf* won international acclaim for its innovative combining of poetry, drama, and dance to tell the stories of seven women. The play was one of the earliest writings in any genre to deal with the anger of black women.

The success of the play gave Shange the financial freedom to explore less financially profitable outlets of expression. She began writing and publishing poetry, and collaborating with musicians and choreographers on improvisational pieces performed in bars and small theaters. She also has taught creative writing and women's studies courses at various colleges across the United States, and has occasionally turned her pen to writing prose fiction, especially for and about adolescent girls.

Shange has often spoken of the responsibilities that inform her writing. As an adolescent she could not find fiction about people like her. As a young woman she did not know how to understand her own pain. She writes many of her works to pass on to younger black women the insights she has gained through her experiences.

for colored girls who have considered suicide

Type of work: Drama
First produced: 1976, pb. 1976

For colored girls who have considered suicide/ when the rainbow is enuf: a choreopoem, Shange's first work, tells the stories of seven women who have suffered oppression in a racist and sexist society. The choreopoem is an innovative combination of poetry, drama, music, and dance. For Shange, the combination is important. She learned about her identity as a woman through words, songs, and literature; she learned about her identity as an African through dance.

The seven women are not named; they are meant to stand for the women who make up the rainbow. They are called "lady in brown," "lady in red," and so on. Each tells her own story. The stories are interwoven together. As the women tell their stories, they reflect on what it means to be a woman of color, what chances and choices they have. These women are in pain; they are angry. They have been abused by their lovers, their rapists, their abortionists, and they have been driven to the brink of despair. What strength they have left they find in music and in one another.

Ntozake Shange (Jules Allen)

Many have criticized the play for being too negative toward black men, but Shange has always attempted to direct the focus of the discussion back on the women. The play is about the women, about who they are and what they have experienced. To insist on a "balanced" view of the men in their lives is to deny these women's experiences. These women deserve a voice. The play, she insists, does not accuse all black men of being abusive. These women are not rejecting men or seeking a life without men. The women desire men and love them, and ache for that love to be returned.

Although the stories these women tell are tales of struggle, the play is ultimately uplifting. The seven women grieve, but they also celebrate their lives, their vitality, their colorfulness. As the play ends, the women recite, one at a time and then together: "i found god in myself/ & i loved her/ i loved her fiercely." These women are not entirely powerless; they have the power of their own voices. They find the courage to tell their stories and thus triumph.

A Photograph

Type of work: Drama
First produced: 1977

In *A Photograph*, a set of meditations and sketches involving an ideal black woman named Michael and her lover Sean, a failed photographer, Shange explores her idea of art—"the poetry of a moment"—as well as representative stages of the African American experience. Photography, dance, and drama are shown to be art forms that capture meaningful moments and present them to viewers and readers so that they might behold and understand the essence and the value of art and life. The young professionals who reside in or pass through Sean's San Francisco apartment-studio are shown to examine the psychological factors that impede and that motivate them and other African Americans.

The five figures of this piece are representative of other aspects of black life than those put forward in her first play. Nevada, a lawyer and lover-supporter of Sean, the struggling artist, sets herself above other "common" African Americans: Her family, she boasts, "was manumitted in 1843/ [when] yall were still slaves/ carrying things for white folks. . . ." The upwardly mobile Earl, also a lawyer, former lover of Claire and longtime friend of Sean, pleads Nevada's case to Sean when the latter rejects her. Claire is a dancer who dances seductively for Sean as he photographs and then ravishes her. Michael is a dancer and the woman Sean comes truly to love as she shares herself and her ideas of art and the African experience with him.

Early in the drama Sean tells Michael, "i'm a genius for unravelling the mysteries of the darker races/ . . . i know who we are." After he rejects Nevada and is rejected by her, Sean reveals his insecurities as a son, a man, an African American, and an artist. The self- and race-assured artist Michael challenges her temporarily broken lover. Sean soon responds to this and to a poetic story danced and told by Michael with his own story and assurances:

> yes. that's right. me. i'ma be it. the photographer of all time. look out ansel
> . . . i can bring you the world shining grainy focused or shaking
> a godlike phenomenon
> sean david . . . i realize you're not accustomed to the visions of a man of color
> who has a gift
> but fear not
> I'll give it to ya a lil at a time. i am only beginning to startle
> to mesmerize and reverse the reality of all who can see. I gotta thing bout niggahs
> my folks
> that just wont stop
> & we are so correct for the photograph
> we profile all the time
> styling
> giving angle & pattern
> shadows & still life. if somebody sides me cd see the line in niggahs
> the texture of our lives
> they wda done it
> but since nobody has stepped forward
> here I am. . . .

Sean seems obviously representative of Shange the artist in his coming-into-his-own response to Michael, who is yet another representative of Shange the artist. This choreopoem seems a particularly significant statement made by Shange, poet and writer: She, like Sean, presents "the contours of life unnoticed" and she, like Michael, speaks "for everybody burdened."

Boogie Woogie Landscapes

Type of work: Drama
First produced: 1979

After examining the identity of isolated young black women in *for colored girls who have considered suicide* and of couples in *A Photograph*, Shange concentrated on one woman's visions, dreams, and memories in *Boogie Woogie Landscapes*, which was first produced as a one-woman poetry piece in 1978 and then cast as a play in 1979, with music and dance. Layla, a young black woman, entertains in her dreams a series of nightlife companions who exemplify her perceptions of herself and her memories. "Layla" in Arabic means "born at night," and the entire drama exists in Layla's nighttime subconscious. Layla's dreams of Fidel Castro's Cuba, of primitive cruelties to African women, and of rock and roll and blues interweave with her feelings about growing up, family, brothers and sisters, parents, maids (some of which appear later in Shange's semiautobiographical novel *Betsey Brown*).

From Okra to Greens

Type of work: Drama
First produced: 1978, pb. 1985

Shange's *From Okra to Greens* draws together and expands on the themes of her earlier theater pieces. The discovery by the lovers Okra and Greens of the beauty and strength—the god—within the individual is like that of the women who populate *for colored girls who have considered suicide*. Similarly, the lovers' discovery of what is sacred—of the fullness and color of life versus the "skinny life" of black and white—is the goal of Layla in *Boogie Woogie Landscapes*, of the actors in *Spell #7*, and of the artists of *A Photograph*. The love between two fully realized human beings, like that experienced by Sean and Michael in *A Photograph*, is fully expanded on in this two-character drama of Okra and Greens. The theme of the responsibility of the artist touched on by Sean and by Michael is also fully developed by the poets Okra and Greens.

In the opening scenes of *From Okra to Greens*, Greens speaks of Okra's plight as single black woman as Okra acts/dances the role. This scene is reminiscent of Sean and Michael speaking in unison about Sean's and then Michael's art in the final scene of *A Photograph* and Ross's talking while Maxine acts out the role that the two are creating together, on the spot, in *Spell #7*. In *From Okra to Greens*, as in her other choreopoems, Shange turns her dramatic poetry into staged drama. She presents verbatim much of the poetry of her collection *A Daughter's Geography*. Although her feminist protests are dramatized in this play as in *for colored girls who have considered suicide/ when the rainbow is enuf* and in *Boogie Woogie Landscapes*, here her feminist protest is given voice by the male character Greens. That both Okra and Greens are poets allows them to have an understanding of each other and of the roles forced on too many African American women and men as well as an understanding of the role that human beings *should* play in the world.

Okra first dances as "the crooked woman" as Greens speaks, showing his and society's distorted view of black women. Okra's dance reflects both her pain and her potential strength and beauty. As the two come together, Greens admits his own crookedness in telling Okra that before their encounter he had not known "what a stood/up straight man felt like." Together the two characters create and present portraits of "some men" who degrade women (as they are encouraged to do by the patriarchy). Once married, the two continue their dialogue, which includes their consideration of one another and of the sociopolitical climate in which they and, later, their daughter must reside.

Shange's *Okra and Greens* celebrates, as do Sean and Michael in *A Photograph*, the richness of African American life. Her love story extends to the poor of not only her own country but also the world. Okra pleads for the return of Haitian liberators Dessalines, Petion, and L'Ouverture with their visions of "*la liberte, l'egalite, la fraternite*." As in her other theater pieces, Shange calls here, too, for the return of American visionaries, among them monologues.

As the hope of the world's visionaries is shown to have dimmed, so the relationship between the lovers Okra and Greens dims momentarily. Abandoned by Greens, Okra says that "the moon cracked in a ugly rupture." Joined once more, the two encourage each other and others to "rise up" and to "dance with the universe." This story of the love between two poets is a love song to a universe in sad need of hope.

The refrain of *Boogie Woogie Landscapes*, that "we don't recognize what's sacred anymore," is revealed in *From Okra to Greens* in the portrait of the "pretty man" whose pretty floors are covered with the kind of rug that "little girls spend whole/ lives tying." Lack of recognition of the sacred is a theme repeated throughout the work. However, the love between Okra and Greens and their hope for their daughter and for the oppressed peoples of the world shows that recognition of the sacred is possible for aware, thinking, and caring individuals. The memory of other visionaries also shows the poets' and others' recognition of the sacred. It is clear here and throughout her writing that Shange would have her audience recognize the sacred in themselves and in others and do their part in telling the story—in spreading the word—and in fighting for liberty, equality, and fraternity for all.

Spell #7

Type of work: Drama
First produced: 1979, pb. 1981

Shange's 1979 play *Spell #7*, like *for colored girls who have considered suicide*, is structured like a highly electric poetry reading, but this time the cast is mixed male and female. A huge blackface mask forms the backdrop for actors of an imitation old-time minstrel show, where actors did skits, recited, and joked, all under the direction of a Mr. Interlocutor. The actors come offstage, relax at an actors' bar, and gradually remove their masks, revealing their true selves. Lou, the "practicing magician," reveals that his father gave up his role as magician when a colored child asked for a spell to make her white. The actors tell each other and the audience tall stories. One of these involves a child who thought blacks were immune to dread diseases and disease-ridden passions such as polio and pedophilia. She is disillusioned when, as an adult, she finds that blacks not only can but also do hurt one another, so she buys South African gold "to remind the black people that it cost a lot for us to be here/ our value/ can be known instinctively/ but since so many black people are having a hard time not being like white folks/ i wear these gold pieces to protest their ignorance/ their disconnect from history." Another woman loves her baby, which she names "myself," while it is in the womb but kills it after it is born. Still another girl vows to brush her "nappy" hair constantly so that she can toss it like white girls. By these contrasts and by wry lists and surprising parallels, Shange shows the pain and difficulty, as well as the hopefulness, of being black. Lou refers to the spell that caused his father to give up magic as he (Lou) casts the final spell of Spell #7:

> aint no colored magician in his right mind
> gonna make you white
> cuz this is blk magic you lookin at
> & i'm fixin you up good/ fixin you up good & colored
> & you gonna be colored all yr life
> & you gonna love it/ bein colored

The others join him in celebration of "bein colored"; but the minstrel mask drops down and Lou's final words contain anger as well as celebration:

> crackers are born with the right to be
> alive/ i'm making ours up right here
> in yr face/ & we gonna be
> colored & love it

Betsey Brown

Type of work: Novel
First published: 1985

Betsey Brown tells the story of its thirteen-year-old title character's struggles with adolescence, with discovering who she is and who she might become. Shange wrote the novel specifically to provide reading matter for adolescent African American girls. In her own youth, Shange could find no books to help her sort out her life: Books about young women were written by whites for whites, and most books by blacks were by and about men.

Betsey Brown is the oldest of five unruly children in a middle-class family. Like most adolescent girls, she feels separated from the rest of her family: They do not understand her; they do not appreciate her. Betsey's father wants her to grow up to lead her people to freedom. He wakes the children every morning with a conga drum and chanting and then leads them through a quiz on black history. All of the children can recite poetry by Paul Laurence Dunbar and Countée Cullen; they know the music of Dizzy Gillespie, Chuck Berry, and Duke Ellington. Betsey herself was once rocked to sleep by W. E. B. Du Bois. Betsey's mother, Jane, fears that this exposure will limit her children instead of expanding them. She would like the children to grow up with nice middle-class manners and tastes. In many ways, she has denied her own heritage, her own identity. Eventually, she leaves the family for a time.

The story is firmly rooted in its specific time and place. In 1959, St. Louis took its first steps toward integrating its public schools, and the Brown children are among the first black children bussed to formerly all-white schools. The father has tried to prepare the children by giving them a firm sense of self and heritage. He is eager for them to enter the struggle for civil rights, even as the mother fears that they will be in danger if they become too involved.

A central issue of the novel is the importance of passing down one's cultural heritage. It is not until the mother decisively embraces her heritage that she can again join the family. While she is absent, the housekeeper assumes her role as mother and guide and teaches Betsey and the other children how to follow the dreams of both parents. They learn to stand up for themselves and honor their culture and history and also to be well-mannered and self-sufficient. When Jane returns, it is to a new Betsey, one who has taken the first steps in forging her adult identity.

Suggested Readings

Effiong, Philip Uko. *In Search of a Model for African American Drama: A Study of Selected Plays by Lorraine Hansberry, Amiri Baraka, and Ntozake Shange*. New York: University Press of America, 2000.

Lester, Neal A. *Ntozake Shange: A Critical Study of the Plays*. New York: Garland, 1995.

Olaniyan, Tejumala. *Scars of Conquest/Masks of Resistance: The Invention of Cultural Identities in African, African-American, and Caribbean Drama*. New York: Oxford University Press, 1995.

Russell, Sandi. *Render Me My Song: African American Women Writers from Slavery to the Present*. New York: St. Martin's Press, 1990.

Shange, Ntozake. Interview. In *Interviews with Contemporary Women Playwrights*, edited by Kathleen Betsko. New York: Beech Tree Books, 1987.

Shange, Ntozake, and Emily Mann. "The Birth of an R&B Musical." Interview by Douglas J. Keating. *The Philadelphia Inquirer*, March 26, 1989.

Sommers, Michael. "Rays of Hope in a Sky of Blues." Review of *The Love Space Demands* by Ntozake Shange. *Star-Ledger* (Newark, N.J.), March 12, 1992.

Contributors: Cynthia A. Bily, Anne Mills King, Judith K. Taylor, and Thomas J. Taylor

Bapsi Sidhwa

Born: Karachi, India (now in Pakistan); August 11, 1938

South Asian American

Pakistan was carved from India, and the country had no established literary tradition in English. Urdu was the official language, and many would have preferred that the former colonizers' language disappear altogether. Sidhwa invented English-language fiction in Pakistan.

Principal works

LONG FICTION: *The Crow-Eaters*, 1978; *The Bride*, 1983; *Ice-Candy-Man*, 1988 (pb. in U.S. as *Cracking India*); *An American Brat*, 1993; *Water*, 2006 (based on Deepa Mehta's film)

EDITED TEXT: *City of Sin and Splendour: Writings on Lahore*, 2005

Born into a wealthy family, Bapsi Sidhwa (BAHP-see SIH-dwah) spent her first seven years as an Indian citizen in the plains city of Lahore. In 1945, after India was divided, she became a Pakistani. The tremendous turmoil and bloodshed she observed as a child left its mark on Sidhwa, and later in her fiction she revived those powerful memories of Partition (as the division of India has come to be known). That she was born a Parsee also affected her writing. A Zoroastrian religious group of fewer than 200,000, the Parsees had long exerted enormous influence on the subcontinent through their business and professional standing. They also tended to be more Westernized than other Pakistanis.

At age two, Sidhwa contracted polio, and she did not attend school until she was fourteen. Tutored at home in English, she read British literature extensively, a practice that encouraged her to become a writer. Her parents, however, had other ideas, and at nineteen she entered an arranged marriage and soon bore three children. As an upper-class wife and mother, Sidhwa broke tradition by starting to write; she once admitted in an interview that at first she wrote in secret. Otherwise her friends would have thought her "pretentious," she said: "After all, I was only a businessman's wife."

Her first novel, *The Bride*, was initiated by a story she heard during a family vacation in Pakistan's tribal regions in the Himalayas. A young woman had made an arranged marriage with a tribal man. Unable to cope with the harsh treatment accorded women in that society, she ran away, only to be pursued, then murdered by her husband and his relatives. Sidhwa felt compelled to tell this story, which to her symbolized the plight of many women on the subcontinent. A friend helped her to place the manuscript with an agent, who tried for seven years to find a publisher.

In the meantime Sidhwa wrote *The Crow-Eaters*, a boisterous and earthy account of the Parsee community in pre-Partition India. Although warned that Pakistan was too remote for international audiences to consider it interesting, Sidhwa eventually found a British publisher for the book. In 1983, *The Bride* was published in London, followed by American editions. While both novels were well received overseas and on the subcontinent, the closely knit Parsee community at first objected to *The Crow-Eaters*, condemning it as an irreverent portrayal of their customs, religious beliefs, and attitudes. Once Sidhwa had established herself internationally as an important writer, the Parsees, proud of one of their own, forgave her for treating them in a comic manner.

Divorced and remarried, Sidhwa moved to the United States during the early 1980's. In 1992 she became an American citizen and settled in Houston, Texas. Although far removed from the world of her childhood, soon after her arrival in America she began writing one of her finest works, *Ice-Candy-Man*. Sidhwa was seven when Partition came about, and violence erupted once millions of Muslims and Hindus were uprooted to turn Pakistan into an Islamic nation, India into a Hindu nation. The number of deaths has never been determined, but it is estimated that several hundred thousand died. Lahore, which had been assigned to Pakistan, witnessed some of the fiercest battles during this struggle for territory and possessions. In *Ice-Candy-Man* a seven-year-old female narrator recalls Lahore on the eve of Partition, then reveals the bloody aftermath of the political acts that brought about what she calls the "cracking" of India. Even though many Indian novelists in English have focused on Partition, Sidhwa's novel carries a greater immediacy—perhaps because she was there and was able four decades later to re-create that tumultuous period through a singular act of memory. In 1991 Sidhwa received the *Liberatur* Prize for *Ice-Candy-Man*, a yearly award given by Germany to a distinguished writer from a non-Western country. In her next novel, *An American Brat*, Sidhwa depicts the Pakistani immigrant in America.

Sidhwa received in 1994 the Lila Wallace-Reader's Digest Fund Award of $105,000 for her fiction. This recognition proves that the Pakistani-Parsee experience, remote and foreign though it may be to the Western reader, carries universal significance when viewed through the eyes of a perceptive writer.

An American Brat

Type of work: Novel
First published: 1993

An American Brat follows Feroza, a Parsee girl from Lahore, through her uncertain start in the United States and her adjustments as a college student. Partially set in Pakistan, the novel also introduces Feroza's colorful family—her mother, in particular, who visits Colorado to break up a romance between Feroza and a non-Parsee. The novel gets off to a fast and amusing start with Zareen Ginwalla anxiously awaiting the arrival of her husband, Cyrus, owner of a sporting-goods store. The place is Lahore, the year 1978. General Zia has seized power, and the liberal Zulfikar Ali Bhutto is in jail, soon to be executed. Zareen's problem is related but more immediate: A Bhutto supporter, she sees that her sixteen-year-old daughter Feroza is becoming, like Pakistan under Zia's military-Islamic fundamentalist rule, increasingly conservative. The solution: to send her daughter to the United States for a few months, where she will stay with her only slightly older Uncle Manek, a doctoral candidate at the Massachusetts Institute of Technology (MIT).

Despite his own early difficulties adjusting to life in America, Manek convinces Feroza to stay on as a student majoring in hotel management, a suitably practical field, at a junior college in Idaho. American enough to become Mike and work for NASA in Houston, Manek is traditional enough to return to Pakistan to find a suitable, and suitably submissive, wife. Feroza goes much further when she decides to marry David Press, an American Jew, thus precipitating her mother's frantic flight to the United States to stop the marriage.

Zareen is more than merely a closet conservative, a comic caricature of the "Indian" mother: She is a Parsee, one of only 120,000 in the world. She knows what Feroza's marrying outside the small Parsee community will mean, both for her daughter (spiritual exile) and for the Parsees (its hold on the world, particularly in Muslim Pakistan under Zia, made still more tenuous). Thus, Sidhwa's comedy serves serious purposes. The mother-daughter relationship is the perfect disguise, or alibi, for considering a number of related issues, some feminist, others having to do with religious, ethnic, national, and personal identity.

An American Brat is more successful in its conception than its execution. The plot is as melodramatic as a Ballywood film, and the prose at times no less improbable. Sidhwa's work includes passages such as "The wine coursed through Feroza like a mellow happiness" and "while he spoke, David's eyes, alight with elation, also spoke." Would that Sidhwa had received the kind of editorial assistance she clearly deserves. Nevertheless, the novel succeeds in honestly presenting the various conflicts and tensions between husbands and wives, mothers and daughters, young and old, conservative and progressive, East and West, India and Pakistan, Parsee and Muslim, the sacred and the profane, haves and have-nots. Sidhwa noted in an interview that she was partially attempting to define her own experiences and reactions as she herself worked to know a new country. At the novel's conclusion, Feroza realizes there is no going back, and she accepts that even while retaining her roots in the Parsee community she has become the product of two cultures.

Suggested Readings

Afzal-Khan, Fawzia. "Women in History." In *International Literature in English: Essays on the Major Writers*, edited by Robert L. Ross. New York: Garland, 1991.

Daiya, Kavita. "'Honorable Resolutions': Gendered Violence, Ethnicity, and the Nation." *Alternatives: Global, Local, Political* 27 (April, 2002): 219-247.

Dhawan, R. K., and Novy Kapadia, eds. *The Novels of Bapsi Sidhwa*. New Delhi: Prestige Books, 1996.

Hai, Ambreen. "Border Work, Border Trouble: Postcolonial Feminism and the Ayah in Bapsi Sidhwa's *Cracking India*." *Modern Fiction Studies* 46 (Summer, 2000): 379-427.

Jussawalla, Feroza, and Reed Way Dasenbrock. *Interviews with Writers of the Post-Colonial World*. Jackson: University Press of Mississippi, 1992.

Contributor: Robert L. Ross

Leslie Marmon Silko

Born: Albuquerque, New Mexico; March 5, 1948

Native American

Silko's short stories and novels represent some of the finest writing of what has been called the Native American Renaissance.

Principal works

DRAMA: *Lullaby*, pr. 1976 (with Frank Chin)
LONG FICTION: *Ceremony*, 1977; *Almanac of the Dead*, 1991; *Gardens in the Dunes*, 1999
POETRY: *Laguna Woman: Poems*, 1974
SHORT FICTION: *Yellow Woman*, 1993
NONFICTION: *The Delicacy and Strength of Lace: Letters Between Leslie Marmon Silko and James Wright*, 1986; *Sacred Water: Narratives and Pictures*, 1993; *Yellow Woman and a Beauty of the Spirit: Essays on Native American Life Today*, 1996; *Conversations with Leslie Marmon Silko*, 2000 (Ellen L. Arnold, editor)
MISCELLANEOUS: *Storyteller*, 1981 (includes poetry and prose)

Leslie Marmon Silko (SIHL-koh) creates characters that reflect the tensions and cultural conflicts of her experience. Born of mixed European American and Navajo blood, Silko spent her formative years learning the stories of her white ancestors and their relationship with the native population into which they married. Her great-grandfather, Robert Marmon, had come to the Laguna pueblo, New Mexico, in the early 1870's as a surveyor and eventually married a Laguna woman. Even more important to Silko's development as a writer was the later generation of Marmons—half European American and half Native American—who continued to transmit the oral traditions of the Laguna pueblo people. One such source was the Aunt Susie of Silko's autobiographical writings. The wife of Silko's grandfather's brother, she was a schoolteacher in the Laguna pueblo during the 1920's and years afterward passed on to the young Silko the oral heritage of her race. So intimate was Silko's imagination with the elements of Laguna culture that her father's family photographs serve as visual commentary on the sketches and stories of *Storyteller*.

Like the Inuit woman in *Storyteller*, Silko attended the local school operated by the Bureau of Indian Affairs, but she remained there only a short time, moving on to Catholic schools in Albuquerque, eventually receiving a B.A. in English from

Leslie Marmon Silko (Courtesy, University Press of Mississippi)

the University of New Mexico in 1969. Like her ancestors, she taught school at Navajo Community College in Tsaile, Arizona, where she wrote *Ceremony*, her first novel. One of the best-known of her works and one of the best novels written by a Native American, the book tells the story of Tayo, a World War II veteran who tries to cope with the conflicts of his mixed-blood heritage.

Her short stories were beginning to appear in the early 1970's, and she quickly gained a reputation as one of the leading writers in the Native American Renaissance. The term is applied to the literary movement beginning in the 1960's that features works by Native American writers using tribal customs and traditions as literary material. Stories such as "Yellow Woman," in which a mortal is seemingly abducted by spiritual beings, and "Uncle Tony's Goat," which retells an old Laguna beast fable, are typical of Silko's handling of traditional indigenous material. One of her best stories, "Lullaby," treats the conflict of an elderly Navajo couple as they seek to come to terms with the dominant culture and how that conflict strengthens their traditional values.

Storyteller

Type of work: Autobiography, poetry, and short fiction
First published: 1981

A collection of autobiographical sketches, poems, family photographs, and short stories, *Storyteller* fuses literary and extraliterary material into a mosaic portrait of cultural heritage and of conflict between the two ethnic groups composing her heritage, the European American and the Native American.

The title story, "Storyteller," presents that conflict from the point of view of a young Inuit woman who is fascinated with and repulsed by white civilization. Set in Alaska—the only major work of the author not in a southwestern setting—the story follows her thoughts and observations as she spends her days amid these contrasting cultures. The old man with whom she lives and who has used her sexually—"she knew what he wanted"—is the storyteller. Now bedridden with age and the cold, subsisting on dried fish, which he keeps under his pillow, the old man narrates a tale, carefully, insistently, about a hunter on the ice facing a challenge from a bear.

Between the beginning and end of his own tale, the Inuit woman's story unfolds. She went to the government school, but largely out of curiosity, and although she remembers being whipped by one of the teachers, her fascination with whites—the "Gussucks," as she calls them—only deepened when she observed their oil rigs, their large yellow machines, and their metal buildings. Gradually she learns that the Gussucks are not so much to be respected or feared but rather scorned because of their insensitivity and greed. The old man calls them thieves, and she herself laughs at the smug confidence they place in their machines, which are almost useless in the Alaskan cold.

Her physical curiosity about the Gussucks leads to her being sexually exploited by one of them, and the turning point of the story occurs when the Inuit woman learns that a Gussuck storekeeper was responsible for the death of her parents by giving them nonpotable alcohol in exchange for their rifles. In revenge, she lures the storekeeper onto the ice, where he falls through and drowns.

At the conclusion, the old man, now on his deathbed, finishes his tale of the hunter and the bear. The two stories, the old man's and the Inuit woman's, thus comment on each other. The woman's vengeance bears a double victory, one the triumph of her people, the other a vindication of her sexuality over its abuses by whites. Yet the old man's story ends menacingly for the hunter, suggesting that the Native American's fate is—like the hunter—perilous amid the alien culture that both attracts and repels.

Almanac of the Dead

Type of work: Novel
First published: 1991

Part Native American history, part mythic prophecy, part contemporary cultural analysis, *Almanac of the Dead* is more and less than all of these. Its focus is on the recent present, and on what has happened to people—white, Mexican, and Native American—who have been corrupted by the greed and violence of the contemporary world, but it hops back and forth between the present and the past, to trace the history of this world and to describe the myths that reside below it.

If the novel seems a disparate mix of elements, it is. Silko's map on the inside and back covers of the book lists dozens of major characters in stories that take place in Tucson, San Diego, and points south. However, this "Five Hundred Year Map" also "foretells the future of all the Americas" and the violent prophecy that is yet to be: "the disappearance of all things European."

The novel is divided into six parts, each part comprising one to eight books, and each book containing from four to twenty chapters. There are at least half a dozen major sets of characters who dominate the different parts of the novel, often for hundreds of pages at a time, and readers may lose touch with other characters in some sections. But, by the end, most of the major characters have touched each other's lives (often sexually, usually violently), and many will gather in the final apocalyptic ending. It is a gripping and frightening fictional vision.

Suggested Readings

Allen, Paula Gunn. "The Feminine Landscape of Leslie Marmon Silko's *Ceremony*." In *Studies in American Indian Literature: Critical Essays and Course Design*. New York: Modern Language Association of America, 1983.

Barnett, Louise K., and James L. Thorson, eds. *Leslie Marmon Silko*. Albuquerque: University of New Mexico Press, 1999.

Chavkin, Allan, ed. *Leslie Marmon Silko's "Ceremony": A Casebook*. New York: Oxford University Press, 2002.

Fitz, Brewster E. *Silko: Writing Storyteller and Medicine Woman*. Norman: University of Oklahoma Press, 2004.

Graulich, Melody, ed. *Leslie Marmon Silko: A Study of the Short Fiction*. New York: Twayne, 1998.

_______. *"Yellow Woman": Leslie Marmon Silko*. New Brunswick, N.J.: Rutgers University Press, 1993.

Krumholz, Linda J. "'To Understand This World Differently': Reading and Subversion in Leslie Marmon Silko's 'Storyteller.'" *Ariel* 25 (January, 1994): 89-113.

Krupat, Arnold. "The Dialogic of Silko's *Storyteller*." *Narrative Chance: Postmodern Discourse on Native American Indian Literature*, edited by Gerald Vizenor. Albuquerque: University of New Mexico Press, 1989.

Salyer, Gregory. *Leslie Marmon Silko*. New York: Twayne, 1997.

Seyersted, Per. *Leslie Marmon Silko*. Boise, Idaho: Boise State University, 1980.

Contributor: Edward A. Fiorelli

Isaac Bashevis Singer

Born: Leoncin, Poland; July 14 or November 21, 1904
Died: Surfside, Florida; July 24, 1991

Jewish

Singer, who was awarded the Nobel Prize in Literature in 1978, is perhaps the most influential, prolific, and admired Jewish American author of the twentieth century.

Principal works

CHILDREN'S LITERATURE: *Zlateh the Goat, and Other Stories*, 1966; *The Fearsome Inn*, 1967; *Mazel and Shlimazel: Or, The Milk of a Lioness*, 1967; *When Shlemiel Went to Warsaw, and Other Stories*, 1968; *A Day of Pleasure: Stories of a Boy Growing Up in Warsaw*, 1969; *Elijah the Slave*, 1970; *Joseph and Koza: Or, The Sacrifice to the Vistula*, 1970; *Alone in the Wild Forest*, 1971; *The Topsy-Turvy Emperor of China*, 1971; *The Wicked City*, 1972; *The Fools of Chelm and Their History*, 1973; *Why Noah Chose the Dove*, 1974; *A Tale of Three Wishes*, 1975; *Naftali the Storyteller and His Horse, Sus, and Other Stories*, 1976; *The Power of Light: Eight Stories*, 1980; *The Golem*, 1982; *Stories for Children*, 1984

DRAMA: *The Mirror*, pr. 1973; *Shlemiel the First*, pr. 1974; *Yentl, the Yeshiva Boy*, pr. 1974 (with Leah Napolin); *Teibele and Her Demon*, pr. 1978

LONG FICTION: *Der Sotn in Gorey*, 1935 (*Satan in Goray*, 1955); *Di Familye Mushkat*, 1950 (*The Family Moskat*, 1950); *Der Hoyf*, 1953-1955 (*The Manor*, 1967, and *The Estate*, 1969); *Shotns baym Hodson*, 1957-1958 (*Shadows on the Hudson*, 1998); *Der Kuntsnmakher fun Lublin*, 1958-1959 (*The Magician of Lublin*, 1960); *Der Knekht*, 1961 (*The Slave*, 1962); *Sonim, de Geshichte fun a Liebe*, 1966 (*Enemies: A Love Story*, 1972); *Der Bal-Tshuve*, 1974 (*The Penitent*, 1983); *Neshome Ekspeditsyes*, 1974 (*Shosha*, 1978); *Reaches of Heaven: A Story of the Baal Shem Tov*, 1980; *Der Kenig vun di Felder*, 1988 (*The King of the Fields*, 1988); *Scum*, 1991; *The Certificate*, 1992; *Meshugah*, 1994

SHORT FICTION: *Gimpel the Fool, and Other Stories*, 1957; *The Spinoza of Market Street*, 1961; *Short Friday, and Other Stories*, 1964; *The Séance, and Other Stories*, 1968; *A Friend of Kafka, and Other Stories*, 1970; *A Crown of Feathers, and Other Stories*, 1973; *Passions, and Other Stories*, 1975; *Old Love*, 1979; *The Collected Stories of Isaac Bashevis Singer*, 1982; *The Image, and Other Stories*, 1985; *The Death of Methuselah, and Other Stories*, 1988

TRANSLATIONS: *Romain Rolland*, 1927 (of Stefan Zweig); *Die Volger*, 1928 (of Knut Hamsun); *Victoria*, 1929 (of Hamsun); *All Quiet on the Western Front*, 1930 (of Erich Remarque); *Pan*, 1931 (of Hamsun); *The Way Back*, 1931 (of Remarque); *The Magic Mountain*, 1932 (of Thomas Mann); *From Moscow to Jerusalem*, 1938 (of Leon Glaser)

NONFICTION: *Mayn Tatn's Bes-din Shtub*, 1956 (*In My Father's Court*, 1966); *The Hasidim*, 1973 (with Ira Moskowitz); *A Little Boy in Search of God: Mysticism in a Personal Light*, 1976; *A Young Man in Search of Love*, 1978; *Isaac Bashevis Singer on Literature and Life*, 1979 (with Paul Rosenblatt and Gene Koppel); *Lost in America*, 1980; *Love and Exile*, 1984; *Conversations with Isaac Bashevis Singer*, 1985 (with Richard Burgin); *More Stories from My Father's Court*, 2000

The son and grandson of rabbis, Isaac Bashevis Singer (I-zak bah-SHEH-vihs SIHN-gur) was born into a pious Hasidic household in Poland, which he would imaginatively portray in his memoir *In My Father's Court*. He began his literary career writing for a Hebrew newspaper and proofreading for a journal that his brother, novelist Israel Joshua Singer, coedited. In 1925, Singer made his fiction debut with a prizewinning short story, "In Old Age." In 1932, he began co-editing *Globus*, which serialized *Satan in Goray*, his novel of messianic heresy.

In 1935, Singer immigrated to New York, where he wrote for the *Jewish Daily Forward*. Several years went by before Singer found the full strength of his writer's voice. He believed that an author needed roots, but he had lost his. Never easily placed within any tradition, Singer wrote first in Yiddish and then translated his work into English. His decision to write in Yiddish, which he knew was a dying language, was linked to his identification with a world that was destroyed by the Nazis.

Singer's first significant recognition in the United States came in 1950, with the English-language publication of *The Family Moskat*, a family saga modeled on his brother's work. Saul Bellow's translation of "Gimpl Tam" as "Gimpel the Fool" in the *Partisan Review* three years later added to Singer's growing reputation. Singer went on to win Newbery Awards for his children's stories (which he did not begin writing until he was sixty-two years old), National Book Awards, and the Nobel Prize in Literature in 1978.

Singer's work not only recalls that lost world, but his questions about the meaning of life reflect modern existential concerns. In *Enemies: A Love Story*, Herman Broder protests against suffering and the anguish of abandonment. Harry Bendiner of the story "Old Love" dreams of meditating in a solitary tent with the daughter of a dead love on why people are born and why people must die. *Neshome Ekspeditsyes* (1974; *Shosha*, 1978) concludes as two friends, reunited after the Holocaust, sit in a darkening room, waiting, as one says with a laugh, for an answer. It seems that Singer's characters all await a moment of revelation that will be more than a faint glimmer in a darkened room.

Singer's work achieved popular success in 1983 with the release of the film *Yentl*, directed by Barbra Streisand and based on one of Singer's short stories. Again, in 1989, a film, *Enemies: A Love Story*, brought international attention to Singer's fiction. During his later life, Singer lived with his wife Alma in New York and then Florida, where he died of a stroke on July 24, 1991, just after turning eighty-seven years old.

"A Crown of Feathers"

Type of work: Short fiction
First published: 1973, in *A Crown of Feathers, and Other Stories*

"A Crown of Feathers" is the title story of a collection, which won the National Book Award for 1973. Like many of Singer's stories, it depicts an individual pulled between belief and disbelief, between the religious and the secular, and between self and others. The story concerns an orphan, Akhsa, whose own emerging identity becomes entangled with the conflicting values of her wealthy grandparents.

Her grandfather is a traditionally religious man, a community leader in the Polish village of Krasnobród, while her grandmother, from the sophisticated city of Prague, is more worldly and possibly, it is learned after her death, a follower of false messiahs. These differences, presented very subtly at first, become more pronounced when, after her grandparents' deaths, Akhsa internalizes their warring voices.

Each voice accuses the other of being a demon, while both battle over Akhsa's soul. Her grandmother assures her that Jesus is the Messiah and encourages Akhsa to convert. As a sign, she has Akhsa rip open her pillowcase, where she finds an intricate crown of feathers topped by a tiny cross. Akhsa converts, makes an unhappy marriage with an alcoholic Polish squire, and sinks into melancholy. Her despair is not mere unhappiness but a continuing crisis of faith. A demon tells her, "The truth is there is no truth," but her saintly grandfather appears and tells her to repent.

Isaac Bashevis Singer (© The Nobel Foundation)

Her grandfather's advice leads Akhsa to return to Judaism and to seek out and marry the man her grandfather had chosen for her years before. This embittered man, however, humiliates her mercilessly. On her deathbed, Akhsa tears open her pillowcase and finds another crown of feathers, this one with the Hebrew letters for God in place of the cross. "But, she wondered, in what way was this crown more a revelation of truth than the other?"

Akhsa never grasps with certainty the truth she has sought, nor is she ever able, like Singer's Gimpel the

Fool, to accept the ambiguity of uncertainty. Akhsa's conversion and subsequent exile, her repentance and journey back to her grandfather's faith—her entire life—have constituted an agonized quest for truth. Torn between two voices of authority, Akhsa has never been certain of her own voice, has never understood her own wants, needs, or beliefs. While Gimpel, when finding his vocation as wandering storyteller, ultimately finds a faith to which he can firmly adhere, Akhsa finds neither self nor truth. Moving from one pole of certain faith to its opposite, and back again, Akhsa never accepts Singer's own truth, which is that "if there is such a thing as truth it is as intricate and hidden as a crown of feathers."

"Gimpel the Fool"

Type of work: Short fiction
First published: "Gimpel Tam," 1945 (English translation, 1953)

The publication of "Gimpel the Fool," in a translation from the Yiddish by Saul Bellow, launched Singer's career. During the 1950's and thereafter, his work appeared widely in English, and throughout the history of Singer studies, "Gimpel the Fool" has held a place of honor. Gimpel belongs to a brotherhood of literary characters—that of the schlemiels. In this work, Singer explores the nature of belief, which, in the modern, secular world, is often considered foolish.

Gimpel believes whatever he is told: that his parents have risen from the dead, that his pregnant fiancé is a virgin, that her children are his children, that the man jumping out of her bed is a figment of his imagination. Gimpel extends his willingness to believe to every aspect of his life, because, he explains: "Everything is possible, as it is written in the Wisdom of the Fathers, I've forgotten just how."

When, on her deathbed, his wife of twenty years confesses that none of her six children are his, Gimpel is tempted to disbelieve all that he has been told and to enact revenge against those who have participated in his humiliation. His temptation is a central crisis of faith. His faith in others, who have betrayed him, is challenged, as is his faith in himself and in God, because among the stories he has believed are those pertaining to the existence of God. Gimpel's belief has always been riddled with doubt; only after he concretizes his spiritual exile by becoming a wanderer does he resolve his faith.

In Singer's fictional worlds, God is the first storyteller who, through words, spoke or wrote the world into being. Belief in God is linked to belief in stories. Thus, when Gimpel is tempted to disbelieve in God, he responds by becoming a wandering storyteller. In so doing Gimpel links himself with the great storyteller and transforms what was once simple gullibility into an act of the greatest faith. As a storyteller, Gimpel opens himself fully to the infinite possibilities of the divine word as it is transformed into the world. At the end, Gimpel still yearns for a world where even he cannot be deceived. He never finds this world. Despite the void he may face, he chooses to believe, and he finds, in his final great act of suspending disbelief, a faith to which he can firmly adhere.

Suggested Readings

Alexander, Edward. *Isaac Bashevis Singer: A Study of the Short Fiction*. Boston: Twayne, 1990.

Allentuck, Marcia, ed. *The Achievement of Isaac Bashevis Singer*. Carbondale: Southern Illinois University Press, 1969.

Farrell, Grace, ed. *Critical Essays on Isaac Bashevis Singer*. New York: G. K. Hall, 1996.

_______. *Isaac Bashevis Singer: Conversations*. Jackson: University Press of Mississippi, 1992.

Hadda, Janet. *Isaac Bashevis Singer: A Life*. New York: Oxford University Press, 1997.

Kresh, Paul. *Isaac Bashevis Singer: The Magician of West Eighty-sixth Street*. New York: Dial Press, 1979.

Noiville, Florence. *Isaac B. Singer: A Life*. Translated by Catherine Temerson. New York: Farrar, Straus and Giroux, 2006.

Sinclair, Clive. *The Brothers Singer*. London: Allison and Busby, 1983.

Wolitz, Seth L., ed. *The Hidden Isaac Bashevis Singer*. Austin: University of Texas Press, 2001.

Zamir, Israel. *Journey to My Father, Isaac Bashevis Singer*. New York: Arcade, 1995.

Contributor: Grace Farrell

Cathy Song

Born: Honolulu, Hawaii; August 20, 1955

Chinese American, Korean American

Song, who was the first Asian American writer to win, in 1982, a Yale Younger Poets Award, has established a formidable reputation as a chronicler of personal experience in multiplicity.

Principal works

POETRY: *Picture Bride*, 1983; *Frameless Windows, Squares of Light*, 1988; *School Figures*, 1994; *The Land of Bliss*, 2001; *Cloud Moving Hands*, 2007
EDITED TEXT: *Sister Stew: Fiction and Poetry by Women*, 1991 (with Juliet S. Kono)

Having grown up in the culturally and ethnically diverse society of Hawaii in a family that had been there for at least two generations, Cathy Song does not write about racial or ethnic anxieties or the pains of being an outsider in an Anglo world. Her poems reflect a family that has been close and nurturing. The title of her first book, *Picture Bride*, refers to her Korean grandmother, who immigrated to Hawaii to marry a man who knew her only from a photograph. Song's paternal grandfather was also Korean; her mother is Chinese. Song's original title for the book, "From the White Place," refers to the paintings of Georgia O'Keeffe, which she encountered while at Wellesley College, from which she graduated in 1977. She went on to receive a master's degree in creative writing from Boston University in 1981. Her vivid imagery and interest in the subject of perspective indicate her fascination with visual art. The dominant strain in *Picture Bride* is the connection between the first-person speaker and her relatives. Song's poems show little interest in political or social issues per se. Song's appreciation of her Asian heritage, however, appears powerfully in poems such as "Girl Powdering Her Neck," which concerns a painting by the eighteenth century Japanese artist Kitagawa Utamaro and ends with a haiku: "Two chrysanthemums/ touch in the middle of the lake/ and drift apart."

Song appears as a somewhat distant narrator in poems such as "Chinatown" and "Magic Island," which are found in *Frameless Windows, Squares of Light*. These poems concern the immigrant experience, which she knows only secondhand. The deft beauty of a poem such as "Magic Island" does not compare with the personally felt experience of "Living Near the Water," in which the poet watches her father give his dying father a drink of water. Her own children appear in these poems: Her blond son in "Heaven," for example, thinks, "when we die we'll go to China."

The blended worlds of Cathy Song are celebrated in her third book, *School Figures*, which opens with a poem on Ludwig Bemelmans's Madeline series of children's books. "Mother on River Street" depicts the poet's mother and aunts eating at a Vietnamese restaurant and recalling Sei Mui, who, as a girl, fell out of Mrs. Chow's car. In the title poem, Western painters such as Piet Mondrian and Pieter Bruegel merge with Katsushika Hokusai. Song's poems portray not a simple multiculturalism but rather—as in "Square Mile," in which she sees her son sitting in the same classroom she once sat in and herself on the same hill her father once was on—a profound and affectionate personal unity.

Picture Bride

Type of work: Poetry
First published: 1983

The content and form of *Picture Bride*, Song's first book of poems, reflect intimately the personal background and interests of its author. Therefore, many of these poems have their locations in Hawaii, where she was born and reared, and the continental United States, where she attended university and married. Song's poems are valuable repositories of an Asian American woman's sensibilities as they experience the intricate varieties of familial and personal relationships—as daughter, wife, mother, lover, and friend. Art, too, is an informing interest of Song's, especially that of the Japanese ukiyo-e master Utamaro and that of the American feminist painter Georgia O'Keeffe, whose life and works lend inspiration and shape to this book of poems.

Picture Bride is organized into five sections, each deriving its title from a painting by O'Keeffe. The book begins with an initial statement of themes and an imagistic setting of scenes in "Black Iris" (familial relationships and home); continues with the development of these themes and scenes in "Sunflower"; moves into a contemplation of the effort and achievement of art in the central "Orchids"; renders scenes suggesting a darker, perhaps Dionysian, side to art and life in "Red Poppy"; and proceeds to a final affirmation of the validity and variety of human creativity and productivity in "The White Trumpet Flower." The central section of the book also contains the key poem "Blue and White Lines After O'Keeffe," whose speaker is Song's imaginative re-creation of Georgia O'Keeffe and which is itself divided into five subsections with subtitles that replicate the titles of the sections of the book itself.

The title poem, "Picture Bride," is a young Korean American woman's meditation on the feelings, experience, and thoughts of her immigrant grandmother, who came to Hawaii to be married to a worker in the sugarcane fields. This piece strikes a chord present in many of the book's poems: a woman's (and especially an ethnic woman's) experience of family. Because Song's feminism is so imbued with ethnicity, some readers may prefer to call her work "womanist," the term coined by African American author Alice Walker in *In Search of Our Mothers' Gardens* (1983). That Song should choose to meditate on her grandmother in "Picture Bride" may seem natural enough to contemporary American readers, but in terms of traditional Confucian and Asian hierarchy, Song should have memorialized and venerated her male ancestor. Instead, the grandfather is devalorized into a mere "stranger."

Cathy Song (Courtesy, Smith College)

Therefore, Song's choice of subject in this poem is itself a break from traditional Asian patriarchy and a declaration of allegiance to a feminist hierarchy of family history.

Many of Song's poems elude a rigid thematic categorization that would separate, for example, poems of women's experience from those about ethnicity or from those about art. In fact, these themes are sometimes organically and inextricably intertwined. For example, one will happen on poems about ethnic women's experience and about women artists/artisans, such as "The Seamstress," whose speaker is a Japanese American woman who makes dolls and creates wedding gowns but who seems condemned to remain in the background, a silent spinster (and spinner), or "For A. J.: On Finding That She's on Her Boat to China," which addresses an Asian ballerina manqué returning to Asia to become a materfamilias.

Women's experience, ethnicity, and art are therefore the main spheres of interest in *Picture Bride*, while the works of feminist artist O'Keeffe provide it with an encompassing structure and indwelling spirit.

Suggested Readings

Bloyd, Rebekah. "Cultural Convergences in Cathy Song's Poetry." *Peace Review* 10 (September, 1998): 393-400.

Fujita-Sato, Gayle K. "'Third World' as Place and Paradigm in Cathy Song's *Picture Bride*." *MELUS* 15, no. 1 (Spring, 1988): 49-72.

Kyhan, Lee. "Korean-American Literature: The Next Generation." *Korean Journal* 34, no. 1 (Spring, 1994): 20-35.

Song, Cathy. "Cathy Song: Secret Spaces of Childhood Part 2: A Symposium on Secret Spaces." *Michigan Quarterly Review* 39, no. 3 (Summer, 2000): 506-508.

Sumida, Stephen H. "Hawaii's Local Literary Tradition." In *And the View from the Shore: Literary Traditions of Hawai'i*. Seattle: University of Washington Press, 1991.

Wallace, Patricia. "Divided Loyalties: Literal and Literary in the Poetry of Lorna Dee Cervantes, Cathy Song, and Rita Dove." *MELUS* 18, no. 3 (Fall, 1993): 3-20.

Contributors: Ron McFarland, Laura Mitchell, and C. L. Chua

Gary Soto

BORN: Fresno, California; April 12, 1952

MEXICAN AMERICAN

Soto's poems, short stories, memoirs, young adult novels, and children's stories bring to life the joys and pains of growing up in the barrio.

PRINCIPAL WORKS

CHILDREN'S LITERATURE: *Baseball in April, and Other Stories*, 1990; *Taking Sides*, 1991; *Neighborhood Odes*, 1992 (poetry); *Pacific Crossing*, 1992; *The Skirt*, 1992; *Local News*, 1993; *Too Many Tamales*, 1993; *Crazy Weekend*, 1994; *Jesse*, 1994; *Boys at Work*, 1995; *Canto Familiar*, 1995 (poetry); *The Cat's Meow*, 1995; *Chato's Kitchen*, 1995; *Off and Running*, 1996; *Buried Onions*, 1997; *Novio Boy*, 1997 (play); *Big Bushy Mustache*, 1998; *Petty Crimes*, 1998; *Chato and the Party Animals*, 1999; *Chato Throws a Pachanga*, 1999; *Nerdlania*, 1999 (play); *Jesse De La Cruz: A Profile of a United Farm Worker*, 2000; *My Little Car*, 2000; *Fearless Fernie: Hanging out with Fernie and Me*, 2002 (poetry; also known as *Body Parts in Rebellion*); *If the Shoe Fits*, 2002; *The Afterlife*, 2003; *Chato Goes Cruisin'*, 2004; *Help Wanted*, 2005; *Worlds Apart: Traveling with Fernie and Me*, 2005; *Accidental Love*, 2006; *Mercy on These Teenage Chimps*, 2007

LONG FICTION: *Nickel and Dime*, 2000; *Poetry Lover*, 2001; *Amnesia in a Republican County*, 2003

POETRY: *The Elements of San Joaquin*, 1977; *The Tale of Sunlight*, 1978; *Where Sparrows Work Hard*, 1981; *Black Hair*, 1985; *A Fire in My Hands*, 1990; *Who Will Know Us?*, 1990; *Home Course in Religion*, 1991; *New and Selected Poems*, 1995; *A Natural Man*, 1999; *One Kind of Faith*, 2003; *A Simple Plan*, 2007

NONFICTION: *Living up the Street: Narrative Recollections*, 1985; *Small Faces*, 1986; *Lesser Evils: Ten Quartets*, 1988; *A Summer Life*, 1990 (39 short vignettes based on his life); *The Effect of Knut Hamsun on a Fresno Boy*, 2000

EDITED TEXTS: *California Childhood: Recollections and Stories of the Golden State*, 1988; *Pieces of the Heart: New Chicano Fiction*, 1993

Gary Soto (SOH-toh) was born to American parents of Mexican heritage and grew up in the Spanish-speaking neighborhoods in and around Fresno, California. Soto's father died when Soto was five years old; he and his siblings were reared by his mother and grandparents. After graduating from high school in 1970, Soto attended the University of California, Irvine, where he later earned an M.F.A.

Soto's life provides much of the material for his writing. He uses his cultural heritage and neighborhood traditions as the setting for stories and poems about growing up poor and Chicano. In *The Elements of San Joaquin*, his first book, he focuses on Fresno of the 1950's. He chronicles the lives of migrant workers, of oppressed people caught in cycles of poverty and violence. In the later poetry collection, *Who Will Know Us*, Soto draws again on his life. In "That Girl," for example, he is the young "Catholic boy" at the public library, while in "Another Time," he is an adult reconsidering the death of his father.

Soto turns to prose with *Living up the Street: Narrative Recollections*, a volume of twenty-one autobiographical stories. His talent in this work is in the minute: Soto is concerned with the small event, with the everyday. In this book he explores racism through vignettes from his own life. Rather than tackle racism in the abstract, he instead offers the concrete: the fight after being called a "dirty Mexican," the anger after an Anglo child wins a beauty contest. Soto also writes books for children and young adults. His matter-of-fact use of Spanish expressions as well as his references to the sights and sounds of the Latino community provide young readers with a sense of cultural identity.

Perhaps Soto's greatest success is his ability to assert his ethnicity while demonstrating that the experiences of growing up are universal. His bittersweet stories remind his readers of their passages from childhood to adulthood, of their search for identities that began up the street.

A Summer Life

Type of work: Short fiction
First published: 1990

A Summer Life is a collection of thirty-nine short vignettes based on Soto's life that chronicle his coming-of-age in California. The book is arranged in three sections covering Soto's early childhood, preadolescence, and the time prior to adulthood. Soto is the writer of the everyday. In the first section, his world is bounded by his neighborhood, and his eyes see this world in the sharp, concrete images of childhood. In "The Hand Brake," for example, he writes, "One afternoon in July, I invented a brake for a child's running legs. It was an old bicycle hand brake. I found it in the alley that ran alongside our house, among the rain-swollen magazines, pencils, a gutted clock and sun-baked rubber bands that cracked when I bunched them around my fingers."

Soto's Latino heritage forms the background. Soto identifies himself with this community in the descriptions he chooses for the everyday realities: his grandfather's wallet is "machine tooled with 'MEXICO' and a *campesino* and donkey climbing a hill"; his mother pounds "a round steak into *carne asada*" and crushes "a heap of beans into *refritos*."

Soto's experiences include the sounds of Spanish and the objects of the barrio, but they seem universal. At heart, the book is a child's movement toward self-awareness. Through *A Summer Life*, Soto paints his growing self-consciousness and increasing awareness of life and of death. "I was four and already at night thinking of the past," he writes, "The cat with a sliver in his eye came and went. . . . [T]he three sick pups shivered and blinked twilight in their eyes. . . . [T]he next day they rolled over into their leaf-padded graves."

In the last story in *A Summer Life*, "The River," Soto is seventeen. He and his friend Scott have traveled to Los Angeles to find themselves amid the "mobs of young people in leather vests, bell-bottoms, beads, Jesus thongs, tied-dyed shirts, and crowns of flowers." As the two of them bed down that night in an uncle's house, Soto seems to find that instant between childhood and adulthood, between the past and the present: "I thought of Braley Street and family, some of whom were now dead, and how when Uncle returned from the Korean War, he slept on a cot on the sunporch. . . . We had yet to go and come back from our war and find ourselves a life other than the one we were losing." In this moment, Soto speaks for all readers who recall that thin edge between yesterday and today.

New and Selected Poems

Type of work: Poetry
First published: 1995

In this collection, Soto records the textures and meanings of his life and those of friends and strangers with whom he shares the San Joaquin Valley, Fresno, California, and trips (sometimes) to Mexico as a tourist. He seeks and finds evocations of meaning in the details of those lives, those places, those avatars of the quotidian, exploring themes of childhood awareness; of place—fields, lots, streets, houses, and nature in mostly quite small segments—and its impact on people; of work, particularly the hard physical work of the Mexican field hand of hoeing and picking, often in contrast with the hard mental labor of the poet; of the consequences of that work on the people and the community; of nature expressed in rain, insects, clouds, heat; of the life of poverty; of eating and feeding; of religion and belief, the manifestations of something beyond the physical.

Gary Soto (M. L. Martinelle)

In its close and attentive observation of the details of nature both urban and rural, Soto's poetry is full of such images as "a windowsill of flies" or "the leaves of cotton plants/Like small hands waving good-bye." Taken together, it seems clear that the insect images, especially those of ants, suggest the Mexican and Chicano workers themselves and the complex of meanings that they have as a result of society's particular construction of them and of the workers' construction of themselves. A strong narrative line characterizes most of his poems; images of impressive clarity and spiritual force evoke ecstatic visions of the Godhead as pure light and the sacrifices of the curious faithful as they seek to understand the "blank eye" of God toward the suffering of the Mexican fieldworker whom the ants know "For what I gave." Indeed, Soto throughout this collection demonstrates his impressive power to transform gritty, closely observed reality into images that inform one of the sacramental through the power of his poetic vision.

Suggested Readings

De La Fuente, Patricia. "Entropy in the Poetry of Gary Soto: The Dialectics of Violence." *Discurso Literario* 5, no. 1 (Autumn, 1987): 111-120.

Erben, Rudolf, and Ute Erben. "Popular Culture, Mass Media, and Chicano Identity in Gary Soto's *Living up the Street* and *Small Faces*." *MELUS* 17, no. 3 (Fall, 1991/1992): 43-52.

Lannan Foundation. *Gary Soto: With Interview by Alejandro Morales*. Videorecording. Santa Fe, N.Mex.: Author, 1995.

Mason, Michael Tomasek. "Poetry and Masculinity on the Anglo/Christian Border: Gary Soto, Robert Frost, and Robert Hass." In *The Calvinist Roots of the Modern Era*, edited by Aliki Barnstone, Michael Tomasek Manson, and Carol J. Singley. Hanover, N.H.: University Press of New England, 1997.

Olivares, Julian. "The Streets of Gary Soto." *Latin America Literary Review* 18, no. 35 (January-June, 1990): 32-49.

Soto, Gary. "Interview with Gary Soto." *Journal of Adolescent and Adult Literacy* 47, no. 3 (November, 2003): 266.

Wojahn, David. Review of *Black Hair*, by Gary Soto. *Poetry* 146 (June, 1985): 171-173.

Contributor: Diane Andrews Henningfeld

Shelby Steele

Born: Chicago, Illinois; January 1, 1946

African American

Steele's writings and lectures forced public debate on new ways to view radical discrimination and civil rights matters.

Principal works

NONFICTION: *The Content of Our Character: A New Vision of Race in America*, 1990; *A Dream Deferred: The Second Betrayal of Black Freedom in America*, 1998; *White Guilt: How Blacks and Whites Together Destroyed the Promise of the Civil Rights Era*, 2006; *A Bound Man: Why We Are Excited About Obama, Why He Can't Win*, 2007

Shelby Steele grew up in Chicago under the guidance of strong parents who provided a stable family relationship for him, his twin brother, and his two sisters. Having interracial parents, Steele was influenced by two races, although he more strongly identified with his black heritage. As a college student, he became involved in the Civil Rights movement of the 1960's, following, at different times, the leads of Martin Luther King, Jr., and Malcolm X. Steele led civil rights marches at Coe College in Cedar Rapids, Iowa, and protested that African Americans were victimized by white society.

After the completion of his education, his marriage to a white woman, and the births of their two children, Steele developed new thoughts about African Americans in America. He came to the conclusion that opportunities are widely available to all citizens if they have personal initiative and a strong work ethic. Upon reaching this conclusion, which ran counter to his earlier ideas, Steele began to publish his ideas in major magazines and journals. His philosophy was often harshly dismissed by leaders in the Civil Rights movement, but it also garnered much praise, especially from African American political conservatives.

Steele was one of a few African Americans willing to challenge what was called the civil rights orthodoxy. When his work was published, he quickly became the subject of magazine and journal articles and was interviewed widely on radio and television, all the while drawing fire from numerous civil rights leaders.

In 1990, his first book, *The Content of Our Character*, was published. With this collection of his essays on race relations in America, Steele became recognized as a leading spokesman for political conservatives of all races. The main thesis of his book is that individual initiative, self-sufficiency, and strong families are what black America needs. Although labeled conservative by many, Steele refuses the label and calls himself a "classical Jeffersonian liberal."

The Content of Our Character

Type of work: Essays
First published: 1990

With *The Content of Our Character: A New Vision of Race in America*, Steele created a debate on the merits of affirmative action, the direction of the Civil Rights movement, and the growing ranks of African American political conservatives. Although certainly not the first to challenge views held by African American leaders, Steele pushed his challenge onto center stage more forcefully than others had before. Coming at a time when the United States was awash in conservative radio and television talk shows, the book quickly became a source of contention among political groups of all races and philosophies. Steele, through his television appearances, became a familiar figure throughout America as he explained and defended his ideas on race problems in America.

The book, titled after a line in Martin Luther King, Jr.'s famous speech, is a collection of essays, most of which appeared earlier in various periodicals. Central to Steele's book is a call for the African American community to examine itself and look to itself for opportunities. He calls for African Americans to look not to government or white society but to themselves for the solutions to their problems. Steele contends that African Americans enjoy unparalleled freedom; they have only to seize their freedom and make it work for them. He suggests that such programs as affirmative action contribute to the demoralization or demeaning of African Americans because preferential treatment denies them the opportunity to "make it on their own."

Shelby Steele (Hoover Institution, Stanford University)

Steele, calling for a return to the original purpose of the Civil Rights movement, says that affirmative action should go back to enforcing equal opportunity rather than demanding preferences. The promised land is, he writes, an opportunity, not a deliverance. Steele's ideas were strongly challenged by African Americans who believe that affirmative action and other civil rights measures are necessary for minority groups to retain the advancements that have been forged and to assure an open path for further progress. Opposition to Steele and other African American conservatives has led to charges that traditional African American civil rights leaders' intolerance of different voices within the black community is itself a form of racism.

Suggested Readings

Cooper, Matthew. "Inside Racism." *The Washington Monthly* 23, no. 9 (October, 1990).

Loury, Glenn C. "Why Steele Demands More of Blacks than of Whites." *Academic Questions* 5 (Fall, 1992): 19-23.

Prager, Jeffrey. "Self Reflection(s): Subjectivity and Racial Subordination in the Contemporary African American Writer." *Social Identities* 1 (August, 1995): 355-371.

Vassallo, Phillip. "Guarantees of a Promised Land: Language and Images of Race Relations in Shelby Steele's *The Content of Our Character*." *ETC: A Review of General Semantics* 49 (Spring, 1992): 36-42.

Contributor: Kay Hively

Virgil Suárez

Born: Havana, Cuba; 1962

Cuban American

Suárez voices the experience of Cuban immigrants who, though having spent the majority their lives in the United States, still do not feel completely acclimated and in some sense remain cultural exiles.

Principal works

LONG FICTION: *Latin Jazz*, 1989; *The Cutter*, 1991; *Havana Thursdays*, 1995; *Going Under*, 1996

POETRY: *You Come Singing*, 1998; *Garabato Poems*, 1999; *In the Republic of Longing*, 1999; *Banyan*, 2001; *Palm Crows*, 2001; *Guide to the Blue Tongue*, 2002; *Ninety Miles: Selected and New Poems*, 2005

SHORT FICTION: *Welcome to the Oasis, and Other Stories*, 1992

EDITED TEXTS: *Iguana Dreams: New Latino Fiction*, 1992 (with Delia Poey); *Paper Dance: Fifty-five Latino Poets*, 1995 (with Victor Hernández and Leroy V. Quintana); *Little Havana Blues: A Cuban-American Literature Anthology*, 1996 (with Poey); *American Diaspora: Poetry of Displacement*, 2001 (with Ryan G. Van Cleave); *Like Thunder: Poets Respond to Violence in America*, 2002 (with Van Cleave); *Vespers: Contemporary American Poems of Religion and Spirituality*, 2003 (with Van Cleave); *Red, White, and Blues: Poets on the Promise of America*, 2004 (with Van Cleave)

MISCELLANEOUS: *Spared Angola: Memories from a Cuban-American Childhood*, 1997 (short stories, poetry, and essays); *Infinite Refuge*, 2002 (sketches, poetry, memories, and fragments of short stories)

Virgil Suárez (VEER-hihl SWAH-rehs), the son of a pattern cutter and a piecemeal seamstress who worked in the sweatshops of Havana, left Cuba in 1970 with his family. After four years in Madrid, Spain, they went to Los Angeles. A man of many interests and prolific literary output, Suárez raised three daughters with his wife in Florida. His multitude of works in numerous genres deal with immigration, exile, and acclimatization to life and culture in the United States as well as the hopes and struggles of Cubans and Cuban Americans who had to abandon their island home under political duress.

A self-confessed obsessive, whether about his family, his hobbies, or his writing, Suárez is preoccupied by voice. He cites physical place as paramount in the process of finding and producing his voice, whether in prose or poetry. Initially recognized for his fiction, Suárez has written poetry since 1978, though he did not begin to publish it until the mid-1990's. He believes that voice is most important in poetry because of poetry's space limitations. He feels so strongly about maintaining the authenticity of his personal voice that he discards any poem he believes does not respect and represent his voice.

That voice is of an immigrant who, although he has spent the majority of his life in his adopted land and does not expect to return to Cuba, still does not feel completely acclimated. Suárez writes about what he knows: the nature and travails of exile. Appropriately, given his mixed feelings, Suárez writes in English and includes a sprinkling of Spanish, reiterated in English. Nonetheless, critics characterize Suárez's style as unwavering, definitive, and direct.

Suárez finished his secondary schooling in Los Angeles and received a B.A. in creative writing from California State University, Long Beach, in 1984. He studied at the University of Arizona and received an M.F.A. in creative writing from Louisiana State University in 1987. In addition to having been a visiting professor at the University of Texas in Austin in 1997, Suárez has taught at the University of Miami, Florida International University, Miami-Dade Community College, and Florida State University in Tallahassee.

Suárez's poems alone have appeared in more than 250 magazines and journals. He has also been a book reviewer for the *Los Angeles Times*, *Miami Herald*, *Philadelphia Inquirer*, and *Tallahassee Democrat*. He is a member of PEN, the Academy of American Poets, the Associated Writing Programs, and the Modern Language Association.

Nominated for five Pushcart Prizes, Suárez was a featured lecturer at the Smithsonian Institution in 1997. He received a Florida State Individual Artist grant in 1998 and a National Endowment for the Arts Fellowship in 2001-2002 to write a poetry work. His volume *Garabato Poems* was named *Generation Ñ* magazine's Best Book of 1999. He served as a National Endowment for the Arts Fellowship panel judge in 1999 and a Mid-Atlantic Arts Foundation panelist in 2000.

The Cutter

Type of work: Novel
First published: 1991

The Cutter is the story of a young man's desperate attempt to leave Cuba and its Communist regime. The novel is divided into five sections that mark the stages of his journey away from the island. The book begins when the protagonist, Julian Campos, is twenty years old. Julian is a university student who has recently returned to Havana after having completed his years of mandatory military service. He has been waiting to leave Cuba ever since his parents left five years earlier, and he thinks that the time has finally come—until the government tells him he must do additional "voluntary work" if he wants to leave Cuba.

The work is slave labor, and Julian and his coworkers are mistreated. Suárez depicts Cuba at its worst, leading the reader to understand why Julian is compelled to leave the country. Julian grows increasingly despondent about his prospects for leaving Cuba, particularly when he receives the belated news of his grandmother's death.

When Julian is finally released from the fields and permitted to go home, he realizes that he will never receive an exit notice. His neighbors plan to escape, and Julian joins them. Their group is infiltrated by a government spy, however, and his neighbors are killed. In the novel's final section, Julian reaches the United States. In contrast to most of the Cuban characters, those in the United States are kind to him and are eager to help him adjust to his new country. Julian clearly enjoys his newfound freedom, and, though he appears reluctant to search for his parents, the novel ends with a suggestion that ultimately he will find refuge with them.

Suarez's own family left Cuba in 1970, about the time at which this novel is set. *The Cutter* is his attempt to come to grips with his native Cuba and reflects his bitterness toward the country from which he and his parents were exiles. The novel focuses mainly on the desire for independence, but it is also about the loss of innocence and of the belief that if one does the right thing, good will necessarily be the end result.

Suggested Readings

Alvarez-Borland, Isabel. *Cuban-American Literature of Exile: From Person to Persona*. Charlottesville: University of Virginia Press, 1998.

_______. "Displacements and Autobiography in Cuban American Fiction." *World Literature Today* 68, no. 1 (1994): 43-49.

Cortina, Rodolfo. "A Perfect Hotspot." In *Hispanic American Literature*. Lincolnwood, Ill.: NTC, 1998.

Herrera, Andrea O'Reilly, ed. "Song for the Royal Palms of Miami." In *ReMembering Cuba: Legacy of a Diaspora*. Austin: University of Texas Press, 2001.

Contributors: Debra D. Andrist and Margaret Kent Bass

Amy Tan

Born: Oakland, California; February 19, 1952

Chinese American

Tan's novels are among the first to bring literary accounts of Asian American women to a broad audience.

Principal works

CHILDREN'S LITERATURE: *The Moon Lady*, 1992; *The Chinese Siamese Cat*, 1994

LONG FICTION: *The Joy Luck Club*, 1989; *The Kitchen God's Wife*, 1991; *The Hundred Secret Senses*, 1995; *The Bonesetter's Daughter*, 2001; *Saving Fish from Drowning*, 2005

NONFICTION: "The Language of Discretion," 1990 (in *The State of the Language*, Christopher Ricks and Leonard Michaels, editors); *The Opposite of Fate: A Book of Musings*, 2003

Amy Tan was born to parents who emigrated from China to California two years before she was born, and her work is influenced by the Asian American people and community she knew in her childhood. Each of her novels features characters who have either emigrated from China or who, like Tan, are the children of those immigrants. Like many immigrants to the United States, Tan's parents had high expectations for their daughter. Tan writes: "I was led to believe from the age of six that I would grow up to be a neurosurgeon by trade and a concert pianist by hobby." In her first two novels, especially, Tan writes of the pressures her young Chinese American characters feel as they try to meet high parental expectations while also craving a normal carefree childhood. Tan struggled with her Chinese heritage; as a girl, she contemplated cosmetic surgery to make her look less Asian. She was ashamed of her cultural identity until she moved with her mother and brother to Switzerland, where Tan attended high school. There, Asians were a rarity, and Tan was asked out on dates because she was suddenly exotic.

Tan did not initially plan to be a writer of fiction. She was working long hours as a technical writer, and sought psychological therapy to help her with her workaholic tendencies. When she became dissatisfied with her therapist, who sometimes fell asleep during her sessions, she decided to use fiction writing as her therapy instead. Experiences from her life thus find their way into her novels, especially *The Joy Luck Club*. Like the characters Rose Hsu and Waverly Jong, Tan experienced the death of a brother. Waverly, like Tan, is married to a tax attorney of European descent. Tan and her husband, Lou DeMattei, married in 1974. In fact, several of Tan's Chinese American women characters are married to European American husbands.

The Joy Luck Club

Type of work: Novel
First published: 1989

The Joy Luck Club, Tan's first novel, debuted to critical acclaim. It takes its place alongside Maxine Hong Kingston's *The Woman Warrior* (1976) as a chronicle of a Chinese American woman's search for and exploration of her ethnic identity. *The Joy Luck Club* is the best-selling, accessible account of four Chinese-born mothers and their four American-born daughters. One of the women, Suyuan Woo, has died before the story opens, but the other seven women tell their own stories from their individual points of view. Critics have noted that this approach is an unusually ambitious one. Nevertheless, the novel has reached a wide audience, especially since it was made into a feature film in 1992.

At the center of the story is Jing-mei "June" Woo, who has been asked to replace her dead mother as a member of the Joy Luck Club, a group of four women who meet for food and mah-jongg. Although Americanized and non-Chinese-speaking June is initially uncertain whether she wishes to join her mother's friends, she discovers that these women know things about her mother's past that she had never imagined. Her decision to become part of the Joy Luck Club culminates in a visit to China, where she meets the half sisters whom her mother was forced to abandon before she fled to the United States. The other Chinese-born women have similarly tragic stories, involving abandonment, renunciation, and sorrow in their native country. June says of her mother's decision to begin the club: "My mother could sense that the women of these families also had unspeakable tragedies they had left behind in China and hopes they couldn't begin to express in their fragile English." Each of these women's hopes includes hopes for her daughter. Each American daughter feels that she has in some way disappointed her mother. Waverly Jong fulfills her mother's ambitions by becoming a chess prodigy, then quits suddenly, to her mother's sorrow. June can never live up to her mother's expectations, and she rebels by refusing to learn the piano. Rose Hsu turns away for a moment, and her youngest brother drowns. Lena St. Clair makes a marriage based on false ideals of equality, and only her mother understands its basic injustice. These American-born daughters insist that they are not Chinese; as June says, she has no "Chinese whatsoever below my skin." By the end of the novel, they find themselves realizing how truly Chinese they are.

The Kitchen God's Wife

Type of work: Novel
First published: 1991

The Kitchen God's Wife, Tan's second novel, is concerned with a young, Americanized Chinese American woman's quest to accept her heritage, and in so doing accept her family, especially her mother. The first section of the novel, told from the daughter Pearl's point of view, concerns Pearl's difficult relationship with her mother, Winnie. Pearl perceives Winnie only as an old, unfashionable woman with trivial concerns. Pearl is troubled by a secret that she believes she cannot tell her mother. Pearl has been diagnosed with multiple sclerosis but dreads her mother's reaction, her reproaches, her list of ways Pearl could have prevented her disease.

Amy Tan (AP/Wide World Photos)

Pearl comes to recognize that her mother has secrets of her own, which Winnie finally decides to share with her daughter. Most of the novel, which is also the part that has received the most critical praise, is Winnie's first-person account of her childhood. The reader discovers along with Pearl that her mother has not always been the penny-pinching part-owner of a dingy, outdated florist's shop. Instead, Winnie has had a life of tragedy and adventure before immigrating to the United States. She lived another life in China, complete with another husband and three long-dead children. Winnie's mother disappeared when Winnie was a child, leaving her with her father and his other wives, who promptly sent her to live with an uncle. That uncle married her to Wen Fu, a sadistic, adulterous pilot, and Winnie soon began the nomadic life of a soldier's wife during wartime. By the end of the war, Winnie found love with the man Pearl knows as her father, the Chinese American serviceman Jimmie Louie. Wen Fu had Winnie imprisoned for adultery when she tried to divorce him, then raped her upon her release. Pearl learns the secret her mother has been hiding—Jimmie Louie, who died when Pearl was fourteen, is not her biological father after all. When Pearl learns these secrets about her mother's past, she is finally able to reveal the secret of her illness.

The title refers to an altar that Pearl inherits from a woman Winnie had known in China, and it symbolizes the growing closeness that Winnie and Pearl develop after sharing their secrets. The final scene shows Winnie buying her daughter a deity for the altar. This statue, whom Winnie names Lady Sorrowfree, the kitchen god's wife, represents Winnie and her care for her daughter. By the end of the novel, Pearl achieves a greater understanding of her mother and of their often-trying relationship.

The Hundred Secret Senses

Type of work: Novel
First published: 1995

The Hundred Secret Senses, Tan's third novel, continues her interest in Chinese and Chinese American culture, especially the strife between family members who are traditionally Chinese and those who are more Americanized. Half-Caucasian, half-Chinese Olivia meets, at age six, her eighteen-year-old Chinese half sister, Kwan, the daughter of her father's first marriage. Kwan instigates Olivia's struggle with her Chinese identity. Olivia is alternately embarrassed, annoyed, and mystified by this sister who claims that she has daily communication with "yin people"—helpful ghosts—many of whom are the spirits of friends from Kwan's past lives. Despite her ambivalence, however, Olivia gains most of her awareness about her Chinese background from Kwan. The sisters' Chinese father has died, and Olivia is being raised in the United States by a Caucasian mother and an Italian American stepfather. After Kwan's arrival from China, the older girl is largely responsible for her sister's care. Thus, Olivia resentfully learns Chinese and learns about her Chinese heritage, including knowledge about the ghosts who populate her sister's world. Olivia is understandably skeptical about the presence of these yin people. In Olivia's culture, such ghosts are the stuff of scary films, while for Kwan, they are a part of everyday life. The title, then, refers to the hundred secret senses that, Kwan asserts, enable one to perceive the yin people. Kwan's stories about a past life are the fairy tales with which Olivia grows up.

Later, Olivia marries a half-Hawaiian, half-Caucasian man, Simon, and as the novel opens, they are beginning divorce proceedings after a long marriage. Olivia begins these proceedings in part because she believes that Simon is still in love with a former girlfriend, who died shortly before Simon and Olivia met. Olivia must develop her own sense of personal and ethnic identity in order to release this ghost from her past. She must begin to believe that she is worthy of Simon's love, and in order to discover her self-worth, she must travel to the tiny Chinese village where her sister grew up.

Although Olivia believes herself to be very American, she begins to feel much closer to her Chinese heritage once she, Simon, and Kwan arrive in China, and in the storytelling tradition of all Tan's novels, Olivia learns about her family's past while talking to residents of the village in which Kwan grew up. Olivia also is able to confront her difficulties with Simon as a result of the trip.

Saving Fish from Drowning

Type of work: Novel
First published: 2005

Told through the narrative voice of murdered tour director, San Francisco antiquarian Bibi Chen, *Saving Fish from Drowning* explores what happens when a group of Americans take a trip to East Asia, where political unrest can erupt into violence.

Left to the bumbling direction of Harry Bailey, a man hiding his epilepsy and more concerned about looking "bad" than about working effectively to help his fellow travelers, these twelve Americans soon manage to desecrate a sacred tribal shrine, become separated from one another, and are kidnapped by a small band of Karen tribespeople hiding in the dense Burmese jungle to avoid political persecution and, most likely, extermination at the hands of Myanmar's dictatorship.

This ugly comedy highlights the embarrassing arrogance of these pampered Americans abroad. These people believe they can manipulate their captors, when, in fact, they have misunderstood everything, including that they have been taken prisoner because the Karen people believed one of them to be the reincarnation of their lost savior. They saw him do "magic" (sleight-of-hand card tricks) and he carries what they believe to be their savior's "sacred" text, in this case, a tattered copy of a Stephen King novel. Things go from bad to worse as the days stretch into weeks and the tourists remain prisoners in the jungle. Out in the "civilized world" plans to find the missing tourists run amok thanks to ineptitude and hatred of Americans.

Although Amy Tan's novel could end as brutally as a reader aware of international incidents like this one might fear, it does not conclude with a bloodbath. The actual ending is far more troubling: Despite the ordeal that these people have managed, through little skill on their part, to survive, once they are back in the "civilized" world it is clear that their experience has not changed them.

Suggested Readings

Benanni, Ben, ed. *Paintbrush: A Journal of Poetry and Translation* 22 (Autumn, 1995).

Bloom, Harold, ed. *Amy Tan*. Philadelphia: Chelsea House, 2000.

Cheung, King-Kok, ed. *An Interethnic Companion to Asian American Literature*. New York: Cambridge University Press, 1997.

Cooperman, Jeannette Batz. *The Broom Closet: Secret Meanings of Domesticity in Postfeminist Novels by Louise Erdrich, Mary Gordan, Toni Morrison, Marge Piercy, Jane Smiley, and Amy Tan*. New York: Peter Lang, 1999.

Ho, Wendy. *In Her Mother's House: The Politics of Asian American Mother-Daughter Writing*. Walnut Creek, Calif.: AltaMira Press, 1999.

Huh, Joonok. *Interconnected Mothers and Daughters in Amy Tan's "The Joy Luck Club."* Tucson, Ariz.: Southwest Institute for Research on Women, 1992.

Huntley, E. D. *Amy Tan: A Critical Companion*. Westport, Conn.: Greenwood Press, 1998.

Pearlman, Mickey, and Katherine Usher Henderson. "Amy Tan." In *Inter/View: Talks with America's Writing Women*. Lexington: University Press of Kentucky, 1990.

Snodgrass, Mary Ellen. *Amy Tan: A Literary Companion*. Jefferson, N.C.: McFarland, 2004.

Tan, Amy. "Amy Tan." Interview by Barbara Somogyi and David Stanton. *Poets and Writers* 19, no. 5 (September 1, 1991): 24-32.

Contributor: J. Robin Coffelt

Sheila Ortiz Taylor

Born: Los Angeles, California; September 25, 1939

Mexican American

Taylor is often considered the first Chicana lesbian novelist.

Principal works

LONG FICTION: *Faultline*, 1982; *Spring Forward/Fall Back*, 1985; *Southbound*, 1990; *Coachella*, 1998

POETRY: *Slow Dancing at Miss Polly's*, 1989

NONFICTION: *Emily Dickinson: A Bibliography, 1850-1966*, 1968; *Imaginary Parents*, 1996

Sheila Ortiz Taylor (SHEE-lah ohr-TEES TAY-lur) is often considered the first Chicana lesbian novelist. Her first and most acclaimed novel, *Faultline*, was republished in 1995 because of increased awareness of its importance not only in lesbian and Chicano literature but as a significant work of fiction. The novel has been published in British, German, Greek, Italian, and Spanish translations, and in 1995 film rights were bought by Joseph May Productions. The novel also won several awards, although it was often neglected by critics and mainstream reviewers.

Ortiz Taylor grew up in a Mexican American family in Southern California, an experience she records in *Imaginary Parents*. The book, a mixture of fact and fiction, is true to the spirit of her childhood in the 1940's and 1950's. Her older sister's color prints accompany the text and represent a different version of the shared past. In her preface Ortiz Taylor writes that the book could be called autobiography, memoir, poetry, nonfiction, creative nonfiction, fiction, or codex (a manuscript book); she herself calls it an *ofrenda*, an offering of small objects with big meanings set out in order. The book reimagines the past and re-creates the parents and extended family who have since died; it also provides an insightful Chicana perspective into what she calls the strange Southern California culture of the war years.

It was during the post-World War II years of the early 1950's that Ortiz Taylor, then twelve or thirteen years old, realized that she wanted to write. She attended California State University at Northridge and graduated magna cum laude. She earned her M.A. from the University of California, Los Angeles, in 1964, and her Ph.D. in English from the same university in 1973 with a dissertation on form and function in the picaresque novel.

Taylor's own novels often follow the episodic traditions of the picaresque, although they transform the rogue hero into an adventurous lesbian protagonist who challenges boundaries and resists stereotyped categorization. In *Faultline* the main character, Arden Benbow, who was an English major in college, is the mother of six when she falls in love with another woman. A similar sense of hopefulness and triumph in the face of opposition, which some reviewers have referred to as utopian, pervades *Spring Forward/Fall Back*, and the same spirit informs Taylor's poetry and other writings. Taylor has a keen eye for detail and is clear about oppression and stagnated prejudicial attitudes. Her writings also show survival techniques in a hostile culture, among them the invocation of humor, love, and goodwill toward others. Her protagonists refuse to be beaten down, and they enjoy and respect life.

Taylor's professional career has been in teaching at several universities, most notably at Florida State University, where she began teaching literature in the early 1970's. Her courses include many on women writers, and she has served as director of Women's Studies. She has given many public readings nationally and internationally, and in 1991 she was awarded a Fulbright Fellowship to teach at the University of Erlangen-Nürnberg.

Taylor's work shows a continuing fascination with the novel form and its many variations. She sees herself as an author who creates convincing forgeries that are intended to illuminate life. Her works show her challenging herself by shifting subject matter, style, and approach. She never repeats simple patterns or formulas from previous works. This approach to writing is also reflected in her central characters, who meet challenges with creativity and vitality and accept risk as a part of life.

Many readers have found Taylor's texts to be engaging. Her work is therefore not restricted to special audiences. Like the literal lesson of the geological faultlines where earthquakes appear, Taylor's works illustrate that chance and change are inevitable, that for individuals and societies it is important to avoid rigidity, and that challenges must be met actively with love, humor, and imagination.

Faultline

Type of work: Novel
First published: 1982

Faultline is a comic novel with a serious message conveyed by example and implication rather than by preaching. Sheila Ortiz Taylor creates a shining cast of characters who speak about their relationships to the protagonist, Arden Benbow, as Arden battles her former husband, Malthus, for custody of their six children. Malthus has never considered women equal to men, and his ego is hurt when Arden prefers living with a woman to staying with him in their dull marriage.

The theme of acceptance of individual differences runs throughout the novel. It is not until Arden and Alice Wicks fall in love that Arden can see what it means to free oneself to live fully and to develop the creative spirit. Alice too has married because that is what society expected of her, but she learns that she must be herself and follow her own spirit. Together the two women create a loving home life, which includes an African American gay male drag queen as a babysitter, an assortment of pets (as many as three hundred rabbits), and various friends and neighbors who are attracted by Arden's energy and enthusiasm. Although he himself is involved with another woman and does not want to be bothered with the children, Arden's former husband files a custody suit on the grounds that Arden's lesbianism makes her an unfit mother. Arden refuses to pretend to be someone she is not, and her life-affirming spirit triumphs. The book ends with a legally nonbinding double wedding between Arden and her lover Alice and between two of their gay male friends.

The faultline of the title refers to the geography of the setting in Southern California, but it is also a metaphor for unpredictability and the need for adaptability and acceptance of reality. One chapter is in the words of a professor of geophysics who specializes in plate tectonics, which includes the study of the faultlines where earthquakes occur. Earthquakes, he says, are dynamic reactions to changes in the earth's crust that remind people of their mortality and the need to live with enthusiasm. People should not waste their time being prejudiced against others. Although he is a scientist, the professor knows—as Malthus does not—that there is more to life than "facts." In *Faultine*, characters who are rigid and domineering prove to be unhappy, whatever material wealth they may have. Malthus will not accept Arden's love for a woman and thus turns his own children against him; they do not want to live with an angry and spiteful father.

Faultline emphasizes the need for people to celebrate life rather than to oppress others. Arden Benbow is, after all, not only a fit mother but an outstanding one who brings to her children and to all around her a sense of fairness and decency and, especially, a joy in living and loving.

Suggested Readings

Aldama, Frederick Luis. *Brown on Brown: Chicano/a Representations of Gender, Sexuality, and Ethnicity*. Austin: University of Texas Press, 2005.

Bruce-Novoa, Juan. "Sheila Ortiz Taylor's *Faultline:* A Third Woman Utopia." *Confluencia: Revista Hispánica de Cultura y Literatura* 6 (Spring, 1991).

Christian, Karen. "Will the 'Real Chicano' Please Stand Up? The Challenge of John Rechy and Sheila Ortiz Taylor to Chicano Essentialism." *Americas Review* 20 (Summer, 1992).

Zimmerman, Bonnie. *Safe Sea of Women*. Boston: Beacon Press, 1990.

Contributor: Lois A. Marchino

Piri Thomas

Born: New York, New York; September 30, 1928

Puerto Rican

Thomas's Down These Mean Streets *gave many Americans a window into the lives of people in New York's Puerto Rican ghetto and became an inspiration for the "Nuyorican" literary movement.*

Principal works

SHORT FICTION: *Stories from El Barrio*, 1978 (juvenile)

NONFICTION: *Down These Mean Streets*, 1967 (autobiographical novel); *Savior, Savior, Hold My Hand*, 1972; *Seven Long Times*, 1974

Piri Thomas (PIH-ree TAH-muhs) was born in 1928, just before the Great Depression struck, the first child of a Puerto Rican couple, Juan (also known as Johnny) and Dolores Montañez Tomás. In 1941, when Piri was thirteen, his father, whom he called "Poppa," lost his job and went to work with the Works Progress Administration (WPA), a Depression-era government jobs program. The work was hard manual labor, and Poppa became distant and cool toward his son, who desperately wanted paternal affection and approval.

At an early age, Thomas became conscious of the problems of having dark skin. His own mother was light-skinned, and his brothers and sisters were light in color, with straight hair. Only the narrator and his father had the hair with tight curls and the dark brown skin that marked them as members of a disadvantaged race. The young narrator's awareness of race increased when his family moved out of Harlem to an Italian neighborhood, where he was subjected to racial slurs and had to fight the Italian boys. Standing up to the Italians gradually won him acceptance, though, and he learned to make his way in the world by fighting.

Thomas's family returned to Harlem, where the boy became a member of a Puerto Rican youth gang. In 1944, the family moved to Long Island, enjoying the prosperity of Poppa's wartime job. Thomas's own stay in the suburbs did not last, though. The snubs of his schoolmates made him even more conscious of his color than he had been in the Italian neighborhood, and he dropped out of school and returned to Harlem. He became friends with Brew, a black man from the South, and Thomas's puzzlement about his own racial identity led him to ask Brew to take him south. The two men went to Virginia, where they took work on a merchant ship.

After his travels, Thomas returned to Harlem, where he fell in love with a young woman from Puerto Rico who was waiting for him. He also, however, began to use heroin and developed a serious habit. After kicking his heroin habit with the help of a friend from his boyhood gang days and his friend's mother, he took up another dangerous pursuit: armed robbery. Another Puerto Rican introduced him to two white men who had been in prison, and the four began robbing small businesses. A daring attempt to rob a nightclub full of patrons ended with Thomas shooting a policeman and being shot himself. Barely escaping death, he was sentenced to five to fifteen years at Sing Sing Prison.

Soon transferred from Sing Sing to Comstock State Prison, Thomas remained behind bars from 1950 to 1956. His youth on the mean streets of New York served him well in prison, where only the strong and aggressive could avoid being raped and exploited. In prison, he also began to think seriously about his life and to read widely. For a time, he explored the religious beliefs of the Black Muslims. Thomas finally won parole and found himself back in New York, ready to turn his life around.

Down These Mean Streets is Thomas's own story, and questions of identity and race lie at its core. Psychologically, it is the coming-of-age story of a young man who must struggle with the conflicts in his family and in his own mind in order to make sense of his life. Through gang involvement, drug addiction, a criminal career, and a prison sentence, the protagonist wrestles with his own versions of the problems that confront all people: problems of self-definition, of tension with parents, of sexual relationships, and of religious meaning.

As a Puerto Rican, Thomas is a member of a group that has an ambiguous status. Puerto Rico is not a state or a part of any state, yet it is still part of the United States. Puerto Ricans are culturally different from the people of the mainland United States, but they are U.S. citizens. As a blend of national and racial ancestries, Puerto Ricans often do not fit neatly into the racial categories used by North Americans. Both of Thomas's parents are from Puerto Rico, but Thomas grew up in New York; thus, there is a gap between him and his parents. To make matters even more complicated, Thomas and his father are dark-skinned, while Thomas's mother and his brothers and sisters are light-skinned. This would not be a problem in Puerto Rico, where racial consciousness is less pronounced than in the mainland United States, but it proved to be a big problem for the young Piri. He continually felt "hung up between two sticks," in his phrase. In his novel, there are continual hints that his father's own discomfort about having dark skin is a source of the coldness the son feels from his father.

Upon its publication, *Down These Mean Streets* was both controversial and influential. It was criticized for its violence, explicit sexuality, and expression of strong racial feelings. During the 1970's, the book was banned from the shelves of school libraries in a number of communities, including Queens in New York; Levittown, Long Island; Darien, Connecticut; and Salinas, California. Responding to these attempts at book banning, Thomas became an opponent of censorship and an advocate for the poor and disenfranchised.

Down These Mean Streets

Type of work: Autobiographical novel
First published: 1967

Down These Mean Streets is an autobiographical novel that tells of the author's experiences growing up as a dark-skinned Puerto Rican in New York, becoming involved in drugs and crime, and going to prison. The book's thirty-five chapters are divided into eight sections, with each of the sections devoted to an important place and time in the author's life. The first section, consisting of eight chapters and entitled "Harlem," deals with Thomas's childhood in and around New York's Spanish Harlem. The two chapters of the second section, "Suburbia," deal with life in the suburbs of Long Island, where the family moves after Thomas's father gets a wartime job at an airplane factory. The third, fifth, and final chapters all concern Harlem, the site of the "mean streets" of the book's title and a place that keeps drawing Thomas back.

Thomas is the narrator of the book, and the style draws heavily on the speech of New York's Puerto Rican and black populations, evoking the urban environment. Racism and prejudice, both as sociological forces and as sources of psychological pain, are central themes in the work. Some of Thomas's difficulties in fitting in with American society are the result of poverty, but he also experiences real discrimination, and opportunities are closed to him because of his skin color. His anger and resentment at being continually rejected, though, are his true reasons for becoming a drug addict and a criminal. His story is ultimately the story of his ability to rise above his anger.

Down These Mean Streets was the first work by a Puerto Rican author writing in English to attract a large readership. A best seller when it appeared in 1967, it gave many Americans a window into the lives of people in New York's Puerto Rican ghetto and became an inspiration for the "Nuyorican" literary movement. The book was criticized for its violence, explicit sexuality, and expression of strong racial feelings, and was banned from the shelves of many school libraries in the 1970's. In response, Thomas has become an outspoken opponent of all forms of censorship. As he says in the afterword to the thirtieth anniversary edition of *Down These Mean Streets:*

> In writing *Down These Mean Streets*, it was my hope that exposure of such conditions in the ghetto would have led to their improvement. But, thirty years later, the sad truth is that people caught in the ghettoes have not made much progress, have moved backwards in many respects—the social safety net is much weaker now. Unfortunately, it's the same old Mean Streets, only worse. I was taught that justice wears a blindfold, so as not to be able to distinguish between the colors, and thus make everyone equal in the eyes of the law. I propose we remove the blindfold from the eyes of Lady Justice, so for the first time she can really see what's happening and check out where the truth lies and the lies hide. That would be a start. *Viva* the children of all the colors! *Punto!*

Suggested Readings

Caminero-Santangelo, Marta. "'Puerto Rican Negro': Redefining Race in Piri Thomas's *Down These Mean Streets*." *MELUS* 29, no. 2 (Summer, 2004): 205ff.

Flores, Juan. *Divided Borders: Essays on Puerto Rican Identity*. Houston, Tex.: Arte Público, 1993.

Fox, Geoffrey E. *Hispanic Nation: Culture, Politics, and the Constructing of Identity*. Tucson: University of Arizona Press, 1997.

Hernandez, Carmen Dolores. *Puerto Rican Voices in English: Interviews with Writers*. New York: Praeger, 1997.

Rivero, Eliana. "Hispanic Literature in the United States: Self-Image and Conflict." *Revista Chicano-Riqueña* 13, nos. 3/4 (1985): 173-192.

Rodriguez de Laguna, Asela, ed. *Images and Identities: The Puerto Rican in Literature*. New Brunswick, N.J.: Transaction, 1987.

Santiago, Roberto, ed. *Boricuas: Influential Puerto Rican Writings—An Anthology*. New York: Ballantine Books, 1995.

Thomas, Piri. "Piri Thomas: An Interview." *MELUS* 26, no. 3 (Fall, 2001): 77ff.

Turner, Faythe, ed. *Puerto Rican Writers at Home in the USA: An Anthology*. Seattle: Open Hand, 1991.

Contributor: Carl L. Bankston III

Jean Toomer

Born: Washington, D.C.; December 26, 1894
Died: Doylestown, Pennsylvania; March 30, 1967

African American

Toomer's goal was to articulate a new identity beyond individual racial identities, a "universal human being" or American "race" beyond the divisions of white and black, East and West, religion, race, class, sex, and occupational classification.

Principal works

DRAMA: *Balo*, pb. 1927
POETRY: "Banking Coal," 1922; "Blue Meridian," 1936; *The Collected Poems of Jean Toomer*, 1988
SHORT FICTION: "Mr. Costyve Duditch," 1928; "York Beach," 1929
NONFICTION: "Race Problems and Modern Society," 1929; "Winter on Earth," 1929; *Essentials: Definitions and Aphorisms*, 1931; "The Flavor of Man," 1949
MISCELLANEOUS: *Cane*, 1923 (prose and poetry); *The Wayward and the Seeking*, 1980 (prose and poetry; Darwin T. Turner, editor)

Nathan Eugene Toomer (TEW-mur) spent most of his life resisting a specific racial label for himself. His childhood and youth were spent in white or racially mixed middle-class neighborhoods in Washington, D.C., and his parents were both light-skinned. Jean's father left shortly after his birth and his mother died after remarrying, so that the most potent adult influences on his life were his maternal grandparents, with whom he lived until his twenties. His grandfather, P. B. S. Pinchback, had been elected lieutenant-governor in Reconstruction Louisiana and served as acting governor in 1873. Toomer believed that his victory was helped by his announcement that he had black blood, although Toomer denied knowing whether it was true. One thing is clear: Pinchback had indeed served the Union cause in the "Corps d'Afrique."

Later in life Toomer denied that he was a "Negro"—a term he defined as one who identifies solely with the black race. At the same time, despite the fact that he had a great deal of nonblack ancestry, he saw himself as not white, but rather as "American," a member of a new race that would unify conflicting racial groups through a mixture of racial strains. The attainment of such an "American" race remained his goal throughout most of his life after *Cane*.

Toomer's education after high school was varied, from agriculture at the University of Wisconsin to the American College of Physical Training in Chicago. Rather than completing courses toward a formal degree, however, he pursued his own reading in literature and social issues while working at assorted jobs until he decided to devote all his efforts to writing. He began writing and was published in a few magazines before moving south to become a schoolteacher in rural Georgia, an experience which he uses in *Kabnis*, a novella that forms the final part of *Cane*.

The real nudge came in the form of a three-month stint as substitute principal of a school in a small Georgia town in the fall of 1921. He returned to Washington in November with material for a whole book. He published several poems and stories in assorted periodicals the following year and then gathered most of them and many new ones into a carefully structured book called *Cane*, published in 1923 by Boni and Liveright. The book caused a considerable stir among the influential white literati with whom he associated (such as Waldo Frank, Sherwood Anderson, and Hart Crane) and among black writers and intellectuals as well. Yet in its two printings (the second in 1927) it sold fewer than a thousand copies.

That same year, Toomer met the Russian mystic George Gurdjieff and embraced his philosophy of higher consciousness. After studying with him in France, Toomer returned to spread his teachings in America. A ten-month marriage to a white poet, Margery Latimer, ended with her death in childbirth in 1932. Two years later he married another white woman, Marjorie Content; he would spend the rest of his life with her. This period in Toomer's life was largely devoted to self-improvement and to writing philosophical and spiritually oriented work. He continued to publish some literary works until 1936, when his career came virtually to an end, despite attempts to have other works published. He became a Quaker and maintained no further identity with the black race, dying in 1967 largely forgotten.

Cane

Type of work: Short fiction, novella, and poetry
First published: 1923

Divided into three parts, Toomer's *Cane* consists of short stories, sketches, poems, and a novella. The first section focuses on women; the second on relationships between men and women; and the third on one man. Although capable of being read discretely, these works achieve their full power when read together, coalescing to create a novel, unified by theme and symbol.

Like all of Toomer's work, *Cane* describes characters who have within a buried life, a dream that seeks expression and fulfillment; *Cane* is a record of the destruction of those dreams. Sometimes the dreams explode, the fire within manifesting itself violently; more often, however, the world implodes within the dreamer's mind. These failures have external causes, like the inadequacy or refusal of the society to allow expression, the restrictions by what Toomer calls the herd. They also have internal causes, primarily because of fears and divisions within the dreamer himself as he struggles unsuccessfully to unite will and mind, passion and intellect. In the later story "York Beach," Toomer describes this as the conflict between the wish for brilliant experience and the wish for difficult experience.

The one limitation on the otherwise thoroughgoing romanticism of this vision is Toomer's rigorous separation of humankind into those who dream, who are worth bothering about, and those who do not. While the struggle of Toomer's characters is for unity, it is to unify themselves or to find union with one other dreamer, never to merge with humankind in general. Like Kabnis, many find their true identity in recognizing their differences, uniqueness, and superiority. At the end of "York Beach," the protagonist tells his listeners that the best government would be an empire ruled by one who recognized his own greatness.

Toomer's dreamers find themselves in the first and third sections of *Cane* in a southern society which, although poor in compassion and understanding, is rich in supportive imagery. In the second part, set in the North, that imagery is absent, so the return of the protagonist to the South in part 3 is logical, since the North has not provided a nurturing setting. Although the return may be a plunge back into hell, it is also a journey to an underground where Kabnis attains the vision that sets him free.

The imagery is unified by a common theme: ascent. Kabnis says, "But its the soul of me that needs the risin," and all the imagery portrays the buried life smoldering within, fighting upward, seeking release. The dominant image of the book, the one that supplies the title, is the rising sap of the sugarcane. Cane whispers enigmatic messages to the characters, and it is to cane fields that people seeking escape and release flee. Sap rises, too, in pines, which also whisper and sing; and at the mill of part 1, wood burns, its smoke rising. The moon in "Blood-Burning Moon" is said to "sink upward," an oxymoronic yoking that implies the difficulty of the rising in this book.

A second pattern of imagery is that of flowing blood or water, although generally in the pessimistic *Cane*, water is not abundant. In "November Cotton Flower," dead birds are found in the wells, and when water is present, the characters, threatened by the life it represents, often fear it. Rhobert, in a sketch of that name, wears a diver's helmet to protect him from water, life which is being drawn off. Dreams denied, blood flows more freely than water.

"Esther"

Type of work: Short fiction
First published: 1923, in *Cane*

"Esther," the most successful story in *Cane*, comes early and embodies many of the book's major themes. It opens with a series of four sentences describing Esther as a girl of nine. In each, the first clause compliments her beauty, the second takes the praise away; the first clauses of each are progressively less strong. Esther represents the destruction of potential by a combination of inner and outer forces. On the outside there is her father, "the richest colored man in town," who reduces Esther to a drab and obsequious life behind a counter in his dry goods store. "Her hair thins. It

Jean Toomer (The Beinecke Rare Book and Manuscript Library, Yale University)

looks like the dull silk on puny corn ears." Then there is King Barlo, a black giant, who has a vision in the corner of town known as the Spittoon. There, while townspeople gather to watch (and black and white preachers find momentary unity in working out ways to rid themselves of one who threatens their power), Barlo sees a strong black man arise. While the man's head is in the clouds, however, "little white-ant biddies come and tie his feet to chains." The herd in Barlo's vision, as in Toomer's, may destroy the dreamer.

Many, however, are affected by what Barlo has seen, none more so than Esther, who decides that she loves him. The fire begins to burn within. As she stands dreaming in her store, the sun on the windows across the street reflect her inner fire, and, wanting to make it real, Esther calls the fire department. For the next eighteen years, Esther, the saddest of all Toomer's women, lives only on dreams, inventing a baby, conceived, she thinks, immaculately. Sometimes, like many of his characters, sensing that life may be too much for her, knowing that "emptiness is a thing that grows by being moved," she tries not to dream, sets her mind against dreaming, but the dreams continue.

At the end of the story, Esther, then twenty-seven, decides to visit Barlo, who has returned to town. She finds the object of her dream in a room full of prostitutes; what rises is only the fumes of liquor. "Conception with a drunken man must be a mighty sin," she thinks, and, when she attempts to return to reality, she, like many Toomer characters, finds that the world has overwhelmed her. Crushed from without, she has neither life nor dreams. "There is no air, no street, and the town has completely disappeared."

"Blood-Burning Moon"

Type of work: Short fiction
First published: 1923, in *Cane*

The main character undergoes a similar emotional destruction in "Blood-Burning Moon," Toomer's most widely anthologized short story (also found in the woman-centered first section). Here, however, the destructive force is primarily internal.

Among the most conventional of Toomer's stories, "Blood-Burning Moon" has both a carefully delineated plot and a familiar one at that: a love triangle. What is inventional is the way Toomer manages the reader's feelings about the woman whom two men love. Both men are stereotypes. Bob Stone is white and repulsively so. Himself divided and content to be, he makes his mind consciously white and approaches Louisa "as a master should." The black, Tom Burwell, is a stereotype too: Having dreams, he expresses his love sincerely, but inarticulately; denied or threatened, he expresses himself violently.

The first two sections open with rhythmic sentences beginning with the word "up"; Louisa sings songs against the omen the rising moon portends, seeking charms and spells but refusing the simple act of choosing between the two men. Because Louisa does not choose, the story comes to its inevitable violent climax and the death of both men. There is more, however: When Louisa is last seen she too has been destroyed, mentally, if not physically. She sings again to the full moon as an omen, hoping that people will join her, hoping that Tom Burwell will come; but her choice is too late. Burwell is dead, and the lateness of her decision marks the end of her dreams. Like Esther, she is separated from even appropriate mental contact with the world that is.

"Cane, Section 2"

Type of work: Short fiction
First published: 1923, in *Cane*

Barlo's vision (in "Esther") is accurate but incomplete as a description of what happens to Toomer's protagonists. While it is true that the herd will often destroy the dreamer, it is just as likely that the dreamer, from inaction, fear, and division, will destroy himself. The four stories of section 2 all focus on pairs of dreamers who can isolate themselves from the rest of society but who cannot get their dreams to merge. In "Avey" it is the man who, focused on his own dreams, refuses to listen to and accept the value of Avey's dreams. In "Bona and Paul," Paul takes Bona away from the dance, not, as everyone assumes, to make love to her, but to know her; but knowing a human is denied him because Bona assumes she already knows him, "a priori," as he has said. Knowing he is black, she "knows" that he will be passionate. When he is interested in knowledge before passion, she discovers that to know a priori is not to know at all and flees him, denying his dream of knowing her.

In "Theater" the divided main character, sitting half in light, half in shadow, watches another dreamer, the dancer on stage, Dorris. She is dreaming of him, but, although "mind pulls him upward into dream," suspicion is stronger than desire, and by the end of the story John has moved wholly into shadow. When Dorris looks at him, "She finds it a dead thing in the shadow which is his dream." Likewise, in "Box Seat" Muriel is torn between the dreamer Dan, who stands with one hand lying on the wall, feeling from below the house the deep underground rumbling of the subway, literal buried life, and Mrs. Pribby, the landlady, rattling her newspaper, its thin noise contrasting with the powerful below-ground sound. Muriel chooses respectability. At the theater, to which Dan has followed her, she is repelled by a dwarf who offers her a rose; Dan rises to his feet to proclaim that Jesus was once a leper. This last, insistent image, suggesting the maimed sources of beauty that Muriel is too timid to accept, also indicates the overexplicit inflation of claims that damages some of Toomer's fiction. Although in *Cane* most of the stories are under control, some seem rather too sketchy; "Box Seat," however, foreshadows the fault that mars all of Toomer's later fiction: the sacrifice of dramatic ideas in favor of often pallid, philosophical ones.

Kabnis

Type of work: Novella
First published: 1923, in *Cane*

The last and longest story in *Cane* integrates the themes, making explicit the nature of the destructive forces. The story is *Kabnis*, a novella, and the force is sin, a word contained backward in Kabnis's name. It is the story of a black man out of place in the rural South, threatened not so much by whites as by his own people, by his environment, and by his sense of himself.

As the story opens, Kabnis is trying to sleep, but he is not allowed this source of dream; instead, chickens and rats, nature itself, keep him awake. He wants to curse it, wants it to be consistent in its ugliness, but he senses too the beauty of nature, and, because that prevents him from hating it entirely, he feels that even beauty is a curse. Intimidated by nature, Kabnis is also attacked by society, by the local black church, from which the shouting acclamations of faith torture Kabnis, and by the black school superintendent who fires him for drinking. As in "Box Seat," the protagonist is thus caught between expressions of life, which are yet too strong for him, and its repression, which traps him. So positioned, Kabnis, like Rhobert, is a man drowning, trying vainly to avoid the source of life. From this low point, for the only time in the book, Toomer describes the way up, and Kabnis gains enough strength to throw off his oppression.

He has three friends: Halsey, an educated black man who has been playing Uncle Tom; Layman, a preacher, whose low voice suggests a canebrake; and Lewis, a doppelgänger who suggests a version of what a stronger Kabnis might have become and who drops out of the story when Kabnis does indeed become stronger. Once fired, Kabnis takes up residence with Halsey, a Vulcan-like blacksmith who gives him work repairing implements, work for which Kabnis is ill-suited. In his basement, however, Halsey has his own buried life, an old man, Father John, and in the climactic scene, the three men descend into the underground for a dark night of the soul, for the Walpurgisnacht on which Kabnis confronts his own demons. Prefiguring the descents in such black fiction as Richard Wright's "Man Who Lived Underground" and Ralph Ellison's *Invisible Man* (1952), this is likewise a descent during which the values of the world above, met on unfamiliar terrain, are rethought. It is a night of debauchery, but also the night when the destructive illusions and fears of the men are exposed.

Father John represents those fears; when he speaks, his message is sin; but Kabnis knows, and for the first time can say, that because of sin the old man has never seen the beauty of the world. Kabnis has, and as he says, "No eyes that have seen beauty ever lose their sight." Kabnis then proclaims a new role for himself: If he is not a blacksmith, he may be, having known beauty, a wordsmith. "I've been shapin words after a design that branded here. Know whats here? M soul." If sin is what is done against the soul and if the soul of Kabnis is what needs the rising, then, as Kabnis says, the world has conspired against him. Now, however, Kabnis acknowledges and confronts that conspiracy, no longer fearing it or Father John. Exhausted by his effort, Kabnis sinks back, but Halsey's sister, Carrie K, lifts him up, and together they ascend the stairs into the daylight, as the risen sun sings a "birth-song" down the streets of the town.

The end is not unequivocally optimistic: It is too small and too tentative a note in this large catalog of the defeated and destroyed. *Cane* does, however, suggest finally that as destructive as dreams may be, once one has seen beauty, if he can free himself from repression, from sin, he may re-create himself. "Kabnis is me," wrote Toomer to Waldo Frank, and he had more in mind than just his use of his experiences. What Toomer has done in *Cane* is to chart the varieties of damage that society has done to people and, more important, since individuals are always more interesting than society to Toomer, that people have done to themselves. Wholeness is the aim, a wholeness that breaks down barriers between mind and will, man and woman, object and subject, and that allows the potential of dreams to be fulfilled. That the wholeness is so difficult to achieve is the substance of Toomer's short fiction; that Toomer achieves it, both for a character in *Kabnis* and more permanently in his only successful work, a book uniting fiction and poetry, songs and narration, images of fire and water, of descent and ascent, is his testimony that wholeness can be achieved by those who dream of it.

"Blue Meridian"

Type of work: Poetry
First published: 1936

Too often, unfortunately, Toomer's later poetry drops the effective devices used in *Cane* and becomes didactic, explicitly philosophical, lacking *Cane*'s brilliantly realized images of concrete reality or its sharp, often startling metaphors. Toomer was mightily inspired by his few months in Georgia, and his sojourn even affected his interpretations of his own more familiar Washington and New York life; but after he had said what he had to say about the South, and the North in relation to the South, he seems to have exhausted his inspiration, except for his more "universal" themes, with only a little sense of poetry left, to be used in "Blue Meridian" and his stories "Winter on Earth" and "Withered Skin of Berries." The latter story returned

Toomer to the lyrical style and poetic sense of structure of the *Cane* stories, but for the most part, Toomer preferred to ignore stylistic and literary matters and chose to express his spiritual and philosophical beliefs, largely influenced by George Gurdjieff's teachings, urging a regeneration of humanity that would eliminate the differences imposed by racial and other categories and bring people closer to God, one another, and the natural world.

This is the point that Toomer makes explicitly in his last major work, the long poem "Blue Meridian," first published in full in *New American Caravan* (1936) after a selection from an earlier version had appeared in *Adelphi* and *Pagany*. A further revised version is printed in Langston Hughes and Arna Bontemps's anthology *The Poetry of the Negro, 1746-1949* (1949), which places more emphasis on God and more clearly reveals Toomer's notion of the transformed America. A few of the more minor revisions are for the better. This is the version published in *The Wayward and the Seeking*, with some incidental changes.

"Blue Meridian" follows a structure much like that of Walt Whitman's longer poems, such as "Passage to India" or "Crossing Brooklyn Ferry," with recurring phrases or stanzas, often significantly altered. While it is not divided into individual sections, as T. S. Eliot's *The Waste Land* (1922) and Stephen Crane's *The Bridge* (1930) are—nor does it use the range of poetic forms of which Eliot and Crane availed themselves—it nevertheless follows those poems in being an examination and criticism of the twentieth century world, achieving a multifaceted view by varying tone and form.

Written largely in a hortatory, exalted style in an effort to invoke Toomer's higher spiritual goals for a better world and unified humankind, "Blue Meridian" explores the past and current conditions of America. The European, African, and "red" races are presented in appropriate images—even stereotypes—each being shown as incomplete. Toomer's goal, as in much of his prose, is to achieve a new race beyond individual racial identities, a "universal human being" to be called the "blue meridian," the highest stage of development beyond white and black, beyond divisions of East and West, of religion, race, class, sex, and occupational classification, and transcending the materialism of a commercial culture and the private concerns of individuals. The message is not so different from that of Whitman, except for greater criticism of modern business and the insistence on the mingling of the races.

Suggested Readings

Benson, Joseph, and Mabel Mayle Dillard. *Jean Toomer*. Boston: Twayne, 1980.

Byrd, Rudolph. *Jean Toomer's Years with Gurdijieff: Portrait of an Artist, 1923-1936*. Athens: University of Georgia Press, 1990.

Fabre, Geneviève, and Michel Feith, eds. *Jean Toomer and the Harlem Renaissance*. New Brunswick, N.J.: Rutgers University Press, 2001.

Hajek, Friederike. "The Change of Literary Authority in the Harlem Renaissance: Jean Toomer's *Cane*." In *The Black Columbiad: Defining Moments in African American Literature and Culture*, edited by Werner Sollors and Maria Diedrich. Cambridge, Mass.: Harvard University Press, 1994.

Jones, Robert B. Introduction to *The Collected Poems of Jean Toomer*, edited by Robert B. Jones and Margery Toomer Latimer. Chapel Hill: University of North Carolina Press, 1988.

Kerman, Cynthia. *The Lives of Jean Toomer: A Hunger for Wholeness*. Baton Rouge: Louisiana State University Press, 1988.

Moore, Lewis D. "*Kabnis* and the Reality of Hope: Jean Toomer's *Cane*." *North Dakota Quarterly* 54 (Spring, 1986): 30-39.

Scruggs, Charles, and Lee VanDemarr. *Jean Toomer and the Terrors of American History*. Philadelphia: University of Pennsylvania Press, 1998.

Taylor, Paul Beekman. *Shadows of Heaven*. York Beach, Me.: S. Weiser, 1998.

Wagner-Martin, Linda. "Toomer's *Cane* as Narrative Sequence." In *Modern American Short Story Sequences*, edited by J. Gerald Kennedy. New York: Cambridge University Press, 1995.

Contributors: Howard Faulkner, Scott Giantvalley, and Earl Paulus Murphy

Luis Miguel Valdez

Born: Delano, California; June 26, 1940

Mexican American

A political activist, playwright, director, essayist, and founder of El Teatro Campesino, Valdez became the seminal figure in Chicano theater.

Principal works

DRAMA: *The Theft*, pr. 1961; *Las dos caras del patroncito*, pr. 1965, pb. 1971; *The Shrunken Head of Pancho Villa*, pr. 1965, pb. 1967; *La quinta temporada*, pr. 1966, pb. 1971; *Dark Root of a Scream*, pr. 1967, pb. 1973; *Los vendidos*, pr. 1967, pb. 1971; *La conquista de México*, pr. 1968, pb. 1971 (puppet play); *The Militants*, pr. 1969, pb. 1971; *No saco nada de la escuela*, pr. 1969, pb. 1971; *Bernabé*, pr. 1970, pb. 1976; *Huelguistas*, pr. 1970, pb. 1971; *Vietnam campesino*, pr. 1970, pb. 1971; *Actos*, pb. 1971 (includes *Las dos caras del patroncito*, *La quinta temporada*, *Los vendidos*, *La conquista de México*, *No saco nada de la escuela*, *The Militants*, *Vietnam campesino*, *Huelguistas*, and *Soldado razo*); *La Virgen del Tepeyac*, pr. 1971 (adaptation of *Las cuatro apariciones de la Virgen de Guadalupe*); *Las pastorelas*, pr. 1971 (adaptation of a sixteenth century Mexican shepherd's play); *Soldado razo*, pr., pb. 1971; *Los endrogados*, pr. 1972; *Los olivos pits*, pr. 1972; *El baille de los gigantes*, pr. 1973; *La gran carpa de los rasquachis*, pr. 1973; *Mundo*, pr. 1973; *El fin del mundo*, pr. 1975; *Zoot Suit*, pr. 1978, pb. 1992; *Bandido!*, pr. 1981, pb. 1992, revised pr. 1994; *Corridos*, pr. 1983; *"I Don't Have to Show You No Stinking Badges!"*, pr., pb. 1986; *Luis Valdez—Early Works: Actos, Bernabé, and Pensamiento Serpentino*, pb. 1990; *Zoot Suit, and Other Plays*, pb. 1992; *Mummified Deer*, pr. 2000

SCREENPLAYS: *Zoot Suit*, 1982 (adaptation of his play); *La Bamba*, 1987

TELEPLAYS: *Fort Figueroa*, 1988; *La Pastorela*, 1991; *The Cisco Kid*, 1994

EDITED TEXT: *Aztlan: An Anthology of Mexican American Literature*, 1972 (with Stan Steiner)

MISCELLANEOUS: *Pensamiento Serpentino: A Chicano Approach to the Theatre of Reality*, 1973

Luis Miguel Valdez (lwees mih-GEHL VAL-dehz), political activist, playwright, director, essayist, and founder of El Teatro Campesino, is the most prominent figure in modern Chicano theater. Born on June 26, 1940, to migrant farmworker parents, he was second in a family of ten brothers and sisters. In spite of working in the fields from the age of six, Valdez completed high school and received a scholarship to San Jose State College, where he developed his early interest in theater. *The Shrunken Head of Pancho Villa* was written while Valdez was a student there. After receiving a bachelor's degree in English and drama in 1964, he joined the San Francisco Mime Troupe, whose work was based on *commedia dell'arte* and the theater of Bertolt Brecht. These experiences heavily influenced Valdez's work, especially in terms of style and production.

A 1965 meeting with César Chávez, who was organizing migrant farmworkers in Delano, California, led to the formation of El Teatro Campesino, the cultural and propagandistic arm of the United Farm Workers (UFW) union. Valdez created short improvisational pieces, called *actos*, for the troupe. All the *actos* are characterized by the use of masks, stereotyped characters, farcical exaggeration, and improvisation. *Las dos caras del patroncito* (the two faces of the boss) and *La quinta temporada* (the fifth season) are *actos* from this early period that highlight the plight of the farmworkers and the benefits of unionization. Valdez left the union in 1967, bringing El Teatro Campesino with him to establish El Centro Campesino Cultural. He wanted to broaden the concerns of the troupe by fostering Chicanos' pride in their cultural heritage and by depicting their problems in the Anglo culture. *Los vendidos* (the sellouts), for example, satirizes Chicanos who attempt to assimilate into a white, racist society, and *La conquista de Mexico* (the conquest of Mexico) links the fall of the Aztecs with the internal dissension of Chicano activists. In 1968 El Teatro Campesino moved toward producing full-length plays, starting with Valdez's *The Shrunken Head of Pancho Villa*. Expressionistic in style, the play explores the conflict between two brothers—an assimilationist and a *pachuco*, a swaggering street kid—and the impact this extremism has on the tenuous fabric of a Chicano family. Recognition followed, with an Obie Award in New York in 1969 for "creating a workers' theater to demonstrate the politics of survival" and an invitation to perform at the Theatre des Nations festival in Nancy, France. Later in 1969, Valdez and the troupe moved to Fresno, California, where they founded an annual Chicano theater festival, and Valdez began teaching at Fresno State College.

Luis Miguel Valdez (Courtesy, UCLA Library/ Alice Greenfield McGrath Papers)

In 1971 Valdez moved his company permanently to the small town of San Juan Bautista in California. There, Teatro Campesino underwent a fundamental transformation, as the group began increasingly to emphasize the spiritual side of their work, as derived from prevalent Christian as well as newfound Aztec and Mayan roots. This shift from an agitational focus to a search for spiritual solutions was met with anger by formerly admiring audiences in Mexico City at the Quinto Festival de los Teatros Chicanos in 1974. The company continued to flourish, however, touring campuses and communities yearly and giving financial support and advice to other theater troupes.

Fame came with *Zoot Suit*, the first Chicano play to reach Broadway. Although its run was relatively brief, owing to negative criticism, the play was very popular on the West Coast and was made into a film in 1981, with Valdez both the director and the writer of the screenplay. During the 1980's, Valdez and El Teatro Campesino continued to tour at home and abroad, presenting works by Valdez and collectively scripted pieces that interpret the Chicano experience. The 1986 comedy *"I Don't Have to Show You No Stinking Badges!"* is about the political and existential implications of acting, both in theater and in society. In 1987 Valdez wrote the screenplay for the successful film *La Bamba*, the story of Ritchie Valens, a young Chicano pop singer who died in an airplane crash in the late 1950's. This work reached a large audience.

After a gap in playwriting of almost fifteen years, Valdez wrote *Mummified Deer*. This play reaffirms his status as the "father of Chicano drama" and continues his exploration of his heritage through the juxtaposition of ritual and realism. The play takes its inspiration from a newspaper article concerning the discovery of a sixty-year-old fetus in the body of an eighty-four-year old woman. According to scholar Jorge Huerta, the mummified fetus serves as a metaphor for "the Chicanos' Indio heritage, seen through the lens of his own Yaqui blood." The play's major dramatic action operates in the historical/fictional past.

Valdez's contributions to contemporary Chicano theater are extensive. Writing individually and with others, he has redefined the cultural forms of the barrio: the *acto*, a short comic piece intended to move the audience to political action; the *mito* (myth), which characteristically takes the form of an allegory based on Indian ritual, in an attempt to integrate political activism and religious ritual; and the *corrido*, a reinvention of the musical based on Mexican American folk ballads. He has placed the Chicano experience onstage in all of its political and cultural complexity, creating what no other American playwright has, a genuine workers' theater that has made serious drama popular, political drama entertaining, and ethnic drama universal.

Zoot Suit

Type of work: Drama
First produced: 1978, pb. 1992

The first Chicano play on Broadway, *Zoot Suit* grew out of California Chicano guerrilla theater, incorporating bilingual dialogue and ultimately alienating Mexican Americans. In it, Valdez questions the Los Angeles newspaper accounts of the Columbus Day "Zoot Suit" riots and the related Sleepy Lagoon murder trial (1942). The drama uses song, dance, and a unifying narrative based on the traditions of the Mexican *corrido* (a ballad form that often reflects on social issues).

A zoot-suiter "master of ceremonies" called Pachuco narrates the action, dispelling illusion, showing reality, and providing flashbacks that characterize the protagonist, Henry Reyna, who is vilified in the white media, as heroic. This defiant, existential street actor wears the colors of Testatipoka, the Aztec god of education.

Reyna, a loyal American about to ship out for the war in the Pacific, becomes a scapegoat for the Los Angeles police. When a minor scuffle with a rival gang interrupts his farewell celebration, he bravely steps in to break up a one-sided attack. Newsboys shouting inflammatory headlines and a lawyer predicting mass trials prepare viewers for legal farce. The prosecution twists testimony proving police misunderstandings and Henry's heroism to win an unjust conviction. White liberals distort the conviction of the zoot-suiter "gang" for personal ends, and even Pachuco is ultimately overpowered and stripped by servicemen. The play ends as it began: with the war over, the incarcerated scapegoats released, and police persecution renewed.

Leaving viewers with the choice of multiple possible endings, Valdez not only reflects the Mayan philosophy of multiple levels of existence but also offers alternate realities dependent on American willingness to accept or deny reality: a calm Henry and supportive family group united against false charges, Henry as victim of racist stereotypes reincarcerated and killed in a prison fight, Henry the born leader dying heroically in Korea and thereby winning a posthumous Congressional Medal of Honor, Henry a father with several children, Henry merged with El Pachuco, a living myth and symbol of Chicano heritage and Chicano oppression. Thus, Reyna the individual portrays Chicanos in crisis in general. The plays shows Chicanos undermined by a prejudiced press, racist police, and an unjust legal system that distorts facts and denies Chicanos their rights.

Suggested Readings

Broyles-Gonzales, Yolanda. *El Teatro Campesino: Theater in the Chicano Movement*. Austin: University of Texas Press, 1994.

Elam, Harry J., Jr. *Taking It to the Streets: The Social Protest Theatre of Luis Valdez and Amiri Baraka*. Ann Arbor: University of Michigan Press, 2001.

Flores, Arturo C. *El Teatro Campesino de Luis Valdez*. Madrid: Editorial Pliegos, 1990.

Huerta, Jorge A. *Chicano Theatre: Themes and Forms*. Ypsilanti, Mich.: Bilingual Press, 1982.

_______. "Labor Theatre, Street Theatre, and Community Theatre in the Barrio, 1965-1983." In *Hispanic Theatre in the United States*, edited by Nicolás Kanellos. Houston: Arte Público, 1984.

Kanellos, Nicolás. *Mexican American Theater: Legacy and Reality*. Pittsburgh: Latin American Literary Review Press, 1987.

Morales, Ed. "Shadowing Valdez." *American Theatre* 9 (November, 1992): 14-19.
Pottlitzer, Joanne. *Hispanic Theater in the United States and Puerto Rico: A Report to the Ford Foundation*. New York: Ford Foundation, 1988.
Valdez, Luis Miguel. "*Zoot Suit* and the Pachuco Phenomenon: An Interview with Luis Valdez." Interview by Roberta Orona-Cordova. In *Mexican American Theatre: Then and Now*, edited by Nicolás Kanellos. Houston: Arte Público, 1983.

Contributors: Lori Hall Burghardt and Gina Macdonald

José Antonio Villarreal

Born: Los Angeles, California; July 30, 1924

Mexican American

Villarreal is recognized as one of the first American writers of Mexican descent to portray the experiences of Mexican families who immigrated to the United States.

Principal works

LONG FICTION: *Pocho*, 1959; *The Fifth Horseman*, 1974; *Clemente Chacón*, 1984
SHORT FICTION: "The Last Minstrel in California" and "The Laughter of My Father" in *Iguana Dreams*, 1992

The early life of José Antonio Villarreal (hoh-ZAY ahn-TOH-nyoh vee-yah-ray-AL) strongly resembles that of Richard Rubio, the hero of his first novel. Both had fathers who fought in the Mexican Revolution; both were born and raised in California. Villarreal also enjoyed, in childhood innocence, the few pleasures of the nomadic life of the migrant farmworker: living in tents, listening to Spanish stories around a campfire, absorbing Mexican lore and culture that was invisible in the white world. Like Richard, Villarreal learned English quickly but retained his fluency in Spanish. Love of language and books led him to early discovery of his desire to become a writer. Circumstances took both into the Navy in World War II. Although *Pocho* appears autobiographical in many ways, it is sometimes criticized as unrealistic in its portrayal of Richard's conscious intention to be a writer and as inattentive to the racism and injustice of American society. Villarreal rejects such pronouncements by declaring himself an American writer, not a Chicano writer. To the creator of *Pocho*, Richard's ethnic and ideological identities are only part of a greater quest for his identity as a man, an artist, and a human being.

Villarreal graduated from the University of California at Berkeley, and since 1950 he has continued to write while supporting a family with a variety of jobs, including technical writer, magazine publisher, and teacher at a number of universities in California, Texas, and Mexico. During the Chicano movement of the 1970's, Villarreal published *The Fifth Horseman*, a novel that explores the Mexican Revolution sympathetically, suggesting its ideals are worthy of preservation in Mexican identity, although its excesses ought to be condemned.

Professional recognition and financial success have come hard to Villarreal, and perhaps as a result, the themes of work, money, and social mobility have become more dominant in his examination of the processes of acculturation. For example, *Clemente Chacón*, set in 1972, contrasts the life of the young insurance man

Clemente, who hustles desperately to succeed in American business and society, with the life of the adolescent Mario Carbajal, who hustles desperately simply to survive another day in Ciudad Juárez, Mexico. Exploitation of the poor and amoral ambition are qualities of both these characters and of their societies. Villarreal's creative focus on individual lives rather than on social institutions suggests that ultimately each person's choice is the origin of good or the origin of evil.

Pocho

Type of work: Novel
First published: 1959

Pocho is generally regarded as the first novel by an American of Mexican descent to represent the experiences of emigration from Mexico and acculturation to the United States. Although this pioneering work went out of print shortly after publication, a second edition appeared in 1970 during the Chicano Renaissance, and it has since become part of many multicultural literature classes. Set in the years between 1923 and 1942, the novel recounts the quest for personal and cultural identity by Richard Rubio, son of a soldier exiled after the Mexican Revolution and now a migrant farmworker in Santa Clara, California. As a *pocho*, a member of the first generation born in the United States, Richard grows up deeply attached to the traditions of his family and very attracted to the values and lifestyles of his American peers.

In addition to trials faced by every young person while growing up, such as the struggle with authority, the search for independence, the thirst for knowledge, and the hunger for sexual experience, Richard faces special challenges in self-definition. He confronts poverty, family instability, a blighted education system, racial prejudice, a society torn by economic crises, and world war.

Richard's passage from childhood into adulthood is given unique shape not only by the circumstances of the Depression but also by the turmoil of life as an itinerant farmworker and the powerful tensions between Mexican and American cultures. Poverty inspires his dreams of success. A life of physical labor belies his intellectual nature. He identifies intensely with his macho father but cannot abide his violence, coldness, and self-destructiveness. Drawn to the beauties of the church, he nonetheless rejects faith. He is deeply attached to his mother but finds her helplessness repugnant. Obliged to become the man of the family as a teenager, he finds that his responsibilities clash with his solitary nature, his love of books, and his emerging personal identity as a writer. His choice to join the Navy is more personal than patriotic. To resolve his conflicts he chooses exile from his shattered family, escapes from his poverty without prospects, and seeks release from the fragments of the two cultures he has not yet pieced together. He leaves to face what he knows will be a struggle for a new identity as a man, as an artist, and as an American.

Suggested Readings

Alarcón, Daniel Cooper. *The Aztec Palimpsest: Mexico in the Modern Imagination*. Tucson: University of Arizona Press, 1997.

Bruce-Novoa, Juan. *Chicano Authors: Inquiry by Interview*. Austin: University of Texas Press, 1980.

Leal, Luis. "*The Fifth Horseman* and Its Literary Antecedents." Introduction to *The Fifth Horseman*. Garden City, N.Y.: Doubleday, 1974.

Saldívar, Ramón. *Chicano Narrative*. Madison: University of Wisconsin Press, 1990.

Contributor: Virginia M. Crane

Victor Villaseñor

Born: Carlsbad, California; May 11, 1940

Mexican American

Villaseñor is one of the significant chroniclers of the Mexican American experience, his novel Macho! *was one of the first Chicano novels issued by a mainstream publisher.*

Principal works

CHILDREN'S LITERATURE: *Mother Fox and Mr. Coyote*, 2004; *The Frog and his Friends Save Humanity*, 2005; *Little Crow to the Rescue*, 2005; *Goodnight, Papito Dios*, 2007

LONG FICTION: *Macho!*, 1973

SCREENPLAY: *The Ballad of Gregorio Cortez*, 1982

SHORT FICTION: *Walking Stars: Stories of Magic and Power*, 1994

NONFICTION: *Jury: The People vs. Juan Corona*, 1977; *Rain of Gold*, 1991; *Wild Steps of Heaven*, 1996; *Thirteen Senses: A Memoir*, 2001; *Burro Genius: A Memoir*, 2004; *Crazy Loco Love: A Memoir*, 2006

Victor Edmundo Villaseñor (VEE-tohr ehd-MEWN-doh VEE-yah-sehn-YOHR) is one of the significant chroniclers of the Mexican American experience; his novel *Macho!* was, along with Richard Vásquez's 1970 novel *Chicano*, one of the first Chicano novels issued by a mainstream publisher. Villaseñor was born to Mexican immigrant parents in Carlsbad, California. His parents, Lupe Gomez and Juan Salvador Villaseñor, who had immigrated with their families when young, were middle class, and Victor and his four siblings were brought up on their ranch in Oceanside. Villaseñor struggled with school from his very first day, being dyslexic and having spoken Spanish rather than English at home. He dropped out of high school, feeling that he would "go crazy" if he did not, and went to work on his parents' ranch. He briefly attended college at the University of San Diego, where he discovered that reading books could be something other than drudgery, but left college after flunking most of his courses. He became a boxer for a brief period, then went to Mexico, where he suddenly became aware of Mexican art, literature, and history. He began to be proud of his heritage, rather than confused and ashamed, meeting Mexican doctors and lawyers—"heroes," he says—for the first time. He read extensively.

Returning to California at his parents' insistence, Villaseñor worked in construction beginning in 1965 and painstakingly taught himself how to write. James Joyce's *A Portrait of the Artist as a Young Man* (1916) was particularly inspirational. He wrote extensively, producing many novels and short stories. They were steadily rejected until Bantam Books decided to take a chance and publish *Macho!* in 1973. The novel's protagonist is a young man named Roberto García, and the novel covers roughly a year in his life, first in his home village in Mexico, then in California, then in Mexico again. Somewhat unwillingly, Roberto journeys northward with a group of *norteños* from his village to earn money working in the fields of California. Roberto's personification of—and finally, inability to fully accept—the traditional social code of machismo; his conflicts with others, notably fellow *norteño* Pedro; and the larger labor struggle between migrant workers and landowners in California provide the central action of the book. *Macho!* received favorable reviews. The year of its initial publication Villaseñor married Barbara Bloch, the daughter of his editor; they have two sons, David and Joe. Villaseñor built a house on his parents' property, and as his sons grew older he enjoyed horseback riding with them.

Villaseñor's second major published work was nonfiction. *Jury: The People vs. Juan Corona* details the trial of a serial killer. Villaseñor had read about the case after *Macho!* had been accepted for publication, and it captured his interest—Corona had been arrested for murdering twenty-five derelicts. Villaseñor extensively interviewed the members of the jury that convicted Corona and thoroughly examined the complex and controversial trial. (The jury had deliberated for eight grueling days before reaching a verdict.) After the book's publication, he received some criticism for his interpretations of the events.

Villaseñor subsequently wrote the screenplay for *The Ballad of Gregorio Cortez*, based partly on writer Américo Paredes's account of the adventures of Cortez, a real-life figure, eluding the Texas Rangers around 1900. Villaseñor tells the story using multiple points of view, effectively relating the story of a man driven by circumstances into the life of a bandit while showing the prejudices and racism of the times. Written for television, the film won an award from the National Endowment for the Humanities; it was also released to theaters.

Rain of Gold, published in 1991 after more than ten years of research and writing, is the multigenerational story of Villaseñor's family. The book was almost published two years earlier by G. P. Putnam's, but Villaseñor became unhappy with the company at the last minute for insisting that the book be called "Rio Grande" ("a John Wayne movie," he scoffed) and wanting to cut its length and call it fiction in order to boost sales. The company agreed to let him buy back his book, for which Villaseñor remortgaged his home. Published in its original form and with the original title (a translation of La Lluvia de Oro, his mother's birthplace in Mexico) by Arte Público, it was well received and was widely considered Villaseñor's masterwork.

Wild Steps of Heaven recounts the history of Villaseñor's father's family in the highlands of Jalisco, Mexico, before the events covered in *Rain of Gold*; Villaseñor considered it part two of a "Rain of Gold" trilogy, and he planned to follow it with the story of his mother's family. He draws on stories told by his father and members of his extended family, relating them in a folkloric style that sometimes verges on Magical Realism. *Walking Stars: Stories of Magic and Power*, published two years before *Wild Steps of Heaven*, consists of stories for young readers that attempt both to entertain and to inspire; each of the stories, most based on events in the early lives of his parents, concludes with notes in which the author discusses the stories' meanings, emphasizing the spiritual magic that people's lives embody.

Macho!

Type of work: Novel
First published: 1973

The protagonist of *Macho!* is Roberto, a young Mexican who immigrates illegally into the United States. Victor Villaseñor suggests that Roberto extracts his identity from the soil of the fields that he works. On the first and last pages of the book, Villaseñor describes how volcanic ash has enriched the soil of a Mexican valley. At the end of the novel, Roberto has returned to this valley to work the land, applying what he has learned in the United States.

These homages to volcanic ash suggest that soil is not just the earth's outer covering but also its soul. Likewise, the soil is the soul of the people who work it. The novel refers to the Mexican Revolution, a popular movement to redistribute the ownership of land, to say that land is fundamental to understanding not only the Mexican people but also the country's politics and history.

According to Villaseñor, Mexico's geography dictates the country's indigenous law. Mexico is mountainous, so villages are isolated. As a result of their isolation, these villages developed their own systems of justice and never appeal to a higher authority. This law of the land is a violent code of honor, and the novel documents how this code places a premium on a woman's virginity and on a man's ability to fight. The definition of "macho" must necessarily emanate from an understanding of this law of the land.

The novel makes frequent references to César Chávez's movement in the 1960's to unionize agricultural workers in the United States. Villaseñor offers a complex portrait of Chávez, not allowing him to become a cardboard cutout representative of Mexicans who identify themselves with the soil. Chávez's movement distinguishes between the illegal Mexican immigrants, whom Chávez wanted deported, and the Mexican Americans, whose rights he sought to protect through unionization.

Villaseñor concludes that Chávez is a "true-self hero," one who is not labeled readily as macho, but who trusts his own conscience and is not afraid to have enemies. In this respect, Chávez is like Abraham Lincoln, Benito Juárez, John F. Kennedy, and Martin Luther King, Jr. On the novel's final page, Villaseñor qualifies Roberto also as a true-self hero when the protagonist returns to his native valley to work the fields.

Rain of Gold

Type of work: Family history
First published: 1991

Villaseñor insists that *Rain of Gold* is a work of nonfiction. So insistent is he on this point, in fact, that he reportedly bought back the rights to his book from Putnam's when he determined he could not allow the 550-page work he viewed as memoir to be marketed as a novel. Putnam's had paid Villaseñor $75,000 for the rights, and the work had been selected as a Book-of-the-Month Club alternate.

Regardless of its classification, *Rain of Gold* reads like a novel. It begins in the days before the turbulence of the Mexican Revolution and continues through life after migration to the United States in the early twentieth century, and it is told with some dramatic fictionalization. It starts with the parallel stories of Lupe and Juan Salvador—the author's parents—beginning in 1911 when they are children living in separate places in Revolution-torn Mexico, relating their respective families' journey north to the land of opportunity that is California, and ending with their marriage in 1929. These are chatty family stories of Salvador's days as a maker and seller of bootleg whiskey and tales of good Mexican people's struggles to overcome the prejudice and exploitation that they face at every turn. Some of the stories here are fantastic, employing the Magical Realism that is a hallmark of Latin American fiction: In one instance, a steer is knocked unconscious and skinned for its valuable hide before it is forced to its feet and made to run up the side of a mountain.

Rain of Gold relates much about Mexican history and about anti-Hispanic prejudice in the American Southwest. These are stories told by a man who is a natural storyteller, one who clearly admires and loves his family and his people and who writes with great passion. It was dubbed the "Chicano *Roots*" by those who compared it with Alex Haley's story of his African American family's history. In an appended author's note of half a dozen pages, the author sketches the next sixty-one years of the Villaseñor family chronicles. Indeed, Villaseñor saw the book as the second installment in his family chronicle, between *Macho!* and *Wild Steps of Heaven*.

Suggested Readings

Barbato, Joseph. "Latino Writers in the American Market." *Publishers Weekly*, February 1, 1991, pp. 17-21.

Guilbault, Rose Del Castillo. "Americanization Is Tough on 'Macho.'" In *American Voices: Multicultural Literacy and Critical Thinking*, edited by Dolores Laguardia and Hans P. Guth. Mountain View, Calif.: Mayfield, 1992.

Kelsey, Verlene. "Mining for a Usable Past: Acts of Recovery, Resistence, and Continuity in Victor Villaseñor's *Rain of Gold*." *Bilingual Review* 18 (January-April, 1993): 79-85.

Tatum, Charles M. *Chicano Literature*. Boston: Twayne, 1982.

Contributors: McCrea Adams and Douglas Edward LaPrade

Helena María Viramontes

Born: East Los Angeles, California; February 26, 1954

Mexican American

Viramontes's feminist portrayals of Latinas struggling against patriarchy and poverty condemn classism, racism, and sexism.

Principal works

LONG FICTION: *Under the Feet of Jesus*, 1995; *Their Dogs Came with Them*, 2000
SHORT FICTION: *The Moths, and Other Stories*, 1985; "Miss Clairol," 1987; "Tears on My Pillow," 1992; "The Jumping Bean," 1993
NONFICTION: "Nopalitos: The Making of Fiction," 1989; "Why I Write," 1995
EDITED TEXTS: *Chicana Creativity and Criticism: Charting New Frontiers in American Literature*, 1987, revised 1996 (with María Herrera-Sobek); *Chicana (W)rites: On Word and Film*, 1995 (with Herrera-Sobek)

The work of Helena María Viramontes (HEH-leh-nah mah-REE-ah vee-rah-MAWN-tehs) is shaped by her feminist and Chicano identities. Viramontes presents realistic portrayals of the struggles that women, particularly Chicanas, face as they attempt to grow up, raise families, and discover their identities. As a child, Viramontes attended schools in East Los Angeles with Chicano student bodies. Her parents were hardworking people—her father was a construction worker and her mother raised nine children.

Viramontes attended Immaculate Heart College with a scholarship for underprivileged girls and graduated in 1975. After graduating she began to send her short stories out for publication, and in 1977 one of her first stories, "Requiem for the Poor," won first prize for fiction in a literary contest sponsored by *Statement* magazine of California State University, Los Angeles. Viramontes's work continued winning awards, and in 1981 she enrolled in the creative writing program at the University of California at Irvine. Her first collection of short stories, *The Moths, and Other Stories*, was published in 1985. Perhaps one of Viramontes's greatest achievements was receiving a National Endowment for the Arts Fellowship in 1989 to attend a workshop given by Gabriel García Márquez at the Sundance Institute.

Viramontes's work has been highly influenced by García Márquez, by Chicana feminist writers Ana Castillo and Sandra Cisneros, and by such black writers as Alice Walker, Ntozake Shange, and Toni Morrison. In *The Moths, and Other Stories*, Viramontes offers her reader portrayals of women at various stages in their lives. These women face complex issues such as adolescence, sexuality, politics, family, aging, and religion and must attempt to navigate their way through problems that are often caused by the patriarchal constructs of their cultures.

The Moths, and Other Stories

Type of work: Short fiction
First published: 1985

The Moths, and Other Stories focuses on the lives of Chicana women of various ages and backgrounds. The women in Viramontes's stories often face identity crises—they struggle with religion, adolescence, sexuality, family, and aging.

"The Moths" narrates the growth of a fourteen-year-old girl who cares for her grandmother. The grandmother's home is a refuge for the young woman, whose home is ruled by her father. When her grandmother dies, the girl laments the loss of a strong female figure who has helped shape her identity. "Growing" also focuses on a young Chicana woman who struggles with adolescence. Fifteen-year-old Naomi looks forward to her first date until her parents make her take along her little sister Lucia as a chaperone. Naomi insists that dating is "different" in America, but her parents insist on their own customs and Naomi wonders about the difficulties of growing up in a new country.

In the stories focusing on young women Viramontes raises the issues of religion, reproduction, and marriage. In "Birthday" a young, unmarried woman struggles over her decision to abort a child. "The Broken Web" focuses on a young woman and her struggles with repressed family memories. Martita learns that her father, Tomas, beat and cheated on her mother, and that her mother finally snapped and killed Tomas. "The Broken Web" shows a young woman dealing with the violence of her childhood. In "The Long Reconciliation" Amanda and Chato's marriage falls apart when Amanda refuses to bring children into their meager existence. After Amanda aborts their first child, Chato refuses all sexual contact with her and their marriage ends. "The Cariboo Cafe" focuses on the struggles of a young mother. Two children are kidnapped by a woman who has lost her own child in the political problems in Central America. Eventually the woman is discovered, and the children are taken away from her. She screams for her own son, Geraldo.

The final two stories focus on older women. In "Snapshots" Olga Ruiz, a middle-aged divorcé, attempts to come to terms with her past identities. As she sifts through family photographs, she realizes how little she has left of herself—she was too busy being a good wife and mother. "Neighbors" focuses on a lonely, elderly woman. Aura has nothing but her beautiful garden and her neighbor, Fierro. When a strange woman visits Fierro, Aura is upset by the change in their relationship. In her struggles with loneliness, Aura becomes fearful, and "Neighbors" examines the loneliness, isolation, and fear of being an old, solitary woman.

Women's issues are Viramontes's focus throughout the collection, and her narratives focusing on the struggles of primarily Chicana women are tinged with the complexities of adolescence, sexuality, marriage, poverty, and family.

Under the Feet of Jesus

Type of work: Novel
First published: 1995

Under the Feet of Jesus traces the day-to-day lives of a group of Chicano migrant farmworkers, revealing the struggles they must endure as they attempt to survive on low wages and in poor living conditions. Viramontes dedicated her book to her parents, who had endured similar hardships, and to the memory of César Chávez, a man who fought for the rights of farmworkers.

The narrative focuses on a large family headed by Perfecto Flores, a man in his seventies, and Petra, a woman who is thirty-seven years younger. Perfecto and Petra travel together with Petra's children, finding fieldwork wherever they can. Estrella is Petra's eldest daughter; she is thirteen, and her voice controls much of the narrative. There are two brothers, Ricky and Arnulfo, and twin girls, Perla and Cookie. Estrella works in the fields, as do her brothers and Perfecto.

The story becomes complicated by a young man named Alejo. Alejo and his cousin Gumecindo are also migratory workers employed by the same farms as Estrella and her family. The boys earn extra money by stealing fruit from the orchards at night. One night when they are raiding the orchard, biplanes fly overhead, spraying pesticides. Although Alejo and Gumecindo attempt to run from the orchards to avoid the poisoning pesticides, Alejo is sprayed and eventually becomes very sick. Since Alejo has become friends with Estrella and her family, Petra feels obliged to care for him. She tries all her healing methods, but nothing seems to work. Alejo gets sicker each day. As he grows weaker, love between Alejo and Estrella grows.

Finally Estrella and her family have no choice but to take Alejo to the clinic. The nurse tells Estrella that Alejo must go to the hospital, and charges them ten dollars for the clinic visit. Unfortunately Perfecto only has eight dollars and some change, and their gas tank is empty. He attempts to barter with the nurse, telling her he can do chores for the clinic, but she insists that she cannot give him work. Perfecto reluctantly hands over their last nine dollars, and they leave the clinic, wondering what they are going to do. Finally Estrella goes to the car, takes out the tire iron, and walks back into the clinic. She smashes the tire iron against the nurse's desk and demands the nine dollars back. With the last of their money Perfecto fills the gas tank, and they drive to the hospital. Estrella takes Alejo into the emergency room and is forced to leave him there, knowing they cannot pay the bill but that the doctors will help him.

Suggested Readings

Carbonell, Ana Maria. "From Llarona to Gritona: Coatlicue in Feminist Tales by Viramontes and Cisneros." *MELUS* 24 (Summer, 1999): 53-74.

Green, Carol Hurd, and Mary Grimley Mason. *American Women Writers*. New York: Continuum, 1994, 463-465.

Moore, Deborah Owen. "La Llarona Dines at the Cariboo Cafe: Structure and Legend in the Works of Helena María Viramontes." *Studies in Short Fiction* 35 (Summer, 1998): 277-286.
Richards, Judith. "Chicano Creativity and Criticism: New Frontiers in American Literature." *College Literature* 25 (Spring, 1998): 182.
Saldivar-Hull, Sonia. "Helena María Viramontes." *Dictionary of Literary Biography*. Detroit: Gale Research, 1992.
Swyt, Wendy. "Hungry Women: Borderlands Mythos in Two Stories by Helena María Viramontes." *MELUS* 23 (Summer, 1998): 189-201.
Yarbo-Bejarano, Yvonne. *Introduction to "The Moths, and Other Stories."* Houston, Tex.: Arte Público, 1995.

Contributor: Angela Athy

Gerald R. Vizenor

BORN: Minneapolis, Minnesota; October 22, 1934

NATIVE AMERICAN

Tribal people and tribal identity are the foci of Vizenor's life and literary work.

PRINCIPAL WORKS

LONG FICTION: *Darkness in Saint Louis Bearheart*, 1978, revised 1990 (as *Bearheart: The Heirship Chronicles*); *Griever: An American Monkey King in China*, 1987; *The Trickster of Liberty: Tribal Heirs to a Wild Baronage*, 1988; *The Heirs of Columbus*, 1991; *Dead Voices: Natural Agonies in the New World*, 1992; *Chancers*, 2000; *Hiroshima Bugi: Atomu 57*, 2003

POETRY: *Matsushima: Pine Islands*, 1984 (originally pb. as four separate volumes of haiku during the 1960's); *Almost Ashore: Selected Poems*, 2006; *Bear Island: The War at Sugar Point*, 2006

SCREENPLAY: *Harold of Orange*, 1984;

SHORT FICTION: *Anishinabe Adisokan: Stories of the Ojibwa*, 1974; *Wordarrows: Indians and Whites in the New Fur Trade*, 1978; *Earthdivers: Tribal Narratives on Mixed Descent*, 1981; *Landfill Meditation: Crossblood Stories*, 1991; *Wordarrows: Native States of Literary Sovereignty*, 2003 (originally pb. as *Wordarrows: Indians and Whites in the New Fur Trade*)

NONFICTION: *Thomas James White Hawk*, 1968; *The Everlasting Sky: New Voices from the People Named the Chippewa*, 1972; *Tribal Scenes and Ceremonies*, 1976; *Crossbloods: Bone Courts, Bingo, and Other Reports*, 1990; *Interior Landscapes: Autobiographical Myths and Metaphors*, 1990; *Manifest Manners: Postindian Warriors of Survivance*, 1994; *Fugitive Poses: Native American Indian Scenes of Absence and Presence*, 1998; *Postindian Conversations*, 1999

EDITED TEXTS: *Summer in the Spring: Ojibwe Lyric Poems and Tribal Stories*, 1981 (revised as *Summer in the Spring: Anishinaabe Lyric Poems and Stories*, 1993); *Native American Perspectives on Literature and History*, 1992 (with Alan R. Velie); *Narrative Chance: Postmodern Discourse on Native American Indian Literatures*, 1993; *Native American Literature: A Brief Introduction and Anthology*, 1995

MISCELLANEOUS: *The People Named the Chippewa: Narrative Histories*, 1984; *Shadow Distance: A Gerald Vizenor Reader*, 1994

An original voice in postmodern literature, Native American author Gerald Vizenor (VIHZ-nuhr) is a brilliant novelist, poet, and essayist, as well as an influential critic. He has received the Josephine Miles PEN award for *Interior Landscapes*, 1990, the Illinois State University/Fiction Collective Prize, 1986, and the American Book Award in 1988 for *Griever: An American Monkey King in China*.

Vizenor believes that Native American imagination foreshadows many common postmodern literary strategies regarding identity. He uses the concept of "survivance" to denote the trickster's playful attitude, which undercuts domination-victimization oppositions and produces new worldviews. The trickster uses stories and humor to tease out contradictions between good and evil in the world. *The Heirs of Columbus* uses trickster storytelling to revise the history of relations between whites and tribal peoples. Always on the move, the trickster destabilizes "pure" identities. Tribal identities pass through tribal stories.

Vizenor, who claims a mixed Native American and European American heritage, belongs to the first generation of his family born off the reservation. When he was a child, his father was murdered, and his mother left him with foster families. At eighteen, he enlisted in the Army and went to Japan. In *Interior Landscapes*, Vizenor describes his discovery of Japanese haiku as a liberating, eye-opening experience important to his development as a writer.

Besides being a writer, Vizenor worked as a social worker, a mental hospital orderly, a camp counselor, and a reporter for the *Minneapolis Tribune*, where he was a staunch advocate for human rights. He established the American Indian Employment Center in Minneapolis and directed the first Native American studies program at Bemidji State University.

Wordarrows

Type of work: Short fiction
First published: 1978

Wordarrows: Indians and Whites in the New Fur Trade is Vizenor's collection of autobiographical short stories. It stems from Kiowa novelist N. Scott Momaday's belief that storytelling is a means of situating oneself in a particular context in order to better understand individual and collective experiences. Vizenor's stories recount cultural "word wars" in which Native Americans cannot afford to be victims in "one-act terminal scenarios," but must become survivors, relying on their own words to preserve their sacred memories and represent the bitter facts. In *Wordarrows*, the trickster, a figure from Native American oral traditions, who appears in most of Vizenor's writing, uses stories and humor to balance the forces of good and evil in the world.

Wordarrows describes the reality of urban Indians, who are denied services and shuttled between various government programs. Vizenor's persona, Clement Beaulieu, directs the American Indian Employment and Guidance Center in Minneapolis, where he is caught between politicians who want to restrict his radical activities and desperate Indians who need his help. At the center, Beaulieu encounters Marleen American Horse, who has been stereotyped as a drunken Indian. He helps

Gerald Vizenor

her free herself from "the language of white people" so that she can create her own identity. He also meets Laurel Hole In The Day, a woman who struggles to move her family to a white neighborhood in the city. Ultimately, loneliness makes the parents turn to drink, lose their jobs, and return to the reservation.

In another story, Beaulieu and a friend visit an Indian boarding school, where the superintendent makes a boy perform a simulated tribal dance to the music of the Lord's Prayer. Outraged by the administrator's idiotic attempt to teach the child racial pride, Beaulieu fumes that white corruption of this dance makes the Indian a spectacle and erases his tribal identity.

The last section of *Wordarrows* contains four stories centering on the case of Thomas James White Hawk, a death-row inmate in South Dakota. As a staff writer for the *Minneapolis Tribune*, Vizenor covered White Hawk's hearing to commute his death sentence to life in prison. Beaulieu blames society for creating the conditions that drove White Hawk to commit his crime and argues that "a man cannot be condemned by an institution of that dominant culture which has actually led to the problems he has to live with." The "cultural schizophrenia" experienced by Beaulieu and other characters in *Wordarrows* represents the dilemma of many contemporary Native Americans.

Interior Landscapes

Type of work: Autobiography
First published: 1990

Mixed-blood Native American novelist, poet, essayist, and critic Vizenor's imaginative autobiography *Interior Landscapes: Autobiographical Myths and Metaphors*, winner of the 1990 Josephine Miles PEN Award, recounts the author's triumphs, tragedies, and confrontations with racism. Throughout his autobiography, Vizenor adopts the mythic identity of the Native American trickster, who uses humor and stories to reinvent his world. "My stories are interior landscapes," Vizenor writes, and, as trickster autobiography, these stories about Vizenor's life enable him to mold his experience of his own life.

Vizenor had a rough childhood by any standard. After his father was stabbed to death, his mother left him with foster families while she vanished for years at a time. Later, she returned and married an alcoholic who beat him. When he was eighteen, Vizenor escaped into the Army. In the Army, Vizenor traveled to Japan, one of the most important experiences of his life. Views of Mount Fuji, a romance with a Japanese woman, and his first visit to a brothel inspired him to write haiku. After his discharge from the Army, Vizenor stayed in Japan. He later returned to the United States to study at New York University and the University of Minnesota, where he discovered writers such as Lafcadio Hearn, Jack London, and Thomas Wolfe. He also studied haiku in translation. Vizenor calls his discovery of Japanese literature his "second liberation." His haikus won for him his first college teaching job, and his continuing fascination with the haiku form is demonstrated in the collections *Two Wings the Butterfly* (1962), *Raising the Moon Vines* (1964), *Seventeen Chirps* (1964), *Empty Swings* (1967), and *Matsushima: Pine Islands* (1984).

Vizenor relates his experience as a community activist. As a *Minneapolis Tribune* reporter Vizenor organized civil rights protests and exposed illegal domestic operations by the Central Intelligence Agency. He wrote key articles about the funeral of Dane Michael White and the trial of Thomas James White Hawk. As a founding director of the American Indian Employment and Guidance Center, he combated the "new urban fur traders" and worked to get services for urban Indians who chose to leave the reservation.

Interior Landscapes ends in a haunted house in Santa Fe, New Mexico, where Vizenor's dreams are invaded by skinwalkers, lost souls from the world of the dead. This dream begins a meditation on the rights of remains that informs Vizenor's writing of his autobiography, a "crossblood remembrance," motivated by a trickster's desire to weave the myths and metaphors of his own life.

The Heirs of Columbus

Type of work: Novel
First published: 1991

Published shortly before the quincentennial of Christopher Columbus's 1492 voyage, Vizenor's *The Heirs of Columbus* proclaims, "I am not a victim of Columbus!" The novel tells of the nine tribal descendants of Christopher Columbus, including Stone Columbus, a late-night talk radio personality, and Felipa Flowers, a "liberator" of cultural artifacts. For the heirs, tribal identity rests in tribal stories, and they are consummate storytellers. "We are created in stories," the heirs say, and "language is our trick of discovery." Their trickster storytelling rewrites and renews the history of white and tribal peoples. Stone tells a story, central to the novel, asserting Columbus's Mayan, not Italian, ancestry. The Mayans brought their civilization to the Old World savages long ago, Stone argues. Columbus escaped Europe's "culture of death" and brought his "tribal genes" back to his homeland in the New World. Columbus did not discover the New World; he returned to it.

For some readers, *The Heirs of Columbus* might recall African American novelist Ishmael Reed's *Mumbo Jumbo* (1972). Both works have a fragmented style and are concerned with the theft and repatriation of tribal property. Felipa Flowers undertakes a mission to recapture sacred medicine pouches and the remains of her ancestor Christopher Columbus from the Brotherhood of American Explorers. After Felipa's successful raid, the heirs are taken to court to tell their story. They win their court case, but Felipa is later kidnapped and murdered in London when she tries to recapture the remains of Pocahontas.

After Felipa's death, the heirs create a sovereign nation at Point Assinika, "the wild estate of tribal memories and the genes of survivance in the New World." Theirs is a natural nation, where tricksters heal with their stories and where humor rules. Stone plans "to make the world tribal, a universal identity" dedicated to healing, not stealing, tribal cultures. To this end, the heirs gather genetic material from their tribal ancestors. They devise genetic therapies that use these healing genes to combat the destructive war herbs, which have the power to erase people from memory and history. Soon, Point Assinika becomes a place to heal abandoned and abused children with the humor of their ancestors.

Stories and genes in *The Heirs of Columbus* operate according to trickster logic, which subverts the "terminal creeds" of cultural domination and signals the reinvention of the world.

Suggested Readings

Barry, Nora Baker. "Postmodern Bears in the Texts of Gerald Vizenor." *MELUS* 27 (Fall, 2002): 93-112.

Blaeser, Kimberly. *Gerald Vizenor: Writing in the Oral Tradition*. Norman: University of Oklahoma Press, 1996.

Coltelli, Laura, ed. *Winged Words: American Indian Writers Speak*. Lincoln: University of Nebraska Press, 1990.

Isernhagen, Hartwig. *Momaday, Vizenor, Armstrong: Conversations on American Indian Writing*. Norman: University of Oklahoma Press, 1999.

Lee, A. Robert, ed. *Loosening the Streams: Interpretations of Gerald Vizenor*. Bowling Green, Ohio: Bowling Green State University Popular Press, 2000.

Monsma, Bradley John. "'Active Readers . . . Obverse Tricksters': Trickster-Texts and Cross-Cultural Reading." *Modern Language Studies* 26 (Fall, 1996): 83-98.

Owens, Louis, ed. *Studies in American Indian Literatures: The Journal of the Association for the Study of American Indian Literatures* 9 (Spring, 1997).

Vizenor, Gerald. "'I Defy Analysis': A Conversation with Gerald Vizenor." Interview by Rodney Simard, Lavonne Mason, and Ju Abner. *Studies in American Indian Literatures: The Journal of the Association for the Study of American Indian Literatures* 5 (Fall, 1993): 42-51.

_______. "Mythic Rage and Laughter: An Interview with Gerald Vizenor." Interview by Dallas Miller. *Studies in American Indian Literatures: The Journal of the Association for the Study of American Indian Literatures* 7 (Spring, 1995): 77-96.

_______. "On Thin Ice, You Might as Well Dance: An Interview with Gerald Vizenor." Interview by Larry McCaffery and Tom Marshall. *Some Other Fluency: Interviews with Innovative American Authors*. Philadelphia: University of Pennsylvania Press, 1996.

Contributor: Trey Strecker

Alice Walker

BORN: Eatonton, Georgia; February 9, 1944

AFRICAN AMERICAN, NATIVE AMERICAN

Walker's poetry, short stories, essays, and novels protest racism, sexism, and mistreatment of the earth while offering affirmation and hope.

PRINCIPAL WORKS

CHILDREN'S LITERATURE: *Langston Hughes: American Poet*, 1974; *To Hell with Dying*, 1988; *Finding the Green Stone*, 1991; *There Is a Flower at the Tip of My Nose Smelling Me*, 2006; *Why War Is Never a Good Idea*, 2007

LONG FICTION: *The Third Life of Grange Copeland*, 1970; *Meridian*, 1976; *The Color Purple*, 1982; *The Temple of My Familiar*, 1989; *Possessing the Secret of Joy*, 1992; *By the Light of My Father's Smile*, 1998; *Now Is the Time to Open Your Heart*, 2004

POETRY: *Once: Poems*, 1968; *Five Poems*, 1972; *Revolutionary Petunias, and Other Poems*, 1973; *Goodnight, Willie Lee, I'll See You in the Morning: Poems*, 1979; *Horses Make a Landscape Look More Beautiful*, 1984; *Her Blue Body Everything We Know: Earthling Poems, 1965-1990, Complete*, 1991; *Absolute Trust in the Goodness of the Earth: New Poems*, 2003; *A Poem Traveled Down My Arm*, 2003

SHORT FICTION: *In Love and Trouble: Stories of Black Women*, 1973; *You Can't Keep a Good Woman Down*, 1981; *The Complete Stories*, 1994; *Alice Walker Banned*, 1996 (stories and commentary)

NONFICTION: *In Search of Our Mothers' Gardens: Womanist Prose*, 1983; *Living by the Word: Selected Writings, 1973-1987*, 1988; *Warrior Marks: Female Genital Mutilation and the Sexual Blinding of Women*, 1993 (with Pratibha Parmar); *The Same River Twice: Honoring the Difficult*, 1996; *Anything We Love Can Be Saved: A Writer's Activism*, 1997; *The Way Forward Is with a Broken Heart*, 2000; *Sent by Earth: A Message from the Grandmother Spirit After the Attacks on the World Trade Center and Pentagon*, 2001; *We Are the Ones We Have Been Waiting For: Light in a Time of Darkness*, 2006

EDITED TEXT: *I Love Myself When I Am Laughing . . . and Then Again When I Am Looking Mean and Impressive: A Zora Neale Hurston Reader*, 1979

Alice Walker wrote her first book of poetry and published her first short story in her final year at Sarah Lawrence College in 1968. She grew up in poverty, in which seven brothers and sisters and her sharecropping parents occupied impossibly cramped quarters and worked for profit that was never their own. She saw the failure of her college, Spelman, to offer courses in African American authors. This experience prompted her to write and to teach courses on black women writers whose works needed to be read by Americans of all ethnicities.

Walker, like the character Meridian in her second novel, considered physical violence a solution to the inequities with which she and other Americans were expected to live. She studied the Cuban Revolution and its effects. She, like Meridian, found herself unable, however, to perpetuate the violence she loathed. In *The Third Life of Grange Copeland*, *The Color Purple*, and *The Temple of My Familiar* she dramatizes the conditions that occasion violence and the horrors that result from violence. In *Possessing the Secret of Joy* she graphically describes the life-crippling effects of the ritualized and continued violence of female genital mutilation. Meridian chooses, as Walker has chosen, a political activism that is peaceful and positive. Meridian goes to the American South to educate, enlist, and assist prospective but fearful African American voters. Walker returned to the South with a similar purpose in the mid-1960's. Walker's writing, her study of world cultures, and her speaking engagements around the world show her continued peaceful political activism.

Once: Poems

Type of work: Poetry
First published: 1968

Once, Walker's first collection of poetry, communicates her youthful impressions of Africa and her state of mind during her early travels there, as well as the melancholy she felt upon her return to a racist United States, when thoughts of death, particularly by suicide, tormented her. Perhaps the epigram from French philosopher Albert Camus, which prefaces the book, expresses its mood best: "Misery kept me from believing that all was well under the sun, and the sun taught me that history wasn't everything."

The title poem of the collection contains several loosely connected scenes of injustice in the American South, small black children run down by vans, because "they were in the way," Jewish Civil Rights workers who cannot be cremated according to their requests because their remains cannot be found, and finally a black child waving an American flag, but from "the very/ *tips*/ of her/ fingers," an image perhaps of irony or perhaps of hope.

There are meditations on white lovers—blond, Teutonic, golden—who dare kiss this poet who is "brown-er/ Than a jew." There are memories of black churches, where her mother shouts, her father snores, and she feels uncomfortable.

The most striking poem is certainly "African Images," an assortment of vignettes from the ancestral homeland: shy gazelles, the bluish peaks of Mount Kenya, the sound of elephants trumpeting, rain forests with red orchids. Yet even glimpsed in the idealism of youth, Africa is not total paradise. The leg of a slain elephant is fashioned into an umbrella holder in a shop; a rhinoceros is killed so that its horn may be made into an aphrodisiac.

The Third Life of Grange Copeland

Type of work: Novel
First published: 1970

Writing in 1973, Walker observed that her first novel, *The Third Life of Grange Copeland*, "though sometimes humorous and celebrative of life, is a grave book in which the characters see the world as almost entirely menacing." This dark view of life is common to Grange Copeland, the patriarch of a family farming on shares in rural Georgia, his son Brownfield, and the wives and daughters of both men. For all these characters, the world is menacing because of the socioeconomic position they occupy at the bottom of the scale of the sharecropping system. Father and son menace each other in this novel because they are in turn menaced by rage born out of the frustration of the system. Although the white people of the book are nearly always vague, nameless, and impersonal, they and the system they represent have the ability to render both Grange and Brownfield powerless.

It is not accidental that these characters' names have agricultural connotations. "Grange" suggests a late nineteenth century association of farmers, a feudal farm and grain storage building, and a combination of graze and range, while "Brownfield" and "Copeland" are self-explanatory—for the inability to cope with the land is what leads both male characters along virtually parallel paths. For the father, the mere appearance of the white farm boss's truck is enough to turn his face "into a unnaturally bland mask, curious and unsettling to see." The appearance of the truck causes the son to be "filled with terror of this man who could, by his presence alone, turn his father into something that might as well have been a pebble or a post or a piece of dirt." Although Grange is, in this same image, literally a piece of land, he eventually returns to the South and learns to live self-sufficiently, farming a section of soil he tricked his second wife into giving to him. Brownfield, in contrast, is never able to escape the sharecropping system, although he sees that, like his father, he is "destined to be no more than overseer, on the white man's plantation, of his own children." Brownfield is able to live obliviously on a farm in Georgia, content to blame all of his problems on others. The poor rural black workers of this novel are themselves little more than a crop, rotated from farm to farm, producing a harvest of shame and hunger, cruelty and violence.

Unlike the men of the novel, the women are menaced by both blacks and whites, by both the agricultural system and the "strange fruit" it produces. Margaret, Grange's first wife, is both physically and mentally degraded by her husband and then sexually exploited by a white truck driver, resulting in her second pregnancy. Unable to cope with this situation, Grange deserts his family, after which his wife poisons both her child and herself. Following his father's pattern, Brownfield marries and begins to work the land, but after "a year when endless sunup to sundown work on fifty rich bottom acres of cotton land and a good crop brought them two diseased shoats for winter meat," he too begins to abuse his wife. Although Brownfield's wife, Mem, is a schoolteacher intelligent enough to try to break the cycle of raising others people's crops, her brief rebellion against her husband's malevolent beatings and mental tortures is a failure: He is able to subjugate her through repeated pregnancies that sap her rebellion as they turn her once rich and strong body into a virtual wasteland of emaciation. Because her body, which represents the land of the South, is still able to produce children despite its depleted condition, Brownfield is enraged enough to murder her in retaliation for her physical shape: "he had murdered his wife because she had become skinny and had not, with much irritation to him, reverted, even when well-fed, to her former plumpness. . . . Plumpness and freedom from the land, from cows and skinniness, went all together in his mind." Despite his irrational abuse of her, Mem is not ashamed "of being black though, no matter what he said. . . . Color was something the ground did to the flowers, and that was an end to it."

What the ground did to these generations of southern black people is the subject of Walker's novel—the whole lurid history of violence, hatred, and guilt that she chronicles in this story of one family's griefs. By the book's end, Brownfield Copeland has murdered his wife and an unnamed albino baby, while Grange Copeland has murdered his son Brownfield—first spiritually, then physically—and indirectly has killed his first wife and her infant.

Walker's characters are allegorical representations of the classic modes of survival historically adopted by black Americans in dealing with their oppression. Brownfield identifies with whites by daydreaming of himself on a southern plantation, sipping mint juleps, and then by bargaining for his freedom with the sexual favors of black women. Both of Grange's wives attempt to be true to the white stereotype of black women as promiscuous sexual beings, free of any moral restraints. Brownfield's wife, Mem, attempts the passive resistance advocated by Martin Luther King, Jr., but she is destroyed by what her husband calls "her weakness . . . forgiveness, a stupid belief that kindness can convert the enemy." Brownfield's daughter, Daphne, who calls herself the Copeland Family Secret Keeper, tries the strategy of inventing a falsely romantic history of the past, of the good old days when her father was kind, echoing those historical revisionists who try to argue that slavery was not that bad. Brownfield's other daughters try to stay away from their father altogether, regarding him "as a human devil" of whom they were afraid "in a more distant, impersonal way. He was like bad weather, a toothache, daily bad news."

Each of the title character's three lives (at home in the South as a sharecropper married to Margaret; in the North as a hustler of alcohol, drugs, and women; and finally back in the South as a farmer married to Josie and rearing his granddaughter Ruth) parallels a traditional survival strategy, which Grange summarizes as follows, "The white folks hated me and I hated myself until I started hating them in return and loving myself. Then I tried just loving me, and then you, and *ignoring* them much as I could." To put it another way, Grange tries at first to adapt to the system by believing what whites say about blacks; then he turns to the classic escape of the runaway slave—heading North to freedom; finally, he tries the technique of praising black life while ignoring whites altogether. A large part of the novel's devastation is caused by the repeated use of these techniques, not against whites but against other members of the Copeland family. Only Ruth, the granddaughter through whom Grange seeks redemption, is able to deal with whites in an intelligent, balanced, nondestructive yet independent way. She has learned from her grandfather, and from her family history, that pure hatred becomes self-hatred, and violence begets self-violence; she therefore becomes the novel's symbol of the new black woman, ready to assume her place in black history as a courageous worker in the Civil Rights movement which the rest of her family has been groping to discover.

Meridian

Type of work: Novel
First published: 1976

Walker's second novel, *Meridian*, picks up chronologically and thematically at the point where her first novel ended. *Meridian* describes the struggles of a young black woman, Meridian Hill, about the same age as Ruth Copeland, who comes to an awareness of power and feminism during the Civil Rights movement, and whose whole life's meaning is centered in the cycles of guilt, violence, hope, and change characteristic of that dramatic time. Thematically, *Meridian* picks up the first novel's theme of self-sacrificial murder as a way out of desperate political oppression in the form of the constant question that drives Meridian Hill—"Will you kill for the Revolution?" Meridian's lifelong attempt to answer that question affirmatively (as her college friends so easily do), while remaining true to her sense of responsibility to the past, her sense of ethics, and her sense of guilt of having given to her mother the child of her teenage pregnancy, constitutes the section of the novel entitled "Meridian." The second third of the novel, "Truman Held," is named for the major male character in the narrative. The third major section of the novel, "Ending," looks back at the turmoil of the Civil Rights movement from the perspective of the 1970's. Long after others have given up intellectual arguments about the morality of killing for revolution, Meridian is still debating the question, still actively involved in voter registration, political activism, and civil rights organization, as though the movement had never lost momentum. Worrying that her actions, now seen as eccentric rather than revolutionary, will cause her "to be left, listening to the old music, beside the highway," Meridian achieves release and atonement through the realization that her role will be to "come forward and sing from memory songs they will need once more to hear. For it is the song of the people, transformed by the experiences of each generation, that holds them together."

In 1978, Walker described *Meridian* as "a book 'about' the Civil Rights movement, feminism, socialism, the shakiness of revolutionaries and the radicalization of saints." Her word "about" is exact, for all of these topics revolve not chronologically but thematically around a central point—the protagonist, Meridian Hill. In some ways, Meridian *is* a saint; by the book's end she has sustained her belief in the Civil Rights movement without losing faith in feminism and socialism, despite family pressures, guilt, literally paralyzing self-doubts, the history of the movement, and the sexism of many of its leaders. In contrast, Truman Held represents those males who were reported to have said that "the only position for a woman in the movement is prone." Although Truman Held is Meridian's initial teacher in the movement, she eventually leaves him behind because of his inability to sustain his initial revolutionary fervor, and because of his misogyny. Unlike Brownfield Copeland, Truman argues that women are of less value than they should be, not because of skinniness, but because "Black women let themselves go . . . they are so fat." Later in the novel, Truman marries a white civil rights worker whose rape by another black man produces disgust in him, as much at his wife as at his friend. When Truman seeks out Meridian in a series of small southern hamlets where she continues to persuade black people to register to vote and to struggle for civil rights, he tells her that the movement is ended and that he grieves in a different way than she. Meridian answers, "I know how you grieve by running away. By pretending you were never there." Like Grange Copeland, Truman Held refuses to take responsibility for his own problems, preferring to run away to the North.

Meridian's sacrificial dedication to the movement becomes a model for atonement and release, words that once formed the working title of the book. *Meridian* could also have been called "The Third Life of Meridian Hill" because of similarities between Meridian's life and Grange Copeland's. Meridian leads three lives: as an uneducated child in rural Georgia who follows the traditional pattern of early pregnancy and aimless marriage, as a college student actively participating in political demonstrations, and as an eccentric agitator—a performer, she calls herself—unaware that the movement is ended. Like Grange Copeland in another sense, Meridian Hill is solid proof of the ability of any human to change dramatically by sheer will and desire.

Meridian is always different from her friends, who, filled with angry rhetoric, ask her repeatedly if she is willing to kill for the revolution, the same question that Grange asked himself when he lived in the North. This question haunts Meridian, because she does not know if she can or if she should kill, and because it reminds her of a similar request, posed in a similar way by her mother: "Say it now, Meridian, and be saved. All He asks is that we acknowledge Him as our Master. Say you believe

Alice Walker (Jeff Reinking/Picture Group)

in Him . . . don't go against your heart." In neither case is Meridian able to answer yes without going against her heart. Unlike her college friends and Truman Held, who see the movement only in terms of future gains for themselves, Meridian is involved with militancy because of her past: "But what none of them seemed to understand was that she felt herself to be, not holding on to something from the past, but *held* by something in the past."

Part of the past's hold on her is the sense of guilt she feels about her relationships with her parents. Although her father taught her the nature of the oppression of minorities through his knowledge of American Indians, her strongest source of guilt comes from her mother, who argues, like Brownfield Copeland, that the responsibility for *all* problems stems from outside oneself: "The answer to everything," said Meridian's mother, "is we live in America and we're not rich." Meridian's strongest sense of past guilt comes from the knowledge she gains when she becomes pregnant: "it was for stealing her mother's serenity, for shattering her mother's emerging self, that Meridian felt guilty from the very first, though she was unable to understand how this could possibly be her fault."

Meridian takes the form of a series of nonchronological sections, some consisting of only a paragraph, some four or five pages long, that circle around the events of Meridian's life. The writing is clear, powerful, violent, lyrical, and often symbolic. Spelman College, for example, is here called Saxon College. The large magnolia tree in the center of the campus, described with specific folkloric detail, is destroyed by angry students during a demonstration: "Though Meridian begged them to dismantle the president's house instead, in a fury of confusion and frustration they worked all night, and chopped and sawed down, level to the ground, that mighty, ancient, sheltering music tree." This tree (named The Sojourner, perhaps for Sojourner Truth) expands symbolically to suggest both the senseless destruction of black ghettos by blacks during the turmoil of the 1960's, and also Meridian Hill herself, who receives a photograph years later of The Sojourner, now "a gigantic tree stump" with "a tiny branch, no larger than a finger, growing out of one side." That picture, suggesting as it does the rebirth of hope despite despair, also evokes the last vision of Meridian expressed by the now-shamed Truman Held: "He would never see 'his' Meridian again. The new part had grown out of the old, though, and that was reassuring. This part of her, new, sure and ready, even eager, for the world, he knew he must meet again and recognize for its true value at some future time."

Goodnight, Willie Lee, I'll See You in the Morning

Type of work: Poetry
First published: 1979

Goodnight, Willie Lee, I'll See You in the Morning, Walker's fourth poetry collection, expands on earlier themes and further exploits personal and family experiences for lessons in living. The title poem is perhaps the most moving and characteristic of the collection. Walker shared it again on May 22, 1995, in a commencement day speech delivered at Spelman College. As a lesson in forgiveness, she recalled the words her mother, who had much to endure and much to forgive, uttered above her father's casket. Her last words to the man with whom she had lived for so many years, beside whom she had labored in the fields, and with whom she had raised so many children were, "Good night, Willie Lee, I'll see you in the morning." This gentle instinctive act of her mother taught Walker the enduring lesson that "the healing of all our wounds is forgiveness/ that permits a promise/ of our return/ at the end."

You Can't Keep a Good Woman Down

Type of work: Short fiction
First published: 1981

You Can't Keep a Good Woman Down is Walker's salute to black women who are pushing ahead, those who have crossed some barriers and are in some sense champions. There are black women who are songwriters, artists, writers, students in exclusive eastern schools; they are having abortions, teaching their men the meaning of pornography, coming to terms with the death of a father, on one hand, or with the meaning of black men raping white women, on the other. Always, they are caught up short by the notions of whites. In other words, all the political, sexual, racial, countercultural issues of the 1970's are in these stories, developed from what Walker calls the "womanist" point of view.

This set of stories, then, is explicitly sociological and apparently autobiographical, but in a special sense. Walker herself is a champion, so her life is a natural, even an inescapable, source of material. Walker-the-artist plays with Walker-the-college-student and Walker-the-idealistic-teacher, as well as with some of the other roles she sees herself as having occupied during that decade of social upheaval. Once a writer's experience has become transformed within a fictive world, it becomes next to impossible to think of the story's events as either simply autobiography or simply invention. The distinction has been deliberately blurred. It is because Walker wants to unite her public and private worlds, her politics and her art, life as lived and life as imagined, that, instead of poetry, these stories are interspersed with autobiographical parallels, journal entries, letters, and other expressions of her personality.

Walker writes free verse, employing concrete images. She resorts to few of the conceits, the extended metaphors, the latinate language, and other devices often found in poetry. Readers frequently say that her verses hardly seem like poetry at all; they resemble the conversation of a highly articulate, observant woman. While her poetry often seems like prose, her fiction is highly poetic. The thoughts of Miss Celie, the first-person narrator of *The Color Purple*, would not have been out of place in a book of poetry. Boundaries between prose and poetry remain thin in the work of Walker. Her verse, like her prose, is always rhythmic; if she rhymes or alliterates, it seems only by accident. The poetry appears so effortless that its precision, its choice of exact image or word to convey the nuance the poet wishes, is not immediately evident. Only close scrutiny reveals the skill with which this highly lettered poet has assimilated her influences, chiefly E. E. Cummings, Emily Dickinson, Robert Graves, Japanese haiku poems, Li Bo, Ovid, Zen epigrams, and William Carlos Williams.

Walker's poetry is personal and generally didactic, generated by events in her life, causes she has advocated, and injustices over which she has agonized. The reader feels that it is the message that counts, before realizing that the medium is part of the message. Several of her poems echo traumatic events in her own life, such as her abortion. She remembers the words her mother uttered over the casket of her father, and makes a poem of them. Other poems recall ambivalent emotions of childhood: Sunday school lessons which, even then, were filled with discrepancies. Some poems deal with the creative process itself: She calls herself a medium through whom the Old Ones, formerly mute, find their voice at last.

Some readers are surprised to discover that Walker's poems are both mystical and socially revolutionary, one moment exuberant and the next reeking with despair. Her mysticism is tied to reverence for the earth, a sense of unity with all living creatures, a bond of sisterhood with women throughout the world, and a joyous celebration of the female principle in the divine. On the other hand, she may lament that injustice reigns in society: Poor black people toil so that white men may savor the jewels that adorn heads of state.

The Color Purple

TYPE OF WORK: Novel
FIRST PUBLISHED: 1982

The Color Purple, awarded the Pulitzer Prize in fiction in 1983 and made into a successful film, is ultimately a novel of celebration. Initially, however, it is the tragic history of an extended African American family in the early and middle years of the twentieth century. Its tragedy is reflective of the country's and its characters' illness, and its celebration is of the characters' and the country's cure.

The story is written as a series of letters by two sisters, Celie and Nettie. The first letters reveal the fourteen-year-old Celie's miserable existence as caretaker of her parents' household. She bears two children to the man she believes to be her father (he is her stepfather), who immediately takes the children from her.

Celie is subject to the same situation in marriage: She is made caretaker for the children of a deceased woman and a stand-in sexual partner for yet another woman. When Celie and Nettie's father seeks to make Nettie his next victim, Nettie follows Celie to her new home, only to be victimized there by Celie's husband.

Nettie finds a home with the minister and his wife, who have become parents to Celie's children, Adam and Olivia. The five move to Africa to bring their Christian message to the Olinka. When Shug, the woman for whom Celie is stand-in partner, enters her home, the note of harmony which will swell to the final chorus of celebration is sounded. Celie comes to love and to learn from Shug. She learns that she must enter Creation as loved creature of her Creator, who, neither white nor male, creates out of love and a desire to please "Its" creatures. Reverence for all of Creation—trees, the color purple, humanity—is the cure, finally, to her and the novel's ills. Nettie's letters show Celie that she and her minister husband have come independently, in Africa, to know the same loving Creator who loves all and repudiates no part of Creation.

Celie leaves her abuser, Albert, who is slow to learn and sing the novel's song. He finally helps to bring Nettie, Samuel, Adam, Olivia, and Tashi, Adam's wife, back to Celie. He tells Celie, as they, finally, establish a friendship, that the more he wonders at and about Creation the more he loves. Celie, now lover of self and Creation, is reunited in middle age with her sister and grown children.

The Temple of My Familiar

Type of work: Novel
First published: 1989

Though written from a "womanist" viewpoint, *The Temple of My Familiar* follows both women and men through what becomes a history of the evolution of humankind. This evolutionary aspect is especially found in the chapters that tell the tales of Miss Lissie's various incarnations, including a brief, horrifying stint as a white man in a black tribe. The intertwining of all the separate narratives takes place as people only mentioned in passing in one chapter become the focal character in another chapter. For example, the white woman (Mary Jane) who rescues Carlotta and her mother, Zede, from a prison camp in South America ends up in Africa married to Fanny and Nzingha's black African father, Ola. Fanny is the granddaughter of Mama Shug and Mama Celie, both characters from *The Color Purple*.

Though Shug and Celie play a background role in the narrative, they are two of the most likable and human characters in the book, palpably real in a way that the novel's more prominent characters are not. Shug and Celie are warm, down-to-earth (especially in expounding "the gospel according to Shug"), and very human. For example, Celie is not very nice to her dog until Shug teaches him to bite the hand that beats him. They are fallible, but not in the strained way that other characters are. When, for example, Carlotta's husband, Arveyda, leaves her for her mother, Zede, the reader is likely to feel cheated, for no credible motivation has been supplied—a recurring problem throughout the novel. It is hard to feel any deep connection with Walker's characters, and the resolution of their conflicts is too pat to be satisfying.

Nevertheless, readers who are interested in the theories of University of California at Los Angeles archaeologist Marija Gimbutas, who posits an Edenic prehistoric era marked by worship of female deities, will find in *The Temple of My Familiar* a kindred spirit.

Possessing the Secret of Joy

Type of work: Novel
First published: 1992

Possessing the Secret of Joy expresses, in fictional and direct statements, its author's resistance to the practice of female circumcision. According to Walker, in 1991 ninety to a hundred million women and girls living in African, Far Eastern, and Middle Eastern countries were genitally mutilated, and the practice of "female circumcision" in the United States and Europe was growing among immigrants from countries where it was a part of the culture.

Three characters from Walker's *The Color Purple* (1982) and *The Temple of My Familiar* (1989) assume major roles in *Possessing the Secret of Joy*. The ritual mutilation of Tashi, childhood African friend to Celie's children Adam and Olivia and later wife to Adam, is graphically described, and its physical and emotional effects are explored in this novel.

Olivia speaks first, as others speak later, of her own, Adam's, and her missionary parents' introduction to the six-year-old Tashi. Tashi was inconsolable, having just witnessed the death of her sister Dura, victim of genital mutilation. The novel's action moves back and forth between Dura's death and the trial of Tashi for the murder of M'Lissa, Dura's killer and her own mutilator. It ends with the roar of rifle fire as Tashi is punished for her crime.

The aged Carl Jung is introduced to the novel's list of characters. While he appears only briefly, his psychological and mythological probing of Tashi's and the world's problem is carried on by his female and male successors, Raye and Pierre.

The recurrent imagery of Tashi's subconscious is finally interpreted by Pierre (son of Adam, Tashi's husband) and Lisette, Jung's niece. Pierre, having grown up with his parents' accounts of Tashi's physical and emotional suffering (continual pain, impeded motion, difficult and aborted childbirth; recurrent nightmares, truncated relationships, frequent confinement to mental institutions), studies anthropology and continues his great uncle's intellectual pursuits.

In Pierre's account, the myth is simple, and it is full of Walker's condemnation of the mutilation and subjugation of women. It is a story the aging Tashi remembers overhearing in bits from covert conversations among the male African elders. The male god descends from the sky to overcome, enjoy, and rape the female earth. Challenged by the earth's response to his advance, he cuts down the source (the mound or hill) of her pleasure.

"*RESISTANCE* IS THE SECRET OF JOY!" is the novel's final statement. Adam, Olivia, Benny (mildly retarded son to Tashi and Adam), Pierre, Raye, and Mbate (servant to M'Lissa and friend to Tashi) hold it up as a banner for Tashi's viewing as she is killed for the murder of M'Lissa. The novel is Walker's act of resistance to male domination and the physical and emotional disabling of women.

By the Light of My Father's Smile

Type of work: Novel
First published: 1998

By the Light of My Father's Smile engenders passionate, often conflicting, opinions. Some praise it as a long-overdue celebration of female sexuality; others are vehemently opposed to its basic tenants. Even some readers predisposed toward Walker's views acknowledge that the explicit sexual detail in the novel may undermine its own message.

Literary merit, too, sparks debate. Lauded by many as brilliant, original writing, *By the Light of My Father's Smile* has also been criticized for flat characterization and confusing jumps in perspective. Certainly, the throbbing talents of its Pulitzer Prize-winning author are not being called seriously into question. Yet, the threads of this work, in some ways more a parable than a traditional novel, may not weave together for everyone.

Celebrating the absolute usefulness of sexuality "in the accessing of one's mature spirituality," Walker focuses on the father's role "in assuring joy or sorrow in this arena for his female children." The story begins with an African American family from the United States living in a remote area of Mexico. The father catches one of his two teenage daughters with a local Mundo boy and beats her; his other daughter witnesses the beating. The rest of the novel investigates the repercussions. It is told mostly from the point of view of the deceased father, as he watches his daughters reap the consequences throughout their lives.

Ultimately, it is the Mundo way of life—considered "primitive" by Eurocentric standards—that holds out the possibility for reconciliation. *By the Light of My Father's Smile* seeks to open doors—between parents and children; between lovers; between cultures; even, perhaps, from one millennium to the next. The subject matter is controversial, but few would probably disagree with Walker's underlying belief that "it is the triumphant heart, not the conquered heart, that forgives."

Suggested Readings

Bates, Gerri. *Alice Walker: A Critical Companion*. Westport, Conn.: Greenwood Press, 2005.

Bloom, Harold, ed. *Alice Walker*. New York: Chelsea House, 1989.

Dieke, Ikenna, ed. *Critical Essays on Alice Walker*. New York: Greenwood Press, 1999.

Gates, Henry Louis, Jr., and K. A. Appiah, eds. *Alice Walker: Critical Perspectives Past and Present*. New York: Amistad, 1993.

Gentry, Tony. *Alice Walker*. New York: Chelsea, 1993.

Lauret, Maria. *Alice Walker*. New York: St. Martin's Press, 2000.

Montelaro, Janet J. *Producing a Womanist Text: The Maternal as Signifier in Alice Walker's "The Color Purple."* Victoria, B.C.: English Literary Studies, University of Victoria, 1996.

Petry, Alice Hall. "Walker: The Achievement of the Short Fiction." In *Alice Walker: Critical Perspectives Past and Present*, edited by Henry Louis Gates, Jr., and K. A. Appiah. New York: Amistad, 1993.
White, Evelyn C. *Alice Walker: A Life*. New York: Norton, 2004.
Winchell, Donna Haisty. *Alice Walker*. New York: Twayne, 1992.

Contributors: Judith K. Taylor, Timothy Dow Adams, Mary A. Blackmon, Rebecca R. Butler, and Theodore C. Humphrey

Joseph A. Walker

Born: Washington, D.C.; February 23, 1935
Died: Washington, D.C.; January 25, 2003

African American

Walker examined issues of personal identity, relationship strife, and racism of particular importance to black American men.

Principal works

DRAMA: *The Believers*, pr., pb. 1968 (with Josephine Jackson); *The Harangues*, pr. 1969, revised pb. 1971 (as *Tribal Harangue Two*); *Ododo*, pr. 1970, pb. 1972; *The River Niger*, pr. 1972, pb. 1973; *Yin Yang*, pr. 1972; *Antigone Africanus*, pr. 1975; *The Lion Is a Soul Brother*, pr. 1976; *District Line*, pr. 1984
SCREENPLAY: *The River Niger*, 1976 (adaptation of his play)
NONFICTION: "Broadway's Vitality," 1973; "Black Magnificance," 1978; "The Hiss," 1980; "Themes of the Black Struggle," 1982

Joseph A. Walker was born in Washington, D.C., in 1935. His father, Joseph Walker, was a house painter and his mother, Florine Walker, a housewife. Walker graduated from Howard University in 1956 with a B.A. in philosophy and a minor in drama, having acted in several student productions (he portrayed Luke in James Baldwin's *Amen Corner* in May of 1955). Although he had realized that his real love was the theater, his fear of poverty drew him, after graduation, to the United States Air Force, where he enlisted as a second lieutenant and reached the rank of first lieutenant by the time of his discharge in 1960. His desire to become a high-ranking officer caused Walker to initially pursue navigators' training, but he later quit when he found himself spending more time writing poetry than studying for his navigator's exams.

This dramatic shift of career was the source for a famous scene in *The River Niger*, when navigator-school student Jeff Williams is belittled by a white airman for his poetry writing in exactly the same way as Walker himself described being insulted during his military career. Trying to establish a balance between his fear of financial dependence and his inner desire to compose poetry, Walker decided to devote his full attention to the study of drama and poetry rather than to achieving high rank in the military. Further education gave him time to clarify his goals. Walker received an M.F.A. from Catholic University in 1963 and began teaching in a Washington, D.C., high school.

Walker followed this teaching position with one at City College of New York.

He combined the role of instructor and playwright during his year as a playwright-in-residence at Yale University and then returned to Howard University, where he became a full professor of drama. While teaching, Walker continued his study of the stage and film by continuing to act. This personal line of study had a profound effect on the young actor-playwright. In 1969, the Negro Ensemble Company produced *The Harangues*. This was a personal milestone for the young Walker, who had, at this point, been studying other people's dramatic work for more than a decade. In 1970, Walker and his second wife, Dorothy Dinroe, started the acting troupe The Demi-Gods, a professional music-dance repertory company with Walker serving as artistic director. Walker's play *Ododo*, which The Demi-Gods later presented at Howard University in 1973, opened the Negro Ensemble Company's 1970 season. This work further examined racial strife and prepared audiences for the African American history that would be so vehemently elucidated in *The River Niger* and his later writings.

After the 1970's, Walker continued to write, albeit infrequently, about minority issues derived from his own personal experiences. One play, *District Line*, used his personal experience as a cab driver to demonstrate universal themes of racial strife and harmony. Essays submitted to *The New York Times*—"Themes of the Black Struggle" (1982) and "Black Magnificence" (1980), for example—and interviews conducted during the 1980's documented more recent difficulties that minorities faced in the mainstream world of the theater. Walker said that mainstream theaters were not willing to produce works from minority authors and there had not been adequate funding of minority-interest theater companies to make up for the lack of mainstream interest. According to Michele DiGirolamo in *Afro-American*, Walker stated that he had little success in getting his plays produced in the 1980's and 1990's because of shrinking budgets and an apathetic public. In 1995, he made an appearance at the National Black Theatre Festival in Winston-Salem, North Carolina, to encourage more young African American authors to write for the stage in the hope that the number of minority-run theater groups would continue to grow and present greater numbers of minority-interest plays. He died in 2003 following a stroke.

Like many other African American authors, Joseph A. Walker examined issues close to the black community and, in particular, those dealing with black American men. Issues of personal identity, relationship strife, and racism play dominant roles in influencing both the thinking and the actions of the black male characters portrayed in his dramas. Lacking a homeland and history, repressed by both whites and assimilationist blacks, and dissociated from the comforts of stable male-female relationships, Walker's black protagonists lead desperate and often destructive lives. Walker's critical success derived from his realistic portrayals of African American men. Working from his own, personal experiences as a black man in the United States, Walker examined interracial relationships, conflicts between people and society, and the struggle that many blacks have in achieving inner peace and acceptance.

The Harangues

Type of work: Drama
First produced: 1969, revised pb. 1971

The Harangues is made up of two closely paired one-act plays, each introduced by an episode designed purely to serve as the medium for the author's invective. In the first episode, a fifteenth century West African man observes the presence of slave traders' ships sitting in the nearby harbor and, foreseeing a life of slavery for his newborn son, chooses to drown him rather than have him captured by the traders.

The one-act that follows this violent episode presents the story of a young interracial couple. A young black man wishes to marry a young white woman who has fallen deeply in love with him and become pregnant with his child. Because the woman's wealthy father opposes the match and threatens to disinherit his daughter, the young man decides that he and his fiancé must kill her father. Seemingly lacking any familial feeling, the white woman agrees to assist her lover in the murder of her father. However, the plan backfires while still in the planning stages. A traitorous black "friend" reveals the couple's intentions to the girlfriend's father and causes the death of the young black man, bringing an end to his plan to marry his white girlfriend and, with her, inherit her father's estate.

The second episode, echoing the first in theme and purpose, presents a contemporary black American revolutionary who, depressed by his vision of the repression inherent in modern society, decides that he has no future. Knowing that he himself will die, he nevertheless convinces his wife not to die with him but to live on to raise their son as a freedom fighter.

The one-act play that follows centers on a deranged black man in a bar who has taken captive three people—a white liberal man, a black conservative man sympathetic to white society, and the black man's white girlfriend—and has threatened to kill them unless they can justify their existence. After the captives are subjected to numerous humiliations, it becomes apparent that, according to the protagonist's ideas of "worthiness," only the white woman may be allowed to live. When the "executions" take place, however, the woman takes a bullet meant for her black lover. In the ensuing struggle, the black conservative gains control of his captor's gun and kills him. Once again, Walker demonstrates that the black man who resorts to violence to achieve his goals is destroyed by his own violence.

The River Niger

Type of work: Drama
First produced: 1972, pb. 1973

Walker wrote four major plays before writing *The River Niger*, but it is this work that brought Walker nationwide recognition (it won many awards, including an Obie and a Tony) and revealed both his strengths and his weaknesses as a playwright. *The River Niger*, rather than being an entirely original work, is more a reworking and refinement of the ideas and issues developed in his earlier plays for a broader audience.

Although the plot and themes of *The River Niger* deal with African American life and issues, the play has been seen as having a far more universal relevance. Mel Gussow, in *Time* magazine, said that the play was powerful and compassionate and has an appeal beyond the borders of black experience. Both the play's realism and this global appeal arise from the fact that it is derived in part from Walker's own experiences and family—experiences that many outside the black community can also appreciate. As Gussow noted, "The playwright knows his people and we grow to know them, too, to understand their fears, appetites, frustrations, and vulnerabilities."

In *The River Niger*, Jeff Williams, who has dropped out of U.S. Air Force navigators' school because of the racist comments of a colleague, returns home to determine what to do with the rest of his life. Everyone has a different opinion on the direction he should take. His friends demand that he join them in defying the established order of white society and take part in the "revolution," while his family is disappointed that he ended his promising military career (his father's first question is "Where is your uniform?") and wants him to continue becoming an officer. Williams, however, is starting to recognize his own, inner desire to become a lawyer. Williams's hesitation and ambivalence can be readily understood by anyone who has had to make dramatic changes in his or her life.

Yin Yang

Type of work: Drama
First produced: 1972

Walker's play *Yin Yang*, first produced in 1972, was his least traditional. Walker designed the play to represent the age-old struggle between good and evil. In an article published in *The New York Times*, Walker said that "Good is represented by God, a hip swinging, fast-talking black mama . . . in conflict with Miss Satan, who is also a black female swinger." Although the play may seem to have been directed for a children's audience, with its reliance on archetypical figures and simple language, Walker claimed that the play draws on the biblical books of Job and Revelation. Walker had long seen a symbolic parallel between Job and blacks because, he said, both believe in their society and their religion even when such institutions seemingly cause them to suffer.

Yin Yang operates on the Chinese philosophy that everything in existence is the result of the combination of two opposing principles: the yin, the feminine, "evil," passive principle; and the yang, the masculine, "good," active principle. Thus, the characters of *Yin Yang* themselves represent the balance of good and evil, masculine and feminine.

District Line

Type of work: Drama
First produced: 1984

District Line offers an interesting discussion of how individuals of differing viewpoints and backgrounds can find common ground. A Washington, D.C., taxi stand serves as the setting, which depicts a day in the lives of six cab drivers: two white men, three black men, and one black woman. Each of the drivers comes from a different background, but each has similar hopes for the future and similar reactions to his or her past experiences. The issues and concerns of the black male characters, however, dominate this play, as they had most of Walker's earlier plays. The scenes concerning two of the black drivers (who are, by far, the most developed characters)—Doc, a moonlighting Howard University professor, another of Walker's alter egos, and Zilikazi, an exiled South African revolutionary—are the ones that receive the greatest amount of attention. Despite this focus on black men's issues, in *District Line*, Walker's presentation of the white characters—the two white drivers—seems more balanced. These white men, compared with white characters in Walker's earlier plays, are complex individuals rather than stereotypical white liberals or oppressors.

Suggested Readings

Barthelemy, Anthony. "Mother, Sister, Wife: A Dramatic Perspective." *Southern Review* 21, no. 3 (Summer, 1985): 770-789.

Clurman, Harold. "Theater: *The River Niger*." *The Nation* 215, no. 21 (December 25, 1972): 668.

Kauffmann, Stanley. "Theater: *The River Niger*." *The New Republic* 169, no. 12 (September 29, 1973): 22.

Lee, Dorothy. "Three Black Plays: Alienation and Paths to Recovery." *Modern Drama* 19, no. 4 (December, 1975): 397-404.

Contributor: Julia M. Meyers

Booker T. Washington

Born: Near Hale's Ford, Virginia; April 5, 1856
Died: Tuskegee, Alabama; November 14, 1915

African American

Washington's autobiography brought national attention to the need for education for African Americans at a time when most schools were segregated.

Principal works

NONFICTION: *The Future of the American Negro*, 1899; *The Story of My Life and Work*, 1900; *Up from Slavery*, 1901; *Working with the Hands*, 1904; *The Story of the Negro*, 1909; *My Larger Education*, 1911

Booker T. Washington rose to national prominence early in the twentieth century for promoting mutual interests as the foundation for better race relations. His views were rejected as limited and harmful by African American activists in the 1960's because he concentrated on economic rather than social equality. His achievements have been given renewed consideration in light of historical perspective.

Washington was born on a Virginia plantation, the son of a white plantation owner and a slave woman. At the end of the Civil War, he moved with his mother and his stepfather to Malden, West Virginia, where he worked in the salt mines and grew up in poverty. Determined to get an education, he made a five-hundred-mile journey, mostly by foot, to Virginia's Hampton Institute, a school set up to educate poor African Americans.

These early experiences influenced Washington's dedication to an ethic of self-help and self-discipline as the means of achievement, principles that became the foundation for his educational philosophy. In 1881, he became the first principal of a fledgling school in Tuskegee, Alabama, established to give industrial training to African Americans. At Tuskegee, Washington took a pragmatic approach to education, stressing personal cleanliness, correct behavior, and industrial education to improve students' economic condition. In a Deep South state where legal restrictions relegated African Americans to second-class citizenship and where injustice and lynching were common, Washington successfully recruited students, promoted education, and raised funds. As Tuskegee prospered, Washington emerged as a national spokesman for race relations.

His circle of influence widened after his 1895 address at the Cotton States and International Exposition in Atlanta. Later called the Atlanta Compromise by his critics, the speech argued in favor of economic gains, while ignoring the white community's denial of black political rights. As a man who understood his times, Washington believed that a materialistic society eventually would respond to economic equality, that social equality would follow. After his address, his fame increased; he was invited to the White House, was awarded an honorary degree from Harvard University, and won the financial support of leading industrial figures for Tuskegee Institute.

In the last years of his career, however, he was sharply criticized by younger, intellectual African Americans who rejected his policies. Washington's contributions are nevertheless remarkable. His autobiography, *Up from Slavery*, is an inspiring record of achievements in the face of overwhelming social handicaps, and even his sharpest critics pay tribute to Washington's singleness of vision.

The Story of My Life and Work

Type of work: Autobiography
First published: 1900

The Story of My Life and Work is not among Washington's most notable works. A collaborator presumably did most of the writing, and it has been speculated that the book went to press when Washington was too occupied with other concerns to reread it and revise it for publication. It is of interest, however, for what it reveals about Washington's career and early use of media, as well as for what it says about the status of African Americans at the time the book was published.

Written with a black audience in mind, the book contains episodes designed to establish a rapport between the author and his black audience. For example, Washington includes in this book an account of how he witnessed the beating of his uncle by his white master and of how the uncle cried out for help. Scenes like this are clearly designed to create empathy with the book's intended audience.

The book presents the details of Washington's early life. Homage is paid to the white people who were most instrumental in helping him receive an education and in aiding him in his rise to becoming the founder and principal of Tuskegee. Among his white patrons were the Ruffners. General Lewis Ruffner owned the salt factory in which Washington's father worked, as well as the coal mines in which Washington himself was employed before he became the Ruffners' house servant. Viola Ruffner encouraged Washington to sharpen his literacy skills and to read as widely as possible. Her faith in him provided the youth with an underpinning that enabled him to continue his education against great odds. Because Viola Ruffner had insisted on Washington's keeping her house immaculate, he developed an appreciation for cleanliness. He also became concerned with personal hygiene and, throughout his early years at Tuskegee, insisted that students pay close attention to washing their bodies.

When he arrived at Hampton, the head teacher, Mary F. Mackie, had already admitted as many students as she could, but, when Washington expertly swept her floor, she allowed him to enter and enabled him to pay for his education by doing

Booker T. Washington (Library of Congress)

janitorial work, which he did with great dedication.

Washington returned to Malden to teach after completing his studies at Hampton, but soon went to Washington, D.C., for additional training. When Washington completed these studies, General Samuel Chapman Armstrong, Hampton Institute's principal, employed him to teach a group of Native American students at Hampton. So well did he succeed in this endeavor that Armstrong appointed him director of the night school for adults.

Therefore, it is not surprising that when a civic group from Tuskegee, Alabama, asked Armstrong to recommend someone to establish an institute in their town, Armstrong recommended Washington, even though the group making the request had not expected that Armstrong would consider a black person suitable for such a job.

The Story of My Life and Work emphasizes the need for African Americans, many of whom were former slaves whose formal education had been prohibited, to make themselves indispensable to the dominant white society. Whereas some of the era's black reformers urged equality for blacks, Washington thought that such demands were unrealistic. He sincerely believed that if blacks could make themselves useful to society, the matter of gaining equality would eventually resolve itself.

In this book, Washington expands on a memorable analogy he used in one of his most celebrated speeches, delivered before the Atlanta Cotton Exposition in 1895. In this speech, which many attacked because of its implied support of the concept of separate but equal societies, Washington likened the races to the fingers of the hand. These fingers are separate, but they are all part of the same entity, so that in time of need, they form themselves into a fist. He was convinced that the races could work together in some critical situations, but that they could also remain separate.

Up from Slavery

Type of work: Autobiography
First published: 1901

Up from Slavery: An Autobiography is an account of Washington's life, which began in slavery and ended with his being a renowned educator. It is written in a simple style with an optimistic tone that suggests to African Americans that they can succeed through self-improvement and hard work. Although *Up from Slavery* has been ranked along with Benjamin Franklin's *Autobiography of Benjamin Franklin* (1791) as a classic story of personal achievement, critics disagree about its central theme. Some scholars complain of its conciliatory stance, while others see the work as a justification for black pride.

The book opens with Washington's boyhood hardships, beginning with his life as a slave on a Virginia plantation where the lack of a family name and a history that would give identity to his existence was painful and difficult to understand. He mentions the slaves' fidelity and loyalty to the master, but he stresses the brutality of the institution: A lack of refinement in living, a poor diet, bad clothing, and ignorance were the slave's lot.

A struggle for literacy is the focus in the intermediate chapters. Leaving the plantation with his mother and stepfather after the Civil War, Washington moved to West Virginia to work in salt and coal mines, where he learned letters while doing manual labor and used trickery to escape work and get to school on time. His situation improved after he was employed as a house servant by a Mrs. Ruffner, who taught him the value of cleanliness and work, lessons he put to good use when he sought admission to Hampton Institute, a Virginia school for poor African Americans. There Washington received an education that led to a teaching job. Throughout these chapters, he gives the impression that his early hardships were a challenge that gave impetus to his later success. He stresses the dignity of labor and the importance of helping others as the means of getting ahead.

Beginning with chapter seven, Washington discusses his work at Tuskegee Institute, where classes were first taught in a stable and a hen house, and he takes pride in the growth of the school from an original enrollment of thirty students to a large body of students from twenty-seven states and several foreign countries. His educational theories conform to his belief in manual labor rather than intellectual pursuit, and he stresses economic growth as the important goal.

The later portion of the book is primarily a chronicle of fund-raising and an account of grants and gifts. His image as a national leader is firmly established, and he includes newspaper comments on his speeches as well as answers to the critics regarding his Atlanta address. In "Last Words," Washington expresses his hope for an end to racial prejudice.

Suggested Readings

Baker, Houston A. *Turning South Again: Re-thinking Modernism/Re-reading Booker T.* Durham, N.C.: Duke University Press, 2001.

Harlan, Louis R. *Booker T. Washington: The Making of a Black Leader, 1856-1901*. New York: Oxford University Press, 1972.

_______. *Booker T. Washington: The Wizard of Tuskegee, 1901-1915*. New York: Oxford University Press, 1983.

Harlan, Louis R., et al., eds. *The Booker T. Washington Papers*. 13 vols. Urbana: University of Illinois Press, 1972-1984.

McElroy, Frederick L. "Booker T. Washington as Literary Trickster." *Southern Folklore* 49, no. 2 (1992).

Mansfield, Stephen. *Then Darkness Fled: The Liberating Wisdom of Booker T. Washington*. Nashville: Cumberland House, 1999.

Munslow, Alan. *Discourse and Culture*. New York: Routledge, 1992.

Verney, Kevern. *The Art of the Possible: Booker T. Washington and Black Leadership in the United States, 1881-1925*. New York: Routledge, 2001.

Contributors: Joyce Chandler Davis and R. Baird Shuman

Wendy Wasserstein

Born: Brooklyn, New York; October 18, 1950
Died: New York, New York; January 30, 2006

Jewish

Wasserstein's plays have helped define the feminist experience of the baby boom generation.

Principal works

CHILDREN'S LITERATURE: *Pamela's First Musical*, 1996

DRAMA: *Any Woman Can't*, pr. 1973; *Happy Birthday, Montpelier Pizz-zazz*, pr. 1974; *Uncommon Women, and Others*, pr. 1975 (one act), pr. 1977 (two acts), pb. 1978; *When Dinah Shore Ruled the Earth*, pr. 1975 (with Christopher Durang); *Isn't It Romantic*, pr. 1981, revised pr. 1983, pb. 1984; *Tender Offer*, pr. 1983, pb. 2000 (one act); *The Man in a Case*, pr., pb. 1986 (one act; adaptation of Anton Chekhov's short story); *Miami*, pr. 1986 (musical); *The Heidi Chronicles*, pr., pb. 1988; *The Heidi Chronicles, and Other Plays*, pb. 1990; *The Sisters Rosensweig*, pr. 1992, pb. 1993; *An American Daughter*, pr. 1997, pb. 1998; *Waiting for Philip Glass*, pr., pb. 1998 (inspired by William Shakespeare's Sonnet 94); *The Festival of Regrets*, pr. 1999 (libretto); *Old Money*, pr. 2000, pb. 2002; *Seven One-Act Plays*, pb. 2000; *Psyche in Love*, 2006

LONG FICTION: *Elements of Style*, 2006

SCREENPLAY: *The Object of My Affection*, 1998 (adaptation of Stephen McCauley's novel)

TELEPLAYS: *The Sorrows of Gin*, 1979 (from the story by John Cheever); *"Drive," She Said*, 1984; *The Heidi Chronicles*, 1995 (adaptation of her play); *An American Daughter*, 2000 (adaptation of her play)

NONFICTION: *Bachelor Girls*, 1990; *Shiksa Goddess: Or, How I Spent My Forties*, 2001; *Sloth*, 2005

Wendy Wasserstein (WAH-zur-steen) attended college at Mount Holyoke. Her first play to gain critical attention, *Uncommon Women and Others*, relates the experiences six alumni from that all-female college have upon graduating from their supportive environment and entering the "real world," where their abilities and identities as intelligent women were often denigrated or denied.

Wasserstein was raised by an extraordinary and flamboyant mother, Lola, and a quieter, though no less supportive, father, Morris. She used them as models for the pushy Jewish parents in *Isn't It Romantic*, which is about a woman who chooses to remain single rather than marry the Jewish doctor of her mother's dreams. This play entertainingly dramatizes how liberated women hoped to attain equality and fulfillment.

The Heidi Chronicles won not only the Pulitzer Prize in drama in 1989 but also a Tony Award and several other prestigious awards. This play explores the life of a feminist art historian from grade school dances, through woman's consciousness-raising, the acquired immunodeficiency syndrome (AIDS) crisis, her problems with men, and her eventual decision to adopt a child. Wasserstein, who considered herself a "professional malcontent," was suddenly inundated with flowers and awards. The play was hailed as a milestone in feminist playwriting, documenting a generation's sadness after the disappointing outcome of the women's movement.

Along with Wendy, Lola and Morris reared three other children, all of whom became exceptionally successful in the high-pressure fields of business and banking. Wasserstein uses the worlds her siblings inhabit, and the bonds they formed as adults, to good effect in *The Sisters Rosensweig*. The play shows how Jews still perceive themselves as outsiders in modern society. Wasserstein, having enjoyed the success of *The Heidi Chronicles*, specifically set out to create a hopeful, romantic ending to this crowd-pleasing work, the most highly structured of her plays.

In the 1990's Wasserstein began working on more innovative theater events. In 1998 she contributed to the production of *Love's Fire*, based on Shakespearean sonnets, and in 1999 she and two other playwrights created librettos for *Central Park*, a New York City Opera production presented at Glimmerglass Opera and Lincoln Center. During this time, at the age of forty-eight, Wasserstein became a single mother after treatment with fertility drugs. Her daughter, Lucy Jane, weighed only one pound, twelve ounces at birth. Wasserstein's essay about her struggle to conceive and her daughter's birth is one of the most moving pieces in *Shiksa Goddess*. Wasserstein died in New York City at the age of fifty-five.

Although early critics saw Wasserstein's plays as period pieces, she established a voice as a feminist pioneer. Her plays dramatize both a unique perspective on the women's movement and a search for religious identity.

The Heidi Chronicles

Type of work: Drama
First produced: 1988, pb. 1988

The Heidi Chronicles, which won the Pulitzer Prize in drama in 1989, focuses on the women's movement of the late twentieth century from the point of view of Heidi Holland, feminist art historian. The two acts each open with a prologue about overlooked women painters. The action of the play begins at a dance in 1965 where Heidi meets Peter Patrone, who charms her with his wit. They promise to know each other all their lives.

Several years later during a Eugene McCarthy rally, Heidi encounters Scoop

Rosenbaum. Scoop is obnoxious and extremely arrogant, and he has a tendency to grade everything, yet Heidi leaves the party to go to bed with him. At a consciousness-raising session a lesbian explains to Heidi that in feminism, "you either shave your legs or you don't." Heidi considers body hair in the range of the personal, but she participates in the group, detailing her pathetic attachment to Scoop. Distraught, she begs the women to tell her that all their daughters will feel more worthwhile than they do.

Next, Heidi attends a rally at the Chicago Art Institute, protesting the opening of a major retrospective containing no women artists. Peter arrives and confesses his homosexuality. Act 1 closes with Scoop's wedding to another woman. Although he claims to love Heidi, Scoop does not promise her equality. At the wedding he knowingly marries a woman he considers his lesser. By act 2 Heidi has written her book, *And the Light Floods in from the Left.* She attends a baby shower for Scoop's wife held on the same day as the memorial service for John Lennon. In 1982, Heidi appears on a talk show with Peter, now a popular pediatrician, and Scoop, owner of *Boomer* magazine. The men continually interrupt her. Later, when Heidi tries to tell an old friend how unhappy she is, the woman is too involved with her own career to care.

In 1986, Heidi gives an address to the alumni of her alma mater, divulging how sad she is. She feels stranded, and she thought the whole point of the feminist movement was that they were all in it together. In 1987, Peter explains that her kind of sadness is a luxury after all the memorial services for those who have died of acquired immunodeficiency syndrome (AIDS). The play's final scene occurs in 1989, when Scoop comes to meet Heidi's adopted child. He has sold *Boomer* and is planning to run for Congress. Heidi hopes that Scoop's son and her daughter will someday find a truer equality. The final image of the play is Heidi and child in front of a banner displaying a major Georgia O'Keeffe retrospective.

By turns heartwrenching and hilarious, the play captures the angst, admittedly sometimes whiny, of a generation of women who could not understand why the world would not accept them as they were and as they wanted to be.

The Sisters Rosensweig

Type of work: Drama
First produced: 1992, pb. 1993

The Sisters Rosensweig, a play intended to echo Russian playwright Anton Chekhov's *Tri sestry* (1901, revised 1904; *The Three Sisters*, 1920), is set in August of 1991 as the Soviet Union is dissolving. To celebrate Sara Goode's birthday, her two sisters, Pfeni Rosensweig and "Dr." Gorgeous Teitelbaum, come to England. Also invited are Sara's teenage daughter, Tessie; Pfeni's lover, the bisexual play director Geoffrey Duncan; Sara's aristocratic lover, Nicholas Pymn; and Tessie's working-class Catholic boyfriend, Tom.

As the play opens, Tessie is listening to recordings of Sara's college chorus for a school project. Pfeni, a globe-trotting feminist journalist, arrives and embraces Geoffrey, whose friend, Mervyn Kant, "world leader in synthetic animal protective covering"—a fake furrier—meets them at Sara's house. Mervyn becomes smitten with Sara and invites himself to dinner.

Dr. Gorgeous, a radio personality who funded her trip from Newton, Massachusetts, by leading a tour for the Temple Beth El sisterhood, enters, her feet aching from cheap shoes. Before dinner Nicholas baits Mervyn about his Jewishness, and Tom and Tessie, who want to go to the celebration in Lithuania, are entranced by Mervyn's political views. After dinner Sara and Mervyn discuss their similar American pasts until he charms her into bed. When Mervyn asks for a song, however, Sara refuses. In act 2 Gorgeous arranges for Geoffrey to entertain her sisterhood. Then everyone questions Sara about Mervyn until she gets annoyed, offends Gorgeous, and sends Mervyn away. When Geoffrey returns he tells Pfeni he misses men. Pfeni replies, "So do I" and allows him to depart.

Pfeni turns to Sara for comfort. Gorgeous enters wearing new, expensive, accidentally broken, shoes. Pfeni suggests Gorgeous's husband should buy her replacements, and Gorgeous reveals she now supports her family. The sisters share revelations and finally relax together.

Mervyn, responding to a call from Sara, returns. He delivers a designer suit to Gorgeous, a gift from her sisterhood. Gorgeous is ecstatic, but will return it and use the money for her children's tuition. Pfeni decides to return to work, and leaves. Sara and Mervyn agree to continue their relationship. Tessie avoids the Lithuanian celebration, realizing she would be an outsider, and cajoles her mother into joining her in song.

While Wasserstein's play was a Broadway success, reviews were frequently lukewarm. Although blessed with witty dialogue, the sisters often seem like caricatures. Yet this is less a character drama than an exploration of issues, specifically those relating to identity, the fears common to middle-aged women, and the self-loathing, self-loving attitudes Jews have toward their culture. Not a classic like Chekhov's masterpiece, Wasserstein's play is nevertheless a triumph of substance and style over structure.

Suggested Readings

Arthur, Helen. "Wendy Wasserstein's *The Heidi Chronicles*." Review of *The Heidi Chronicles*, by Wendy Wasserstein. *Nation* 261, no. 12 (October 16, 1995): 443-445.

Barnett, Claudia, ed. *Wendy Wasserstein: A Casebook*. New York: Garland, 1999.

Ciociola, Gail. *Wendy Wasserstein: Dramatizing Women, Their Choices, and Their Boundaries*. Jefferson, N.C.: McFarland, 1998.

Frank, Glenda. "The Struggle to Affirm: The Image of Jewish-Americans on Stage." In *Staging Difference: Cultural Pluralism in American Theatre and Drama*, edited by Marc Maufort. New York: P. Lang, 1995.

Hoban, Phoebe. "The Family Wasserstein." *New York*, January 4, 1993.

Keyssar, Helene. "Drama and the Dialogic Imagination: *The Heidi Chronicles* and *Fefu and Her Friends*." In *Feminist Theater and Theory*, edited by Keyssar. New York: St. Martin's Press, 1997.
Whitfield, Stephen. "Wendy Wasserstein and the Crisis of (Jewish) Identity." In *Daughters of Valor: Contemporary Jewish American Women Writers*, edited by Jay Halio and Ben Siegel. Newark: University of Delaware Press, 1997.

Contributor: Shira Daemon

James Welch

Born: Browning, Montana; November 18, 1940
Died: Missoula, Montana; August 4, 2003

Native American

Welch's poems, novels, films, and nonfiction present the viewpoint of Native Americans.

Principal works

LONG FICTION: *Winter in the Blood*, 1974; *The Death of Jim Loney*, 1979; *Fools Crow*, 1986; *The Indian Lawyer*, 1990; *The Heartsong of Charging Elk*, 2000 (also known as *Heartsong*, 2001)

POETRY: *Riding the Earthboy Forty*, 1971, revised 1975

NONFICTION: *Killing Custer: The Battle of Little Bighorn and the Fate of the Plains Indians*, 1994 (with Paul Stekler)

James Welch received his Indian bloodline from his mother, of the Gros Ventre tribe, and from his father, of the Blackfeet tribe. Although his parents had as much Irish as Indian ancestry, for the most part he grew up near reservations. He attended Indian high schools in Browning and in Fort Belknap, Montana.

In 1965, while Welch was a student at the University of Montana, his mother, a stenographer at the reservation agency, brought home copies of annual reports from the Fort Belknap Indian agents for 1880, 1887, and 1897. These documents excited Welch, for they offered statistics on the numerical decline of Indians and showed agents' purposeful efforts to control Indians. Of greater interest was evidence that an agent had reported communication with Chief Sitting Bull who had been for a time within a few miles of the house where Welch lived. This revelation ignited Welch's interest in the history of his people.

"I wanted to write about that Highline Country in an extended way," says Welch in describing the impetus for *Winter in the Blood*. Welch captures the feeling of vast openness of Northeastern Montana's rolling plains. The novel is about a young Indian who lacks purpose in life until he discovers how Yellow Calf saved and protected an Indian maiden, an intriguing, heroic tale of his Indian grandparents. The novel's locale is Welch's parents' ranch, and it suggests Welch's own discovery of Indian forebears.

Welch married Lois Monk, a professor of comparative literature, in 1968. In 1976, he held the Theodore Roethke Chair in Poetry at the University of Washington. He later served as a visiting professor there and at Cornell University. The year 1979 saw the appearance of *The Death of Jim Loney*, in which Welch portrays a young Indian tied by heritage to his reservation, unable to find opportunity there, endlessly drinking at lonely bars. Then came the historical novel *Fools Crow*, which would become his most successful book, especially in Western Europe. It also won the *Los Angeles Times* Book Prize for fiction, the American Book Award, and the Pacific Northwest Booksellers Award. A fourth novel, *The Indian Lawyer*, followed in 1990, suggested in part by Welch's ten-year service on the Montana State Board of Pardons.

James Welch (Marc Hefty)

In 1992 Welch was asked to coauthor the script of the documentary *Last Stand at Little Bighorn*, for the public television series *The American Experience*. This film script, and the tribal research it required, inspired his only nonfiction book, *Killing Custer: The Battle of Little Bighorn and the Fate of the Plains Indians* (1994), written with Paul Stekler, which presented an account of the 1876 massacre of General George Custer's army from an Indian perspective. Author Sherman Alexie praised this as "the first history book written for Indians."

Welch was named a Chevalier of the Order of Arts and Letters by the French government for *Fools Crow* in 1995; in later years, the Welches traveled often in France. His final novel, *The Heartsong of Charging Elk* (2000), based on a historical incident, replaced his customary Montana setting with that of nineteenth century France. At his death from a heart attack (while battling lung cancer), he had been working on a sequel to bring Charging Elk home.

Fools Crow

Type of work: Novel
First published: 1986

Fools Crow dramatizes Native American life on the plains of eastern Montana toward the end of the era of the free, nonreservation tribe. This novel follows an Indian coming to manhood, his free life, his romantic marriage, his daring attack on an enemy, his struggle with the dilemma of whether to fight the white man and be slain or to submit to humiliating poverty and confinement on a reservation. Welch inherited sympathy for Native Americans from his Gros Ventre mother and from his Blackfoot father. His mother showed Welch documents from the Indian agency where she worked. The tales of his paternal grandmother concerning the awful massacre at Marias River, Montana, provided basic material and a viewpoint from which to write. Welch's grandmother, a girl at the time of the massacre, was wounded but escaped with a few survivors. She spoke only her tribal language.

In *Fools Crow*, White Man's Dog yearns to find respect. At eighteen he has three puny horses, a musket without powder, and no wife. He joins in a raid, in which he proves himself. He woos beautiful Red Paint. His young wife fears he may be killed yet yearns for his honor as a warrior; in a war raid, he outwits and kills the renowned Crow chief, thereby winning the mature name of Fools Crow. Names such as that of his father, Rides-at-the-door, and of the medicine man, Mik-Api, suggest an Indian culture. The people pray to The Above Ones—the gods—and to Cold Maker, winter personified. These gods sometimes instruct warriors such as Fools Crow in dreams.

Fools Crow follows Raven—a sacred messenger—to free his animal helper, a wolverine, from a white man's steel trap. Later the Raven requires that Fools Crow lure to death a white man who shoots animals and leaves the flesh to rot. Smallpox ravages the teepees. Settlers push into the treaty territory, reducing buffalo, essential for food, shelter, and livelihood. Fools Crow finds a few of his people running in the northern winter away from the Army slaughter of an entire village. In a vision experience, he sees his people living submissively with the powerful whites. Hope for his people resides in such children as his infant son Butterfly.

The Heartsong of Charging Elk

Type of work: Novel
First published: 2000

The Heartsong of Charging Elk opens when Charging Elk wakes up in a hospital in Marseille in 1889 and slowly realizes where he is. A member of Buffalo Bill's touring Wild West Show, Charging Elk has fallen off his horse and broken his ribs, and now the show has moved on, and Charging Elk is left to the mercy of the French governmental bureaucracy. What follows is a fascinating account of the adventures of a true stranger in a strange land.

Welch alternates this main narrative with long flashbacks, as Charging Elk remembers his earlier life. After Red Cloud and the other Oglalas were defeated by the U.S. Army in 1877, Charging Elk and his friend Strikes Plenty stayed free for another decade, and many of his memories center on that last period of freedom for western American Indians. His earlier life seems tame and peaceful in contrast to the present, however: He has been arrested, tried, imprisoned, and treated as a savage by the provincial French authorities. By staying true to his Indian spirit, however, Charging Elk survives the hardships and suffering, eventually finding love and happiness in France.

The Heartsong of Charging Elk is based on historical precedent, for both Black Elk and Standing Bear left accounts of the European tour of Buffalo Bill's Wild West Show. What Welch's novel does is to render Charging Elk's experiences in such detailed and different settings that readers view Native American life without the mediation of white America, and the result is a sad but powerful story.

Suggested Readings

Beidler, Peter G., ed. *American Indian Quarterly* 4 (May, 1978).

Gish, Robert F. "Word Medicine: Storytelling and Magic Realism in James Welch's *Fools Crow*." *American Indian Quarterly* 14, no. 4 (Fall, 1990).

McFarland, Ronald E. *Understanding James Welch*. Columbia: University of South Carolina Press, 2000.

Nelson, Robert M. *Place and Vision: The Function of Landscape in Native American Literature*. New York: P. Lang, 1993.

Schort, Blanca. *Storied Voices in Native American Texts: Harry Robinson, Thomas King, James Welch, and Leslie Marmon Silko*. New York: Routledge, 2003.

Velie, Alan R. "Blackfeet Surrealism: The Poetry of James Welch." In *Four American Indian Literary Masters*. Norman: University of Oklahoma Press, 1982.

Wild, Peter. *James Welch*. Boise, Idaho: Boise State University Press, 1983.

Contributor: Emmett H. Carroll

Ida B. Wells-Barnett

Born: Holly Springs, Mississippi; July 16, 1862
Died: Chicago, Illinois; March 25, 1931

African American

Wells-Barnett's work in civil rights and in feminism was central to the struggle for African Americans' participation in American life.

Principal works

NONFICTION: *Crusade for Justice: The Autobiography of Ida B. Wells*, 1970; *The Memphis Diary of Ida B. Wells*, 1995; *Southern Horrors, and Other Writings: The Anti-Lynching Campaign of Ida B. Wells, 1892-1900*, 1997
MISCELLANEOUS: *Selected Works of Ida B. Wells-Barnett*, 1991

Ida B. Wells-Barnett was a prolific author whose work covered a wide range of subjects: civil rights, suffrage, social justice, feminism, race riots, social settlements, women's organizations, travel, and voluntary associations. Many of these works were published in newspapers, pamphlets, and journals.

From 1889 to 1892 she was the editor of a newspaper, *Free Speech*, in Memphis, Tennessee. When she wrote an editorial criticizing a white mob who lynched three men who were her friends, her newspaper was destroyed and she had to flee for her life. She continued to protest against lynching for the rest of her life. She documented the horrors of the practice in a series of writings, especially in pamphlets, and three of these pamphlets were reprinted in the book *On Lynchings*.

Wells-Barnett witnessed injustice toward African Americans in a wide range of other settings and institutions, for example, in employment, housing, voting, and politics. Many of her writings on these subjects were published in African American newspapers that have been lost, so the full range of her thought remains to be documented. She was active in founding many civil rights organizations, such as the National Association for the Advancement of Colored People, the Equal Rights League, and the Negro Fellowship League. Two important allies on numerous issues were Frederick Douglass and Jane Addams. Wells-Barnett opposed the gradual approach to changing race relations advocated by Booker T. Washington, and this stand was courageous during the height of Washington's influence.

Wells-Barnett was a leader in women's clubs, although she fought with many white and African American women about the pace and direction of their protests. She was active for several years in the National Association of Colored

Women's Clubs and founded the Ida B. Wells Clubs and the Alpha Suffrage Club, among others.

Although Wells-Barnett was born into slavery, she conquered racism, sexism, and poverty to become an articulate and forceful leader. Her autobiography documents not only these public struggles but also her personal decisions to help rear her orphaned siblings, marry, and rear five children.

Crusade for Justice

Type of work: Autobiography
First published: 1970

Crusade for Justice: The Autobiography of Ida B. Wells is the inspiring story of an African American feminist and civil rights leader. Wells-Barnett documents her individual struggles, her accomplishments, and her major activities to promote equality for women and African Americans. Born into slavery in 1862, she lived through the Reconstruction era after the U.S. Civil War, the battle for suffrage, World War I, and its aftermath. Wells-Barnett's reflections provide a critical review of American racial and sexual relations. She did not simply observe the American scene; she also altered it as a leader in the women's movement and the African American Civil Rights movement.

The autobiography is especially important in documenting the widespread patterns of lynchings of African American men by white mobs. In protests and writings about these horrors, Wells-Barnett fought against any acceptance of these illegal and violent acts. She struggled with many people to have her radical and unflinching stands represented. Her struggles included arguments with other leaders such as the suffragist Susan B. Anthony, the civil rights activist W. E. B. Du Bois, and the African American leader Booker T. Washington. She presents her side of these differences in the autobiography, which reflects her occasional unwillingness to compromise and her hot temper.

Wells-Barnett published in formats such as small-circulation newspapers, pamphlets, and journals, so the autobiography is vital in providing obscure information about her life and ideas. She did not complete the autobiography, however, and her daughter Alfreda Duster helped fill in many missing pieces for the publication of the manuscript almost four decades after her mother's death. In addition, Wells-Barnett lost many of her writings in two different fires, so her daughter did not have access to the full range of her mother's publications and thoughts. As a result, major areas of Wells-Barnett's life and ideas are not covered or explained. Wells-Barnett's life is remarkable in its courage and influence. She refused to be limited by her battles with personal poverty, sexism, and racism, and her valiant spirit is apparent in her life story.

Suggested Readings

Apteker, Bettina. Introduction to *Lynching and Rape: An Exchange of Views*, by Jane Addams and Ida B. Wells-Barnett. San Jose, Calif.: American Institute for Marxist Studies, 1977.

Bedermank, Gail. " 'Civilization,' The Decline of Middle-Class Manliness, and Ida B. Wells's Antilynching Campaign (1892-94)." *Radical History Review*, no. 52 (1992): 5-30.

Broschart, Kay. "Ida B. Wells-Barnett." In *Women in Sociology*, edited by Mary Jo Deegan. Westport, Conn.: Greenwood Press, 1991.

Giddings, Paula. *When and Where I Enter: The Impact of Black Women on Race and Sex in America*. New York: William Morrow, 1984.

Hendricks, Wanda. "Ida Bell Wells-Barnett." In *Black Women in America: An Historical Encyclopedia*, edited by Darlene Clark Hine. Brooklyn, N.Y.: Carlson, 1993.

Loewenberg, Bert James, and Ruth Bogin, eds. *Black Women in Nineteenth Century American Life*. University Park: Pennsylvania State University Press, 1976.

Sterling, Dorothy. "Ida B. Wells: Voice of a People." In *Black Foremothers: Three Lives*. Old Westburg, N.Y.: The Feminist Press, 1979.

Tucker, David M. "Miss Ida B. Wells and Memphis Lynching." *Phylon* 32 (Summer, 1971): 112-22.

Wells, Ida B. *Crusade for Justice: The Autobiography of Ida B. Wells*. Edited by Alfreda M. Duster. Chicago: University of Chicago Press, 1970.

Contributor: Mary Jo Deegan

Cornel West

Born: Tulsa, Oklahoma; June 2, 1953

African American

Best known for his works of political and social philosophy, West is among the most significant intellectuals in the United States.

Principal works

NONFICTION: *Prophesy Deliverance! An Afro-American Revolutionary Christianity*, 1982; *Prophetic Fragments*, 1988; *The American Evasion of Philosophy: A Genealogy of Pragmatism*, 1989; *Breaking Bread: Insurgent Black Intellectual Life*, 1991 (with Bell Hooks); *The Ethical Dimensions of Marxist Thought*, 1991; *Beyond Eurocentrism and Multiculturalism*, 1993 (2 volumes); *Keeping Faith: Philosophy and Race in America*, 1993; *Race Matters*, 1993; *Jews and Blacks: Let the Healing Begin*, 1995 (with Michael Lerner; rev. as *Jews and Blacks: A Dialogue on Race, Religion, and Culture in America*, 1996); *The Future of the Race*, 1996 (with Henry Louis Gates, Jr.); *Restoring Hope: Conversations on the Future of Black America*, 1997 (Kelvin Shawn Sealey, editor); *The Future of American Progressivism: An Initiative for Political and Economic Reform*, 1998 (with Roberto Mangabeira Unger); *The War Against Parents: What We Can Do for America's Beleaguered Moms and Dads*, 1998 (with Sylvia Ann Hewlett); *The Cornel West Reader*, 1999; *The African-American Century: How Black Americans Have Shaped Our Country*, 2000 (with Gates); *Cornel West: A Critical Reader*, 2001 (George Yancy, editor); *Democracy Matters*, 2004

EDITED TEXTS: *Theology in America: Detroit II Conference Papers*, 1982 (with Caridad Guidote and Margaret Coakley); *Post-Analytic Philosophy*, 1985 (with John Rajchman); *Out There: Marginalization and Contemporary Cultures*, 1991; *White Screens, Black Images: Hollywood from the Dark Side*, 1994 (with James Snead and Colin MacCabe); *Encyclopedia of African-American Culture and History*, 1996 (with Jack Salzman and David Lionel Smith); *Struggles in the Promised Land: Towards a History of Black-Jewish Relations in the United States*, 1997 (with Salzman); *The Courage to Hope: From Black Suffering to Human Redemption*, 1999 (with Quinton Hosford Dixie); *Taking Parenting Public: The Case for a New Social Movement*, 2002 (with Sylvia Ann Hewlett and Nancy Rankin); *Racist Traces and Other Writings: European Pedigrees/African Contagions*, 2003 (by James Sneak; with Kera Keeling and Colin MacCabe)

Cornel Ronald West was the son of a civilian Air Force administrator Clifton L. West, Jr., and his wife, Irene Bias West, a teacher and school principal after whom an elementary school in Sacramento, California, is named. He was an early achiever: student body president of both his junior and senior high schools and a violinist in his school orchestra. He placed first in the two-mile track contest at the all-city meet and was on his school's seventh-grade football team. Upon graduation from John F. Kennedy High School in Sacramento, he entered Harvard University, where, in 1973, he received his bachelor's degree magna cum laude after three years. Originally he majored in philosophy, but he soon switched to Near Eastern languages so that he could read the biblical languages Hebrew and Aramaic. West studied history extensively and pursued both formal course work and independent reading in social thought. At Harvard, West was surrounded by exciting intellectuals, and he drew fully upon the intellectual resources they offered.

He continued his education in philosophy at Princeton University, receiving his master's degree in 1975 and his doctorate in 1980. In that year he married his first wife, the mother of his only child, Clifton L. West III; he would later remarry, to Elleni Gebre Amlak. Richard Rorty, generally considered the most significant philosophical pragmatist in the United States, became one of West's mentors at Princeton and taught him a great deal about American pragmatism. West contrived

Cornel West (AP/Wide World Photos)

his own version of what he termed "prophetic pragmatism," creating a new pragmatism that avoided Rorty's ethnocentricity and the conservatism that was inherent in Rorty's political pessimism.

While he was completing his doctoral studies, West was appointed assistant professor of the history of religion at New York City's Union Theological Seminary. At that time, Union was considered by many the most intellectually exciting seminary in the United States. West remained there for six years and spent another year affiliated with the school in 1988. In 1984, he joined the staff of Yale University's Divinity School, where he remained until 1987. He spent the spring semester of 1988 teaching at the University of Paris.

The following year, Princeton University appointed West professor of religion and made him director of its African American studies program. He served in that capacity from 1988 to 1994, when he was appointed professor of African American studies and the philosophy of religion at Harvard. In 2002, after a dispute with Harvard's president, Lawrence Summers, West returned to Princeton, this time as Class of 1943 University Professor of Religion.

West's religious stance, which postulates a union between Christianity and Marxism, has been truly ecumenical. Although clinging to his Baptist roots, he has reached out to people of other faiths in his attempts to understand the roots of religious divisions. In 1982, he collaborated with two Roman Catholic nuns in editing *Theology in the Americas: Detroit II Conference Papers*. He also has been extremely interested in the relationship between Jewish and African Americans, and has collaborated with two Jewish scholars on books that address this issue: *Jews and Blacks: A Dialogue on Race, Religion, and Culture in America*, with Michael Lerner, and *Struggles in the Promised Land: Towards a History of Black-Jewish Relations in the United States*, with Jack Salzman.

Much of West's writing is devoted to the development of a new pragmatism that runs somewhat counter to that of his Princeton mentor, Rorty. West has read the work of the most significant philosophers of Western civilization—Immanuel Kant, David Hume, Ludwig Wittgenstein, Karl Marx, Leon Trotsky, Blaise Pascal, and Søren Kierkegaard—all of whom have influenced his thinking and led him to original insights. West's writing is essentially a quest to understand the position and role of African Americans in society and to analyze their roles in relation to the roles of other groups.

Prophesy Deliverance!

Type of work: Speeches
First published: 1982

West made his publishing debut in 1982 with *Prophesy Deliverance!*, a collection of addresses he delivered at Brooklyn's Lord Pentecostal Church. In these addresses, West stresses the inherent value of all humanity regardless of race, class, gender, and other arbitrary distinctions. The prophetic Christianity that West espouses views knowledge as being communally created, a view that certainly speaks to the unity of all humans despite their obvious individual differences.

West outlines the steps prophetic Christianity must take in order to affect society. He recognizes and encourages the significant role that individualism plays, but he tempers it by insisting upon an acceptance of the supremacy of divine grace. He contends that prophetic Christianity must critically examine and seek to redirect the prevailing supremacy of a white society, which he believes is undermining African American society. He calls on blacks to honestly and objectively assess their responses to white domination and oppression.

Perhaps the most startling of West's proposals is his call for "thoughtful engagement" between prophetic Christianity and progressive Marxism. He calls on blacks to construct a model for advancing the progress and liberation of black Americans. His linking of Christianity and Marxism may seem a drastic alliance, but West's contention here and in much of his later writing is that a redistribution of wealth is essential to reforming society equitably. Certainly nothing could challenge white supremacy more pointedly than a move toward the Marxism that West champions.

Perhaps the most challenging insight in this book is West's understanding of where African Americans stand in relation to other immigrants in American society. During the nineteenth century, waves of immigrants from Europe flooded the United States, but, unlike American blacks, they were free.

West asserts that European modernity was in decline from 1871 until 1950 and that this decline resulted in postmodernism. He finds that African Americans were becoming a part of the modern world at precisely the time that European immigrants to America and their progeny were being drawn into the postmodern world. West's reasoning goes far in explaining and illuminating some of the black-white conflicts that have led to considerable racial strife in the United States, particularly in the decade immediately preceding the publication of this book.

The American Evasion of Philosophy

Type of work: Philosophy
First published: 1989

Having studied at Princeton with a man reputed to be America's greatest living pragmatic philosopher, Richard Rorty, and having a profound understanding of the works of such other American pragmatists as C. S. Peirce, William James, and John Dewey, it is not surprising that in 1989 West turned his attention to presenting his own take on pragmatism. Although he greatly admires Rorty, he is unable to unquestioningly accept Rorty's version of pragmatism, which espouses many ideals with which West can agree but some that he cannot.

Although Rorty is appalled by human cruelty and argues for a pluralistic society in which racial harmony exists, he argues from a white perspective and is unable to view racism the way West can, having been exposed to racism throughout his life. West's book is cautionary, arguing, however gently, against the new pragmatism that Rorty espouses. He argues that American pragmatism has evaded important aspects of its Cartesian predecessors.

West asserts that once one begins to demythologize philosophy, the result is the introduction of the complexities of both politics and culture. He takes Rorty to task for his reading of the pragmatism of John Dewey, who is in many respects the most significant pragmatic philosopher of the twentieth century. He faults Rorty's Dewey as being much more intellectually playful and politically tame than the Dewey West has gleaned from his extensive reading of Dewey's work. This book is essentially an argument in favor of West's prophetic pragmatism, which is a vital concomitant of his Christianity.

Race Matters

Type of work: Essays
First published: 1993

Race Matters was published in April, 1993, one year following the Los Angeles riots sparked by the trials of four police officers who had participated in the beating of Rodney King. To West, the case and its aftermath demonstrated the pain and distress the public feels in dealing seriously with any matter involving race. People would rather sweep such matters under the carpet than consider them with an eye toward bringing about much-needed change.

This collection presents essays with such titles as "Nihilism in Black America," "The Pitfalls of Racial Reasoning," "The Crisis of Black Leadership," "Demystifying the New Black Conservatism," "Beyond Affirmative Action: Equality and Identity," "On Black-Jewish Relations," and "Malcolm X and Black Rage." Throughout his text, West urges readers to work toward building a communal spirit.

West contends that the way people deal with situations determines their response to these situations, suggestive of Marshall McLuhan's contention in the mid-1960's that the medium is the message. Blacks and whites, liberals and conservatives have, according to West, been responsible for the failure of race relations in the United States. The white community appears limited to viewing the black community from a white perspective. West urges the building of black-white coalitions, a more equitable distribution of resources, public intervention to provide for the needs of all citizens (particularly their health and educational needs), and the implementation of a system that prepares people, especially young people, to assume the leadership roles that will make his ideal society a reality.

West chides intellectually gifted blacks who choose to attend prestigious, predominantly white institutions of higher learning, suggesting that they do so for their own betterment rather than for the betterment of their race. He questions why they do not attend predominantly black schools and help to elevate the quality of such institutions. Coming from a writer whose degrees are from Harvard and Princeton, this suggestion has struck many readers as disingenuous.

The Rodney King debacle certainly brought racial tensions in Los Angeles to the boiling point, but West contends, probably quite validly, that race was the obvious and visible cause of the eruption, but not the fundamental cause. Rather, he blames a combination of economic decline, cultural decay, and political lethargy.

Democracy Matters

Type of work: Essays
First published: 2004

In this sequel to *Race Matters*, published eleven years after that best-selling collection of essays, Cornel West scrutinizes the democratic tradition in the United States and America's attempts to impose democracy upon sovereign Middle Eastern countries. His democracy would emphasize justice and love, would foster a worldwide sense of community built on Socratic dialogue and prophetic practices.

West decries America's attempts to impose a political system on the Middle East through military force and authoritarianism on the part of the United States government. As in much of his work, he cringes at the narrow perspectives through which America views the world. He recalls some of the greatest thinkers of the past, citing their historical, religious, and philosophical ideas, and he then compares their ideals with the current leadership of the United States.

Nine pages of this book are devoted to West's account of why he, after locking horns with Harvard president Lawrence Summers, resigned from his tenured professorship and, in 2002, returned to Princeton. His move from Harvard was highly controversial and resulted in other departures among some notable black scholars.

In this book, West writes analytically about America's youth culture and about hip-hop, in which he has a considerable interest. This interest was in part responsible for his rift with Summers and his departure from Harvard. He also analyzes American Christianity and somewhat softens but does not abandon his early contention that Christianity and Marxism must combine for the betterment of society.

Suggested Readings

Anderson, Jervis. "The Public Intellectual." *The New Yorker* 69 (January 17, 1994): 39-46.

Appiah, K. Anthony. "A Prophetic Pragmatism." *The Nation* 250 (April 9, 1990): 496-498.

Berube, Michael. "Public Academy." *The New Yorker* 70 (January 9, 1995): 73-80.

Cowan, Rosemary. *Cornel West: The Politics of Redemption*. Malden, Mass.: Blackwell, 2002.

Johnson, Clarence Shole. *Cornel West and Philosophy*. New York: Routledge, 2002.

Nichols, John. "Cornel West." *The Progressive* 61 (January, 1997: 26-29.
West, Cornel. "Cornel West." Interview by John Nichols. *The Progressive* 61 (January, 1997): 26-29.
White, Jack E. "Philosopher with a Mission." *Time* 141 (June 7, 1993): 60-62.
Wood, Mark David. *Cornel West and the Politics of Prophetic Pragmatism.* Urbana: University of Illinois Press, 2000.
Yancy, George, ed. *Cornel West: A Critical Reader.* Cambridge, Mass.: Blackwell, 2001.

Contributor: R. Baird Shuman

Phillis Wheatley

Born: West Coast of Africa (possibly the Senegal-Gambia region); 1753(?)
Died: Boston, Massachusetts; December 5, 1784

African American

America's first black poet and only its second published woman poet, Wheatley produced sophisticated, original poems whose creative theories of the imagination and the sublime anticipate the Romantic movement.

Principal works

POETRY: *Poems on Various Subjects, Religious and Moral*, 1773; *The Poems of Phillis Wheatley*, 1966, 1989 (Julian D. Mason, Jr., editor)

MISCELLANEOUS: *Memoir and Poems of Phillis Wheatley: A Native African and a Slave*, 1833; *The Collected Works of Phillis Wheatley*, 1988 (John Shields, editor)

From the time of her first published piece to the present day, controversy surrounded the life and work of Phillis Wheatley (WEET-lee), America's first black poet and only its second published woman poet (after Anne Bradstreet). Few poets of any age have been so scornfully maligned, so passionately defended, so fervently celebrated, and so patronizingly tolerated.

The known details of Wheatley's life are few. A slave, she was, according to her master, John Wheatley of Boston, "brought from Africa to America in the Year 1761, between Seven and Eight Years of Age [sic]." Her parents were apparently sun worshippers, for she is supposed to have recalled to her white captors that she remembered seeing her mother pouring out water to the sun every morning. If such be the case, it would help to explain why the sun is predominant as an image in her poetry.

Her life with the Wheatleys, John and Susanna and their two children, the twins Mary and Nathaniel, was probably not too demanding for one whose disposition toward asthma (brought on or no doubt exacerbated by the horrible "middle passage") greatly weakened her. The Wheatleys' son attended Harvard, so it is likely that Nathaniel served as the eager young girl's Latin tutor. At any rate, it is certain that Wheatley knew Latin well; her translation of the Niobe episode from book 6 of Ovid's *Metamorphoses* displays a learned knowledge and appreciation of the Latin original. Wheatley's classical learning is evident throughout her poetry, which is thick with allusions to ancient historical and mythological figures.

During the years of her young adulthood, Phillis Wheatley was the toast of

England and the colonies. For years before she attempted to find a Boston publisher for her poems, she had published numerous elegies celebrating the deaths of many of the city's most prominent citizens. In 1770, she wrote her most famous and most often-reprinted elegy, on the death of "the voice of the Great Awakening," George Whitefield, chaplain to the countess of Huntingdon, who was one of the leading benefactors of the Methodist evangelical movement in England and the colonies.

Not finding Boston to be in sympathy with her 1772 proposal for a volume, Wheatley found substantial support the following year in the countess of Huntingdon, whose interest had been stirred by the young poet's noble tribute to her chaplain. Subsequently, Wheatley was sent to London, ostensibly for her health; this trip curiously accords, however, with the very weeks that her book was being printed. The turning point of Wheatley's career, not only as an author but also as a human being, came when her *Poems on Various Subjects, Religious and Moral* was published in London in 1773. It is likely that she proofread the galleys herself. At any rate, she was much sought after among the intellectual, literary set of London, and Sir Brook Watson, who was to become Lord Mayor of London within a year, presented her with a copy of John Milton's *Paradise Lost* (1667) in folio. The earl of Dartmouth, who was at the time secretary of state for the colonies and president of the board of Trade and Foreign Plantations, gave her a copy of Tobias Smollett's translation of *Don Quixote* (1755). Benjamin Franklin, to whom she would later inscribe her second book of poetry (never published), has even recorded that, while in London briefly, he called on Wheatley to see whether "there were any service I could do her."

After she returned from England, having been recalled because of Susanna Wheatley's growing illness, she was manumitted sometime during September, 1773. It is probable that Wheatley was freed because of the severe censure that some English reviewers of her *Poems* had directed at the owners of a learned author who "still remained a slave."

In the opening pages of her 1773 volume appears a letter of authentication of Wheatley's authorship which is signed by still another of the signatories of the Declaration of Independence, John Hancock. Added to the list of attesters are other outstanding Bostonians, including Thomas Hutchinson, then governor of Massachusetts, and James Bowdoin, one of the founders of Bowdoin College. Later, during the early months of the revolution, Wheatley wrote a poem in praise of General George Washington titled "To His Excellency General Washington." As a result, she received an invitation to visit the general at his headquarters, and her poem was published by Tom Paine in *The Pennsylvania Magazine*. John Paul Jones, who also appreciated Wheatley's celebration of freedom, even asked one of his officers to secure him a copy of her *Poems*.

Nevertheless, she did not continue to enjoy such fame. A country ravaged by war has little time, finally, for poetry, and Wheatley regrettably, perhaps tragically, faced the rejection of two more proposals for a volume of new poems. In 1778, at the height of the war and after the deaths of both John and Susanna Wheatley, she married John Peters, a black man of some learning who failed to rescue the poet from poverty.

Wheatley died alone and unattended in a hovel somewhere in the back streets of the Boston slums in 1784, truly an ignominious end for one who had enjoyed such favor. She was preceded in death by two of her children, as well as by the third, to whom she had just given birth. She was only thirty-one years old. Given Wheatley's vision of the world "Oppress'd with woes, a painful endless train," it should not be surprising that her most frequently adopted poetic form is the elegy, in which she always celebrates death as the achievement of ultimate freedom—suggesting the thanatos-eros (desire for death) motif of Romanticism. Along with Philip Freneau, she is arguably the most important poet of America's Revolutionary War era.

The Political Poems

Type of work: Poetry
Written: 1768-1784

Wheatley's political poems document major incidents of the American struggle for independence. In 1768, she wrote "To the King's Most Excellent Majesty on His Repealing the American Stamp Act." When it appeared, much revised, in *Poems on Various Subjects, Religious and Moral*, the poet diplomatically deleted the last two lines of the original, which read, "When wars came on [against George] the proudest rebel fled/ God thunder'd fury on their guilty head." By that time, the threat of the king's retaliation did not seem so forbidding nor the injustice of rebellion against him so grave.

"America," a poem probably written about the same time but published only recently, admonishes Britain to treat "americus," the British child, with more deference. According to the poem, the child, now a growing seat of "Liberty," is no mere adorer of an overwhelming "Majesty," but has acquired strength of his own: "Fearing his strength which she [Britain] undoubted knew/ She laid some taxes on her darling son." Recognizing her mistake, "great Britannia" promised to lift the burden, but the promise proved only "seeming Sympathy and Love." Now the Child "weeps afresh to feel this Iron chain." The urge to draw an analogy here between the poem's "Iron chain" and Wheatley's own predicament is irresistible; while America longs for its own independence, Wheatley no doubt yearns for hers.

The year 1770 marked the beginning of armed resistance against Britain. Wheatley chronicles such resistance in two poems, the second of which is now lost. The first, "On the Death of Mr. Snider Murder'd by Richardson," appeared initially along with "America." The poem tells how Ebenezer Richardson, an informer on American traders involved in circumventing British taxation, found his home surrounded on the evening of February 22, 1770, by an angry mob of colonial sympathizers. Much alarmed, Richardson emerged from his house armed with a musket and fired indiscriminately into the mob, killing the eleven- or twelve-year-old son of Snider, a poor German colonist. Wheatley calls young Christopher Snider, of whose death Richardson was later found guilty in a trial by jury, "the first martyr for the common good," rather than those men killed less than two weeks later in the

Phillis Wheatley (Library of Congress)

Boston Massacre. The poem's fine closing couplet suggests that even those not in sympathy with the quest for freedom can grasp the nobility of that quest and are made indignant by its sacrifice: "With Secret rage fair freedom's foes beneath/ See in thy corse ev'n Majesty in Death."

Wheatley does not, however, ignore the Boston Massacre. In a proposal for a volume which was to have been published in Boston in 1772, she lists, among twenty-seven titles of poems (the 1773 volume had thirty-nine), "On the Affray in King Street, on the Evening of the 5th of March." This title, naming the time and place of the Massacre, suggests that the poet probably celebrated the martyrdom of Crispus Attucks, the first black man to lose his life in the American struggle, along with the deaths of two white men. Regrettably, the poem has not yet been recovered. Even so, the title alone confirms Wheatley's continued recording of America's struggle for freedom. This concern shifted in tone from obedient praise for the British regime to supplicatory admonition and then to guarded defiance. Since she finally found a publisher not in Boston but in London, she prudently omitted "America" and the poems about Christopher Snider and the Boston Massacre from her 1773 volume.

She chose to include, however, a poem dedicated to the earl of Dartmouth, who was appointed secretary of state for the colonies in August, 1772. In this poem, "To the Right Honourable William, Earl of Dartmouth, His Majesty's Principal Secretary of State for North America," she gives the earl extravagant praise as one who will lay to rest "hatred faction." She knew of the earl's reputation as a humanitarian through the London contacts of her mistress, Susanna. When the earl proved to support oppressive British policies, the poet's expectations were not realized; within four years of the poem's date, America had declared its independence. Since her optimism was undaunted by foreknowledge, Wheatley wrote a poem that was even more laudatory than "To the King's Most Excellent Majesty on His Repealing the American Stamp Act." Perhaps she was not totally convinced, however; the poem contains some unusually bold passages for a colonist who is also both a woman and a slave.

For example, she remarks that, with Dartmouth's secretaryship, America need no longer "dread the iron chain,/ Which wanton *Tyranny* with lawless hand/ Had made, and with it meant t'enslave the land." Once again Wheatley uses the slave metaphor of the iron chain. Quite clearly she also accuses the Crown of "wanton *Tyranny*," which it had wielded illegally and with the basest of motives—to reduce the colonies to the inhuman condition of slave states. Here rebellious defiance, no longer guarded, is unmistakable; the tone matches that of the Declaration of Independence. It is a mystery how these lines could have gone unnoticed in the London reviews, all of them positive, of her 1773 volume. Perhaps the reviewers were too bedazzled by the "improbability" that a black woman could produce such a volume to take the content of her poetry seriously.

In this poem, Wheatley also presents a rare autobiographical portrait describing the manner in which she was taken from her native Africa. The manuscript version of this passage is more spontaneous and direct than the more formally correct one printed in the 1773 volume, and thus is closer to the poet's true feelings. It was "Seeming cruel fate" which snatched her "from Afric's fancy'd happy seat." Fate here is only apparently cruel, since her capture has enabled her to become a Christian; the young poet's piety resounds throughout her poetry and letters. Her days in her native land were, nevertheless, happy ones, and her abduction at the hands of ruthless slavers doubtless left behind inconsolable parents. Such a bitter memory of the circumstances of her abduction fully qualifies her to "deplore the day/ When Britons weep beneath Tyrannic sway"; the later version reads: "And can I then but pray/ Others may never feel tyrannic sway?" Besides toning down the diction, this passage alters her statement to a question and replaces "Britons" with the neutral "others." The question might suggest uncertainty, but it more probably reflects the author's polite deportment toward a London audience. Since, in the earlier version, she believed Dartmouth to be sympathetic with her cause, she had no reason to exercise deference toward him; she thought she could be frank. The shift from "Britons" to "others" provokes a more compelling explanation. In the fall of 1772, Wheatley could still think of herself as a British subject. Later, however, after rejoicing that the earl's administration had given way to restive disillusionment, perhaps the poet was less certain about her citizenship.

Three years after the publication of her 1773 volume, Wheatley unabashedly celebrated the opposition to the "tyrannic sway" of Britain in "To His Excellency General Washington," newly appointed commander in chief of the Continental Army; the war of ideas had become one of arms. In this piece, which is more a paean to freedom than a eulogy to Washington, she describes freedom as "divinely fair,/ Olive and laurel bind her golden hair"; yet "She flashes dreadful in refulgent arms." The poet accents this image of martial glory with an epic simile, comparing the American forces to the power of the fierce king of the winds:

> As when Eolus heaven's fair face deforms,
> Enwrapp'd in tempest and a night of storms;
> Astonish'd ocean feels the wild uproar,
> The refluent surges beat the sounding shore.

For the young poet, America is now "The land of freedom's heaven-defended race!" While the eyes of the world's nations are fixed "on the scales,/ For in their hopes Columbia's arm prevails," the poet records Britain's regret over her loss: "Ah! cruel blindness to Columbia's state!/ Lament thy thirst of boundless power too late." The temper of this couplet is in keeping with Wheatley's earlier attitudes toward oppression. The piece closes as the poet urges Washington to pursue his objective with the knowledge that virtue is on his side. If he allows the fair goddess Freedom to be his guide, Washington will surely emerge not only as the leader of a victorious army but also as the head of the newly established state.

In Wheatley's last political poem, "freedom's heaven-defended race" has won its battle. Written in 1784 within a year after the Treaty of Paris, "Liberty and Peace" is a demonstrative celebration of American independence. British tyranny, the agent of American oppression, has now been taught to fear "americus" her child, "And new-born *Rome* shall give *Britannia* Law." Wheatley concludes this piece with two pleasing couplets in praise of America, whose future is assured by heaven's approval:

> Auspicious Heaven shall fill with favoring Gales,
> Where e'er *Columbia* spreads her swelling Sails:
> To every Realm shall *Peace* her Charms display,
> And Heavenly *Freedom* spread her golden Ray.

Personified as Peace and Freedom, Columbia (America) will act as a world emissary, an emanating force like the rays of the sun. In this last couplet, Wheatley has captured, perhaps for the first time in poetry, America's ideal mission to the rest of the world.

The fact that Wheatley so energetically proclaims America's success in the political arena certainly attests her sympathies—not with the neoclassic obsession never to challenge the established order nor to breach the rules of political and social decorum—but with the Romantic notion that a people who find themselves unable to accept a present, unsatisfactory government have the right to change that government, even if such a change can be accomplished only through armed revolt. The American Revolution against Britain was the first successful such revolt and was one of the sparks of the French Revolution. Wheatley's steadfast literary participation in the American Revolution clearly aligns her with such politically active English Romantic poets as Percy Bysshe Shelley and Lord Byron.

The Elegies

Type of work: Poetry
Written: 1770's

In her elegies, on the other hand, Wheatley displays her devotion to spiritual freedom. As do her political poems, her elegies exalt specific occasions, the deaths of people usually known to her within the social and religious community of the poet's Old South Congregational Church of Boston. Also in the manner of her poems on political events, her elegies exceed the boundaries of occasional verse. The early, but most famous of her elegies, "On the Death of the Rev. Mr. George Whitefield, 1770," both illustrates the general structure in which she cast all seventeen of her extant elegies and indicates her recurring ideological concerns.

Wheatley's elegies conform for the most part to the Puritan funeral elegy. They include two major divisions: First comes the portrait, in which the poet pictures the life of the subject, then follows the exhortation, encouraging the reader to seek the heavenly rewards gained by the subject in death. The portrait usually comprises three biographical steps: vocation or conversion; sanctification, or evidence of good works; and glorification, or joyous treatment of the deceased's reception into heaven. Wheatley's elegy on Whitefield surprisingly opens with the glorification of the Great Awakener, already in Heaven and occupying his "immortal throne." She celebrates the minister's conversion or vocation in an alliterative line as "The greatest gift that ev'n a God can give." Of course, she writes many lines describing the good works of a man wholly devoted to the winning of souls during the seven visits which he made to America during and after the period of the Great Awakening.

Whitefield died in Newburyport, Massachusetts, on September 30, 1770, having left Boston only a week or so before, where he had apparently lodged with the Wheatley family. Indeed, the young poet of sixteen or seventeen appears to recollect from personal experience when she observes that the minister "long'd to see *America* excel" and "charg'd its youth that ev'ry grace divine/ Should with full lustre in their conduct shine." She also seizes this opportunity to proclaim to the world Whitefield's assertion that even Africans would find Jesus of Nazareth an "*Impartial Saviour*." The poem closes with a ten-line exhortation to the living to aspire toward Whitefield's example: "Let ev'ry heart to this bright vision rise."

As one can see, Wheatley's elegies are not sad affairs; quite to the contrary, they enact joyful occasions after which deceased believers may hope to unite, as she states in "On the Death of the Rev. Dr. Sewell, 1769," with "Great God, incomprehensible, unknown/ By sense." Although one's senses may limit a firsthand acquaintance with God, these same senses do enable one to learn *about* God, especially about God's works in nature. The poem in the extant Wheatley canon that most pointedly addresses God's works in nature is "Thoughts on the Works of Providence." This poem of 131 lines opens with a ten-line invocation to the "Celestial muse," resembling Milton's heavenly muse of *Paradise Lost*.

Identifying God as the force behind planetary movement, she writes, "Ador'd [is] the God that whirls surrounding spheres" which rotate ceaselessly about "the monarch of the earth and skies." From this sublime image she moves to yet another: "'Let there be light,' he said: from his profound/ Old chaos heard and trembled at the sound." It should not go unremarked that Wheatley could, indeed, find much in nature to foster her belief, but little in the mundane world of ordinary people to sustain her spiritually. The frequency of nature imagery but the relative lack of scenes drawn from human society (with the exception of her political poems, and even these are occasions for abstract departures into the investigation of political ideologies) probably reflects the poet's insecurity and uncertainty about a world which first made her a slave and then gave her, at best, second-class citizenship.

In "An Hymn to the Morning," one of her most lyrical poems, Wheatley interprets the morn (recall her mother's morning ritual of pouring out water to the rising sun) as the source of poetic afflatus or inspiration. The speaker of the poem, Wheatley herself, first perceives the light of the rising sun as a reflection in the eye of one of the "feather'd race." After she hears the song of the bird which welcomes the day, she turns to find the source of melody and sees the bird "Dart the bright eye, and shake the painted plume." Here the poet captures with great precision the bird's rapid eye movement. The bird, archetypal symbol of poetic song, has received the dawn's warm rays which stimulate it to sing. When the poet turns to discover the source of melody, however, what she sees first is not Aurora, the dawning sun, but Aurora the stimulus of song reflected within the "bright eye" of the bird.

In the next stanza the poet identifies the dawn as the ultimate source of poetic inspiration when she remarks that the sun has awakened Calliope, here the personification of inspiration, while her sisters, the other Muses, "fan the pleasing fire" of the stimulus to create. Hence both the song of the bird and the light reflected in its eye have instructed her to acknowledge the source of the bird's melody; for she aspires to sing with the same pleasing fire that animates the song of the bird. Like many of the Romantics who followed her, Wheatley perceives nature both as a means to know ultimate freedom and as an inspiration to create, to make art.

It is in her superlative poem, "On Imagination," however, that Wheatley most forcefully brings both aspirations, to know God and to create fine poetry, into clear focus. To the young black poet, the imagination was sufficiently important to demand from her pen a fifty-three-line poem. The piece opens with this four-line apostrophe:

> Thy various works, imperial queen, we see,
> How bright their forms! how deck'd with pomp by thee!
> Thy wond'rous acts in beauteous order stand,
> And all attest how potent is thine hand.

Clearly, Wheatley's imagination is a regal presence in full control of her poetic world, a world in which her "wond'rous acts" of creation stand in harmony, capturing a "beauteous order." These acts themselves testify to the queen's creative power. Following a four-line invocation to the Muse, however, the poet distinguishes the imagination from its subordinate fancy:

> Now, here, now there, the roving Fancy flies;
> Till some lov'd object strikes her wand'ring eyes,
> Whose silken fetters all the senses bind,
> And soft captivity involves the mind.

Unlike the controlled, harmonious imagination, the subordinate fancy flies about here and there, searching for some appropriate and desired object worthy of setting into motion the creative powers of her superior.

Poems of Fancy and Memory

Type of work: Poetry
Written: 1770's

In "Thoughts on the Works of Providence," the poet describes the psychology of sleep in similar fashion. Having entered the world of dreams, the mind discovers a realm where "ideas range/ Licentious and unbounded o'er the plains/ Where Fancy's queen in giddy triumph reigns." Wheatley maintains that in sleep the imagination, once again "Fancy's queen," creates worlds which lack the "beauteous order" of the poet sitting before a writing desk; nevertheless, these dream worlds provoke memorable images. In "On Recollection" Wheatley describes the memory as the repository on which the mind draws to create its dreams. What may be "long-forgotten," the memory "calls from night" and "plays before the fancy's sight." By analogy, Wheatley maintains, the memory provides the poet "ample treasure" from her "secret stores" to create poetry: "in her pomp of images display'd,/ To the high-raptur'd poet gives her aid." "On Recollection" asserts a strong affinity between the poet's memory, analogous to the world of dreams, and the fancy, the associative faculty subordinate to the imagination. Recollection for Wheatley functions as the poet's storehouse of images, while the fancy channels the force of the imagination through its associative powers. Both the memory and the fancy, then, serve the imagination.

Wheatley's description of fancy and memory departs markedly from what eighteenth century aestheticians, including John Locke and Joseph Addison, generally understood as the imagination. The faculty of mind which they termed "imagination" Wheatley relegates to recollection (memory) and fancy. Her description of recollection and fancy closely parallels Samuel Taylor Coleridge's in the famous thirteenth chapter of *Biographia Literaria* (1817), where he states that fancy "is indeed no other than a mode of Memory emancipated from the order of time and space." Wheatley's identification of the fancy as roving "Now here, now there" whose movement is analogous to the dream state, where "ideas range/ Licentious and unbounded," certainly frees it from the limits of time and space. Coleridge further limits the fancy to the capacity of choice. "But equally with the ordinary memory," he insists, "the Fancy must receive all its materials ready made from the law of association." Like Coleridge's, Wheatley's fancy exercises choice by association as it finally settles upon "some lov'd object."

If fancy and memory are the imagination's subordinates, then how does the imagination function in the poet's creative process? Following her description of fancy in "On Imagination," Wheatley details the role the imagination plays in her poetry. According to her, the power of the imagination enables her to soar "through air to find the bright abode,/ Th' empyreal palace of the thund'ring God." The central focus of her poetry remains contemplation of God. Foreshadowing William Wordsworth's "winds that will be howling at all hours," Wheatley exclaims that on the wings of the imagination she "can surpass the wind/ And leave the rolling universe behind." In the realm of the imagination, the poet can "with new worlds amaze th' unbounded soul."

Immediately following this arresting line, Wheatley illustrates in a ten-line stanza the power of the imagination to create new worlds. Even though winter and the "frozen deeps" prevail in the real world, the imagination can take one out of unpleasant reality and build a pleasant, mythic world of fragrant flowers and verdant groves where "Fair Flora" spreads "her fragrant reign," where Sylvanus crowns the forest with leaves, and where "Show'rs may descend, and dews their gems disclose,/ And nectar sparkle on the blooming rose." Such is the power of imagination to promote poetic creation and to release one from an unsatisfactory world. Unfortunately, like reality's painful intrusion upon the delicate, unsustainable song of John Keats's immortal bird, gelid winter and its severe "northern tempests damp the rising fire," cut short the indulgence of her poetic world, and lamentably force Wheatley to end her short-lived lyric: "Cease then, my song, cease the unequal lay." Her lyric must end because no poet can indefinitely sustain a mythic world.

In her use of the imagination to create "new worlds," Wheatley's departure from eighteenth century theories of this faculty is radical and once again points toward Coleridge. Although she does not distinguish between "primary" and "secondary" imagination as he does, Wheatley nevertheless constructs a theory which approaches his "secondary" imagination. According to Coleridge, the secondary imagination, which attends the creative faculty, intensifies the primary imagination common to all men. Coleridge describes how the secondary imagination operates in this well-known passage: "It dissolves, diffuses, dissipates, in order to recreate;/ or where this process is rendered impossible, yet still at all/ events it struggles to idealize and to unify." In spite of the fact that Wheatley's attempt to dissolve, diffuse, and dissipate is assuredly more modest than Coleridge's "swift half-intermitted burst" in "Kubla Khan," she does, nevertheless, like the apocalyptic Romantics, idealize, unify, and shape a mythopoeic world. Proceeding in a systematic fashion, she first constructs a theory of mental faculty which, when assisted by the associative fancy, builds, out of an act of the mind, a new world which does indeed stand in "beauteous order." This faculty, which she identifies as the imagination, she uses as a tool to achieve freedom, however momentary.

Wheatley was, then, an innovator who used the imagination as a means to transcend an unacceptable present and even to construct "new worlds [to] amaze the unbounded soul"; this practice, along with her celebration of death, her loyalty to the American struggle for political independence, and her consistent praise of nature, places her firmly in that flow of thought which culminated in nineteenth century Romanticism. Her diction may strike a modern audience as occasionally "got up" and stiff, and her reliance on the heroic couplet may appear outdated and worn, but the content of her poetry is innovative, refreshing, and even, for her times, revolutionary. She wrote during the pre-Revolutionary and Revolutionary War eras in America, when little poetry of great merit was produced. Phillis Wheatley, laboring under the disadvantages of being not only a black slave but also a woman, nevertheless did find the time to depict that political struggle for freedom and to trace her personal battle for release. If one looks beyond the limitations of her sincere if dogmatic piety and her frequent dependence on what Wordsworth called poetic diction, one is sure to discover in her works a fine mind engaged in creating some of the best early American poetry.

Suggested Readings

Barker-Benfield, G. J., and Catherine Clinton, comps. *Portraits of American Women: From Settlement to the Present*. New York: St. Martin's Press, 1991.

Bassard, Katherine Clay. *Spiritual Interrogations: Culture, Gender, and Community in Early African American Women's Writing*. Princeton, N.J.: Princeton University Press, 1999.

Gates, Henry Louis. *The Trials of Phillis Wheatley*. New York: BasicCivitas Books, 2003.

Jones, Jacqueline. "Anglo-American Racism and Phillis Wheatley's 'Sable Veil,' 'Length'ned Chain,' and 'Knitted Heart.'" In *Women in the Age of the American Revolution*, edited by Ronald Hoffman and Peter J. Albert. Charlottesville: University Press of Virginia, 1989.

Richmond, Merle. *Phillis Wheatley*. New York: Chelsea House, 1988.

Rinaldi, Ann. *Hang a Thousand Trees with Ribbons: The Story of Phillis Wheatley*. New York: Harcourt, 1996.

Robinson, William H. *Phillis Wheatley and Her Writings*. New York: Garland, 1984.

_______, ed. *Critical Essays on Phillis Wheatley*. Boston: G. K. Hall, 1982.

Contributor: John C. Shields

John Edgar Wideman

Born: Washington, D.C.; June 14, 1941

African American

John Edgar Wideman's range of style, continual formalistic innovation, and powerful prose warrant his consideration as one of the best American writers of his generation.

Principal works

long fiction: *A Glance Away*, 1967; *Hurry Home*, 1970; *The Lynchers*, 1973; *Hiding Place*, 1981; *Sent for You Yesterday*, 1983; *The Homewood Trilogy*, 1985 (includes *Damballah*, *Hiding Place*, and *Sent for You Yesterday*); *Reuben*, 1987; *Philadelphia Fire*, 1990; *The Cattle Killing*, 1996; *Two Cities*, 1998; *Fanon*, 2007

short fiction: *Damballah*, 1981; *Fever: Twelve Stories*, 1989; *All Stories Are True*, 1992; *The Stories of John Edgar Wideman*, 1992; *God's Gym*, 2005

nonfiction: *Brothers and Keepers*, 1984; *Fatheralong: A Meditation on Fathers and Sons, Race and Society*, 1994; *Conversations with John Edgar Wideman*, 1998 (Bonnie TuSmith, editor); *Hoop Roots*, 2001; *The Island: Martinique*, 2003

edited texts: *My Soul Has Grown Deep: Classics of Early African-American Literature*, 2001; *Twenty: The Best of the Drue Heinz Literature Prize*, 2001

Growing up in Homewood (the African American section of Pittsburgh) and attending public school, John Edgar Wideman (WID-muhn) was every parent's dream. Delivering newspapers after school, he learned to manage finances. He was careful to avoid getting in trouble. He cared about school, did his homework, and he was smart, but his first love was basketball. These were all winning characteristics, and Wideman was successful on and off the court.

In his senior year of high school, Wideman was the captain of the basketball team and the class valedictorian. He earned a four-year scholarship from the University of Pennsylvania. The university gave Wideman choices that would change his life dramatically. In 1963, Wideman was named a Rhodes Scholar, the second black American to receive that honor. Wideman also became a graduate of the University of Iowa Writers' Workshop. Wideman went on to teach at various universities.

In 1966, Wideman accepted a teaching position at the University of Pennsylvania, where he later headed the African American studies program from 1971 to 1973 and rose to the rank of professor of English; he was also assistant basketball coach from 1968 to 1972. Academic appointments brought him to Howard University, the University of Wyoming at Laramie, and the University of Massachusetts at Amherst. The National Endowment for the Humanities in 1975 named him a Young Humanist Fellow; in 1976, the U.S. State Department selected him for a lecture tour of Europe and the Near East. That same year, he held a Phi Beta Kappa lectureship. Wideman married Judith Ann Goldman in 1965, and together they had three children: Daniel, Jacob, and Jamila. The family tragedy of his youngest brother, Rob, who was convicted in 1978 of armed robbery and murder, was grimly reiterated in 1988, when Wideman's son Jacob received a life sentence for the 1986 murder in Arizona of a teenage traveling companion. His daughter Jamila, having inherited her father's basketball prowess, garnered a position playing in the Women's National Basketball Association (WNBA) professional league. In the 1980's and 1990's he frequently contributed articles and review essays to *The New York Times Book Review* and to popular magazines such as *TV Guide*, *Life*, and *Esquire*.

In speaking about the formative influences upon his writing, Wideman asserts that his creative inclinations underwent a transformation upon his arrival as a new faculty member at the University of Pennsylvania, where students of color assumed him to be as well versed in the African American literary legacy as he was in the Anglo-American tradition. His responsiveness to their concerns prompted him not only to create the university's African American studies program but also to recover the cultural identity that he had self-consciously minimized in pursuit of the dominant culture's standards of academic excellence. His subsequent writing, fiction and nonfiction alike, repeatedly sounds the autobiographical theme of "coming home," and Wideman not only dissects the obstacles that thwart such return but also espouses the belief that art can at least make possible a temporary reconciliation between past and present. By paralleling his own multigenerational family history and the community history of Homewood, Wideman fuses personal and collective memory to create a mythology of the human condition at once particular and universal.

A Glance Away

Type of work: Novel
First published: 1967

Dedicated to "Homes," Wideman's first novel, *A Glance Away*, creates thematic excitement with its treatment of two drifting men coming to terms with their pasts. After a year spent at a rehabilitation center for drug addicts, Eddie Lawson, a disillusioned young black man, returns to his listless, decaying urban neighborhood. Rather than celebrating, however, he spends his gloomy homecoming confronting the goblins that drove him to the brink in the first place: his mother Martha Lawson's idealization of his dead older brother, his girlfriend Alice Smalls's rejection of him for sleeping with a white woman, and his own self-disgust over abandoning a secure postal job for menial, marginal employment. Dejected and defeated by nightfall, he drags himself to grimy Harry's Place in order to cloak his memories in a narcotic haze. There, he is reconciled by his albino friend Brother Smalls with another outcast named Robert Thurley, a white college professor struggling with his own record of divorce, alcoholism, and homosexuality. Though discrepancies between wealth and power divide the two homeless men, each manages to urge the other to maintain his faith in people despite his guilt-ridden history.

A Glance Away generated much favorable critical response in particular for Wideman's depiction of the alienated Thurley. In trying to disavow his personal past, this connoisseur of food and art embraces a surfeit of creeds and cultures. "In religion an aesthetic Catholic, in politics a passive Communist, in sex a resigned anarchist," he surrounds himself with treasures from both East and West and indulges in a smorgasbord of the globe's delicacies. Yet as a real measure of the displacement that these extravagances so futilely conceal, he quotes lines from T. S. Eliot's "The Love Song of J. Alfred Prufrock" (1917), in which a similarly solitary speaker searches for intimacy in a world bereft of its cultural moorings.

Emphasizing his protagonists' self-absorption and the estrangement of their family members and friends, Wideman abandons strictly chronological plot development in favor of lengthy interior monologues. Conversations tend to be short; more likely than not they are interrupted by unspoken flashbacks and asides. Using speech to measure isolation, the author portrays both Eddie and Thurley as incapable of communicating adequately. Eddie, for example, becomes tongue-tied around a group of southern travelers, shuddering in his bus seat instead of warning them as he wishes for the reality of the Northern mecca that they seek. Similarly, despite the empowering qualities of a gulp of Southern Comfort, Thurley delivers a lecture on Sophocles' *Oedipus Tyrannus* (c. 429 B.C.E.) fraught with "futility and detachment, . . . introspection and blindness." In one brilliant play on this speechlessness, both men suddenly converse as if they were actors on a stage. This abrupt emphasis on what is spoken—to the exclusion of private thoughts—stresses each person's imprisonment within him- or herself. Flowing from a weaker artist's pen, *A Glance Away* would have become a mere exercise in allusive technique and stream-of-consciousness style. On the contrary, it reads with the effortless ease of a masterfully crafted lyrical poem. Key to its success is Wideman's careful alliance of form and content, not to mention his insightful treatment of a rootlessness that transcends the barriers of race.

Hurry Home

Type of work: Novel
First published: 1970

The same compact length as the novel that precedes it, *Hurry Home* similarly focuses upon the theme of rootlessness. Its ambitious protagonist, the honors graduate Cecil Otis Braithwaite, is in many ways an upscale Eddie Lawson with a wife and an advanced degree. After slaving through law school, supporting himself with

John Edgar Wideman (University of Wyoming)

a meager scholarship and his earnings as a janitor, Cecil has lost his aspirations and his love for his girlfriend, Esther Brown. In search of something more, he escapes from his wedding bed to Europe, where he roams indiscriminately for three years among its brothels as well as its art galleries. In the tradition of Robert Thurley of *A Glance Away*, two white men as displaced as Cecil attempt to guide him: Charles Webb, belatedly in search of an illegitimate son, and Albert, a mercenary in Webb's employ who has also abandoned a wife. Too lost to save themselves, however, this pair can offer no enduring words of solace to Cecil.

Hurry Home is more sophisticated than *A Glance Away* in its treatment of the isolation theme. It suggests, for example, that the upwardly mobile Cecil is not merely disturbed by his personal past; he is estranged as well from his African and European cultures of origin. On the other hand, nowhere does *Hurry Home* convey the hope that pervades its predecessor. Cecil travels more extensively than does Eddie to reclaim his past, yet he gains no meaningful key to it. Confronting his European heritage merely confirms his status as "a stranger in all . . . tongues." He flees to the African continent by boat, "satisfied to be forever possessed," only to be forever rebuffed from a past that "melts like . . . wax . . . as I am nearer . . . the flame." When he returns at last to his Washington, D.C., tenement, the fruitlessness of his journey is underscored. There, he finds all the same as when he first entered following his miserable nuptials. Symbolically limning his rootlessness, he switches vocations, abandoning the tradition-steeped protocol of the bar for the faddish repertoire of a hairdresser. Thus, "hurry home," the catchphrase for his odyssey, is an ironic one. Cecil really can claim no place where a heritage nurtures and sustains him, no history that he can truly call his own.

Hurry Home displays a masterful style commensurate with that of the later Homewood novels. In addition to a more controlled stream-of-consciousness technique, recurring Christian symbols, icons of Renaissance art, and fragments from Moorish legend powerfully indicate Cecil's fractured lineage. This second novel being a more refined paradigm than the first, Wideman seemed next inclined to break new ground, to address intently the racial polarization that had unsettled American society by the early 1970's, producing that period's most influential published works.

The Homewood Trilogy

Type of work: Novels and short fiction

First published: *Damballah*, 1981; *Hiding Place*, 1981; *Sent for You Yesterday*, 1983 (pb. as *The Homewood Trilogy*, 1985)

In *The Homewood Trilogy*, which comprises the short-story collection *Damballah* and the novels *Hiding Place* and *Sent for You Yesterday*, Wideman re-creates Homewood, the black section of Pittsburgh, and describes the myriad relationships among ancestors and a living African American family in the hundred years since slavery. Damballah is an African Voodoo god, "the good serpent of the sky." The hero of the trilogy is John French, who specializes in a kind of benevolent fatherhood. Wideman's return to Homewood through these novels convinces readers of his determination to find and understand his identity through tracing his roots as deep as he can. In *Damballah* and *Hiding Place*, Wideman furnishes a family tree. Readers are told of his great-great-great grandmother, who fled through the Underground Railroad with a white man to safety in Pittsburgh. Biological roots traced, the job of understanding begins.

One sour apple on the family tree is Tommy. The character Tommy is actually Robby, Wideman's brother. Tommy and Wideman are complex dimensions in finding the identity that Wideman seeks. The main character in *Hiding Place*, Tommy, is a fugitive from history as well as the law. He is taken in by Mama Bess, who is family and who represents what family does. Family tries to put together the "scars" and the "stories" that give young people their identities. Essentially, *Hiding Place* is the story of two lost souls, Mama Bess and Tommy. Mama Bess is lost because she has lost her husband and her son; she becomes a recluse, a fugitive living on a hill overlooking Pittsburgh, away from the family. Tommy is lost because he is too headstrong to listen and finds himself on the run after a scheme to rob a ghetto hoodlum ends in murder. Tommy does not want to hear the stories and learn about the scars; he is too absorbed in preservation.

Sent for You Yesterday, through the characters of Doot and Albert Wilkes, the outspoken blues pianist, suggests that creativity and imagination are important means of transcending despair. Creativity also strengthens the common bonds of race, culture, and class. *Homewood Trilogy* is a monumental work of investigating and understanding the origins of self and identity.

Brothers and Keepers

Type of work: Novel

First published: 1984

Brothers and Keepers, Wideman's most popular novel, is a psychologically realistic portrait of two brothers. Although they grow up in the same environment, Homewood, these brothers travel diverse paths. Wideman is a black star pulsing brilliantly in a white universe; his brother, Robby, sinks into a life of crime and drug addiction. Robby's path leads to his serving a life sentence without parole for taking part in a robbery in which a man was killed. *Brothers and Keepers* is a novel of tragic dimensions, grave despair, and spiritual survival.

This novel had to be written as much for Wideman as for Robby. It is a homecoming for Wideman—a return to the community of brotherhood, concern, and understanding. In part 1, "Visits," readers learn that although Wideman never sees his color as an obstacle to his own success, he views Robby as a black victim of society's ills: "A brother behind bars, my own flesh and blood, raised in the same house by the same mother and father; a brother confined in prison has to be a mistake, a malfunctioning of the system."

In the second part of the novel, "Our Time," Wideman describes his growth and maturation while he spends time with his brother on visits to the prison. Wideman is seen as searching for his own identity while he searches for reasons for Robby's fall from grace. Learning that he needs as much help as Robby does, Wideman gains respect for Robby's intelligence. Wideman also learns the truth about the foiled robbery attempt.

In the final section, "Doing Time," a spirituality operates to bring harmony to the two brothers. Especially moving is Robby's graduation speech as he receives his associate degree, and his promise to Wideman that he will "forever pray." From a sociological point of view, it is interesting that prison can rehabilitate someone like Robby and motivate him to work on his education. It is an equally moving experience to see Wideman connect with his own identity and return to his roots. Wideman learns that he cannot escape genetics or the ghetto. Until Robby is free, Wideman is not free.

Reuben

Type of work: Novel
First published: 1987

Traditions preserved and memories presented from black America's African past form the backbeat of *Reuben*, Wideman's next novel of community and interracial struggle. From a rusting trailer that his clients describe as part office, part altar to the gods, the dwarf Reuben serves the poor of Homewood in need of a lawyer, a psychologist, a warrior, or a priest. Like West African *griots* or oral scribes, who commit to unerring memory genealogies, triumphs, faults, and names, Reuben relies upon a mix of law and bureaucratic legerdemain that he has heard from his own employers and remembered. Like an obliging ancestral spirit shuttling prayers from this world to the next, Reuben negotiates pacts between the ghetto's bombed-out streets and the oak, plush, and marble interiors of City Hall. As he prescribes legal strategies and bestows grandfatherly advice, he also steers his clients to confront and abandon the views that have overturned their lives. When words and contracts alone will not do, Reuben rustles deep within collective memory and knots a charm: "A rag, a bone, a hank of hair. Ancient grains of rice. . . ." Reuben transforms garbage into power, excrement into nourishment, gristle into life. He preaches reincarnation and the nature of things dead to rise again, and he catalyzes his clients to seek similar transformations in themselves.

Infused with magic and spiritualism, *Reuben* also is illustrated by the ravaged images of the inner city. Wideman likens ghetto buildings to the rat-infested holds of slave ships and the people in those buildings to roles of both predator and prey. Much of the Homewood population resembles a coffle of freshly branded slaves, slaves who are bound by laws instead of chains, by the welfare system or underworld crime instead of a plantation economy. Others are human versions of rats—snitching, beating, starving, stealing, and otherwise pestering their neighbors with an eat-or-be-eaten mentality. "There were historical precedents, parallels," Reuben understands. "Indian scouts leading long-hairs to the hiding places of their red brethren. FBI informers, double agents, infiltrators of the sixties. An unsubtle variation of divide and conquer." In this bleak landscape, the game of divide and conquer has changed little since enslavement.

Fever

Type of work: Short fiction
First published: 1989

While *Damballah* draws its cumulative power from its unifying narrative sensibility and its consistent focus upon the citizens past and present of Homewood, *Fever: Twelve Stories* demonstrates a much looser internal logic grounded in thematic rather than storytelling interlacings. Once again, Wideman uses the short story to escape the constraints of novelistic continuity and reconfigure—this time through unrelated voices—motifs that assume international proportions. His most striking theme correlates the historical catastrophes of American slavery, the Holocaust, and modern international terrorism, thereby suggesting a common pattern of scapegoating and racist antagonism that transcends the experience of any single group of victims.

"The Statue of Liberty" and "Valaida," for example, both demonstrate how episodes of interracial miscommunication and self-indulgent fantasizing about the imaginary "Other" continually compromise the possibility of real human engagement. Moreover, in the latter story, a Jewish Holocaust survivor relates to his black maid a story of the jazz performer, whose actions in a wartime concentration camp saved his life; her droll response resists the empathy he has attempted to build between them: "Always thought it was just you people over there doing those terrible things to each other." In "Hostages," an Israeli expatriate and daughter of Auschwitz survivors reflects on her first marriage to an Israeli Arab and her current marriage to a wealthy businessman who offers a prime target for Muslim terrorists; finally she sees herself as a hostage to the comfortable but isolated life she leads and meditates on the Talmudic lesson of the Lamed-Vov, or "God's hostages," predestined "sponges drawing mankind's suffering into themselves."

"Fever," the volume's title story—and one of its most accomplished—depicts the 1793 yellow fever epidemic in Philadelphia, a crisis attributed to African slaves brought up north from the Caribbean but in fact resulting from the internally bred corruption of the swamp-ridden city. A metaphor for the pervasive racial contagions of this ironically dubbed "City of Brotherly Love," the fever levels all distinctions of race, gender, and class even as it triggers responses affirming them. The story's protagonist, Richard Allen, is a minister exhausting himself in Christian service to dying whites and blacks alike. Eventually confronted by the angry monologue of an infected Jewish merchant unimpressed by his humanity, he too is told of the Lamed-Vov, the implication being that Allen has been arbitrarily selected "to suffer the reality humankind cannot bear," enduring an unimaginable and unrelieved burden of "earth, grief and misery." A nihilistic voice in the text, Abraham deconstructs Allen's faith and further magnifies the din of conflicting perspectives—past and present, conciliatory and confrontational—that make the story the touchstone of the volume's exploration of compassion as a limited but essential response to incomprehensible suffering, be its origins cosmic or human—or both.

Elsewhere, Wideman contrasts vision versus blindness ("Doc's Story" and "When It's Time to Go") to illustrate very different positionings by African Americans within the racially charged dominant culture through which they try to move. Wideman's attunement to the musical textures of African American culture again asserts itself, as does his interest in the drama of the individual alienated from his root culture by his ambitions. "Surfiction" offers an exercise in postmodern pastiche that is both a self-conscious parody of the imaginative stasis to which contemporary critical and aesthetic practice can lead and a serious study of the ways in which human determination to communicate across the void poignantly subverts even the most sophisticated intellectual distancing devices. Finally, then, the reader of this volume is left musing on the cultural incompatibilities institutionalized by ideologies of difference—racial, gender, ethnic, nationalistic—and the heroic folly of the Richard Allens of the world, who resist them against all odds.

Philadelphia Fire

Type of work: Novel
First published: 1990

Philadelphia Fire, *The Cattle Killing*, and *Two Cities* are framed within a geographic shift from Pittsburgh to Philadelphia. In keeping with Wideman's fluid notion of history and myth as mutually interlocking categories of representation, *Philadelphia Fire* recasts the 1985 police bombing of the building occupied by the radical MOVE organization. John Africa, MOVE's leader, is represented as Reverend King, who is described as "a nouveau Rousseau." King leads a rebellion against the infringement on African American individual and communal rights couched in the guises of "urbanization" and "integration" by espousing an ideology that embraces a return to nature and a rejection of modern material values. Elsewhere, Wideman asserts that "the craziness of MOVE is their sanity; they were saying no to the system . . . it makes perfect sense. So the myth of integration is analogous to the prophecy of the cattle killing."

The Stories of John Edgar Wideman

Type of work: Short fiction
First published: 1992

The Stories of John Edgar Wideman reprints two earlier collections—*Damballah* and *Fever*—and adds ten stories written especially for this volume and collected in it as *All Stories Are True*. The three collections are published here in reverse order, so that the reader begins with Wideman's most recent stories and moves back through the two earlier collections. *The Stories of John Edgar Wideman* in some ways resembles a novel, for many of the stories have the same setting (the black Homewood section of Pittsburgh) and characters (relatives and other residents of Homewood, both now and in the past). Wideman's best stories render twentieth century urban black life in vivid detail and history.

Wideman, as this volume attests, is not always an easy writer. In any one story, he may mix several points of view, and several different narrative voices. Like Toni Morrison and William Faulkner, Wideman focuses on interior life—the thoughts and feelings of characters struggling to get through life. Action and incident are here incidental to the interior experiences of characters caught up in them. Similarly, there are often jumps between incidents and ideas that are not easy to follow, a narrative stream-of-consciousness that readers may find rather difficult. But, as is true of the best short story writers working today—Richard Ford, Joy Williams, Joyce Carol Oates—the difficulties are their own reward, for Wideman renders American life in all its fullness and tragedy.

Fatheralong

Type of work: Memoirs
First published: 1994

The five essays that make up this short memoir are prefaced by "Common Ground," which defines the assumptions of the whole collection, and in which Wideman makes his most important statements about race and society in America. Among its many scars, the "paradigm of race" denies black diversity and transforms color into a sign of class, culture, and inferiority. The antidotes to these distortions are the stories Wideman tells here which can help African Americans in their struggle to "reinvent" themselves by giving them "a glimpse of common ground where fathers and sons, mothers and daughters can sit down and talk, learn to talk and listen together again."

In essence, the five essays of *Fatheralong* describe trips Wideman takes with his father; put in socioeconomic terms, the book is about places, and about the history of African Americans getting to them: to America as slaves in the distant past; to the crossroads town of Promised Land, S.C., as survivors during Reconstruction; to Pittsburgh as black migrants in the beginning of the twentieth century looking for better work; and finally back to South Carolina as adults trying to understand something of "the miracle and disgrace" of this complex history. The trips are also psychological, for they describe Wideman's attempt to understand his father, their common roots, and thus himself, and his relationship to his own sons.

In many ways, these memoirs may remind readers of other contemporary African American writers such as Alice Walker or Toni Morrison. Yet *Fatheralong* also reverberates with works by male writers as well, such as Philip Roth's *Patrimony* (1991) and Richard Rodriguez's *Days of Obligation: An Argument with My Mexican Father* (1993)—both part of an emergent literary consciousness of male roles and gender history. Like Richard Wright and James Baldwin before him, Wideman is making a wake-up call to America about race and racism. Like Roth and Rodriguez, Wideman is also giving a call about the sons who have been abandoned along the roadbed of American history, a renewed call about the responsibilities of fathers for their children—and the responsibility of the culture for that deteriorating relationship. At a time when politicians talk easily about taking children from welfare parents, Wideman's book contains an important message.

The Cattle Killing

Type of work: Novel
First published: 1996

The title for the novel *The Cattle Killing* refers to the lies told to the African Xhosa people in order to make them believe that to combat European oppression they must kill their cattle. The cattle are their life force, and their destruction leads to the near annihilation of Xhosa culture. The people die as their cattle die, struck down because they believed the lie of the prophecy: "The cattle are the people. The people are the cattle." Wideman subtly extends this metaphor to consider the problem of intraracial crime ravaging American inner cities and connects contemporary circumstances with the diseased and disintegrating conditions surrounding the yellow fever outbreak of eighteenth century Philadelphia.

In all three instances—in Africa, in Philadelphia, in black urbania—there is a potential for annihilation because of an epidemic fueled by hysteria, exacerbated by racist ideology and carried out by those who believe the "lie" and perpetrate their self-destruction. The narrator of *The Cattle Killing*, Isaiah, called "Eye," is an obvious recasting of the biblical figure who prophesies the downfall of the nation of Israel. He is a prophet who warns of false prophecies—in this case, the lie of integration, which is, intricately entwined with modernization and its attenuating conspicuous consumption, the theme foregrounded in *Philadelphia Fire*. This text's distinction from *Philadelphia Fire*, however, lies in the vision of hope with which readers are left: *The Cattle Killing* is also a love story.

Two Cities

Type of work: Novel
First published: 1998

The subtitle of this novel, *A Love Story*, creates expectations of romance, but instead readers are thrown into a world of violence, death, and loneliness. Kassima has experienced more loss in her thirty-five years than most people experience in their whole lives. Her husband has died of AIDS; her two sons have been killed by deadly gang violence. Robert Jones confronts the daily threat of violence as he lives his life as normally as one can among gangbangers' turf wars. At age fifty, Robert and his generation can only watch and hold back their anger and despair as young men absurdly kill themselves and others. Old Mr. Mallory, having witnessed death in a world war and the street wars of America's cities, awaits his own end. Love among such ruins—the ruins of neighborhoods, of families, of lives—saves a young woman from despair, a middle-aged man from loneliness, and an old man from meaninglessness.

Wideman's novel is also a story of two cities, Philadelphia and Pittsburgh, run over and run down by violence. In Philadelphia, police attack the barricaded MOVE compound, killing eleven men, women, and children. OD's diner becomes a site of burglary and murder. In Pittsburgh, red- and blue-clad boys in oversized parkas carrying oversized guns tear a world apart. In these two cities, death has become a fact of life. However, when Wideman speaks of two cities, he is not simply referring to geographic locations; he treats death and life as two concomitant modes of existence often indistinguishable one from the other. In Wideman's world, life is shaped by death, by the images of death, and by its constant threat. Memories of times past and people who have died live in those who remain. As the characters in the novel learn, however, they find the strength to live and die through the power of love.

Suggested Readings

Auger, Philip. *Native Sons in No Man's Land: Rewriting Afro-American Manhood in the Novels of Baldwin, Walker, Wideman, and Gaines*. New York: Garland, 2000.

Byerman, Keith Eldon. *John Edgar Wideman: A Study of the Short Fiction*. New York: Twayne, 1998.

Coleman, James W. *Blackness and Modernism: The Literary Career of John Edgar Wideman*. Jackson: University Press of Mississippi, 1990.

Dubey, Madhu. "Literature and Urban Crisis: John Edgar Wideman's *Philadelphia Fire*." *African American Review* 32 (Winter, 1998): 579-595.

Hume, Kathryn. "Black Urban Utopia in Wideman's Later Fiction." *Race & Class* 45, no. 3 (January-March, 2004): 19-35.

Mbalia, Doreatha D. *John Edgar Wideman: Reclaiming the African Personality*. Selinsgrove, Pa.: Susquehanna University Press, 1995.

Rushdy, Ashraf. "Fraternal Blues: John Edgar Wideman's Homewood Trilogy." *Contemporary Literature* 32, no. 3 (Fall, 1991): 312-345.

Samuels, Wilfred D. "Going Home: A Conversation with John Edgar Wideman." *Callaloo* 6 (1983): 40-59.

TuSmith, Bonnie, ed. *Conversations with John Edgar Wideman*. Jackson: University Press of Mississippi, 1998.

Wilson, Matthew. "The Circles of History in John Edgar Wideman's *The Homewood Trilogy*." *CLA Journal* 33 (March, 1990): 239-259.

Contributors: Barbara Cecelia Rhodes, Heather Russell Andrade, Margaret Boe Birns, Barbara A. McCaskill, and Barbara Kitt Seidman

Elie Wiesel

Born: Sighet, Transylvania (now Romania); September 30, 1928

Jewish

Wiesel is the preeminent chronicler of the Holocaust whose fiction, nonfiction, and plays encompass Jewish lore, tradition, and memory, and relate the Jews' unique human legacy. In recognition of his humanism and activism he received the Nobel Peace Prize in 1986.

Principal works

CHILDREN'S LITERATURE: *King Solomon and His Magic Ring*, 1999

DRAMA: *Zalmen: Ou, La Folie de Dieu*, pb. 1968 (*Zalmen: Or, The Madness of God*, 1974); *Le Procès de Shamgorod tel qu'il se déroula le 25 février 1649*, pb. 1979 (*The Trial of God: As It Was Held on February 25, 1649, in Shamgorod*, 1979)

LONG FICTION: *L'Aube*, 1960 (novella; *Dawn*, 1961); *Le Jour*, 1961 (novella; *The Accident*, 1962); *La Ville de la chance*, 1962 (*The Town Beyond the Wall*, 1964); *Les Portes de la forêt*, 1964 (*The Gates of the Forest*, 1966); *Le Mendiant de Jérusalem*, 1968 (*A Beggar in Jerusalem*, 1970); *Le Serment de Kolvillàg*, 1973 (*The Oath*, 1973); *Le Testament d'un poète juif assassiné*, 1980 (*The Testament*, 1981); *Le Cinquième Fils*, 1983 (*The Fifth Son*, 1985); *Le Crépuscule, au loin*, 1987 (*Twilight*, 1988); *L'Oublié*, 1989 (*The Forgotten*, 1992); *Les Juges*, 1999 (*The Judges*, 2002); *Le Temps des déracinés*, 2003 (*The Time of the Uprooted*, 2005)

SHORT FICTION: *Le Chant des morts*, 1966 (essays and short stories; *Legends of Our Time*, 1968); *Entre deux soleils*, 1970 (essays and short stories; *One Generation After*, 1970); *Un Juif aujourd'hui*, 1977 (essays and short stories; *A Jew Today*, 1978)

NONFICTION: *Un di Velt hot geshvign*, 1956 (in Yiddish; 1958, in French as *La Nuit*; *Night*, 1960); *Les Juifs du silence*, 1966 (travel sketch; *The Jews of Silence*, 1966); *Discours d'Oslo*, 1987; *Le mal et l'exil: Recontre avec Élie Wiesel*, 1988 (*Evil and Exile*, 1990); *From the Kingdom of Memory: Reminiscences*, 1990; *A Journey of Faith*, 1990 (with John Cardinal O'Connor); *Tous les fleuves vont á la mer*, 1994 (memoir; *All Rivers Run to the Sea*, 1995); *Et la mer n'est pas remplie*, 1996 (*And the Sea Is Never Full: Memoirs*, 1999); *Le Mal et l'exil: Dix ans après*, 1999; *Conversations with Elie Wiesel*, 2001 (Thomas J. Vinciguerra, editor); *After the Darkness: Reflections on the Holocaust*, 2002; *Elie Wiesel: Conversations*, 2002 (Robert Franciosi, editor); *Wise Men and Their Tales: Potraits of Biblical, Talmudic, and Hasidic Masters*, 2003

MISCELLANEOUS: *Célébration hassidique*, 1972-1981 (2 volumes; biographical sketches and stories; volume 1 *Souls on Fire*, 1972; volume 2 *Somewhere a Master: Further Hasidic Portraits and Legends*, 1982); *Ani Maamin: Un Chant perdu et retrouvé*, 1973 (cantata; *Ani Maamin: A Song Lost and Found Again*, 1973); *Célébration biblique*, 1975 (biographical sketches and stories; *Messengers of God: Biblical Portraits and Legends*, 1976); *Four Hasidic Masters and Their Struggle Against Melancholy*, 1978 (biographical sketches and stories); *Images from the Bible*, 1980 (biographical sketches and stories); *Five Biblical Portraits*, 1981 (biographical sketches and stories); *Paroles d'étranger*, 1982 (biographical sketches and stories); *Somewhere a Master*, 1982 (biographical sketches and stories); *The Six Days of Destruction: Meditations Towards Hope*, 1988 (with Albert H. Friedlander); *Silences et mémoire d'hommes: Essais, histoires, dialogues*, 1989; *Célébration talmudique: Portraits et légendes*, 1991; *Sages and Dreamers: Biblical, Talmudic, and Hasidic Portraits and Legends*, 1991; *Celebrating Elie Wiesel: Stories, Essays, Reflections*, 1998 (Alan Rosen, editor); *Célébration prophétique: Portraits et légendes*, 1998

As a young teen, Elie Wiesel (EH-lee vee-ZEHL) led a sheltered, bookish adolescence that was forever shattered in 1944, when the Nazis invaded Hungary and rounded up all its Jews, including the Wiesel family. The fifteen-year-old Elie was deported to Auschwitz and Buchenwald, from which he was liberated in April, 1945. The horrors he saw there, the despair he felt, the anger he directed at God were later themes in his literary and nonfiction writings.

Shortly after the war, Elie went to France, where he learned the language and developed a lifelong passion for philosophy and literature. When, in 1955, French novelist François Mauriac urged him to bear witness to the six million Jews murdered in Europe's concentration camps, Wiesel wrote the acclaimed *Night*. First published in Yiddish, then French, then English, the book began as an eight-hundred-page manuscript but was cut to about one hundred pages of terrifyingly bald description of what happened to Wiesel. *Night* is a wrenching account of evil and a terrifying indictment of God.

He next published novels presenting the anguished guilt of those who survived the mass slaughter. Central to the protagonists' conduct and outlook is the belief that every act is ambiguous and implies a loss of innocence. By rejoining the religious community, however, the survivor may finally transform despair into joy. *A Beggar in Jerusalem* shows how a tormented people came of age. Celebrating Israel's victory in the Six-Day War, the novel is a memorial to the dead and an appeal for the world's beggars. Although still haunted by the Holocaust, Wiesel could thereafter address other problems confronting the next generation—from madness as an escape from persecution to silence as a means of overcoming horror.

In 1969, Wiesel married Marion Erster Rose, who was to become his principal translator and with whom he would have one son. In the fall of 1972, he began his tenure at the City College of New York as Distinguished Professor of Judaic Studies. This endowed chair gave him the opportunity to teach young students (he considered himself an educator first) the celebrations and paradoxes of Jewish theology and the meaning of modern Jewishness and to continue writing in diverse genres. He left this position in 1976 to become the Andrew Mellon Professor of Humanities at Boston University. In 1982 he was the first Henry Luce Visiting Scholar in Humanities and Social Thought at Yale University, and from 1997 to 1999 he held the Ingeborg Rennert Visiting Professorship of Judaic Studies at Barnard College.

During this period Wiesel also was involved in various social and political activities, from fighting against racism, war, fanaticism, apartheid, and violence to commemorating the Holocaust. In fact, some historians credit him with introducing "Holocaust" as the primary name for the Nazis' death camps policy. (He was a member of the U.S. Holocaust Memorial Council until 1986, when he resigned in protest over U.S. president Ronald Reagan's controversial visit to the military cemetery in Bitburg, West Germany.) For his humanitarian work and his concern for the oppressed everywhere, as well as for his literary achievements, he received numerous honorary degrees, prizes, and awards, including the Congressional Gold Medal, the rank of Commander in the French Legion d'honneur, and, in 1986, the Nobel Peace Prize. It was bestowed both for his practical work in the cause of peace and for his message of "peace, atonement, and human dignity." He used the money from the prize to establish the Elie Wiesel Foundation, which is dedicated to combat indifference and misinformation about the Holocaust through international dialogue and educational programs. Moreover, in 1992 he received the Ellis Island Medal of Honor, was elected to the American Academy of Arts and Letters in 1996, and in 2006 was awarded an honorary knighthood from the United Kingdom for his efforts in Holocaust education there.

Meanwhile, Wiesel continued to publish plays, novels, and nonfiction at a prolific pace, producing more than forty books; in these he again wove post-Holocaust despair and divine cruelty, but above all he denounced the world's forgetfulness of and indifference to humankind's inhumanity to humans. In 1995 he published the first volume of his memoirs, *All Rivers Run to the Sea*, which describes his childhood in Romania, internment in concentration camps, life in France following World War II, and life in the United States until 1969 and his marriage to Marion. The second volume, *And the Sea Is Never Full*, appeared in 1999 and takes up the story of his writing and activism into the late 1990's. In 1999 he also added children's literature to his accomplishments with the publication of *King Solomon and the Magic Ring*.

Among Wiesel's late novels is *The Judges*, a moral fable set in Connecticut, and *Time of the Uprooted*, which concerns a Czech refugee from World War II who was raised in Hungary and moved to New York, working as a ghost writer and struggling with the lasting effects of the Holocaust on his morality, ability to love, and faith.

While writing, Wiesel continued his efforts at peace and reconciliation. He became a member of the Human Rights Foundation, and in 2004 the Romanian government invited him to head what came to be known as the Wiesel Commission to study the history of the Holocaust in Romania. In 2006, with American actor George Clooney, he testified before the United Nations Security Council, urging it to confront the humanitarian disaster wrought by Sudan's civil war. Wiesel also was a popular lecturer, often to the consternation of his critics. In 2007 he was attacked and nearly kidnapped by a Holocaust denier while staying in a hotel in San Francisco, California.

Night

Type of work: Memoir
First published: *Un di Velt hot geshvign*, 1956; *La Nuit*, 1958 (English translation, 1960)

Night, Wiesel's memoir of the Holocaust, tells of his concentration camp experience. Encompassing events from the end of 1941 to 1945, the book ponders a series of questions, whose answers, Moché the Beadle, who was miraculously saved from an early German massacre, reminds the boy, lie "only within yourself."

Moché, who teaches the boy the beauty of biblical studies, is a strange character with a clownish awkwardness, more God's madman than mentally ill; he is also a recurring figure in later Wiesel works. After Moché returns to town to describe the horrible scenes he has witnessed, no one listens to this apparently insane rambler who, like Cassandra, repeats his warnings in vain. The clown, a moving and tragic fool, is unable to convince the Jewish community of its impending doom. Despite arrests, ghettoizations, and mass deportations, the Jews still cannot believe him, even as they embark for Auschwitz.

In 1944, the young narrator is initiated into the horrors of the archipelago of Nazi death camps. There he becomes A-7713, deprived of name, self-esteem, identity. He observes and undergoes hunger, exhaustion, cold, suffering, brutality, executions, cruelty, breakdown in personal relationships, and flames and smoke coming from crematories in the German death factories. In the barracks of terror, where he sees the death of his mother and seven-year-old sister, his religious faith is corroded. The world no longer represents God's mind. Comparing himself to Job, he bitterly asks God for an explanation of such evil. The boy violently rejects God's presence and God's justice, love, and mercy: "I was alone—terribly alone in a world without God and without man."

After a death march and brutally cruel train ride, young Wiesel and his father arrive at Buchenwald, where his father soon dies of malnutrition and dysentery. As in a daze, the son waits to be killed by fleeing German soldiers. Instead, he coolly notes, on April 11, 1945, "at about six o'clock in the evening, the first American tank stood at the gates of Buchenwald."

In addition to wanting to elucidate the unfathomable secret of death and theodicy, the narrator lived a monstrous, stunted, and isolated existence as an adult. He saw himself as victim, executioner, and spectator. By affirming that he was not divided among the three but was in fact all of them at once, he was able to resolve his identity problem. The autobiography's last image shows Wiesel looking at himself in a mirror: The body and soul are wounded, but the night and its nightmares are finally over.

A Beggar in Jerusalem

Type of work: Novel
First published: *Le Mendiant de Jérusalem*, 1968 (English translation, 1970)

A Beggar in Jerusalem is told in the first person by David, heir to a bloody history of anti-Semitic persecutions. It is a novel in which Jewish survivors of destruction must confront their miraculous escape. In the process, although they suffer from guilt and anger, they ultimately forge an identity based on hope.

In June, 1967, the forty-year-old David goes to fight against the united Arab armies. He wishes to die in order to finally overcome the despair caused by God's abandonment of the Jews during World War II and by his own pointless survival. At the front, he meets Katriel, and both soon agree that whoever comes back will tell the other's story. Israel wins a resounding victory in what comes to be called the Six-Day War, and as the narrative opens, there are celebrations all over the land, especially in Jerusalem. Katriel, however, does not come back.

David not only tells his comrade's story—much as King David told of Absalom—but also wonders whether he ought to live it as well. This he does, at the end, by marrying Katriel's widow, not out of love, which would imply a total gift of self and of which he does not feel himself capable, but rather out of affection and sympathy, perhaps out of friendship. The hero has realized that, beyond suffering and bitterness, he can arrive at self-discovery.

Whereas Albert Camus favored revolt in the face of the absurd, Wiesel advocates laughter. By laughing one succeeds in conquering oneself, and by dominating one's fear one learns to laugh: "Let our laughter drown all the noises of the earth, all the regrets of mankind." There is no longer a need to search for an antidote against distress, but simply to abandon oneself to the joy of an event without precedent—the reunion of Israel with Jerusalem, uniting those absent and present, the fighters and mad beggars, in similar euphoria and similar ecstasy: "I want to laugh and it is my laughter I wish to offer to Jerusalem, my laughter and not my tears."

Elie Wiesel (© The Nobel Foundation)

In his tireless attempt to understand the awesome and terrifying mystery of Jewish suffering, the once-tormented David is resolutely optimistic, for the recaptured Jerusalem means the end of despair for Jews in Israel and abroad. The victory celebrations are a memorial to the dead, a song to and of life, and an appeal on behalf of history's wandering outcasts—the allegorical beggars who, after the annihilation of European Jewry, have come to Jerusalem to give God the last chance to save his people.

All Rivers Run to the Sea

Type of work: Autobiography
First published: *Tous les fleuves vont à la mer*, 1994 (English translation, 1995)

Taking the title of his autobiography from Ecclesiastes, Wiesel presents the important people and events of his life, beginning with his childhood in Sighet, Romania, and culminating in his 1969 marriage in Jerusalem. Wiesel, through stories and remembrances, tells of a family full of piety, moral courage, and selfless devotion to Judaism. From his mother and grandmother, Elie learned goodness and love; from his grandfather, the Jewish legends he would later use in fiction and essays; from his father, rectitude and altruism. His teachers, at various times of his life, inculcated in him a reverence for learning, an exactness in biblical or philosophical discourse, and above all the joy, sadness, and truth of the old masters.

World War II and the persecution of the Jews destroyed Wiesel's idyllic world forever. He and his family were taken to Auschwitz. He later was transferred to Buchenwald. Unable to understand German cruelty, angry at those who did not intervene on the victims' behalf, angry too at God for letting it happen, Wiesel emerged alive after terrible trials. At age seventeen he was endowed with a special knowledge of life and death.

Shortly after his liberation from Buchenwald he went to France, where he eventually enrolled at the university, enduring hardship and contemplating suicide. Saved by Zionist fervor, he worked as a journalist for an Israeli newspaper in Paris. A crucial meeting with novelist François Mauriac in 1955 was to decide his literary career: Mauriac encouraged him to break his self-imposed silence about his experience in concentration camps and found a publisher for Wiesel's first novel, *La Nuit* (1958; *Night*, 1960), to which he contributed the foreword.

After Wiesel moved to New York to become his newspaper's American correspondent, he soon applied for U.S. citizenship. In a series of amusing anecdotes he describes his life in a Jewish American milieu. He also tells of his relations with his French publishers and of his meeting with Marion, his future wife and translator. More moving and bittersweet are his return to his native town, where relatives and friends have disappeared and only the ghosts of his youth remain; his personal and literary campaign for Russian Jewry; the fear caused by the Six-Day War of 1967, since it could have meant the end of Israel and the Jewish dream; and his prayer of thanksgiving at the newly liberated Wailing Wall.

Throughout, a celebration of life and of the great Hasidic teachers and thinkers as well as a moral and ethical strength permeates Wiesel's conduct and writings over his first forty years. In memorializing his relatives and friends and in bearing witness to their passing, he leaves his own mark behind.

Suggested Readings

Berenbaum, Michael. *Elie Wiesel: God, the Holocaust, and the Children of Israel.* West Orange, N.J.: Behrman House, 1994.

Bloom, Harold, ed. *Elie Wiesel's "Night."* New York: Chelsea House, 2001.

Horowitz, Rosemary, ed. *Elie Wiesel and the Art of Storytelling*. Jefferson, N.C.: McFarland, 2006.

Horowitz, Sara. *Voicing the Void: Muteness and Memory in Holocaust Fiction*. Albany: State University of New York Press, 1997.

Kolbert, Jack. *The Worlds of Elie Wiesel: An Overview of His Career and His Major Themes*. Selinsgrove, Pa.: Susquehanna University Press, 2001.

Mass, Wendy, ed. *Readings on "Night."* New York: Greenhaven Press, 2000.

Patterson, David. *The Shriek of Silence: A Phenomenology of the Holocaust Novel*. Lexington: University Press of Kentucky, 1992.

Rosen, Alan, ed. *Celebrating Elie Wiesel: Stories, Essays, Reflections*. Notre Dame, Ind.: University of Notre Dame Press, 1998.

Roth, John K., and Frederick Sontag. *The Questions of Philosophy*. Belmont, Calif.: Wadsworth, 1988.

Sibelman, Simon P. *Silence in the Novels of Elie Wiesel*. New York: St. Martin's Press, 1995.

Wiesel, Elie, and Richard D. Heffner. *Conversations with Elie Wiesel*. Edited by Thomas J. Vinciguerra. New York: Schocken, 2001.

Contributor: Pierre L. Horn

John A. Williams

Born: Jackson, Mississippi; December 5, 1925

African American

One of the most prolific and influential writers of his era, Williams infused his works with self-exploration, reflecting the collective social experience of African Americans.

Principal works

DRAMA: *Last Flight from Ambo Ber*, pr. 1981; *Vanqui*, pr. 1999 (libretto)

LONG FICTION: *The Angry Ones*, 1960 (also known as *One for New York*); *Night Song*, 1961; *Sissie*, 1963; *The Man Who Cried I Am*, 1967; *Sons of Darkness, Sons of Light: A Novel of Some Probability*, 1969; *Captain Blackman*, 1972; *Mothersill and the Foxes*, 1975; *The Junior Bachelor Society*, 1976; *!Click Song*, 1982; *The Berhama Account*, 1985; *Jacob's Ladder*, 1987; *Clifford's Blues*, 1998

POETRY: *Safari West*, 1998

NONFICTION: *Africa: Her History, Lands and People*, 1962; *The Protectors: The Heroic Story of the Narcotics Agents, Citizens, and Officials in Their Unending, Unsuing Battles Against Organized Crime in America and Abroad*, 1964 (as J. Dennis Gregory with Harry J. Ansliger); *This Is My Country Too*, 1965; *The King God Didn't Save: Reflections on the Life and Death of Martin Luther King, Jr.*, 1970; *The Most Native of Sons: A Biography of Richard Wright*, 1970; *Flashbacks: A Twenty-Year Diary of Article Writing*, 1973; *Minorities in the City*, 1975; *If I Stop I'll Die: The Comedy and Tragedy of Richard Pryor*, 1991; *Way B(l)ack Then and Now: A Street Guide to African Americans in Paris*, 1992 (with Michel Fabre)

EDITED TEXTS: *The Angry Black*, 1962; *Beyond the Angry Black*, 1966; *Amistad I*, 1970 (with Charles F. Harris); *Amistad II*, 1971 (with Harris); *The McGraw-Hill Introduction to Literature*, 1985 (with Gilbert H. Muller); *Bridges: Literature Across Cultures*, 1994 (with Muller)

John Alfred Williams was born near Jackson, Mississippi, in Hinds County, to Ola and John Henry Williams. Williams's mother, whose African name means "Keeper of the Beautiful House" or "He Who Wants to Be Chief," had been born in Mississippi; his father's roots were in Syracuse, New York, where the couple met. When Williams was six months old, he returned with his mother to Syracuse. The family resided in the multiethnic Fifteenth Ward, and Williams attended Washington Irving Elementary, Madison Junior High, and Central High School. Joining the

Navy in 1943, Williams served in the Pacific, and after discharge in 1946 and his return to Syracuse he completed his secondary education, followed by a brief term at Morris Brown College in Atlanta and then enrollment at Syracuse University, where he studied creative writing. In 1947, he married Carolyn Clopton, with whom he had two sons, Gregory and Dennis. In 1950, Williams earned his B.A. and continued at Syracuse to pursue graduate study. During this period, he worked at a variety of jobs—foundry work, social work, public relations, insurance, radio and television—while developing as a journalist. Following the failure of his marriage in 1952 and a brief stay in California in 1954, he was determined to become a professional writer. In 1946, he contributed pieces to the Syracuse newspaper, the *Progressive Herald*, continuing through 1955 as a reporter for the *Chicago Defender*, the *Pittsburgh Courier*, the *Los Angeles Tribune*, and the *Village Voice*.

After moving to New York in 1954, he worked for a vanity publisher, Comet Press, in 1955-1956 and at Abelard-Schuman in 1957-1958. In 1958, Williams was director of information for the American Committee on Africa, a reporter for *Jet* magazine, and a stringer for the Associated Negro Press. Based in Barcelona for a period, he was employed in 1959 by WOV Radio in New York; his first published novel, *The Angry Ones*, appeared in 1960.

Though Williams was nominated in 1962 for the Prix de Rome by the American Academy of Arts and Letters, his name was withdrawn for reasons that Williams attributed to his upcoming interracial marriage. In 1963 Williams contributed an article to *Ebony* magazine and began writing for *Holiday*. He became an Africa correspondent for *Newsweek* in 1964, and in 1965 he married Lorrain Isaac, with whom he had a son, Adam. Williams began his career in higher education in 1968, teaching at the College of the Virgin Islands and the City College of New York. He held positions at the University of California at Santa Barbara, University of Hawaii, Boston University, New York University, University of Houston, and Bard College. In 1979 he began teaching at Rutgers University; he was named Paul Robeson Professor of English at Rutgers in 1990, and he retired in 1994. *Safari West* won the 1998 American Book Award.

John A. Williams (Library of Congress)

Williams's novels draw on personal experience, though they are not strictly autobiographical; they reflect the racial issues facing American society, especially during the Civil Rights movement. Williams writes in the clear, readable prose of the journalist; his plot structures mix linear time with flashback passages to achieve a seamless continuity. His characters have been writers, jazz musicians, black mothers, and military veterans, and his themes have addressed the hardships of the black writer, the expatriate in Europe, black family life, interracial relationships, and political conspiracy. The presentation of jazz is a frequent element, and New York City is a repeated setting, though Williams has also depicted the Caribbean and Africa.

The Angry Ones

Type of work: Novel
First published: 1960

Williams's first novel is a first-person narrative drawing on autobiographical elements. Like Williams, Stephen Hill, the African American main character, is a World War II veteran who works for a vanity press in New York. Early in the novel, Williams refers to African and Native American origins and jazz contexts. The novel is principally about Steve's relationships with his employer, coworkers, and friends. One of Steve's closest associates is Linton Mason, a white former collegemate and editor at McGraw-Hill. The novel uses Lint's success in publishing to indicate the racial divide, sexual jealousy, and the benefits of being white in America. Another theme is the search for a meaningful relationship, the choice between interracial and intraracial love. The causes of black "anger" are linked to Steve's frustrating attempts to rise within the company run by Rollie Culver and, generally, the treatment of black men in New York's publishing world, symbolized by the suicide of Steve's black friend Obie Roberts. The novel presents racism through the day-to-day experiences of the main character.

Night Song

Type of work: Novel
First published: 1961

Set in Greenwich Village, New York, in the 1950's, *Night Song* is a "jazz novel" that mirrors the life of famed alto saxophonist Charlie Parker through the portrayal of Eagle (Richie Stokes), a drug-addicted musician who retains the capabilities of jazz performance despite his debilitation. Eagle befriends the alcoholic David Hillary, an out-of-work white college professor employed in the jazz café run by Keel Robinson, a former black preacher and Harvard graduate involved in an interracial relationship with Della. Each of the characters is fractured, most notably Eagle, whose alcoholism and addiction are implicitly the result of the racist treatment of the black artist. Williams portrays David as a savior and betrayer of Eagle; David's "healing" is the ironic result of his association with Eagle, Keel, and Della.

Sissie

Type of work: Novel
First published: 1963

Named after the mother of two principal characters, Iris and Ralph, *Sissie* is divided into four parts. Through memories, the novel presents the stories of Iris, Ralph, and Sissie Joplin, with Sissie's history revealed in parts 3 and 4, resulting in a Joplin family saga. Iris's story, her failed marriage, her career in Europe, and her relationship with the jazz musician called Time, is the first extended flashback. Ralph's recollections, his experiences in the military, and his struggle as a writer in New York are presented through psychoanalysis, a device that reveals racial issues from the viewpoint of a white psychologist, a symbol of societal norms. Sissie Joplin, a matriarchal figure, has an affair that threatens the stability of her marriage, which undergoes numerous challenges, such as the difficulty of surviving economic hard times and the struggle to find personal fulfillment through love. Sissie is ultimately the catalyst for Ralph and Iris's recognition of their family's conflicted yet sustaining experiences.

The Man Who Cried I Am

Type of work: Novel
First published: 1967

Williams's best-received and perhaps most influential work, *The Man Who Cried I Am* revolves around Max Reddick, an African American writer reunited in Amsterdam with his Dutch former wife, Margrit. Williams presents, within a twenty-four-hour time period, the downward spiral of Reddick, a Chester Himes figure, who is suffering from colon cancer. Through flashbacks, Reddick's recollections of a thirty-year past present the social experience of black Americans through the civil rights era. The novel portrays Reddick's association with Harry Ames, a character based on black novelist Richard Wright, who has uncovered the King Alfred Plan, a plot to place America's black population in concentration camps. Other characters in the novel also resemble actual black writers or political figures, such as Marion Dawes, a James Baldwin type; Paul Durrell, a Martin Luther King, Jr., replica; and Minister Q, a Malcolm X parallel. Furthermore, Williams develops African characters, such as Jaja Enzkwu, who reveals the King Alfred Plan to Harry Ames. The involvement of the Central Intelligence Agency (CIA) in Reddick's death points to an international conspiracy against black people, demonstrating Williams's tragic vision of global race relations.

Captain Blackman

Type of work: Novel
First published: 1972

An exploration of black contributions in American wars, this novel employs a narrative strategy in which time is fluid. At the outset, Captain Blackman, a Vietnam War soldier who teaches his troops the history of black Americans in the military, is wounded and trapped by the Viet Cong. His hallucinations are used to develop scenes in various periods of American wars, from the American Revolution through Vietnam. In these settings, Blackman experiences battle and the racial circumstances affecting black troops. The novel mixes fictional characterizations with historical fact, as in the reference to the Battle of Bunker Hill in the American Revolution. Williams portrays a possible nuclear armageddon, in which black people become the forces of control, though the reversal of power from black to white is itself part of the dream visions of Blackman.

!Click Song

Type of work: Novel
First published: 1982

Williams *!Click Song* considered to be the novel in which he achieved the most effective coalescence of his literary intentions, and it won the 1983 American Book Award. Named for a vocal sound found in the Xhosa language of South Africa, *!Click Song* follows two writers, one black, the other white and Jewish. Using flashbacks, manipulating linear time, the narrative develops the literary careers of Cato Douglass and Paul Cummings in parallel. Divided into three sections, "Beginnings," "Middle," and "Endings," the narrative uses the first-person point of view of Cato as a representation of the journey of the black American writer. Beginning with the funeral of Paul, who committed suicide, the novel returns to the undergraduate experiences of the two veterans as they pursue their creative writing. Parallels to Williams's life are inescapable, especially in the treatment of Cato's career. However, Williams goes beyond mere autobiography by using Cato to symbolize the black artist who resists cultural falsehood, as in the closing section in which Cato in the 1960's offers a countertext to the withholding of information about black culture by major museums.

Jacob's Ladder

Type of work: Novel
First published: 1987

Jacob's Ladder explores the predicament of an African American military attaché, Jacob Henry (Jake), caught in the turmoil of American destabilizing efforts in Pandemi, a fictitious West African country, where he had spent part of his youth as the son of a black American missionary. Resembling Liberia, Pandemi is ruled by Chuma Fasseke, Jake's childhood friend. The government of Chuma Fasseke has replaced that of the Franklins, a family descended from nineteenth century repatriated African Americans. The novel also offers a parallel to Nigeria in the portrayal of Taiwo Shaguri, the head of state of Temian. Containing elements of an espionage thriller, *Jacob's Ladder* proposes that an African country can attain nuclear capabilities. Williams humanizes Jake and Fasseke, creating a work deeper than clandestine intrigue. The final sections describe the fall of Fasseke and the takeover of the nuclear power plant by his opposition, assisted by the CIA. The epilogue uses the ironic device of the press release to show the perspective of the international press.

Suggested Readings

Cash, Earl A. *John A. Williams: The Evolution of a Black Writer*. New York: Third Press, 1975.

Fleming, Robert. "John A. Williams." *Black Issues Book Review* 4 (July/August, 2002): 46-49.

Gayle, Addison, Jr. *The Way of the New World: The Black Novel in America*. Garden City, N.Y.: Doubleday, 1975.

Muller, Gilbert H. *John A. Williams*. Boston: Twayne, 1984.

Nadel, Alan. "My Country Too: Time, Place, and Afro-American Identity in the Work of John Williams." *Obsidian II: Black Literature in Review* 2, no. 3 (1987): 25-41.

Ramsey, Priscilla R. "John A. Williams: The Black American Narrative and the City." In *The City in African-American Literature*, edited by Yoshinobu Hakutani and Robert Butler. Madison, N.J.: Fairleigh Dickinson University Press, 1995.

Reilly, John M. "Thinking History in *The Man Who Cried I Am*." *Black American Literature Forum* 21, nos. 1/2 (1987): 25-42.

Ro, Sigmund. "Toward the Post-Protest Novel: The Fiction of John A. Williams." In *Rage and Celebration: Essays on Contemporary Afro-American Writing*. Atlantic Highlands, N.J.: Humanities Press, 1984.

Smith, Virginia W. "Sorcery, Double-Consciousness, and Warring Souls: An Intertextual Reading of *Middle Passage* and *Captain Blackman*." *African American Review* 30 (Winter, 1996): 659-674.

Tal, Kali. "'That Just Kills Me.'" *Social Text* 20 (Summer, 2002): 65-92.

Contributor: Joseph McLaren

August Wilson
(Frederick August Kittel)

Born: Pittsburgh, Pennsylvania; April 27, 1945
Died: Seattle, Washington; October 2, 2005

African American

Wilson made an ambitious effort to create a cycle of ten plays examining African American life in each decade of the twentieth century.

Principal works

DRAMA: *Ma Rainey's Black Bottom*, pr. 1984, pb. 1985; *Fences*, pr., pb. 1985; *Joe Turner's Come and Gone*, pr. 1986, pb. 1988; *The Piano Lesson*, pr. 1987, pb. 1990; *Two Trains Running*, pr. 1990, pb. 1992; *Three Plays*, pb. 1991; *Seven Guitars*, pr. 1995, pb. 1996; *Jitney*, pr. 2000, pb. 2001; *King Hedley II*, pr. 2001, pb. 2005; *Gem of the Ocean*, pr. 2003, pb. 2006; *How I Learned What I Learned*, pr. 2003; *Radio Golf*, pr. 2005, pb. 2007
TELEPLAY: *The Piano Lesson*, 1995 (adaptation of his play)
NONFICTION: *The Ground on Which I Stand*, 2000

August Wilson considered contact with one's roots to be a crucial source of strength, and his plays explore and celebrate African American culture. Wilson's plays also acknowledge the white racism that has marked African American history. Black experience in America contains, Wilson has noted, "all the universalities." His work received wide acclaim, winning Pulitzers and numerous other awards.

Wilson's father was a white baker from Germany, and his mother was a black cleaning woman who had moved to Pittsburgh from rural North Carolina. His father "wasn't around much," according to Wilson, and he and his brothers and sisters grew up in a financially strapped single-parent household "in a cultural environment which was black." At age twelve Wilson discovered and read through the small "Negro section" of the public library.

In 1965, Wilson decided to become a writer and adopted his mother's maiden name, becoming August Wilson (which he legally formalized in the early 1970's) instead of Frederick August Kittel. He began living on his own in a rooming house in the black area of Pittsburgh known as the Hill, while writing poetry and supporting himself in a series of menial jobs. In 1965, he also discovered the blues, which he acknowledges as "the greatest source of my inspiration." Wilson identified three other B's as influences: Amiri Baraka, some of whose plays Wilson directed in the 1960's at the Black Horizons Theater Company that Wilson cofounded; the art of Romare Bearden, noted for his collages of black life; and the stories of Argentinean author Jorge Luis Borges. In addition, he acknowledged the influence of South African playwright Athol Fugard.

In 1978, Wilson moved to St. Paul, Minnesota, where, surrounded by white voices, he began to create characters who spoke a poeticized version of the black English he had heard on the Hill. Lloyd Richards—then dean of the Yale School of Drama—directed Wilson's first major dramatic success, *Ma Rainey's Black Bottom*, and began a long-term working relationship with Wilson, who sees Richards as a father figure and professional mentor, with insight into Wilson's plays because of his own roots in black culture.

After *Ma Rainey's Black Bottom* Wilson realized he had written three plays set in different decades and decided to complete a historical cycle, with a play for each decade of the twentieth century. He used Pittsburgh as a setting for his plays after *Ma Rainey's Black Bottom* (which is set in Chicago), causing him to be compared to other artists who cast real locales as near characters in their fiction, such as James Joyce (who used Dublin) and William Faulkner (who used the area around Oxford, Mississippi). This cycle, the Pittsburgh or Century cycle, would eventually include ten plays, each covering a decade, in the following order:

- 1900's: *Gem of the Ocean* (2003)
- 1910's: *Joe Turner's Come and Gone* (1984)
- 1920's: *Ma Rainey's Black Bottom* (1982)
- 1930's: *The Piano Lesson* (1989)
- 1940's: *Seven Guitars* (1995)
- 1950's: *Fences* (1985)
- 1960's: *Two Trains Running* (1990)
- 1970's: *Jitney* (1983)
- 1980's: *King Hedley II* (2001)
- 1990's: *Radio Golf* (2005)

Two of these plays—*The Piano Lesson* and *Fences*—won the Pulitzer Prize in drama.

Divorced in 1990 from his second wife, Wilson moved to Seattle, Washington. There he continued to write his cycle of plays, participated as a dramaturge at the Eugene O'Neill Center, and, with his co-producer, Ben Mordecai, formed a joint venture called Sageworks, which gave Wilson artistic and financial control of his plays. Wilson married a third time, to Constanza Romero, and they had a daughter, Azula. Wilson died in 2005 at the age of sixty after battling liver cancer.

Ma Rainey's Black Bottom

Type of work: Drama
First produced: 1984, pb. 1985

Set in 1927 in a Chicago recording studio, Wilson's play *Ma Rainey's Black Bottom* explores the values and attitudes toward life and music of the classic blues singer Ma Rainey. Their economic exploitation as African American musicians in a white-controlled recording industry, as well as their inferior social status in the majority white culture, become evident in the play's dialogue and action. As Ma Rainey puts it: "If you colored and can make them some money, then you all right with them. Otherwise, you just a dog in the alley."

For Rainey, the blues is "a way of understanding life" that gives folks a sense they are not alone: "This be an empty world without the blues." As such, the blues has been a source of strength for African Americans, and performers like Ma Rainey have been bearers of cultural identity. A major theme of *Ma Rainey's Black Bottom* and of other plays by Wilson is the necessity of acknowledging one's past and connecting with one's culture.

African American identity, however, with its roots in Africa and the rural South, is at times rejected by the members of Ma Rainey's band. The pianist, Toledo, for example, points out the "ancestral retention" involved in the bass player's trying to get some marijuana from another band member by naming things they have done together—in effect, an African appeal to a bond of kinship. Toledo's observation is immediately rejected by the bass player, who replies: "I ain't no African!" and by Levee, the trumpet player, who remarks: "You don't see me running around in no jungle with no bone between my nose." Levee also has a loathing for the South, which he associates with sharecropping and general backwardness. Levee's disregard for African American heritage extends to Ma Rainey's style of blues, which he calls "old jug-band street." He resents her refusal to use his jazzed-up arrangements and, at the tragic end of the play, when his hopes for a recording contract of his own are dashed, his rage is misdirected at Toledo, who happens to step on his shoe, and whom he stabs with his knife.

Fences

Type of work: Drama
First produced: 1985, pb. 1985

Troy Maxson, the protagonist of Wilson's *Fences*, is the son of a frustrated sharecropper whose harshness drove off his wives and Troy. Troy has made his way north to a world where African Americans live in shacks and are unable to find work. Troy takes to stealing, kills a man, and is sent to prison, where he learns how to play baseball, which he loves and at which he excels. Segregation confines Troy, after prison, to the Negro Leagues. He is angry at the racism that frustrates his attempt at achieving the American Dream in the most American of sports, but he remains resilient. *Fences* celebrates his indomitable spirit, while acknowledging his flaws.

August Wilson (AP/Wide World Photos)

The play opens in 1957, when Troy is fifty-three years old. He is appealing in the zest with which he dramatizes his life. A battle with pneumonia becomes a time when he wrestles with a white-robed and hooded Death, and buying furniture on credit from a white man becomes making a deal with the devil. His friend Bono seems to acknowledge the African American tradition of these tall tales when he comments: "You got some Uncle Remus in your blood." The audience learns of Troy's admirable defiance at work in questioning the sanitation department's policy of having all the whites drive while the blacks do the lifting. Troy also has an affectionate teasing relationship with Bono and his wife Rose.

As the play continues, however, Troy erects fences between himself and those he loves. He refuses to allow his son to accept a football fellowship to college and then forces him to leave home. Troy loses contact with Bono after being promoted at work. Troy hurts his wife through an extramarital affair, and he commits his brain-damaged brother, Gabe, to a mental institution so he can collect part of Gabe's government checks.

Although Troy has tragic flaws, the ending of *Fences* is not tragic. A spirit of reconciliation is brought by Gabe, who has been allowed to leave the mental hospital to attend his brother's funeral. Gabe thinks that, when he blows his trumpet, Saint Peter will open the pearly gates and allow Troy into Heaven. Gabe's horn lacks a mouthpiece, however, and, distraught, he performs a dance, connected, presumably, to pre-Christian African ancestors. In performance, the stage is then flooded with light, indicating that the gates have opened.

Joe Turner's Come and Gone

Type of work: Drama
First produced: 1986, pb. 1988

In *Joe Turner's Come and Gone*, Wilson reaches further back into the historical black experience. As in the old blues song of the same title, the brother of the governor of Tennessee, Joe Turner, found and enslaved groups of black men. Herald Loomis, the mysterious central character in this play, was so enslaved in 1901 and not released for seven years. The play dramatizes his search for his wife, which is actually a search for himself. His arrival at a Pittsburgh boardinghouse in 1911 disrupts and disturbs, creating the tension and significance of the drama.

Another boardinghouse resident, Bynum, establishes his identity as a "conjure man" or "rootworker" early in the play. Bynum's search for his "shiny man" becomes a thematic and structural tie for the play. At the end of the first act, during a joyous African call-and-response dance, Loomis has a sort of ecstatic fit, ending with his being unable to stand and walk. Some kind of dramatic resolution must relate Bynum's vision and Loomis's quest. It comes in the final scene when wife Martha returns and Loomis learns that his quest is still unrealized. Wilson describes Loomis's transformation in actions rather than words. His wife does not restore him, nor does her religion restore him. In desperation, he turns a knife on himself, rubs his hands and face in his own blood, looks down at his hands, and says, "I'm standing. My legs stood up! I'm standing now!" It is at this point that he has found his "song of self-sufficiency." Wilson's rather poetic stage directions articulate a redemption that Loomis cannot verbalize, risking audience misinterpretation.

Bynum's final line of the play recognizes Loomis as a shiny man, the shiny man who can tell him the meaning of life. The suggestion of a Christ figure is unmistakable, and yet Loomis's soul is not cleansed through religious belief. He has denied the Christ of the white man, despite Martha's pleading. His epiphany is in finding himself. Joe Turner has come but he has also gone. Herald Loomis finds his identity in his own African roots, not in the slave identity that the white Joe Turner had given him.

The Piano Lesson

Type of work: Drama
First produced: 1987, pb. 1990

With his fourth major play, Wilson crafted a more tightly structured plot. In fact, *The Piano Lesson* is stronger thematically and structurally than it is in character development. The characters serve to dramatize the conflict between the practical use of a family heritage to create a future, and a symbolic treasuring of that heritage to honor the past. The piano, which bears the blood of their slave ancestors, is the focus of the conflict between Boy Willie and his sister, Berniece. Its exotic carvings, made by their great-grandfather, tell the story of their slave ancestors who were sold in exchange for the piano. Its presence in the northern home of Berniece and her Uncle Doaker represents the life of their father who died stealing it back from Sutter.

Berniece is embittered and troubled not only by the piano and her father's death but also by her mother's blood and tears that followed that death and by the loss of her own husband. In contrast, Boy Willie is upbeat and funny, an optimistic, ambitious, and boyish man who is sure he is right in wanting to sell the piano to buy Sutter's land. He has the warrior spirit. Throughout the play, the presence of Sutter's ghost is seen or felt. Sutter's ghost seems to represent the control that the white man still exerts over this family in 1937. Boy Willie chooses to ignore the ghost, to accuse his sister of imagining it, but ultimately it is Boy Willie who must wrestle with the ghost.

Wilson said that this play had five endings because Berniece and Boy Willie are both right. The conflict is indeed unresolved as Boy Willie leaves, telling Berniece that she had better keep playing that piano or he and Sutter could both come back. The lesson of the piano is twofold: Berniece has learned that she should use her heritage, rather than let it fester in bitterness, and Boy Willie has learned that he cannot ignore the significance of this piano, which symbolizes the pain and suffering of all of his ancestors. There is little in the play that deviates from the central conflict. The skill of Wilson's writing is seen in the interplay of characters bantering and arguing, in the indirect quality of questions that are not answered, and in the storytelling. While characters may serve primarily as symbols and plot devices, they are nevertheless vivid and credible.

Two Trains Running

Type of work: Drama
First produced: 1990, pb. 1992

Memphis Lee's small restaurant is the setting of Wilson's *Two Trains Running*. Risa, a young woman who has scarred her legs with a razor to deflect the sexual interest of men, is the restaurant's cook and waitress. The rest of the African American cast are male and include, among others, Sterling, an unemployed young man recently released from prison; Holloway, a retired house painter; and Hambone, who is mentally retarded.

The gossip, debates, philosophizing, and storytelling that take place in Memphis's restaurant reflect the oral tradition of African American culture. Some critics note that the characters engaged in the talk seem detached from the racial riots, assassinations, and antiwar protests that marked the late 1960s, when the play takes place. Wilson responds by saying that he was not interested in writing "what *white* folks think of as American history for the 1960's." He was interested in making the point that "by 1969 nothing has changed for the black man."

One thing not changed by 1969 was economic injustice. Holloway notes that for centuries blacks worked hard for free, enriching white slaveholders. Once blacks have to be paid whites deny them work and call them lazy. The characters in *Two Trains Running* are directly affected by the whites' ability to make and interpret rules, to the disadvantage of blacks. When Hambone painted a fence, the white butcher who hired him offered a chicken in payment instead of the promised ham. When Sterling wins at the numbers, the whites who run the game cut his winnings in half. When Memphis's restaurant is scheduled to be taken over by the city, the whites in charge invoke a clause saying they do not have to pay his price.

Hambone dies without getting his ham, but his persistence in demanding it for more than nine years moves Memphis to donate fifty dollars for flowers for his funeral and moves Sterling to break into the butcher shop and steal a ham for his casket. By the end of the play Sterling has been transformed from a man unwilling to pay the price for love (he is reluctant to accept responsibility for others) to one who is willing to make a commitment to Risa, who seems willing to have a relationship with him. In this he has the blessing of Aunt Ester, reputedly 322 years old and an important offstage character. She symbolizes the wisdom of black experience in America, the wisdom of a people who survived against the odds. Memphis, too, has been transformed. He was run off his land in Mississippi years before, and he vowed one day to return seeking justice. "They got two trains running every day." By the play's end he wins his fight with the city, which agrees to pay more than his price for his restaurant, and he declares he will now follow through on his vow because, as he understands Aunt Ester to have told him: "If you drop the ball, you got to go back and pick it up."

Seven Guitars

Type of work: Drama
First produced: 1995, pb. 1996

Two Trains Running was followed in 1995 by *Seven Guitars*. Set in the 1940's, it tells the tragic story of blues guitarist Floyd Barton, whose funeral opens the play. The action flashes back to re-create the events of Floyd's last week of life. Floyd had arrived in Pittsburgh to try to get his guitar out of the pawnshop and to convince his former lover, Vera, to return with him to Chicago. A record he made years earlier has suddenly gained popularity, and he has been offered the opportunity to record more songs at a studio in Chicago.

The play's central conflicts are Floyd's struggle to move forward in his musical career and his personal strife with Vera and his bandmates. A subplot centers on Floyd's friend Hedley and his deteriorating physical and mental health as his friends attempt to place him in a tuberculosis sanatorium. The play contains some of Wilson's familiar character types, including the mentally aberrant Hedley; the troubled-by-the-law young black male protagonist, Floyd; the capable and independent woman, Louise; and the more needy, younger woman, Ruby. It also contains elements of music, dance, storytelling, violence, and food.

Jitney

Type of work: Drama
First produced: 2000, pb. 2001

In a reworked version of Wilson's earlier, short play *Jitney*, Becker, a retired steel-mill worker, runs a jitney station, serving the unofficial taxi needs of the black community of Pittsburgh's Hill district during early autumn of 1977. The jitney drivers are a rich collection of troubled but hardworking men. The station offers the men a living and a sense of independence that is threatened by the city's plans to tear down the neighborhood in the name of urban renewal. Becker also faces a personal crisis. His son, Booster, is about to leave prison after serving twenty years for murdering his well-to-do white girlfriend. Father and son have not spoken for two decades. Becker is bitter that his son threw away a promising career, and Booster sees his father's lifetime of hard work and submissiveness to white landlords and bosses as demeaning. Father and son never reconcile, but they indirectly attempt to redeem themselves to each other. Becker decides to organize the jitney drivers and fight the urban renewal. Yet, just as Becker begins the move to resistance, he falls victim to his rigorous work ethic and dies unexpectedly. As the dispirited drivers praise his father, Booster begins to respect his father's accomplishments and prepares to carry on Becker's mission to save the jitney station.

King Hedley II

Type of work: Drama
First produced: 2001, pb. 2005

King Hedley II takes place in the backyard of a few ramshackle houses in the Hill District of Pittsburgh in 1985. Its protagonist, King Hedley II, is a petty thief and a former convict engaged in selling stolen refrigerators. Believing that he is being held back while everybody else is moving forward, Hedley dreams of a better life. His partner in crime is a shady character named Mister. Hedley's wife, Tonya, is pregnant with a child she does not want to raise in the rough life she knows. Hedley's mother, Ruby, is a former jazz singer who is reunited with an old lover, the con man Elmore. The next-door neighbor, Stool Pigeon, is a crazy old man who stacks old newspapers in his hovel. He is the play's mystic messenger who buries a dead cat in the backyard and brings to its grave various tokens that he believes will bring the animal back to one of its nine lives. The yard, barren except for weeds and garbage, is a major symbol. Hedley tries to raise plants in it, even fencing off a small patch with barbed wire. However, like Hedley's efforts to better himself, the attempt to grow something is doomed.

Suggested Readings

Bigsby, C. W. E. *Modern American Drama, 1945-1990*. New York: Cambridge University Press, 1992.

Birdwell, Christine. "Death as a Fastball on the Outside Corner: *Fences*' Troy Maxson and the American Dream." *Aethlon* 8 (1990).

Bogumil, Mary L. *Understanding August Wilson*. Columbia: University of South Carolina Press, 1999.

Brustein, Robert. *Reimagining American Theatre*. New York: Hill and Wang, 1991.

Elkins, Marilyn, ed. *August Wilson: A Casebook*. New York: Garland, 1994.

Herrington, Joan. *I Ain't Sorry for Nothin' I Done: August Wilson's Process of Playwriting*. New York: Limelight Editions, 1998.

Hill, Holly. "Black Theatre into the Mainstream." In *Contemporary American Theatre*, edited by Bruce King. New York: St. Martin's Press, 1991.

Nadel, Alan, ed. *May All Your Fences Have Gates*. Iowa City: University of Iowa Press, 1994.

Pereira, Kim. *August Wilson and the African-American Odyssey*. Champaign: University of Illinois Press, 1995.

Rocha, Mark William. "August Wilson and the Four *B*'s: Influences." In *August Wilson: A Casebook*, edited by Marilyn Elkins. New York: Garland, 1994.

Shannon, Sandra G. *The Dramatic Vision of August Wilson*. Washington, D.C.: Howard University Press, 1995.

Wolfe, Peter. *August Wilson*. New York: Twayne, 1999.

Contributors: Jack Vincent Barbera, Rhona Justice-Malloy, and Sally Osborne Norton

Jade Snow Wong

Born: San Francisco, California; January 21, 1922
Died: San Francisco, California; March 16, 2006

Chinese American

Wong's accounts of Chinese life in America break down prejudice and create understanding among cultures.

Principal works

NONFICTION: *Fifth Chinese Daughter*, 1950; *No Chinese Stranger*, 1975

Jade Snow Wong was introduced to writing by her father, who gave her a diary when she was young and encouraged her to record the important events of her life. She continued this habit into her adult life. She also received formal training at Mills College, where she wrote many papers about her life in Chinatown.

Wong began work on her first book, *Fifth Chinese Daughter*, in 1946, at the age of twenty-four. Her goal was to create a "better understanding of the Chinese culture on the part of Americans." She wanted to show non-Chinese Americans the beauty and traditions of her culture and dispel prevalent stereotypes. Although Wong produced two other major works, writing was not her primary occupation. Instead, she saw it as a method for exposing other Americans to her cultural heritage.

As a result of her first book, the U.S. State Department sent her on a four-month tour to speak to various audiences and to relate her experiences of breaking through race and gender barriers in America. Wong and her husband also acted as tour guides and escorted many Americans to China before her husband's death in 1985. Wong's third book, *No Chinese Stranger*, was written in reaction to her first visit to China, in 1972, only one month after Richard M. Nixon's trip. During that trip, she learned what it is like to be part of a homogeneous society, and not a minority.

Influenced by this trip, Wong soon published a second autobiography, *No Chinese Stranger*, which described her life in the 1950's and 1960's before focusing on her trip to China. Again she enjoyed a high public profile, and she returned to Mills College in 1976 to receive an honorary doctorate in humane letters. From 1975 to 1981, she was a member of the California Council for the Humanities, and from 1978 to 1981 she was director of the Chinese Culture Center. After the death of her husband in 1985, Snow lowered her profile although she continued to lead annual tours to China. She died at the age of eighty-four in San Francisco on March 16, 2006.

Wong's works also show that each person must establish an identity regardless of race. Her wish was to share her struggles in order to encourage others who may face similar obstacles. Wong's sense of identity and self-expression was not limited to her writing, however—she was an accomplished potter, and she sold her pottery in her own shop. She also cared for her children—the most important work in her life, according to Snow: "Our basic and greatest value is family cohesiveness."

Fifth Chinese Daughter

Type of work: Autobiography
First published: 1950

Fifth Chinese Daughter, Wong's autobiography, directly and honestly relates the struggles and accomplishments of an American-born Chinese girl. Although it is an autobiography, it is written in the third person, which reflects the Chinese custom of humility. This use of the third person also reminds the reader of how difficult it is for the author to express her individual identity.

The book explains Wong's desire to prove to her parents that she was "a person, besides being a female." Even as a toddler, she was taught to obey her parents and her older brother and sisters without question. She was not allowed to express her opinions; rather, she was forced to comply with the demands of the rest of her family.

When she began school, her parents expected her to earn good grades, yet they refused to praise or even encourage her when she was recognized for her school achievements. In fact, they refused to fund her college education, although they paid her brothers' expenses, because it was not considered wise to educate a girl, who would leave the family when she married. As a result, Wong was forced to work full time throughout her teenage years in order to save the money to go to college. During this time, she was exposed to the "foreign" culture of the whites living in San Francisco, and she was surprised to learn that parents in many Anglo families listened to children and respected their opinions. Further, she learned in a college sociology class that in many families, children were afforded the right to discuss with their parents what they saw as unfair. Learning about the practices of other families caused Wong to question her parents' practices for the first time.

As a result, Wong began a slow and painful struggle to earn her parents' respect while developing her own identity. Unfortunately, her parents were not the only people who would discourage her. She also had to face prejudice and stereotyping in the white world. She refused to be discouraged by this and accepted the challenges that it brought.

Eventually, Jade Snow was able to win her parents' respect. She established her own identity and her independence by beginning a business selling handmade pottery. Although her Chinatown shop was patronized only by white customers, her ability to attract many customers was recognized by her family and by members of Wong's community. The pottery shop venture finally allowed her to find "that niche which would be hers alone."

Suggested Readings

Blinde, Patricia Lin. "The Icicle in the Desert: Perspective and Form in the Works of Two Chinese-American Women Writers." *The Journal of the Society for the Study of the Multi-Ethnic Literature of the United States* 6, no. 3 (1979).

Chin, Frank. "Come All Ye Asian-American Masters of the Real and the Fake." In *The Big Aiiieeeee! An Anthology of Chinese American and Japanese American Literature*, edited by Jeffery Paul Chan et al. New York: Meridian, 1991.

Hong, Maria, ed. *Growing Up Asian American: An Anthology*. New York: W. Morrow, 1993.

Kim, Elaine. *Asian American Literature: An Introduction to the Writings and Their Social Context*. Philadelphia: Temple University Press, 1982.

Lim, Shirley Geok-lin. "Twelve Asian American Writers: In Search of Self-Definition." In *Redefining American Literary History*. New York: Modern Language Association of America, 1990.

Ling, Amy. *Between Worlds: Women Writers of Chinese Ancestry*. New York: Pergamon Press, 1990.

Contributor: Amy Beth Shollenberger

Jay Wright

Born: Albuquerque, New Mexico; May 25, 1935

African American

Wright's intellectually demanding poetry illuminates the African American experience by exploring the philosophies and religious cosmologies that underlie historical events and personal spiritual development.

Principal works

DRAMA: *Balloons*, 1968; *The Death and Return of Paul Batuata*, 1984; *Death as History*, 1989

POETRY: *Death as History*, 1967; *The Homecoming Singer*, 1971; *Dimensions of History*, 1976; *Soothsayers and Omens*, 1976; *The Double Invention of Komo*, 1980; *Explications/Interpretations*, 1984; *Elaine's Book*, 1986; *Selected Poems of Jay Wright*, 1987; *Boleros*, 1991; *Transfigurations: Collected Poems*, 2000; *Music's Mask and Measure*, 2007

Jay Wright was reared in New Mexico and Southern California. Wright became fluent in English and Spanish and knowledgeable regarding African American, Latino, and Native American ways of looking at the world. Extended travels in Mexico and Europe in later years also expanded his cultural literacy and empathy. His poetry expresses his interest in understanding all of the many different cultures that have contributed to modern global identity.

After high school in San Pedro, California, Wright played minor league baseball and served in the U.S. Army. He earned a degree at the University of California at Berkeley in 1961, studied briefly at Union Theological Seminary, and received a master's degree from Rutgers University in 1966. Though he taught at Tougaloo College, Talladega College, and Yale University in the late 1960's and early 1970's, Wright did not pursue a regular academic career. Married in 1971 to Lois Silber, Wright settled in New Hampshire to continue his research and writing.

Wright's serious devotion to poetry and his prolific production brought him numerous awards, including a National Endowment for the Arts Fellowship in 1968, a Guggenheim Fellowship in 1974, and the prestigious MacArthur Fellowship in 1986. These awards allowed Wright time to study and to write. The study of comparative religion, philosophy, and anthropology is central to Wright's poetic work, which explores the history of slavery in the New World by investigating the mythologies and cosmologies of the African, European, and Native American peoples.

The Homecoming Singer

Type of work: Poetry
First published: 1971

Semantic density and formal extravagance are particularly characteristic of the book-length poems that have followed Wright's first collection, *The Homecoming Singer*, which was preceded in 1967 by a chapbook, *Death as History*. These early poems, most of which are reprinted in *Selected Poems of Jay Wright*, tend to be more manageable from both a thematic and a linguistic point of view. *The Homecoming Singer* is important to Wright's canon not only as a record of his early artistic, spiritual, and intellectual development but also because it contains all the seeds of his later writing. The two opening poems, "Wednesday Night Prayer Meeting" and "The Baptism," inspired by the religious zeal of Daisy Faucett, lament the failure of institutionalized African American religions to provide spiritual resources for what Wright, with Harris, calls "the redefinition of the person." The tragic lack of "myths to scale your life upon" results in "the senseless, weightless,/ timedenying feeling of not being there" with which the poet is left at the end of "Reflections Before the Charity Hospital." Yet rather than leading to the despair and violence of LeRoi Jones's "A Poem for Willie Best," a text on which Wright brilliantly meditates in "The Player at the Crossroads" and "Variations on a Theme by LeRoi Jones," this alienation and dispossession heighten the poet's awareness, as in "First Principles," of "the tongues of the exiled dead/ who live in the tongues of the living." In "Destination: Accomplished," this new awareness grows into an abiding emotional and intellectual desire for "something to put in place." It is the death-challenging search for "new categories for the soul/ of those I want to keep" that finally directs Wright toward traditional African societies, their rituals and mythologies, in "A Nuer Sacrifice" and "Death as History."

Like all of Wright's poetry, though more explicitly so, *The Homecoming Singer* draws on autobiographical experience as a catalyst for the persona's introspective inquiries into the possible nature of an African American cultural and literary tradition. Memories of his two fathers, in "A Non-Birthday Poem for My Father," "Origins," "First Principles," and "The Hunting-Trip Cook," become occasions for acknowledging and examining the responsibilities the dead confer upon the living. This is what connects these presences from Wright's personal past, which also include his alcoholic stepmother in "Billie's Blues," to "the intense communal daring" of Crispus Attucks and W. E. B. Du Bois.

The Homecoming Singer also acquaints the reader with geographies to which Wright returns throughout his poetic career. In "An Invitation to Madison County," one of the best poems in this collection, the black American South offers unexpected memories and visions of community to the displaced poet, whose journey in this instance follows that of so many other African American writers in search of their cultural origins. The Southwest, which, along with California, provides the setting for Wright's family remembrances, is another place of origin; its history also connects the persona with the Mexico of "Morning, Leaving Calle Gigantes,"

"Chapultepec Castle," "Jalapeña Gypsies," and "Bosques de Chapultepec." "A Month in the Country" offers a fleeting glimpse of the "New England reticence" of New Hampshire, to which the persona escapes after "The End of an Ethnic Dream" to soothe his "blistered" brain. In later poems, all these places evolve into full-fledged symbolic geographies. "Sketch for an Aesthetic Project" and "Beginning Again," the two poems that close *The Homecoming Singer*, are the initial attempts of the "aching prodigal" at weaving his memories and his discontent into a poetic design that transcends individual experience. These poems are preludes to *Soothsayers and Omens*, the first volume of a poetic cycle that continues with *Explications/Interpretations*, *Dimensions of History*, and *The Double Invention of Komo*. Each of these book-length poems is part of a carefully constructed pattern or dramatic movement, and this is the order in which Wright places them.

Soothsayers and Omens

Type of work: Poetry
First published: 1976

The poem that opens the first of *Soothsayers and Omens*'s four parts is significantly titled "The Charge." Reminiscent of Wright's homages to paternal figures in *The Homecoming Singer*, this poem focuses on fathers and sons "gathered in the miracle/ of our own memories." With "The Appearance of a Lost Goddess" and the rise of a female principle to complement and balance the male presences, the poet identifies himself as an initiate who has accepted the charge to reconstruct neglected and severed ties. This reconstruction takes the initial shape of six short poems titled "Sources" with which Wright inaugurates his systematic exploration of African cosmologies. "Sources" draws heavily on West African precolonial mythologies, both of which become part of a collective memory. The two longer poems that follow and change the pace of the first part, "Benjamin Banneker Helps to Build a City" and "Benjamin Banneker Sends His 'Almanac' to Thomas Jefferson," weave elements of Dogon theology around quotations from the letters of the African American astronomer, an "uneasy" stranger in his own land who bemoans "the lost harmony" and the injustices of slavery.

Dogon ritual becomes even more significant in Part IV, whose title, "Second Conversations with Ogotemmêli," refers directly to Griaule's anthropological exploits. These are poems of apprenticeship that invoke different components and stages of the creation of the universe, represented by the water spirit Nommo, creator of the First Word (that is, language) and his twin Amma, Lébé, guardian of the dead, and the Pale Fox, agent of chaos. Wright's "Conversations" are characterized by exchanges and relationships very different from those that prevail between anthropologist and informer. For Wright's persona, Ogotemmêli is a spiritual guide or "nani" who "will lead me into the darkness" and whose silences promise the speech of redemption with which to mend "the crack in the universe." The terms and trajectory of Wright's journey into darkness, a sort of Middle Passage in reverse that leads back to Africa, are also indebted to Dante's search, even if the spiritual map (the "God") Wright's initiate "designs" is different. It is no coincidence, then, that "Homecoming," the poem that announces "a plan of transformations," is laced with quotations from *La divina commedia* (c. 1320; *The Divine Comedy*).

At the same time that *Soothsayers and Omens* initiates the reader into African mythologies, it also revisits Mexico and New Mexico, geographies already implicit in the pre-Columbian references of the opening poems. The most remarkable of the transitional poems in parts 2 and 3 is "The Albuquerque Graveyard," a place to which Wright's persona returns to worry the dead, the "small heroes," with a quest for patterns that is as "uneasy" as Benjamin Banneker's. The poet's announcement that

> I am going back
> to the Black limbo,
> an unwritten history
> of our own tensions,

is a precise summary of his desire and purpose throughout *Soothsayers and Omens*: both to articulate a history that has not been written and to un-write a history that has neglected, even forgotten—the participation of Africans and African Americans in founding what is deceptively called "Western" civilization.

If *Soothsayers and Omens* is the "first design," the first step toward the articulation of a spiritual order, *Explications/Interpretations* marks the next logical stage in what Wright calls his "African-Hellenic-Judaic discourse." Dedicated to poet Robert Hayden and critic Harold Bloom, this volume generates somewhat different patterns and principles of order and also introduces a set of new players on a new stage in "MacIntyre, The Captain, and the Saints." This central dramatic poem enacts Wright's personal and intellectual ties with Scotland. MacIntyre, the Irish-Scottish clan to which the names Murphy and Wright can be traced, is Wright's autobiographical persona who, instead of conversing with Ogotemmêli, now turns to astronomer David Hume, poet Hugh MacDiarmid, and anthropologist Robert Sutherland Rattray. A new element in this poem is the use of ideograms, a strategy indebted to Ezra Pound's works, which Wright explores more fully in *Dimensions of History* and *The Double Invention of Komo*. Yet dramatic poetry, a form for which Wright has an undoubted preference, is not the only important formal aspect of this volume. *Explications/Interpretations* is also energized by the vital rhythms of African American music. The poem is divided into three parts, "Polarity's Trio," "Harmony's Trio," and "Love's Dozen," titles that already indicate Wright's concern with music and number. "Tensions and Resolutions" introduces dualism or twinning and balance as concepts that inform the poem's thematic and structural organization: "Each act caresses/ the moment it remembers,/ and the moment it desires." This double "act" is of course the act of writing, which makes Wright's poem a "field of action" along the lines of Charles Olson's "projective verse."

Explications/Interpretations

Type of work: Poetry
First published: 1984

Although published after *Dimensions of History*, *Explications/Interpretations* is really the second volume in the poetic cycle that began with *Soothsayers and Omens*. That the rhythms of writing and speaking are formal articulations of the poet's being is crucial to understanding the dynamics of *Explications/Interpretations* and indeed of all of Wright's poems. The arrangement of the poems in groups of three, six, and twelve (plus one) already creates a sense of rhythm, which is rendered most explicit in "The Twenty-two Tremblings of the Postulant," subtitled "Improvisations Surrounding the Body." This poem is a good example of Wright's kind of blues poetry, in which the compositional principle is derived not from the call-and-response structure of the blues lyrics, as is the case, for instance, in the poetry of Langston Hughes and Sterling Brown, but from the arrangement of the twenty-two short poems across a sequence of chords. Each poem corresponds not only to a different part of the human body but also to a musical bar that belongs to a specific chord, I, IV, or V. The last two bars, one is told at the end of the poem, are "tacit," which makes for a total of twenty-four bars, whose musical equivalent is a (doubled) blues line. *Explications/Interpretations* as a whole is a poetic improvisation on this basic blues line, one of the most distinctive rhythms of African American culture. These are the sounds of flesh and bone that constitute the poem's and the poet's "grammar of being." For Wright, who insists on poetry's social and historical responsibilities, these schemes, "the god's elemental bones," are "a launchpad/ into the actual" ("Inscrutability").

Wright's emphasis in *Explications/Interpretations* on the body as a site of knowledge and action is indicative of his rejection of dualisms. The spiritual does not exist in separation from the material any more than male exists without female. They are what Wright conceives of as "twins," and the desired relationship between them is one of balance. This is most clearly articulated in "The Continuing City: Spirit and Body" and "The Body," two poems that lay out aesthetic and philosophical principles indebted to Danquah's *The Akan Doctrine of God*. In his notes, Wright identifies *Explications/Interpretations* as an attempt "to claim this knowledge as part of the continuing creative life of the Americas"; the Americas are what comes into full view in *Dimensions of History*.

Dimensions of History

Type of work: Poetry
First published: 1976

Though *Dimensions of History* is dedicated to the late Francis Ferguson, with whom Wright studied at Rutgers, the book owes perhaps its most significant debt to

Harris's notion of "vision as historical dimension." This third volume of Wright's poetic cycle maintains the tripartite structure of *Explications/Interpretations*, a scheme now more explicitly associated with the three stages of an initiation ritual: separation, transition, (re)incorporation. Part 1, "The Second Eye of the World. The Dimension of Rites and Acts," announces this link not only by being itself divided into three poems but also by offering the reader a Dogon ideogram that, according to Griaule and Dieterlen, represents the separation of the twins, male and female, at the moment of circumcision. The historical dimension of separation within an African American context is (enforced) exile. This historical condition becomes the "special kinship" the poet's persona shares with his other selves, the dead to whose realm he descends and whose claims he seeks to understand in a spiritually barren land from which the god has retreated. Among them are once again Du Bois and Attucks, who are joined by the voices of and allusions to Frederick Douglass, St. Augustine, Toussaint Louverture and many others who congregate in a text brimming with references to Aztec, Mayan, Incaic, Egyptian, Arabic, Christian, Yoruba, Akan, and, of course, Dogon and Bambara mythologies. Ogotemmêli's return in the figure of the blind sage at the beginning of the second poem commences the process of healing: "Anochecí enfermo amanecí bueno" (I went to bed sick, I woke up well) are the words that open the third poem, at the end of which the persona names himself "a dark and dutiful dyēli,/ searching for the understanding of his deeds."

Part 2, titled "Modulations. The Aesthetic Dimension," consists of an assortment of poetic forms, many of them linked to Caribbean and Latin American musical forms and instruments such as the Cuban *son*, the *areito*, and the *bandola*, a fifteen-string Colombian guitar. The shorter poems in "Rhythms, Charts, and Changes," "The Body Adorned and Bare," a section reminiscent of the meditations on the body in *Explications/Interpretations*, and "Retablos" (votive paintings) lead up to Wright's "Log Book of Judgments," a series of ethical and aesthetic formulations distilled from the persona's historical and ritualistic experiences. They culminate in the following lines from "Meta-A and the A of Absolutes": "I am good when I know the darkness of all light,/ and accept the darkness, not as a sing, but as my body."

Dimensions of History closes with "Landscapes. The Physical Dimension," whose themes and poetic architecture return to the history of the conquest of the Americas and to Náhua (Aztec) mythology and poetry. The most notable formal aspects of this final part are the encyclopedic monoliths, block passages that list the vital statistics of five American nations: Venezuela, Colombia, Panama, Mexico, and the United States. The spaces between these building blocks or "stones" are filled with Wright's own enchanted mortar, a possible translation of the Náhuatl-infused Spanish idiom *cal y canto* (literally, mortar and song) that joins Wright's compositional principles with his cross-cultural concerns. This syncretic idiom, which also conjures up such Latin American poets as Pablo Neruda and José María Arguedas, is a miniature representation of the rhizomes Wright's poem uncovers. It is one of his "emblems of the ecstatic connection." His poet's Middle Passages temporarily end with an image of the Great Gate of the ancient Mayan city Labná, a sole triumphal arc in a city without fortifications that is both "a gateway to the beautiful" and "the image of our lives among ourselves."

The Double Invention of Komo

Type of work: Poetry
First published: 1980

The Double Invention of Komo, which is dedicated to the memory of Griaule, may well be called the most African of Wright's poems. Wright's most sustained and ambitious effort in the genre of dramatic poetry, *The Double Invention of Komo* is a poetic reenactment of the initiation ceremonies performed by the all-male Komo society among the Bambara. The object of these highly formalized ceremonies is to maintain the Bambara's traditional intellectual, religious, and social values. *The Double Invention of Komo* "risks ritual's arrogance" to the extent that the logic and the specifics of this ritualistic process inform the poem's conceptual and formal structures. Of special importance to Wright are the 266 great signs, a system of ideograms that organizes Bambara cosmology. Each sign inscribes a different "name" or aspect of the god and binds him to the material objects and substances associated with Komo's altars, as in "*Dyibi*—obscurity—gold." As is evident from "The Initiate Takes His First Six Signs, the Design of His Name," such naming is an exceedingly complex process. What Wright is after is the sacred "grammar" of names that, ultimately, evolve into a secular "alphabet" of creation. *The Double Invention of Komo* is quite explicitly and self-consciously a poem about the metaphysics of writing, and this accounts for much of its difficulty.

The central preoccupation of *The Double Invention of Komo* is how to achieve self-knowledge through writing, how to fashion a language that would redress loss and dispossession. Writing, for Wright, is a process of simultaneous dismemberment and reassembly of meaning and community: It is both "scalpel" and "suture," both excision and circumcision. Like the ritual scars on the body of the initiate, poetic writing confers not only knowledge of traditional values but also kinship. It is as if the poet's pen were a ritual knife "cutting" the initiates (and the readers) into kinship, marking them as members of a special community. As the persona's status changes from that of an initiate to that of a "delegate," the statements made in *Dimensions of History*'s "Meta-A and the A of Absolutes" are reformulated: "What is true is the incision./ What is true is the desire for the incision,/ and the signs' flaming in the wound." It is in this sense that the Middle Passage, which all of the persona's journeys reenact, becomes a rite of passage that compensates for the violent psychic dismemberment and the geographical dispersal of the members of Africa's traditional cultures. Wright's key metaphor, the limbo, refers to Harris, who regards this dance, created on the crowded slave ships, as a form of silent collective resistance. Harris's sense of the limbo as a "structure of freedom" has been an inspiration for Wright since "The Albuquerque Graveyard." It also encapsulates the main concerns that have motivated Wright's explorations of the poetic potential of music and dance.

Elaine's Book

Type of work: Poetry
First published: 1986

Given the usually all-male composition of Wright's imaginary communities and especially the emphasis on male initiation rituals in *The Double Invention of Komo*, the foregrounding of female voices in *Elaine's Book* is almost startling. While women are never entirely absent from his poetry, which frequently identifies creativity as a female principle, this is the first book in which they assume historical, rather than exclusively mythological, stature. They are an integral part of the poetic geographies Wright's persona traverses in his fascinating explorations of female otherness. The female voices in *Elaine's Book* assume many different identities: that of Yemanjá, the Yoruba/Afro-Cuban goddess of the waters; that of Hathor or Aphrodite; that of the Virgin of Guadalupe, whom Wright connects with the Aztec goddess Tonantzin; that of the African American poet Phillis Wheatley; and those of many others who take their places right next to Octavio Paz, Paul Celan, and Friedrich Hölderlin, who now merely provide epigraphs.

Wright's poetic language is as rich as his symbolic geography is varied and extensive. His journey into the night, which begins with the sunset of "Veil, I," not only leads the reader to pre-Columbian Mexico, Spain, Scotland, and back to the United States but also guides the reader across an ever-changing linguistic surface in which even historical documents, such as letters by Wheatley, the former slave Judith Cocks, Louisa Alexander, and the Harvard astronomer Cecilia Payne Yaposchkin take on poetic qualities of their own. *Elaine's Book* can be said to achieve resonance as well as consonance: Each fragment sounds new depths as it becomes part of a "nation," which, like the "city," is also a figure for the poem itself. That a poet who lives in uncertain multiplicities, who knows neither his actual birth date nor his real name, should be fascinated by names and dates is hardly surprising.

Boleros

Type of work: Poetry
First published: 1991

In *Boleros*, a book dedicated to his wife, Lois, Wright's preoccupation is with imagining the fictions that, like his own father's stories, lead to names—in this case, names of Greek muses, of saint's days adorned with "graces and the seasons," and of places. "All names," he writes, "are invocations, or curses." Reinventing these stories and histories of origins is the poetic project of *Boleros* and the point of departure for further journeys across far-flung geographies of the spirit. As in *Elaine's Book*, the poet's guides are mostly female: Erato, Calliope, Euterpe, Thalia, Polyhymnia, Clio, Terpsichore, Urania. Yet the familiar Greek identities of these muses are complicated by the association of each of their personalities with concepts taken from another of Wright's favorite archives, *The Egyptian Book of the Dead* (first published in English in 1894). The resulting Africanization of the muses recalls Martin Bernal's compelling speculations in *Black Athena: The Afro-Asiatic Roots of Classical Civilization* (1987).

Many of the sites the poet's persona revisits in *Boleros* are familiar ones: Edinburgh, Guadalajara, Jalapa, New Hampshire, and always West Africa. The poet also takes up a number of new residences, however, most significant among them the city of Benares in Uttar Pradesh, one of the intellectual and cultural centers of traditional India. "Black spirits such as mine will always come/ to a crossroads such as this," the persona explains at the shores of the Ganges. As always, these geographic journeys become explorations of poetic form. Most striking in this regard are the six poems in "Sources and Roots" and "Coda," which are the title's most concrete reference points. The relatively brief poems in these final sections, many of which open with lines from popular Latin American songs, are daring in their use of Spanish meter and rhyme in an English-language environment. The results of such unexpected contact are wondrous formal hybrids, whose breaks with English accentuation are infused with Wright's wit and humor:

> Esta tierra da de todo.
> Oh, perhaps, you will see no sloe
> plum, or no white-tailed, ginger doe,
> break-dancing at sunset when snow
> shows us its blackberry wine skin.

Poems such as this are testimony to the transformations of vision and language at the many crossroads to which Wright's ceaseless poetic journeys lead. These transformations truly are Wright's "gift," for few poets have dared to bridge the troubled waters of cultural difference. Even fewer have succeeded so splendidly.

Transfigurations

Type of work: Poetry
First published: 2000

Transfigurations collects Wright's work produced over the course of more than twenty-five years of poetic exploration. The volume is hefty, providing more than six hundred pages of densely textured verse, including sixty pages of new poetry. Detailed references to West African, Haitian, Mexican, and European and American Christian religious rituals abound, as well as to the various political and poetic genealogies in which Wright situates himself. Geographic journeys expose the earth itself to the questioning soul of the poet. In a single poem, Wright travels from North Africa to Jamaica to Boston and then on to Spain, dropping historical allusions at every step. The esoteric network of obscure signs and allusions he uses serves to trace his own development in which, for nearly three decades, he has determinedly initiated himself into the mysteries of language, history, and sense.

Transformation and transfiguration act as the axes of this collection. A bulk of the poems in the volume speak to initiation, the human ceremonial act that marks transformation: the Mexican boy to whom a god says, "You must prepare for my eruption/ and the guarded way I have of guarding you," or the West African Dogon boy who undergoes the trials and tribulations of coming into adulthood, "If I were the light's sacred buffoon,/ I could read this meaning and mount/ my own awakening" in the spectacular poem "The Double Invention of Komo." A transfiguration, similarly, is a change of appearance, one that is accompanied with a sense of revelation. A refinement of vision, put to the service of metamorphosis, is one of Wright's most potent forces. For example, in "The Abstract of Knowledge/the First Test," Wright transfigures the scene of the Dogon boy encountering the first phase of his initiation, in which he must undergo a hallucinatory vision of the universe in the light of the knowledge that he will obtain from his vision. That vision changes knowledge, transfiguring it and transforming it. In these lines, a number of the features of Wright's poetry are apparent: the tightly rhythmical free verse—which lacks enjambment for the most part, the voice of the dramatic persona, the physical details, and a cosmological reach.

Suggested Readings

Callaloo 6 (Fall, 1983).

Kutzinski, Vera M. *Against the American Grain: Myth and History in William Carlos Williams, Jay Wright, and Nicolás Guillén*. Baltimore: The Johns Hopkins University Press, 1987.

Okpewho, Isidore. "Prodigal's Progress: Jay Wright's Focal Center." *MELUS* 23, no. 3 (Fall, 1998): 187-209.

Stepto, Robert B. "After Modernism, After Hibernation: Michael Harper, Robert Hayden, and Jay Wright." In *Chant of Saints: A Gathering of Afro-American Literature, Arts, and Scholarship*, edited by Michael S. Harper and Robert B. Stepto. Urbana: University of Illinois Press, 1979.

Welburn, Ron. "Jay Wright's Poetics: An Appreciation." *MELUS* 18, no. 3 (Fall, 1993): 51.

Contributors: Lorenzo Thomas, Vera M. Kutzinski, and Sarah Hilbert

Richard Wright

Born: Natchez, Mississippi; September 4, 1908
Died: Paris, France; November 28, 1960

African American

Wright portrays African Americans entrapped in forms of neo-slavery; he earned national and international acclaim.

Principal works

DRAMA: *Native Son: The Biography of a Young American*, pr. 1941 (with Paul Green)

LONG FICTION: *Native Son*, 1940; *The Outsider*, 1953; *Savage Holiday*, 1954; *The Long Dream*, 1958; *Lawd Today*, 1963; *A Father's Law*, 2008

POETRY: *Haiku: This Other World*, 1998 (Yoshinobu Hakutani and Robert L. Tener, editors)

SHORT FICTION: *Uncle Tom's Children: Four Novellas*, 1938 (expanded as *Uncle Tom's Children: Five Long Stories*, 1938); *Eight Men*, 1961

NONFICTION: *Twelve Million Black Voices: A Folk History of the Negro in the United States*, 1941 (photographs by Edwin Rosskam); *Black Boy: A Record of Childhood and Youth*, 1945; *Black Power: A Record of Reactions in a Land of Pathos*, 1954; *The Color Curtain*, 1956; *Pagan Spain*, 1957; *White Man, Listen!*, 1957; *American Hunger*, 1977; *Richard Wright Reader*, 1978 (Ellen Wright and Michel Fabre, editors); *Conversations with Richard Wright*, 1993 (Keneth Kinnamon and Fabre, editors)

MISCELLANEOUS: *Works*, 1991 (2 volumes)

Richard Wright rose from abject poverty to become one of America's foremost writers. His topics consistently focus on the freedom and self-governance of African Americans in texts before 1950. He chronicled his southern experiences to 1927 in *Black Boy*, and his northern experiences from 1927 to 1937 in *American Hunger*. Wright met with success once he moved to New York City in 1937. He won a literary prize in 1938 that earned him a contract with a major publisher, which published *Uncle Tom's Children*. A Guggenheim Fellowship in 1939 enabled Wright to complete *Native Son*; with that work alone, he earned acclaim as the leading African American writer of his time. The novel is Wright's moral indictment of America for perpetrating neo-slavery among African Americans. In *Native Son*, the ghetto produces Bigger Thomas, who dies as a result of his accidentally killing a white woman.

The 1940's brought personal crises to Wright. He faced America's continuous racial discrimination toward him and toward interracial couples once he married Ellen Poplar in 1941. Ongoing rifts with the Communist Party also added to Wright's tensions. In 1946, he renounced America for France, as did other expatriates who sought freedom abroad. The 1950's marked the emergence of Wright's global consciousness and his writings concerning Western imperialism. His immersion in French existentialism provided the means to assess the effects of Western imperialism on Asian, African, and Spanish cultures. *The Outsider* became the seminal existentialist novel in African American letters. Wright became an existentialist humanist, transformed from what he identified as an "American Negro" to a "Western man of color" and freedom activist. Wright was prolific as well as a writer of high quality; his writings continued to be published after his death in 1960.

"Fire and Cloud"

Type of work: Short fiction
First published: 1938

"Fire and Cloud" in *Uncle Tom's Children* is perhaps the best representative of Richard Wright's early short fiction. It won first prize in the 1938 *Story* magazine contest which had more than four hundred entries, marking Wright's first triumph with American publishers. Charles K. O'Neill made a radio adaptation of the story after it appeared in *American Scenes*.

Unlike the later works concerning black ghetto experience, "Fire and Cloud" has a pastoral quality, recognizing the strong bond of the southern black to the soil and the support he has drawn from religion. Wright reproduces faithfully the southern black dialect in both conversation and internal meditations. This use of dialect emphasizes the relative lack of sophistication of rural blacks. His protagonist, Reverend Taylor, is representative of the "old Negro," who has withstood centuries of oppression, sustained by hard work on the land and humble faith in a merciful God.

Wright's attitude toward religion, however, is ambivalent. Although he recognizes it as contributing to the quiet nobility of the hero, it also prevents Taylor from taking effective social action when his people are literally starving. The final triumph of Reverend Taylor is that he puts aside the conciliatory attitude which was part of his religious training and becomes a social activist. Instead of turning the other cheek after being humiliated and beaten by white men, he embraces the methods of his Marxist supporters, meeting oppression with mass demonstration. Strength of numbers proves more effective and appropriate for getting relief from the bigoted white establishment than all his piety and loving kindness. Early in the story Taylor exclaims "The good Lawds gonna clean up this ol worl some day! Hes gonna make a new Heaven n a new Earth!" His last words, however, are "Freedom belongs t the strong!"

The situation of the story no doubt reflects Wright's early experience when his sharecropper father was driven off the plantation. Taylor's people are starving because the white people, who own all the land, have prohibited the blacks from raising food on it. No matter how Taylor pleads for relief, the local white officials tell him to wait and see if federal aid may be forthcoming. When two communist agitators begin pushing Taylor to lead a mass demonstration against the local government, white officials have Taylor kidnapped and beaten, along with several deacons of his church. Instead of intimidating them, this suffering converts them to open confrontation. As the communists promised, the poor whites join the blacks in the march, which forces the white authorities to release food to those facing starvation.

The story's strength lies in revealing through three dialogues the psychological dilemma of the protagonist as opposing groups demand his support. He resists the communists initially because their methods employ threat of open war on the whites—"N tha ain Gawds way!" The agitators say he will be responsible if their demonstration fails through lack of numbers and participants are slaughtered. On the other hand, the mayor and chief of police threaten Taylor that they will hold him personally responsible if any of his church members join the march. After a humiliating and futile exchange with these men, Taylor faces his own church deacons, who are themselves divided and look to him for leadership. He knows that one of their number, who is just waiting for a chance to oust him from his church, will run to the mayor and police with any evidence of Taylor's insubordination. In a pathetic attempt to shift the burden of responsibility that threatens to destroy him no matter what he does, he reiterates the stubborn stand he has maintained with all three groups: He will not order the demonstration, but he will march with his people if they choose to demonstrate. The brutal horse-whipping that Taylor endures as a result of this moderate stand convinces him of the futility of trying to placate everybody. The Uncle Tom becomes a rebel.

Critics sometimes deplore the episodes of raw brutality described in graphic detail in Wright's fiction, but violence is the clue here to his message. Behind the white man's paternalistic talk is the persuasion of whip and gun. Only superior force can cope with such an antagonist.

Native Son

TYPE OF WORK: Novel
FIRST PUBLISHED: 1940

Native Son parallels Theodore Dreiser's *An American Tragedy* (1925): Both are three-part novels in which there is a murder, in part accidental, in part willed; an attempted flight; and a long concluding trial, in both cases somewhat anticlimactic. Both novels are concerned with the interplay of environment and heredity, of fate and accident, and both have protagonists who rebel against the world which would hold them back.

In the first part of *Native Son*, Bigger Thomas is a black man cut off from family and peers. Superficially like his friends, he is in fact possessed of a different consciousness. To think about that consciousness is for him to risk insanity or violence, so Bigger endeavors to keep his fears and uncertainty at a preconscious level. On the day of the first section, however, he is required by the welfare agency to apply for a job as a menial at the home of the rich Dalton family. Mr. Dalton is a ghetto landlord who soothes his conscience by donating sums of money for recreational purposes. That it is a minuscule part of the money he is deriving from blacks is an irony he overlooks. Mrs. Dalton is blind, a fact that is necessary to the plot as well as being symbolic. Their daughter, Mary, is a member of the Communist Party, and from the moment she sees Bigger, who wants nothing more than to be left alone, she begins to enlist his support.

The first evening, Bigger is to drive Mary to a university class. In reality, she is going with Jan Erlone, her communist boyfriend, to a party meeting. Afterward, they insist that Bigger take them to a bar in the black part of town. Jan and Mary are at this point satirized, for their attitudes toward blacks are as limited and stereotyped as any in the novel. Bigger does not want to be seen by his friends with whites, but that fact does not occur to Mary. After much drinking, Bigger must carry the drunken Mary to her bedroom. He puts her to bed, stands over her, attracted to the woman he sees. The door opens and Mrs. Dalton enters. When Mary makes drunken noises, Bigger becomes frightened that Mrs. Dalton will come close enough to discover him, so he puts a pillow over Mary's face to quiet her. By the time Mrs. Dalton leaves, Mary is dead.

Wright wanted to make Bigger a character it would be impossible to pity, and what follows is extremely grisly. Bigger tries to put Mary's body in the furnace and saws off her head to make her fit. However accidental Mary's death may appear to the reader, Bigger himself does not regard it as such. He has, he thinks, many times wanted to kill whites without ever having the opportunity to do so. This time there was the act without the desire, but rather than seeing himself as the victim of a chance occurrence, Bigger prefers to unite the earlier desire with the present act, to make himself whole by accepting responsibility for the killing. Indeed, he not only accepts the act but also determines to capitalize on it by sending a ransom note. Later, accused of raping Mary as well, an act he considered but did not commit, he reverses the process, accepting responsibility for this, too, even though here there was desire but no act. His only sign of conscience is that he cannot bring himself to shake the ashes in the furnace; this guilt is not redemptive, but his undoing, for, in an implausible scene in the Dalton basement, the room fills with smoke, the murder is revealed to newspaper reporters gathered there, and Bigger is forced to flee.

He runs with his girlfriend, Bessie Mears. She, like Bigger, has a hunger for sensation, which has initially attracted him to her. Now, however, as they flee together, she becomes a threat and a burden; huddled with her in an abandoned tenement, Bigger wants only to be rid of her. He picks up a brick and smashes her face, dumping her body down an airshaft. His only regret is not that he has killed her but that he has forgotten to remove their money from her body.

The rest of the plot moves quickly: Bigger is soon arrested, the trial is turned into a political farce, and Bigger is convicted and sentenced to death. In the last part of the novel, after Bigger's arrest, the implications of the action are developed, largely through Bigger's relations to other characters. Some of the characters are worthy

Richard Wright (Library of Congress)

only of contempt, particularly the district attorney, who, in an attempt at reelection, is turning the trial into political capital. Bigger's mother relies on religion. In a scene in the jail cell, she falls on her knees in apology before Mrs. Dalton and urges Bigger to pray, but toughness is Bigger's code. He is embarrassed by his mother's self-abasement, and although he agrees to pray simply to end his discomfort, his attitude toward religion is shown when he throws away a cross a minister has given him and throws a cup of coffee in a priest's face. In his view, they want only to avoid the world and to force him to accept guilt without responsibility.

Bigger learns from two characters. The first is Boris Max, the lawyer the Communist Party provides. Max listens to Bigger, and for the first time in his life, Bigger exposes his ideas and feelings to another human. Max's plea to the court is that, just as Bigger must accept responsibility for what he has done, so must the society around him understand its responsibility for what Bigger has become and, if the court chooses to execute Bigger, understand the consequences that must flow from that action. He does not argue—nor does Wright believe—that Bigger is a victim of injustice. There is no injustice, because that would presume a world in which Bigger could hope for justice, and such a world does not exist; more important, Bigger is not a victim, for he has chosen his own fate. Max argues rather that all men are entitled to happiness. Like all of Wright's protagonists, Bigger has earlier been torn between the poles of dread and ecstasy. His ecstasy, his happiness, comes from the meaningfulness he creates in his existence, a product of self-realization. Unhappily for Bigger, he realizes himself through murder: It was, he feels, his highest creative act.

If Max articulates the intellectual presentation of Wright's beliefs about Bigger, it is Jan, Mary's lover, who is its dramatic representation. He visits Bigger in his cell and, having at last understood the futility and paucity of his own stereotypes, admits to Bigger that he too shares in the responsibility for what has happened. He, too, addresses Bigger as a human being, but from the unique position of being the one who is alive to remind Bigger of the consequences of his actions, for Bigger learns that Jan has suffered loss through what he has done and that, while Bigger has created himself, he has also destroyed another.

Native Son ends with the failure of Max's appeals on Bigger's behalf. He comes to the cell to confront Bigger before his execution, and the novel closes with Bigger Thomas smiling at Max as the prison door clangs shut. He will die happy because he will die fulfilled, having, however terribly, created a self. *Native Son* is Wright's most powerful work, because his theme, universal in nature, is given its fullest and most evocative embodiment. In the characterization of Bigger, alienated man at his least abstract and most genuine, of Bigger's exactly rendered mind and milieu, and of Bigger's working out of his destiny, *Native Son* is Wright's masterpiece.

"The Man Who Lived Underground"

Type of work: Short fiction
First published: 1942, in *Accent*

Wright's best piece of short fiction is "The Man Who Lived Underground." Although undoubtedly influenced by Fyodor Dostoevski's underground man and by Franz Kafka's "K," the situation was based on a prisoner's story from *True Detective* magazine. The first version appeared in 1942 in *Accent* magazine under the subtitle "Two Excerpts from a Novel." This version began with a description of the life of a black servant, but Wright later discarded this opening in favor of the dramatic scene in which an unnamed fugitive hides from the police by descending into a sewer. This approach allowed the story to assume a more universal, symbolic quality. Although racist issues are still significant, the protagonist represents that larger class of all those alienated from their society. Eventually the fugitive's name is revealed as Fred Daniels, but so completely is he absorbed into his Everyman role that he cannot remember his name when he returns to the upper world. His progress through sewers and basements becomes a quest for the meaning of life, parodying classic descents into the underworld and ironically reversing Plato's allegory of the cave.

Although Plato's philosopher attains wisdom by climbing out of the cave where men respond to shadows on the cave wall, Wright's protagonist gains enlightenment because of his underground perspective. What he sees there speaks not to his rational understanding, however, but to his emotions. He moves among symbolic visions which arouse terror and pity—a dead baby floating on the slimy water whose "mouth gaped black in a soundless cry." In a black church service spied on through a crevice in the wall, the devout are singing "Jesus, take me to your home above." He is overwhelmed by a sense of guilt and intuits that there is something obscene about their "singing with the air of the sewer blowing in on them." In a meat locker with carcasses hanging from the ceiling, a butcher is hacking off a piece of meat with a bloody cleaver. When the store proprietor goes home, Fred emerges from the locker and gorges on fresh fruit, but he takes back with him into the sewer the bloody cleaver—why he does not know.

When Fred breaks through a wall into the basement of a movie house, the analogy to Plato's myth of the cave becomes explicit. He comes up a back stair and sees jerking shadows of a silver screen. The Platonic urge to enlighten the people in the theater, who are bound to a shadow world, merges with messianic images. In a dream he walks on water and saves a baby held up by a drowning woman, but the dream ends in terror and doubt as he loses the baby and his ability to emulate Christ. All is lost and he himself begins to drown.

Terror and pity are not the only emotions that enlarge his sensibilities in this underground odyssey. As he learns the peculiar advantages of his invisibility, he realizes that he can help himself to all kinds of gadgets valued by that shadow world above ground. He collects them like toys or symbols of an absurd world. He acquires a radio, a light bulb with an extension cord, a typewriter, a gun, and finally, through a chance observation of a safe being opened by combination, rolls of hundred dollar bills, containers of diamonds, watches, and rings. His motivation for stealing these articles is not greed but sheer hilarious fun at acquiring objects so long denied to persons of his class.

In one of the most striking, surrealist scenes in modern literature, Fred delightedly decorates his cave walls and floor with these tokens of a society which has rejected him. "They were the serious toys of the men who lived in the dead world of sunshine and rain he had left, the world that had condemned him, branded him guilty." He glues hundred dollar bills on his walls. He winds up all the watches but disdains to set them (for he is beyond time, freed from its tyranny). The watches hang on nails along with the diamond rings. He hangs up the bloody cleaver, too, and the gun. The loose diamonds he dumps in a glittering pile on the muddy floor. Then as he gaily tramps around, he accidentally/on purpose, stomps on the pile, scattering the pretty baubles over the floor. Here, indeed, is society's cave of shadows, and only he realizes how absurd it all is.

When the euphoria of these games begins to pall, Fred becomes more philosophical, perceiving the nihilistic implications of his experience. "Maybe *any*thing's right, he mumbled. Yes, if the world as men had made it was right, then anything else was right, any act a man took to satisfy himself, murder, theft, torture." In his unlettered, blundering way, he is groping toward Ivan Karamazov's dark meditation: "If there is no God, then all things are permissible." Fred becomes convinced of the reality of human guilt, however, when he witnesses the suicide of the jewelry store's night watchman, who has been blamed for the theft he himself committed. At first, the scene in which police torture the bewildered man to force a confession strikes Fred as hilariously funny, duplicating his own experience. When the wretched man shoots himself before Fred can offer him a means of escape, however, Fred is shocked into a realization of his own guilt.

The protagonist ultimately transcends his nihilism, and like Platonic realism's philosopher who returns to the cave out of compassion for those trapped there, Fred returns to the "dead world of sunshine and rain" to bear witness to the Truth. Like the philosopher who is blinded coming out of the light into cave darkness, Fred seems confused and stupid in the social world above ground. When he is thrown out of the black church, he tries inarticulately to explain his revelation at the police station where he had been tortured and condemned. The police think he is crazy, but because they now know they accused him unjustly, they find his return embarrassing. Fred euphorically insists that they accompany him into the sewer so that they too can experience the visions that enlightened him. When he shows them his entrance to the world underground, one of the policemen calmly shoots him, and the murky waters of the sewer sweep him away.

This ironic story of symbolic death and resurrection is unparalleled in its unique treatment of existential themes. Guilt and alienation lead paradoxically to a tragic sense of human brotherhood, which seems unintelligible to "normal" people. The man who kills Fred Daniels is perhaps the only person who perceives even dimly what Daniels wants to do. "You've got to shoot this kind," he says. "They'd wreck things."

Black Boy

Type of work: Autobiography
First published: 1945

Black Boy: A Record of Childhood and Youth is one of Wright's finest achievements: a classic of African American autobiography and a brilliant portrayal of, as Wright put it, the way the environment provides the instrumentalities through which one expresses oneself and the way that self becomes whole despite the environment's conspiring to keep it divided. The book tells of Wright's escape from figurative slavery in the South to freedom in the North.

The text opens in 1912 on Wright's earliest memory at age four. Richard is living in Jackson, Mississippi, in the crowded home of his grandparents. The household includes Richard, his mother, father, brother, and his uncle, and it replicates the subhuman living conditions of slaves. Richard's father is illiterate and an unskilled laborer; in search of work, he moves his family to another state, which initiates Richard's life of emotional and physical instability. These disruptions occur in three cycles. From age four to age twelve, Richard moves frequently from Mississippi to Tennessee to Arkansas and back again. From age twelve to age seventeen, he remains in Jackson. From age seventeen to age nineteen, he escapes, first to Tennessee and then to Illinois. Before age twelve, Richard suffers abandonment by his father, life in an orphanage, street life, heavy drinking, and the illness of his mother.

Wright employs the literary technique of naturalism to portray the racial and environmental factors that create a hostile world for Richard. Whites consider African Americans to be inferior because of their skin color, and Richard hears of violent acts against African Americans in the form of murders, lynchings, and beatings. He personally experiences verbal threats, physical assaults, and animal attacks. Whites pay African Americans low wages to keep them economically enslaved and unable to escape the mandated segregated housing, which is substandard. Richard consistently suffers from hunger, poor housing, insufficient clothing, and erratic schooling.

Richard grows up an isolated figure because he does not fit the servile demeanor required of African Americans to live in the South. He rejects religion since he cannot understand how a white God allows his mother, family, and community to suffer. In turn, they assail his reading and writing of fiction, which his grandmother charges is "Devil's work." The school principal even denounces Richard when he refuses to deliver the stock valedictory speech of humility at his graduation ceremony from ninth grade. Whites, too, attack Richard for being a "smart Negro" when he undertakes menial jobs in private homes or at businesses during his stay in the South.

Richard resists these oppressive forces in his quest for knowledge and for freedom. At nineteen, he discovers the writer H. L. Mencken, and decides that he, too, wants to become a writer to "wage war with words." *Black Boy* concludes in 1927, with Richard's flight to the North in the tradition of former slaves before him.

The Outsider

Type of work: Novel
First published: 1953

Wright's novel *The Outsider*, written in France and published thirteen years after *Native Son*, suffers from a surfeit of internal explanation and a failure to provide a setting as rich as that of *Native Son*. Still, its portrayal of Cross Damon and his struggle to define himself, while too self-conscious, adds new dimensions to Wright's myth.

As the novel opens, Damon is trapped by his life. His post-office job is unfulfilling, his wife is threatening, and his underage mistress is pregnant. He "desires desire," but there is no way for that desire to be completed. "A man creates himself," he has told his wife, but the self Damon has created is a nightmare. He broods, his brooding as close as he comes to religion. Damon gets his chance for new life on the subway. Thought dead after his identification papers are found near the mangled body of another, Damon gets a chance to create himself anew. He must invent, he thinks, not only his future, but also a past to fit with his present; this new opportunity brings with it a different and more potent sense of dread.

From the beginning of this new life, Damon is remarkably successful at the mechanics of creating a past. He easily obtains a birth certificate and a draft card. At a deeper level, however, he traps himself as surely as he has been trapped in his old life, so that his new one becomes a continuous act of bad faith. Even before he leaves Chicago, he hides in a brothel where he encounters a coworker who recognizes him. Damon murders the man and throws his body out a window. The pattern of violence, so typical of Wright's characters, begins in earnest for Damon.

Taking a train to New York, Damon meets two people who will influence his new life, a black waiter who introduces him to the world of communist politics in New York City, and Ely Houston, the district attorney, who is the most articulate person in the novel and the only one to understand Damon fully. Houston asks Damon why, when all blacks are outsiders, so few seem conscious of this fact. Wright suggests that being human is too much to be borne by people, that the struggle to define oneself is too difficult; the novel is a testament to that suggestion.

The Communist Party members, too, are outsiders, and there is nothing unified about their company. Each one that Damon meets is playing god, hoping to protect and extend his personal power. Their awareness of their motives varies, but they are a threat to Damon, and the action of the book is propelled by a series of murders: Damon himself wants to act like a god. Near the end of the book, Houston comes to understand that Damon is the killer, but—rather than indicting and punishing him legally—Houston allows him to go free, alone with his knowledge of what he is. Damon is horrified by his fate, but he is robbed of even that when he is killed by two Communist Party members who fear him.

The Outsider is both an extension and a modification of Wright's earlier views; it is far more pessimistic than *Native Son*, and the influence of the French existentialists is more pervasive. Like earlier Wright heroes, Damon is engaged in defining the world and himself. "The moment we act 'as if' it's true, then it's true," he thinks, because each person, in the absence of a god, is able to create the world and its truth. From Dostoevski, Wright borrows the notion of underground man and the idea that without a god, all is permitted. Yet as each man plays god, as each becomes criminal, policeman, judge, and executioner, there are no longer limits. People desire everything, and desire is described as a floating demon. People are jealous gods here—the worlds they create are petty, their jealousy destructive. Damon is loved in the novel, but that love, unlike the love in *Native Son*, which is held up as potentially meaningful, is here without promise. Although he creates himself and his world in *The Outsider*, all that is made is violent and brutal, a world without redemption even in the act of self-realization.

At the end of the novel, Cross Damon dies, not with Bigger Thomas's smile, but with the knowledge that alone, people are nothing. Searching in his last moments of freedom for a clean, well-lighted place in which to rest before he confronts the world again, Cross finds only death. Before he dies, he admits his final act of bad faith: He has thought that he could create a world and be different from other men, that he could remain innocent. Like Joseph Conrad's Kurtz in *Heart of Darkness* (1902), Damon dies realizing the futility of that hope; having looked into his own heart of darkness, he dies with the word *horror* on his lips. It is Wright's bleakest conclusion, the book his most relentless examination of the consequences of his own philosophy. If *The Outsider* lacks the narrative drive of *Native Son*, it remains a strongly conceived and troubling piece of fiction.

Lawd Today

Type of work: Novel
First published: 1963

Lawd Today, written before *Native Son* but not published until after Wright's death, tells the story of Jake Jackson from his awakening on the morning of February 12, 1936, to that day's violent conclusion. Jackson is Wright's most inarticulate protagonist: He has a banal life, undefined dreams, and a vague sense of discontent which he is unable to explain. Violent and prejudiced, he speaks in clichés, a language as meaningless as his life.

Technically, the book incorporates a montage of radio broadcasts, newspaper articles, and religious and political pamphlets into the narration of Jake's day. Divided into three sections, *Lawd Today* opens with Jake's dream of running up an endless staircase after a disappearing voice. That dream gives way to the reality of his life: hunger, anger, and recrimination. Tricked by Jake into an abortion for which Jake still owes five hundred dollars and now claiming to have a tumor which will cost another five hundred dollars to remove, Jake's wife represents his entrapment. In the first section, "Commonplace," Jake reveals his brutish and trivial character: his anger at his wife, a jealousy and resentment that lead him to bait her so he can hit her, a mock battle straightening his hair, and a meeting with friends who work with him at the post office. As they play bridge to pass the time until work, Wright presents without comment their stupid, cliché-ridden conversation.

Section 2, "Squirrel Cage," shows the men at work. They are all alienated in meaningless, routine jobs, but Jake's position is the most desperate, for his wife has been to see his boss, and he is now threatened with the loss of his job. Falling deeper into debt by borrowing more money and making mistakes on the job, Jake is trapped by his work—despite his own protestations, as a self-proclaimed Republican and capitalist, that work is liberating. This section, too, ends with a long, rambling, and banal conversation among the men at work.

In the concluding section, "Rat's Alley," the men go to a brothel for a good time on some of Jake's borrowed money. There, Jake is robbed and then beaten for his threats of revenge. Finally, Jake stumbles homeward, his day nearing an end. The February weather, pleasant when the book began, has turned bad. All of Jake's frustration and anger finally erupt; he beats his wife, whom he finds kneeling asleep by the bed in an attitude of prayer. As they struggle, he throws objects through the window. She grabs a shard of broken glass and slashes him three times. The book ends with Jake lying in a drunken stupor, bleeding, while his wife is on her knees, also bleeding, praying for death. Outside, the wind blows mercilessly.

Although some of the experimentalism of *Lawd Today* seems artificial, and although the protagonist is too limited to sustain the reader's interest, this early work is powerful and economical. The situation, if not the character, is typical of Wright's work, and the reader understands Jake's violent frustration. *Lawd Today* has its flaws, but it foreshadows the strengths of Wright's best work and in its own right is a daring and fascinating novel.

American Hunger

Type of work: Autobiography
First published: 1977

American Hunger, the second part of Wright's autobiography, published posthumously, focuses on his life in Chicago, Illinois, from 1927 to 1937. The book was written in 1944. The northern experience recurs as a new slave narrative. It demonstrates how modern African Americans were deceived. Wright opens the text in 1927, when nineteen-year-old Richard, his alter ego, arrives in Chicago with his Aunt Maggie. Wright juxtaposes the terms "strange" and "familiar" to express Richard's dismay at seeing African Americans openly consort with whites in public facilities. He learns quickly that appearances are deceptive.

Wright employs literary naturalism to illustrate racial and environmental barriers erected by whites to imprison African Americans in modern slavery. Richard discovers that migrants have traded southern plantations for urban ghettos. They live in the black belt of Chicago and remain racially and economically disfranchised. Richard's economic status soon imitates that of his impoverished southern experience. Richard earns low wages at menial jobs during the following six years. The intermittent checks from his postal service job or the relief agency barely sustain Richard's family.

Consistent with *Black Boy*, Richard becomes the outsider, in conflict with his family, community, and professional affiliations. A major source of conflict is his independent thinking. His attempts at writing cause alarm to his Aunt Maggie, who believes that fiction writing and book reading serve no value unless Richard is studying law. Richard's white employer cannot understand why an African American dishwasher would read newspapers. Once Richard joins professional writing groups, between 1933 and 1935, he discovers that his intelligence poses a threat to members of the John Reed Club of the Communist Party, the Southside Writers' Group, and the Federal Theatre Project. They attack him for being an "intellectual" just as southerners attacked the "smart Negro." The Communists even label Richard a Trotskyite or traitor, and physically assault him at the May Day parade of 1936.

His freedom from slavery culminates with Richard's resignation from the Communist Party. He takes physical flight to New York in 1937. In his ongoing quest for freedom, his psychological emancipation is the real moral to his narrative. It coincides with the successful publication of fiction, which frees Richard to write "art for art's sake," not propaganda, and to accelerate his "war with words."

Suggested Readings

Bloom, Harold, ed. *Richard Wright*. New York: Chelsea House, 1987.

Butler, Robert. *"Native Son": The Emergence of a New Black Hero*. Boston: Twayne, 1991.

Fabre, Michel. *The Unfinished Quest of Richard Wright*. New York: William Morrow, 1973.

_______. *The World of Richard Wright*. Jackson: University Press of Mississippi, 1985.

Felgar, Robert. *Richard Wright*. Boston: Twayne, 1980.

Hakutani, Yoshinobu. *Richard Wright and Racial Discourse*. Columbia: University of Missouri Press, 1996.

Kinnamon, Kenneth, ed. *Critical Essays on Richard Wright's "Native Son."* New York: Twayne, 1997.
Rowley, Hazel. *Richard Wright: The Life and Times*. New York: Henry Holt, 2001.
Walker, Margaret. *Richard Wright: Daemonic Genius*. New York: Warner, 1988.
Webb, Constance. *Richard Wright: A Biography*. New York: Putnam, 1968.

Contributors: Virginia Whatley Smith, Thomas Cassidy, Howard Faulkner, and Katherine Snipes

Mitsuye Yamada

Born: Kyushu, Japan; July 5, 1923

Japanese American

Serving with Amnesty International, Yamada has dedicated her writing to the cause of human rights.

Principal works

POETRY: *Camp Notes, and Other Poems*, 1976

EDITED TEXTS: *The Webs We Weave: Orange County Poetry Anthology*, 1986 (with others); *Sowing Ti Leaves: Writings by Multi-Cultural Women*, 1990 (with Sarie Sachie Hylkema)

MISCELLANEOUS: *Desert Run: Poems and Stories*, 1988; *Camp Notes, and Other Writings*, 1998 (includes *Camp Notes, and Other Poems and Desert Run*)

Mitsuye Yasutake Yamada (miht-sew-yeh yah-sew-tah-keh yah-mah-dah) spent most of her formative years in Seattle, Washington, until a few months after the outbreak of World War II, when her family was removed to a concentration camp at Minidoka, Idaho. Her poems in *Camp Notes, and Other Poems* recount this experience. Her need to integrate her art, her beliefs, and her commitment to human rights stems largely from the impact this event had on her.

Yamada earned a bachelor's degree in English and art at New York University and a master's degree in literature at the University of Chicago. She had a distinguished career as a teacher, working for many years at a community college in Cypress, California, and serving as writer-in-residence at Pitzer College and San Diego State University.

In her writings, Yamada has characteristically focused on her bicultural heritage, women, and human rights. During the early 1960's she began working as a volunteer with Amnesty International, and her continuing commitment to human rights through that organization eventually led to her service on the national board of Amnesty International USA and participation in international committees seeking increased Asian involvement in human rights work. She made several trips to South Korea, Japan, and other countries in Asia on behalf of Amnesty International.

Commitment to diversity in all areas of life has led Yamada to multidisciplinary as well as multicultural commitments. While a community college professor she team-taught an interdisciplinary course in biology and poetry which involved field trips to research and experience the wilderness areas of California. Out of this experience came many of the poems in Yamada's second collection, *Desert Run*. This book returns to the themes of alienation, human rights, and protest against injustice that reverberate through the earlier collection. In *Desert Run*, seeing the desert from a new perspective enables a healing process to take place. The title poem, "Desert Run," makes the comparison explicitly as the speaker returns in memory to an earlier, enforced encampment on the desert, where armed guards stood watch over American men, women, and children, and contrasts it with the silence, agelessness, and demanding beauty of the desert as seen on a class camping trip. Other poems celebrate the beauty of seemingly insignificant flowers and, especially, the strength and endurance of desert plants such as cacti and lichens.

Another avenue of Yamada's activism is her formation of a writers' group, MultiCultural Women Writers, dedicated to raising support for and awareness of diversity in the arts. This group published an anthology, *Sowing Ti Leaves: Writings by Multi-Cultural Women* (1992), coedited by Yamada, which has gone through several editions.

Camp Notes, and Other Poems

Type of work: Poetry
First published: 1976

The poems in *Camp Notes, and Other Poems* originated in the experience of a concentration camp. Yamada and her family were interned with other Japanese Americans from the West Coast during World War II. Yamada spent April, 1942, through September, 1943, at the internment camp near Minidoka, Idaho. Inmates could have few possessions; Yamada brought a tablet of paper on which she recorded her reflections on life in the camp. To the poems from this period she later added others concerning the time preceding and the time following the camp experience.

At the beginning of the book are poems about ancestors and parents: great-grandmother's box of treasured souvenirs, a young bride in a new and precarious environment, a folktale related by a sophisticated father. Following the poems about internment are poems related to the poet's later life. These poems frequently have themes that are a feature of the center section about the internment: justice, equity, and generosity. These themes are continuing threads in these poems, which occasionally have a feminist perspective.

The middle, or "Camp Notes," section contains the angriest poems. With irony, the speaker in the poems expresses and conquers the rage, humiliation, and despair of unjust captivity. A photographer's instruction to "smile" as internees are collected at staging points, the bus ride to the camps, a guard tower seen through the eyes of a child, makeshift furniture of packing crates and straw mattresses, stuffing rags into cracks in the shacklike barracks during a dust storm—each of these moments is crystallized. The poem titled "Curfew" ends in a particularly vivid commentary: After quoting the "block head" giving orders for lights out, the speaker simply remarks, "There must be no light." One of the briefest poems, "In the Outhouse," is also one of the most powerful. The stench of the outhouse becomes a metaphor for the entire camp and the mentality that created it; fear and racism relegate a whole group of people to the domain of "refuse" and "outsider." Many of the poems focus on the absurdity and duplicity of the language and thinking used to justify the camps. In "Desert Storm" the speaker notes the euphemisms that attempted to disguise injustice, noting how the reality of imprisonment was "sanitized" by the term "relocation." The speaker notes in "The Trick Was" that the "mind was not fooled."

Camp Notes, and Other Poems is actually a cooperative and family project. Yamada's husband, Yoshikazu Yamada, contributed the calligraphs that translate titles and text for some of the poems. Her daughters, Jeni and Hedi, produced illustrations for some pages. Yamada also includes a translation of one of her father's poems, written while he was interned apart from his family in a different camp.

Suggested Readings

Cheng, Scarlet. "Foreign All Your Life." *Belles Lettres* 4, no. 2 (Winter, 1989).

Patterson, Anita Haya. "Resistance to Images of the Internment: Mitsuye Yamada's Camp Notes." *MELUS* 23, no. 3 (Fall, 1998).

Schweik, Susan. "A Needle with Mama's Voice: Mitsuye Yamada's *Camp Notes* and the American Canon of War Poetry." In *Arms and the Woman: War, Gender, and Literary Representation*, edited by Helen M. Cooper, Adrienne Auslande Munich, and Susan Merrill Squier. Chapel Hill: University of North Carolina Press, 1989.

Woolley, Lisa. "Racial and Ethnic Semiosis in Mitsuye Yamada's 'Mrs. Higashi Is Dead.'" *MELUS* 24, no. 4 (Winter, 1999).

Yamada, Mitsuye. "A *MELUS* Interview: Mitsuye Yamada." Interview by Helen Jaskoski. *MELUS* 15, no. 1 (Spring, 1988).

Yamada, Mitsuye, and Sarie Sachie Hylkema, eds. *Sowing Ti Leaves: Writings by Multi-Cultural Women*. Irvine, Calif.: MultiCultural Women Writers, 1991.

Contributor: Helen Jaskoski

Hisaye Yamamoto

Born: Redondo Beach, California; 1921

Japanese American

Yamamoto, an accomplished short-story writer, was one of the first Japanese American writers to gain recognition after World War II.

Principal works

SHORT FICTION: *Seventeen Syllables, and Other Stories*, 1988

Born of Japanese immigrant parents, Hisaye Yamamoto (hih-say-yeh yah-mah-moh-toh) began writing in her teens. As a second-generation Japanese American, she was especially interested in the interaction between the Japanese traditions passed on to her and the American experience she encountered. She once cited that her main reason for writing was a desire "to reaffirm certain basic truths which seem to get lost in the shuffle from generation to generation, so that we seem destined to go on making the same mistakes over and over again."

Interest in literary subjects was strong among the generation born in Japan, many of whom wrote traditional Japanese poetry, which appeared in Japanese-language periodicals. The second generation tended to express its literary leanings in English. Yamamoto contributed regularly to *Kashu Mainichi* in Los Angeles and associated herself with the League of Nisei Writers and Artists.

In 1942, President Franklin D. Roosevelt ordered that all people of Japanese descent living on the West Coast be evacuated to internment camps. Interned at Poston, Arizona, until 1945, Yamamoto became a columnist and sometime editor for the camp newsletter. She published her first mystery, "Death Rides the Rails to Poston." The experience of internment looms large in postwar Japanese American writing. In "I Still Carry It Around," Yamamoto describes internment as a painful collective wound.

From 1945 to 1948, she worked for the *Los Angeles Tribune*, a black weekly, thus extending her experience of multiculturalism, before deciding to turn to writing full time. In 1950, she received a John Hay Whitney Foundation Opportunity Fellowship. Three of her short stories received critical attention: "High-Heeled Shoes," dealing with sexual harassment; "The Brown House," dealing with interethnic and interracial encounters; and "Epithalamium," dealing with romance. Yamamoto's themes are multiple, but she is especially sensitive to the life allotted to Japanese American women. Marriage in 1955 and four subsequent children (added to one she had already adopted) curtailed her literary output, but she did not cease to write and to influence other writers. In 1988, the publication of *Seventeen Syllables, and Other Stories*, a collection of fifteen of her short stories, made work easily available.

"Seventeen Syllables"

Type of work: Short fiction
First published: 1949

"Seventeen Syllables," Yamamoto's most acclaimed short story, combines a number of themes that appear frequently in her fiction. These themes include the difficulties faced by Japanese immigrants to the United States, the cultural separation between these immigrants and their children, and the restrictions experienced by Japanese American women within traditional Japanese culture. Important for an understanding of the story are some facts about the Japanese immigrant experience in America. Although the United States welcomed Japanese immigrants after 1885, immigration was stopped with the Asian Exclusion Act of 1924. Many of the first Japanese immigrants were unmarried men, who saved their earnings and sent back to Japan for brides they knew only through letters and photographs. Many of these married couples proved incompatible and were forced to make the best of an unsuitable marriage, keeping their problems concealed from the children. The Alien Land Act of 1913 prohibited Japanese immigrants from buying or leasing land for a period of more than three years. Since one-half of the immigrants lived in rural areas, the law forced families to move constantly and dispersed them often. A Japanese woman frequently had no other woman in whom to confide. In spite of these hardships, literature flourished and many immigrants wrote traditional Japanese poetry.

Yamamoto's story deals with these concerns through a device used often by Yamamoto, the double plot. On one level the plot concerns the adolescent Rosie Hayashi and her secret plan to meet Jesus Carrasco, a member of a Mexican family hired for the harvest. Rosie's inability to speak much Japanese and her failure to understand the interest her mother, Tome, takes in writing haiku, which she submits weekly to a Japanese-language paper in San Francisco, highlight the cultural and intergenerational differences between them. In the midst of the tomato harvest, when all workers are desperately needed, the editor arrives with a prize for Tome's poetry, a print by Hiroshige. Angry, her husband burns the picture. Tome reveals to Rosie that she has married her husband as an alternative to suicide. Rejected by a well-to-do lover, she had given birth to a stillborn son. An aunt in the United States arranged the marriage. Disappointed and disillusioned, Tome asks Rosie to promise never to marry at a time Rosie is experiencing the blissful promise of young romance. The story is a carefully nuanced and technically sophisticated combination of ethnic, feminist, and intergenerational concerns.

Suggested Readings

Cheung, King-Kok. *Articulate Silences: Hisaye Yamamoto, Maxine Hong Kingston, Joy Kogawa*. Ithaca, N.Y.: Cornell University Press, 1993.

Higashida, Cheryl. "Women, Work, and World in the Fiction of Carlos Bulosan and Hisaye Yamamoto." In *Transnational Asian American Literature: Sites and Transits*, edited by Shirley Geok-lin Lim et al. Philadelphia, Pa.: Temple University Press, 2006.

Kim, Elaine H. *Asian American Literature: An Introduction to the Writings and Their Social Context*. Philadelphia: Temple University Press, 1982.

Madsen, Deborah L., ed. *Asian American Writers*. Dictionary of Literary Biography 312. Detroit: Thomson Gale, 2005.

Whitson, Kathy J., ed. *Encyclopedia of Feminist Literature*. Westport, Conn.: Greenwood Press, 2004.

Contributor: Christine R. Catron

Frank Yerby

Born: Augusta, Georgia; September 5, 1916
Died: Madrid, Spain; November 29, 1991

African American

Yerby excelled at creating complicated, fast-moving plots that give vivid impressions of historical eras and periods. Often the novels contradict myths and stereotypes, and suggest the futility of finding real truth in the universal confusion of the human condition.

Principal works

LONG FICTION: *The Foxes of Harrow*, 1946; *The Vixens*, 1947; *The Golden Hawk*, 1948; *Pride's Castle*, 1949; *Floodtide*, 1950; *A Woman Called Fancy*, 1951; *The Saracen Blade*, 1952; *The Devil's Laughter*, 1953; *Benton's Row*, 1954; *Bride of Liberty*, 1954; *The Treasure of Pleasant Valley*, 1955; *Captain Rebel*, 1956; *Fairoaks*, 1957; *The Serpent and the Staff*, 1958; *Jarrett's Jade*, 1959; *Gillian*, 1960; *The Garfield Honor*, 1961; *Griffin's Way*, 1962; *The Old Gods Laugh: A Modern Romance*, 1964; *An Odor of Sanctity*, 1965; *Goat Song*, 1968; *Judas, My Brother*, 1968; *Speak Now: A Modern Novel*, 1969; *The Dahomean: An Historical Novel*, 1971; *The Girl from Storyville*, 1972; *The Voyage Unplanned*, 1974; *Tobias and the Angel*, 1975; *A Rose for Ana Maria*, 1976; *Hail the Conquering Hero*, 1978; *A Darkness at Ingraham's Crest*, 1979; *Western*, 1982; *Devilseed*, 1984; *McKenzie's Hundred*, 1985

SHORT FICTION: "Health Card," 1944

Frank Garvin Yerby (YEHR-bee) was born in Augusta, Georgia, on September 5, 1916. He received a B.A. at Paine College in 1937 and an M.A. at Fisk College in 1938. Subsequently, he did graduate work in education at the University of Chicago. From 1939 to 1941, Yerby taught English, first at Florida A&M and then at Southern University and Agricultural and Mechanical College. Married in 1941, he worked from 1941 to 1944 at the Ford Motor Company in Dearborn, Michigan, as a technician and then as an inspector at Fairchild Aircraft from 1944 to 1945. In 1944, he won an O. Henry Memorial Award for the short story "Health Card," a story that dealt sensitively with black issues. In 1945, he started work on a novel, *The Foxes of Harrow*, which he aimed to make a commercial success. Thereafter, Yerby wrote many similar melodramatic best sellers. His books have sold millions of copies and have been translated into at least fourteen languages.

Divorced in the 1950's, Yerby moved to France and then to Spain, where he died in 1991. He had four children from his first marriage. His second wife was his researcher and general manager; some of his later novels give evidence of their considerable research. He traveled widely, and sometimes his travels involved investigating locales of works in progress. His plots are intricate and involved, although in many of his novels the characterizations are basically flat. His most common setting is the nineteenth century South, yet he wrote about many other places and times in his more than thirty novels. Occasionally, he set a novel in modern times. The superficial reader of best sellers will find in Yerby's novels fast-paced narrative with appropriate amounts of violence and sex.

Yerby was more, however, than a mere best-selling novelist. His early short stories show promise and develop radically different themes from those of his costume novels. In the 1960's, secure after many commercial successes, Yerby began to do his best work, dealing with larger issues of race and religion, which figure less prominently in his earlier novels. The characters in these later novels are no longer cardboard figures, while the backgrounds are as richly detailed and vividly recreated as ever.

Moreover, Yerby's historical novels must be evaluated within the context of that often unappreciated genre. His novels almost always show the conflict between two worlds or orders, as great historical novels do. Yerby rarely deals with actual historical figures but rather creates characters who have to deal with the essential conflicts of their eras. Often his novels, even the early ones, destroy widely held myths and stereotypes; critic Darwin Turner suggests that this revisionism might be Yerby's most significant contribution as a novelist. While extensive research is not evident in his early work, many of Yerby's later novels were thoroughly researched. Yerby was at his best in creating the color and movement of a particular era.

Yerby's typical protagonist is, in the words of his main character in *The Serpent and the Staff*, an *auslander*, or outsider, excluded from the ruling social order. The protagonist experientially develops a philosophy that often approaches modern existentialism, an attitude that life has no answer but that people still must cope with the bleakness of human existence with both dignity and humanity. This pattern emerges in Yerby's first novel, *The Foxes of Harrow*, and is developed in three of his best novels: *Griffin's Way, An Odor of Sanctity*, and *The Dahomean*.

The Foxes of Harrow

Type of work: Novel
First published: 1946

The Foxes of Harrow is set in the South and covers the years from 1825 to just after the end of the Civil War. Superficially, it is a novel about a clever schemer who rises to own a plantation with a neoclassical mansion, Harrow, and who has marriages to beautiful white women and a liaison with a stunning mulatto. Much of the novel is composed of stock devices of pulp fiction, and Yerby himself said of *The Foxes of*

Harrow that he set out to write a popular novel that would make him a lot of money, regardless of literary merit. Yerby added, however, that he became strangely involved with the writing of the novel and, despite himself, exceeded the ambitions of the pulp genre. Stephen Fox, the protagonist, is an outsider, originally shanty Irish. He is not merely the rogue that early reviewers took him for, whose success and eventual fall conform to a predictable pulp outline. Fox sees all values and ideals slip from him, so that at the end, he is a failure despite his humanity and perception. He is superior to the Southerners with whom he sympathetically deals. More than merely a novel of stock devices, *The Foxes of Harrow* is a story about the failure of a culture.

At the opening of the novel, Yerby's authorial voice establishes a pensive tone as he describes a visit to Harrow, now in ruins, in the twentieth century. Harrow is the symbol of a lost cause. Thus, for symbolic purposes, Harrow is cut off from the modern world. Bathed in moonlight, the ruins of Harrow have a decadent grandeur. The visitor feels driven from room to room and finally away from the house, never wanting to look back. The shortness of the opening, six brief paragraphs, makes the tone all the more striking, and the mood shifts quickly into the dialogue and description of the arrival of Stephen Fox in New Orleans in 1825.

Yerby was at his best in the novel in creating vivid images and scenes of the region during the forty or so years the novel spans. New Orleans appears as a lush feudalistic world where color is measured by degrees, given the novel's constant references to mulattos, quadroons, and octaroons, references which are historically true to the setting. New Orleans emerges as a backward society that refuses to drain the marshes where the mosquitoes carrying yellow fever breed and instead fires cannon to disperse the plague. The society also destroys the creativity of freed blacks. In one case, a thoroughly educated black returns from France and is killed for acting as if he were equal to whites. The most poignant scene occurs at the end of the novel, when the young heir to Harrow returns after the war to New Orleans to be confronted by a former slave of Harrow now in control. This former slave presents the heir's unknown half brother (by a beautiful mulatto) to his former master, who sees the image of his father as a young man—but the half brother is mentally retarded. As the scene concludes, Yerby deftly shows the social history of the next one hundred

Frank Yerby (Library of Congress)

years of the South. The former slave, now the ruler, knows that power will again return to the whites but suggests that blacks and whites can live together and respect one another. The heir, a combination of the worst of his father's roguish tendencies and the excesses of New Orleans, emphatically denies that such equality and reconciliation between the races are possible.

Yerby was weakest in his creation of character in *The Foxes of Harrow*, for the characters are one-dimensional and move woodenly through a convoluted, overheated plot. Stephen Fox is the fox, the rogue set off from Southern society by his birth, whose goals are riches and the most beautiful woman in New Orleans, Odalie Arceneaux, a cold, haughty belle. Her sister Aurore is a foil to her, for she is warm and beautiful and in love with Stephen, who is too blind at first to see her love. As is common in pulp fiction, Odalie dies in childbirth, and Stephen then marries gentle Aurore, but only after having fathered a child by a beautiful mulatto when Odalie had spurned his strong sexual drives.

Beneath this claptrap, though, is an author working with social issues not to be found in the typical 1946 pulp novel. In one scene, a black woman recently inducted into slavery throws herself into the Mississippi River rather than live in bondage. Old Calleen, a trusted slave at Harrow, later tells her grandson Inch (the son of the drowned slave) that someday, the rightness of their freedom will be made apparent. More significantly, in understated dialogue Stephen talks to his son Étienne about freeing slaves and says that the country must treat all people equally, including the blacks and the poorest whites. When his son dismisses the poor, white or black, Stephen uses history as a defense, mentioning the French Revolution, Haiti, and insurrectionist Nat Turner. It is in his sympathy and balance in treating social matters that Yerby's "moral mobility" appears, a phrase that a London *Times* writer used in reviewing a later Yerby novel.

Griffin's Way

Type of work: Novel
First published: 1962

Griffin's Way was published in 1962, sixteen years after *The Foxes of Harrow*, and is a departure in some respects from Yerby's work up to that time. It treats the Mississippi of the 1870's unglamorously, highlighting squalor, inbreeding among whites, and the violence of the Ku Klux Klan in a manner more characteristic of William Faulkner than of the standard best-selling author. The novel shows the paralysis of humane white society after the Civil War, a paralysis symbolized by the central hero's amnesia and invalid status.

Much of the novel debunks the grandeur and opulence of the old South, which Yerby himself had occasionally exploited in earlier novels. The ruined South appears first through the eyes of a Northerner, Candace Trevor, a New England minister's daughter married to a paralyzed Southerner and hired as a nurse for Paris Griffin as the novel opens. She despises the Southern "courtesy" to which women are subjected, dismisses the neoclassical architecture in the poorly constructed homes, and comments on how most planters lived in squalor even before the war. Unlike her father, she believes in a Darwinian theory of evolution and sees the darker forces in herself as part of the ape still remaining in people. Candace knows that to cure Paris of his amnesia she must find the key to it from Paris's oversexed wife Laurel. Ferreting out answers with the right leading questions, she discovers the tawdry, twisted story that led to Paris's amnesia and emotional paralysis. It is only her austere moral upbringing that allows her to control her love for Paris to use her knowledge to help him.

When Candace does cure him, Paris tries to return to his home, Griffin's Way, and to his wife Laurel, but while his cure is a rebirth, it does not allow a return. To begin with, he has returned to a world changed by the war, a world of political corruption and violence, a world that has regressed, so that even a sixty-mile trip, once possible in three hours, now involves an arduous three-day journey because the railroads remain unrepaired even five years after the war. Three years later, with the railroad rebuilt, Paris and Laurel visit Vicksburg, where Paris, despite his humanity, appears troubled by the apparent ascendancy of blacks. Yerby balances the situation by having Paris also see the obvious corruption of the black superintendent of schools, who lives in the grand style of the Old South on money intended for the schools. Paris is thus caught between two worlds: He rejects the Klan as apes but resents a black man wearing a suit as if he is accustomed to it. Even renewed, Paris still represents the paralysis of the humane white during the Reconstruction.

Yerby titled the last third of the novel "Apocalypse," and this part has unresolved elements, unresolved on account of Yerby's honesty in dealing with his material. Paris watches the new world tumble around him, powerless to do anything. Black militants and white Klansmen fight all over the South, but Paris can only catalog the battles; he cannot change events. His moment of action does allow him to rescue Samson, a former slave, and Samson's wife by helping them escape to the North. He can do nothing to help his brother, his mulatto wife, and their children, who are burned in their house except for one daughter, who dies after being repeatedly raped, all of them victims of the Klan. He also helps a black minister escape, but only after the dynamiting of the minister's house, which killed a daughter. At his daughter's funeral, the minister delivers a stern sermon to the Klan members, who then threaten his life so that Paris must again help him. The Klan members finally back off from Paris's house when one accidentally shoots Laurel, still very much a symbol of Southern womanhood. The novel ends with dawn imagery, the night having been endured and the humane whites now waiting for the light of morning. Whether the whites threatened by the Klan can start anew is unclear. Given the implied parallel to modern events, Yerby seems to be saying that it is too soon to tell whether the twentieth century can rise above racial violence; nevertheless, the concluding imagery does suggest hope.

An Odor of Sanctity

Type of work: Novel
First published: 1965

In *An Odor of Sanctity*, Yerby is at his best as a historical novelist. It is a long, deftly paced novel which, while using many of the stock elements of Yerby's novels of the 1940's and 1950's, also deals intelligently with a religious theme. Once again, Yerby creates an outsider, Alaric Teudisson, as hero; he is set off by his odor of sanctity, a saintly force in him of which he is not fully aware for most of his life. Teudisson must deal with the complex culture of medieval Spain, a battleground for Christians, Moors, and numerous bands of marauding barbarians.

Like earlier Yerby protagonists, Teudisson is involved in many liaisons and several marriages. Teudisson is a striking blond of Visigoth extraction who, before the male hormones take effect, is so "beautiful" that at one point he is almost made a catamite. Thereafter, Teudisson has numerous sexual encounters, one unconsummated marriage, and finally a marriage to a woman who has been repeatedly raped by bandits, a marriage which shows Teudisson's magnanimity and one which also brings Teudisson genuine happiness and a family.

The religious motif of *An Odor of Sanctity* adds depth to what would otherwise be an entertaining but rather shallow melodrama. Despite himself, Teudisson becomes a saint by the end of the novel. As a man, Teudisson is handsome but scarred by battle, but as a boy, his beauty, so unlike the usual rough Goth face, led his mother and others to think he was marked for the priesthood. He turns from his religious impulses to lead a secular life, however, and while doing so, he finds his saintliness. In dealing with women, he shows a compassion and love that are the basis of his profound sexual appeal; at one point of seeming dissolution, he has numerous prostitutes loving him because he has talked to them and treated them as human beings and not merely as sex objects. Misused by a woman, he always responds with kindness. By the end of the novel, Teudisson becomes the arbiter between Moor and Christian factions when a certain group of fanatic Christians wants to destroy all tolerance for the predominant Moors. Throughout the novel, Teudisson has been a genuine ecumenist. At the end, Teudisson, doubting his saintly powers because he is unable to save his wife, willingly seeks crucifixion and thus enters sainthood and legend. In losing himself, he gains sainthood.

As in most of his novels, Yerby's greatest strength in *An Odor of Sanctity* is his re-creation of a time, invoked through color and action. Again, a humane authorial voice speaks throughout the novel. The book shows that the diversity of medieval Spain is indeed its glory. While the Moorish culture encourages learning and recognizes Christ as a prophet, the contrasting Christian culture (except for Teudisson and a few Church fathers) is dark and intolerant. In showing the clash between these cultures, *An Odor of Sanctity* is first-rate historical fiction.

The Dahomean

Type of work: Novel
First published: 1971

If one of Yerby's novels is destined to last, it is *The Dahomean*, a novel unlike any of his others. It is a simple, moving tale of the life of a black man in his African culture before he was sold into slavery. Yerby neither idealizes nor sensationalizes his material but presents a story composed of love, envy, and hatred that reads as a legend, a story of characters and events drawn larger than life. The protagonist, Nyasanu, is like other Yerby protagonists because he is an alien or outsider: He is far less violent and far more handsome than most men of his society. Caught in the ugliness of the American slave system, he has the tragic quality of some of the great existentialist heroes.

Yerby begins the chronological narrative of Nyasanu as he is about to enter manhood, a passage marked by the painful ritual of circumcision. The early parts of the novel present such rituals in convincing detail. Yerby moves the reader from Nyasanu's initiation to an enemy's attempt to destroy his guardian tree to his wedding and the deflowering of his bride. In "A Note to the Reader," Yerby explains that the novel is based on research into the customs of the Dahomeans of the nineteenth century, but Yerby adds to his research his own respect of this African culture.

As Nyasanu moves through his period of manhood, Yerby depicts the society of the Dahomeans as a stage for the great primal emotions and forces of life. Nyasanu has encounters with numerous women, but his sexual experiences are never merely sensational, the stuff of popular fiction: Nyasanu has a reality which sets him apart from Yerby's typical protagonists. In addition to his sexual encounters, Nyasanu has the experience of real brotherhood, for his society expects each male to have his three closest friends identified in order. Battles with warring tribes give Nyasanu the chance to show bravery and also to distinguish himself as more sensitive to violence than the average Dahomean. In addition, Yerby shows the diversity of Dahomean society, which includes both male homosexuals and Amazonian warriors.

In a moving discussion with his number-one friend, Kpadunu, Nyasanu learns that the generations are all of one fabric. Each generation faces the same problems of love, the family, and death. The old priests, therefore, give answers based on the past to the young and the unsure, and—given the coherence of their society—the answers generally hold. Facing the problem of belief in the gods which these old priests try to inculcate in the young, Nyasanu realizes that their wisdom is not divine but experiential, that the past of his society answers the present needs. Ironically, his friend Kpadunu is trying to help Nyasanu rise above the control of priests by showing where their wisdom resides, yet he actually makes the skeptical Nyasanu believe more than he did, so that he must face the priestly prediction that his life will end in Dahomey but will begin again in another place.

Nyasanu does learn that he can count on the inexorability of fate and not the protection of the gods. In quick succession, he loses his friend Kpadunu, his wife in childbirth, and his father. He comes to see his heroism as mere foolishness in taking risks. Rather than listening to the gods, he simply faces life as chieftain and husband of Kpadunu's widow. Far more than the ritual of circumcision, his acceptance of life and his rejection of the illusion of divine protection mark Nyasanu's adulthood. When Nyasanu next appears in the novel, he is chieftain and has four wives. His life is successful until he is sold into slavery with the aid of his homosexual brother and rival.

The betrayal of Nyasanu has the archetypal pattern of tragedy, the hero fallen from great heights, undone by his own blindness in not facing the evil of his brother and his incestuous brother-in-law and by his pride in not following the past and living with his extended family in the same compound. He faces the guns of his attackers with his sword, only to be told to put his sword down, for in the modern era, swords are powerless against guns. First, he must watch the murder of his mother (the slavers see that she is too old to have children), the subsequent murder of all his children (the slavers know that they would die on the voyage across the Atlantic), and the subjugation of his wives, the rape of some and the suicide of one. His response is disassociation, a silence which lasts the rest of his life.

Like a classical tragedy, *The Dahomean* treats terrible despair in its conclusion but leads to an illumination, Nyasanu's enlightenment. He recognizes the evil of blacks selling blacks into American slavery, although they have no conception of the degradation of this foreign slavery, their domestic slavery being gentle and indulgent. Philosophically, Nyasanu faces the bleakness of life with the realization that there are no answers. Truth is only that there is no truth. Nyasanu acquits himself with honor; like a great tragic hero, he has his dignity, the dignity of silence in the face of the emptiness of the human condition.

Suggested Readings

Glasrud, Bruce. "'The Fishes and the Poet's Hands': Frank Yerby, a Black Author in White America." *Journal of American and Comparative Cultures* 23 (Winter, 2000): 15-21.

Jarreet, Gene Andrew. "'For Endless Generations': Myth, Dynasty, and Frank Yerby's *The Foxes of Harrow*." *Southern Literary Journal* 29, no. 1 (Fall, 2006): 54ff.

Klotman, Phyllis. "A Harrowing Experience: Frank Yerby's First Novel to Film." *College Language Association Journal* 31 (December, 1987): 210-222.

Smiles, Robin V. "Uncovering Frank Yerby." *Black Issues in Higher Education* 21, no. 19 (November 4, 2004): 28ff.

Contributor: Dennis Goldsberry

José Yglesias

Born: Tampa, Florida; November 29, 1919
Died: New York, New York; November 7, 1995

Cuban American

Yglesias is best known for writing about individual lives and hardship in Cuba and in Latin American countries affected by revolutions.

Principal works

DRAMA: *Chattahoochee*, pr. 1989; *The Dictatorship of the Proletariat*, pr. 1989; *You Don't Remember?*, pr. 1989; *New York 1937*, pr. 1990

LONG FICTION: *A Wake in Ybor City*, 1963; *An Orderly Life*, 1967; *The Truth About Them*, 1971; *Double Double*, 1974; *The Kill Price*, 1976; *Home Again*, 1985; *Tristan and the Hispanics*, 1989; *Break-in*, 1996; *The Old Gents*, 1996 (novella)

SHORT FICTION: *The Guns in the Closet*, 1996

TRANSLATIONS: *Island of Women*, 1962 (pb. in England as *Sands of Torremolinos*); *Villa Milo*, 1962; *The Party's Over*, 1966

NONFICTION: *The Goodbye Land*, 1967; *In the Fist of the Revolution*, 1968; *Down There*, 1970; *The Franco Years*, 1977

Of Cuban and Spanish descent, José Yglesias (hoh-SAY ee-GLAY-see-ahs) was born to José and Georgia Milian Yglesias in Tampa, Florida. He worked as a stock clerk and a dishwasher when he moved to New York City at age seventeen. Yglesias then served in the U.S. Navy from 1942 to 1945 during World War II; he received a naval citation of merit. After the war, he attended Black Mountain College in 1946. He married Helen Basine, a novelist, on August 19, 1950. Yglesias held numerous jobs during his lifetime, from assembly line worker to film critic, from assistant to a vice president of a pharmaceutical company to Regents Lecturer at the University of California at Santa Barbara in 1973.

Yglesias's birthplace greatly influenced his literary concern and career. He was born in the section of Tampa called Ybor City. Until Ybor City, a cigar-making town, was founded by V. Martinez Ybor in 1885, there were not many Latinos in Tampa. As Ybor City and its economy grew, Cubans and other Latinos arrived and brought their own cultural activities and vibrant traditions. These aspects of life in Ybor City served as inspiration and material for Yglesias's plays and books. According to him, these events must be documented so that the history and cultural richness of that part of America will not be forgotten.

Descriptions of Ybor City and its history can be found in the pages of Yglesias's first novel, *A Wake in Ybor City*. The novel is a colorful depiction of Cuban immigrants in the Latin section of Tampa on the eve of the Cuban Revolution in 1958. The story deals with family dynamics, class envy, sexual intrigues, and cultural assimilation, along with machismo and matriarchal powers in conflict. This novel started his prolific writing career, in which he would move back and forth between fiction and nonfiction.

Being of Cuban and Spanish ancestry also greatly influenced Yglesias's second book, *The Goodbye Land*. The laborious energy required—as well as personal desire—to travel to the mountainside village of Galacia, Spain, in 1964 in order to trace his father's birth and death there proved to be worthwhile; the book was a great success and was praised by many critics for its authenticity as a travel narrative.

Many of Yglesias's books after *The Goodbye Land* deal with personal statements and individuality amid the revolutionary experience. His nonfiction work *In the Fist of the Revolution* addresses individual lives and hopes amid political and social problems in the town of Miyari, Cuba. *The Franco Years* depicts the living conditions of the author's Spanish acquaintances under the Fascist regime of dictator Francisco Franco, who died in Spain in 1976. (Yglesias was in Spain at the time.) Again, many critics agreed that these two books demonstrate authentic social reporting because the author, while in Cuba and Spain interviewing people, experienced their hardships and turmoil. That authenticity reflects the critical talent and genuine objectivity of Yglesias, who went against the mainstream literary fashion of political and social analysis and moralizing.

Yglesias's talent and honesty in his literary desire to present emotions, aspirations, and disappointments unique to Latino émigrés in the United States led to success and critical acclaim in his novels as well as nonfiction works. His persistent interest in individual lives, the immigrant experience, and cultural assimilation can be seen in novels such as *The Kill Price*, *Home Again*, and *Tristan and the Hispanics*.

Mainly known for writing novels, nonfiction, and translation, Yglesias was also a talented dramatist. He wrote only four plays, three of which—*Chattahoochee*, *The Dictatorship of the Proletariat*, and *You Don't Remember?*—form a trilogy set in Ybor City in 1912, 1920, and 1989, respectively. The fourth play, *New York 1937*, is an autobiographical comedy involving cigar making and the Great Depression, set in Manhattan's Washington Heights. In his plays, Yglesias's creative drive and imagination brings his characters to life upon the stage.

In addition to his efforts as novelist and dramatist, Yglesias contributed major articles for prestigious literary magazines, newspapers, and other periodicals. He was the patriarch of a literary family, which included his former wife and his son Rafael, also a novelist and screenwriter. Yglesias died of cancer in 1995. His body of work places him as one of the pioneers of modern American and Latino literature.

The Truth About Them

Type of work: Novel
First published: 1971

Yglesias's third novel, *The Truth About Them*, focuses on the family history of a Cuban American clan, whose American experience dates from 1890, when the narrator's aristocratic grandmother first arrived in Tampa, Florida. Although much of their life in America is associated with the up-and-down fortunes of Florida's cigar industry, this working-class family displays a pride and cohesiveness that defy all obstacles. During the lean years of the 1930's, some members of the clan are forced to go north to New York City in search of jobs. Before long, however, they find themselves drifting back to Ybor City, owned and controlled by the cigar company. The narrator, much like Roberto of *A Wake in Ybor City*, is truly a Cuban American. Brought up in the very Latin atmosphere of Ybor City, he eventually becomes a left-wing journalist and learns to swim freely in America's traditionless mainstream. Eager to learn more about his Latin roots, however, he visits postrevolutionary Cuba, an experience that engenders a newfound pride in his Cuban background.

The Truth About Them covers a greater time span than that of *A Wake in Ybor City*, filling in the historical background lacking in Yglesias's first novel. Written in an episodic style (several adventures were first published separately in *The New Yorker*), this fictionalized family portrait, with its rich and varied characters, its fast-moving plot, and its free-flowing style, offers a panoramic vision of a part of America generally unknown to non-Cuban Americans. Its detailed and loving depiction of a specific ethnic group suggests that America is greater for having accepted as its own such resolute and distinctive communities.

Suggested Readings

Baskin, Leonard. "José Yglesias." *Tampa Review* 13 (1996).

Booklist. Review of *The Kill Price*. 72 (May 1, 1976): 1244.

Ivory, Ann, ed. "José Yglesias." In *Contemporary Authors*. Vols. 41-44, first revision series. Detroit: Gale Research, 1974.

"José Yglesias." In *Contemporary Novelists*. 6th ed. Detroit: St. James Press, 1996.

Laezman, Rick. *One Hundred Hispanic-Americans Who Shaped American History*. San Mateo, Calif.: Bluewood Books, 2002.

Nelson, Milo G. Review of *Double Double*. *Library Journal* 99 (May 15, 1974): 1410.

Contributors: H. N. Nguyen and Richard Keenan

Al Young

Born: Ocean Springs, Mississippi; May 31, 1939

African American

Young's poetry is inspired by rhythm-and-blues and jazz, and he makes effective use of various American dialects. He also writes about family relationships, his characters and personas often centering their identities in family life, which enables them to cope with the meanness and injustice of contemporary urban American society.

Principal works

LONG FICTION: *Snakes*, 1970; *Who Is Angelina?*, 1975; *Sitting Pretty*, 1976; *Ask Me Now*, 1980; *Seduction by Light*, 1988

POETRY: *Dancing*, 1969; *The Song Turning Back Into Itself*, 1971; *Geography of the Near Past*, 1976; *The Blues Don't Change: New and Selected Poems*, 1982; *Heaven: Collected Poems, 1956-1990*, 1992; *Conjugal Visits, and Other Poems in Verse and Prose*, 1996; *The Sound of Dreams Remembered: Poems, 1990-2000*, 2001; *Coastal Nights and Inland Afternoons: Poems, 2001-2006*, 2006

NONFICTION: *Bodies and Soul: Musical Memoirs*, 1981; *Kinds of Blue: Musical Memoirs*, 1984; *Things Ain't What They Used to Be: Musical Memoirs*, 1987; *Mingus/Mingus: Two Memoirs*, 1989 (with Janet Coleman); *Drowning in the Sea of Love: Musical Memoirs*, 1995

EDITED TEXTS: *Changing All Those Changes*, 1976 (of James P. Girard); *Zeppelin Coming Down*, 1976 (of William Lawson); *Yardbird Lives!*, 1978 (with Ishmael Reed); *Calafia: An Anthology of California Poets*, 1979 (with Reed and Shawn Hsu Wong); *Quilt*, 1981-1986 (with Reed; 5 volumes); *African American Literature: A Brief Introduction and Anthology*, 1996

Albert James Young, the son of Mary (Campbell) and Albert James Young, was born in Ocean Springs, Mississippi, near Biloxi, on the Gulf of Mexico. His childhood, which he characterizes as happy, was divided between rural Mississippi and urban Detroit. Though he moved through several communities and schools, he values the flexibility that he gained by adapting to different subcultures. His father was an auto worker (in part, the model for Durwood Knight's father in *Ask Me Now*), and also a professional musician, like his son. For five years, Young sang and played the flute and guitar professionally, at first while attending the University of Michigan, then while working as a disc jockey at radio station KJAZ-FM in Alameda, California. The character M. C. in *Snakes* reflects some of Young's aspirations as a young jazz musician, and the poem "A Little More Traveling Music" reflects his divided roots in rural and urban music. American blues and jazz and their origins in African music have influenced the themes and the formal structures of Young's fiction and poetry.

Young has credited his interest in writing narratives to his early exposure to the art of southern storytelling, and his fictional and poetic use of regional and ethnic vernacular draws upon his memories of southern speech as well as his wide reading in American literature (especially the works of Zora Neale Hurston, Mark Twain, Langston Hughes, and Jesse Stuart) and British and European literature.

Young attended the University of Michigan from 1957 to 1961 before moving to the San Francisco Bay Area in 1961. There he received his A.B. degree in Spanish from the University of California at Berkeley in 1969. He and his wife, Arline June (Belch), were married in 1963 and have a son, Michael James Young. From 1966 to 1967, Young was a fellow in Advanced Fiction Writing at Stanford University; in 1969, he received his bachelor of arts degree in Spanish at Berkeley. Young taught writing at the San Francisco Museum of Art during the late 1960's and was linguistic consultant for the Berkeley Neighborhood Youth Corps. From 1969 to 1973, he held Stanford University's Edward H. Jones Lectureship in Creative Writing, and he served as consultant to the New York writers' organization Poets and Writers in 1974 and 1975. He was the 1979 director of Associated Writing Programs, an organization of graduate university administrators, teachers, and students of creative writing, was writer-in-residence at the University of Washington from 1981 to 1982.

Young also spent many years in the 1970's and 1980's working as a film screenwriter for various Los Angeles-area studios. He was a writer-in-residence at the University of Washington in Seattle from 1981 to 1982, and served as the vice president of Yardbird Publishing Cooperative, which he had cofounded. He became a familiar face on the lecture circuit at universities throughout the United States. In the 1980's, Young turned increasingly to writing nonfiction, often having to do with music and film. He earned an Outstanding Book of the Year citation from *The New York Times* in 1980 for *Ask Me Now*, a Pushcart Prize in 1980, an American Book Award from the Before Columbus Foundation in 1982 for *Bodies and Soul*, and a Fulbright Fellowship in 1984.

In the 1990's, he continued writing, contributing to anthologies, and creating "musical memoirs." Though he has traveled widely—in Spain, France, Mexico, and the United States—he has made his home in Northern California.

Young's concern for language, a concern that embraces both mistrust and love, is clearly evinced in his prose. His second novel, *Who Is Angelina?*, and his fourth, *Ask Me Now*, have third-person narrative personas who stand distractingly close to their author; they appear hesitant to act freely for want of purpose. Readers of the first and third novels, however, will quickly recognize Young's ability to render in his first-person narrative personas a vibrant male voice of new adulthood (*Snakes*), or sagacious middle age (*Sitting Pretty*).

The author's background as a professional musician enables him to use music descriptively as well as metaphorically; the reader shares the experience of making music and feeling music make life known. The music of language also affects Young's style. He makes careful alterations to standard syntax and diction, sometimes punctuation, in order to set the speech closer to its natural human tone. His objective is not merely to create contemporary dialect but also to create an enduring contemporaneity, to offer rhythmically, as the poet-musician should, the nonverbal meanings that language can carry in its sounds. Young creates this quality of speech through narrative personae who speak softly or stridently, sometimes too literally, yet with voices constant and sincere.

Love, like a curse or a whimper, extends most intensely from the individual to those nearby. The contemporary American social dilemma is thereby represented in Young's prose just as it appears in his poetry: Each person must somehow maintain the unity, fidelity, and consistency love requires while grappling for the freedom and oneness that American mythology promises. Although *Snakes* and *Sitting Pretty* are more successful, all Young's novels contain graphic portrayals of mainstream urban America—middle-class people who try to be good at being themselves. They emote, they dream, and they reason. At worst, they stand too large on the page; at best, they find purpose to complement the dignity they feel. Whether he narrates with commentary from a third-person point of view, or with the immediacy of first-person sensory experience, Young confronts the problems of individuals growing into their individuality, and the qualities of life central to the congregate American family.

Dancing

Type of work: Poetry
First published: 1969

Young's poetry originates in visual and aural memories and in musical forms which are then developed through suitable language and prosody. The music that inspires his poetry includes rhythm and blues and jazz, and he makes effective use of various American dialects. The metaphor of dancing unites the visual images and musical forms, and suggests both the formality and the spontaneity of design in his poetry.

Young also writes about family relationships and does so with insight, humor, and affection. His fictional characters and poetic personas often center their identities in their family life, which enables them, somehow, to cope with the meanness and injustice of contemporary urban American society. The family relationships are hardly idyllic, and characters habitually annoy and occasionally hurt one another; nevertheless, the love they feel for one another transforms their lives. Although his work offers no simplistic ideological solutions, his poems and novels clearly reflect his belief in the writer's function: to change society by expanding the reader's perception of reality.

Dancing, Young's first collection of poems, won the National Arts Council Award for poetry, as well as a Joseph Henry Jackson Award from the San Francisco

Foundation. These poems explore many forms of dance, including "A Dance for Militant Dilettantes," "Dancing Day to Day," "The John Coltrane Dance," "Reading Nijinsky's Diary," "Dancing Pierrot," "A Little More Traveling Music," and "Dancing." Young's rejection of "monocultural values, of whatever hue," is reflected in the diverse cultural backgrounds of the poems in *Dancing*.

At the beginning of his collection, Young places an uncharacteristic poem, perhaps written after the manuscript of *Snakes* had been refused by a series of publishers interested only in black voices that were violently angry and bitter. "A Dance for Militant Dilettantes" implicitly rejects the advice of a friend who urges him to play the stereotypic role of a honky-hating African American activist, writing about bloodying "those fabled wine & urine-/ stained hallways." While modifying the Homeric cliché of wine-dark seas, Young's brilliant epithet exposes the contemporary racism of the publisher who wants to market "a furious nigrah" and of the militant dilettantes willing to sell out.

The poet in "Dancing Day to Day" lives in and writes about a multicultural world, in which people are fearful of violence and yet live, fairly contentedly, one day at a time. In the first four lines of this poem, Young echoes T. S. Eliot, in the "come and go" of his monotonous, trivial, habitual Prufrockian world, but, significantly, without Eliot's contempt:

In my street
the people mostly go.
Very few come
to what I'd call home.

The walking iambic meter of lines 2 and 4 alternates with the emphatic trochees of lines 1 and 3, and his quatrain establishes the dominant metric pattern of the verse paragraphs that follow. This open design, built on no regular line length, perfectly expresses the speaker's relaxed attitude toward his neighbors, as well as the freedom of their daily natural movements.

"The John Coltrane Dance," a tribute to the music of John Coltrane, uses repetition, subtle assonance, and alliteration to suggest the emotional power of Coltrane's musical compositions and performances. The word "sound" occurs seven times, is echoed in "astound" and "surround," and introduces a pattern of sibilants. The line "Mr Love Trane" occurs only twice (lines 2 and 24), but its distinctive concluding spondee, lengthened by the long vowels, sets a metrical pattern that also occurs in lines 8 ("tree dance"), 14 ("smoothed stones"), 16 ("hurt songs"), and 18 ("sound cures"). Against the implied hesitation of this duple meter, Young syncopates rapidly moving feet of triple meter, such as the dactyl ("hovering," line 6), the anapest ("where that sound," line 14) and the tribrach, or three unaccented syllables ("& cleansed the," line 15, and "on all the," line 23). Traditional prosody offers these terms to describe lines of verse, but readers familiar with open forms in American poetry and listeners familiar with Coltrane's extended and complex rhythmic patterns may not need this abstract analysis to hear the musical phrases of Young's poem. The poem first invokes Coltrane as muse ("Fly on into my poem"), imitating

Al Young (© Miriam Berkley)

both the sounds and the impact of one of his solo performances, then places his music within the social and political history of Black America (the migrations from Alabama, the confrontation over segregated schools in Little Rock, Arkansas, and the urban ghettos in the city of brotherly love, Philadelphia, Pennsylvania). Citing the function of the blues, expressing pain to soothe and heal it, Young identifies Coltrane's music as creating and keeping alive both collective and individual history. In a temporal metaphor moving from day to night, Young suggests that Coltrane's music also forecasts the future, as the "sunrise" of line 9 is transformed into the "stars" of the final line. It is an optimistic poem, celebrating the growth of the spirit, through a history and an artistic form that recall dark nights of the soul.

In the playful "Dancing Pierrot," the speaking poet claims to have known the moons of China, Egypt, Mexico, Tokyo, Bahia, San Francisco, Tanzania, and the Moors; further, he claims to have known not merely fat and skinny moons (the lunar phases) but moons that shone "lifetimes ago." Clearly, he claims the international and timeless realm of the poet who speaks to all cultures, to all races, and to all ages. Like Jules Laforgue, whose Pierrot of *L'Imitation de Notre-Dame la Lune* (1886; "Imitation of Our Lady the Moon") appears in the title, Young imagines the poet as a kind of noble lunatic, drunk on moonlight. His dancing seems that of the marionette, jerkily bobbing at the end of his strings, an image reinforced by several short two- and three-syllable lines, and by the many one-syllable words; the lyrical fifth stanza, however, echoing "Drink to me only with thine eyes," breaks the confining strings and creates the feeling of freedom. The poet's function appears in the third of the poem's five stanzas, as he observes the effects of moonlight (imagination) on ordinary working people, whose aspirations the poet powerfully images as "armed to the eyes/ with star guns" (lines 28 and 29). The workers, who might seem imprisoned by repetitive movements, have a vision of self-liberating power, which is articulated by the poet.

"Reading Nijinsky's Diary" also considers the madness of the artist, whose dance plays between the extremes of confinement ("bodily concern/ vinetangled nerve") and freedom ("—cut loose, freed/ to know ever for all"). The visual images that Young employs suggest the surviving photographs of Vaslav Nijinsky in costume for his roles as the faun in *Afternoon of a Faun* and as the rose in *Specter of the Rose*. The identification of the dancer with the dance, like that of the poet with the poem, carries the threat of insanity. For Young, unlike Nijinsky, the descent into madness is only temporary, and he is released by the incantation: "'My madness is my love/ for mankind.'"

"A Little More Traveling Music" is the autobiographical sketch of a poet and singer born in Mississippi, reared on the "Colored music, rhythmic & electrifying" broadcast over the radio, and on the music of a mother's recited family history. His move "up north" introduced him to the external, daily sounds of urban traffic and the internal music of moonlit dreams, and educated him in the sounds of written poetry. The third stanza narrates the return to "motherly music" and the poet's synthesis of that oral tradition with his formal education. The cycle of personal history culminates in his choice of vocation: "I turned to poetry & to singing." Performing and creating are made possible by listening to his "own background music."

The long poem "Dancing," which gives its title to the collection, responds personally and politically to the crises that Americans endured in the late 1960's. Admonitory rhetoric and judgmental images establish the poet as a cultural historian. The four sections of "Dancing," however, do not trace a chronology, since the work begins and ends in the night before a dawn, with the poet in the dark about his life, but hopeful. There are none of the theological issues that Eliot explores in *The Waste Land* (1922), and yet Young claims the same correlation between personal and cultural crises and records a spiritual descent followed by a mystical elevation. Writing in the oracular tradition of Walt Whitman, Allen Ginsberg, Amiri Baraka, and the Old Testament prophets, Young envisions a decade of personal experience in the context of his jeremiad on contemporary American culture. "Dancing" begins as the writer, struggling with his muse in the early evening, thinks of the world outside and of the roads he might have taken (heroin dealer, drunken bum, drifter).

Sobered by his thought that he "is capable of being assassinated/ at any moment" (as were Martin Luther King, Jr., and Robert Kennedy in 1968), and saddened that people continue to live trivial, habitual lives, that the younger generation seeks violent solutions, and that America's commercialism assigns little value to his grandfather's work on a farm, the poet laments the corruption of "Ahhhhhmerica!/ you old happy whore." Sections 1 and 2 present the poet's confusion and the decline of America, culminating in a descent "to these dark places/ to these waters"—but, significantly, the drowning is only apparent. The moon is associated with the heart pumping blood, "washing the way clear for new origins," and the blood that is ritually spattered is, symbolically, that of fish.

At the end of section 2, the speaker recognizes that attempting to bring "the promiseland" to a chosen few by violent means has only polluted his mind: "the knife doubles back." After this self-inflicted death, section 3 offers a new beginning: "Be the mystic/ & wage ultimate revolution." All stereotypic revolutionary roles are rejected, and the short homily concludes with the admonition to "Be yourself." Section 4 makes the connection between the speaker's own past dreams and his projected life. The steps to this new life he learns from a stranger met in April (in Young's calendar, not the cruellest month but the time of resurrection). The poem concludes where it began, at the writer's desk in early evening, but with a new optimism. As he works, he envisions a people newly energized by the night, he hopes for the dawn, and he pronounces a blessing of peace. The final hortatory line—"Let the revolutions proceed!"—rejects the tyranny of any one ideological movement and advocates the proliferation of individual struggles.

Snakes

Type of work: Novel
First published: 1970

The narrative persona of Young's first novel, *Snakes*, is M. C. Moore, who recollects his youth and adolescence in the mature, seasoned voice of the novel's master of ceremonies. A novel of formation, *Snakes* is in the bildungsroman tradition and is rendered in a tone of voice at once nostalgic and fatherly. Although he has only snapshots of his true parents by which to remember them, M. C. gradually finds their love implanted in his own initialed name, "so it sound[s] like you had some status," his first lover explains, "whether you did or not." For M. C., the process of learning who he is becomes the composition of his own music.

M. C. discovers music in his soul, and he makes music the core of his world. He finds music everywhere, "in the streets, in the country, in people's voices," and "in the way they lead their lives." Providing counterpoint, M. C.'s grandmother Claude offers guidance and family history, and M. C. is her captive audience: "I could listen to Claude talk all day long, and did, many a time. Her voice was like music." The association expands as his views of love and music merge, and women ultimately become "lovable fields of musical energy."

While living with relatives in the South, M. C. learns at the age of ten that music will be his life. His Uncle Donald, a "night rambler" with a "talent for getting hold of a dollar," turns their impoverished household into a "blind pig," or a Meridian, Mississippi, version of a speakeasy. During his first exposure to the amoral world of adults, M. C. meets Tull, an itinerant jazz pianist who in effect provides the novel's premise: "You'll get it if you keep at it. Listen, just take your time, one note a time over here with your right hand. Just take your time, that's all it is to playin' the piano or anything else. Take your time and work it on out." The impression lasts; M. C. goes on to structure his life around his love of music and his faith that music will help him grow.

Literature also has a formative effect on him. It is not literature as found in the classroom or in books—M. C. attends high school in body only, and barely earns his diploma—rather, literature personified in Shakes, his closest friend, whose name is short for Shakespeare. Shakes has a "greedy memory and a razor tongue." He is bright, musical, and funny: "You hip to Cyrano de Bergerac? Talk about a joker could talk some trash! Cyrano got everybody told! Didn't nobody be messin with Cyrano, ugly as he was."

Yet there is more to know about life than its music and its literature; such knowledge appears in the person of Champ, who exposes M. C. to contemporary jazz and the business hemisphere of that musical world. In his bemusing, self-sacrificial way, Champ also demonstrates his worsening drug addiction and the consequential brutalization of his sensibilities. "Poor Champ," M. C. soon observes while he learns to jam, to feel his music come alive inside himself and issue forth, "who wanted to play an instrument so badly, would stand around working his arms and fingers for hours sometimes, shaping the smoky air in the room into some imaginary saxophone. . . . We all wanted to get good."

The evil to which Champ submits himself opposes the good that he gives M. C.—music as growth and expression. M. C.'s band, "The Masters of Ceremony," discover in their art a meaning that transcends the music they produce, and although the group separates after one demo and some local gigs, M. C.'s early success provides him with a clearer view of the possibilities of his life and a deep sense of wonder. He emerges from his plain, ordinary background complete, communicative, and capable of more, having also achieved his own narrative voice, that husky, now masculine voice the reader has heard maturing since the story's outset. He boards the New York bus a musician, grown: "I don't feel free . . . but I don't feel trapped." Awkwardly, painfully, naturally, M. C. has learned to look for the subtle ironies that enrich both life and art. Ready at last for the rest of what he will be, the young adult takes with him his guitar, his music, and precious recordings of his song "Snakes," which throughout the novel parallels his experience of youth: "The tune sounded simple the first time you heard it, but it wasn't all that simple to play."

The Song Turning Back into Itself

Type of work: Poetry
First published: 1971

The Song Turning Back into Itself, a collection taking its name from a long poem in seven parts, includes forty-four poems grouped under the five headings "Loneliness," "The Song Turning Back into Itself," "The Prestidigitator," "Everywhere," and "The Move Continuing." In an interview published in *New Orleans Review*, Young explained that *The Song Turning Back into Itself* has three levels of meaning: that history moves in cycles; that American popular music is returning to its roots in folk, African, and other ethnic music; and that the individual, going through changes, nevertheless returns to an original, unique self.

These three returns are all explored in "The Old Fashioned Cincinnati Blues," which appears in the first group of poems. Dedicated to Jesse "Lone Cat" Fuller, and taking its form and its train-ride setting from the blues, the poem is a nostalgic return to the poet's past—to a trip made by rail from Cincinnati, Ohio, to Meridian, Mississippi, by two young brothers, for a summer visit with grandparents and relatives left behind in the South. Vivid sensual images are fixed in his memory: "RC Cola coolers" and "tin tub baths" and "swapping ghost stories." The adult sees himself as essentially the same as the boy he was in 1949. The poet experiences his journey not just as a personal reminiscence but as part of the American tradition, for the voice of

Walt Whitman can be heard in Young's lines: "O Americana!/ United Statesiana!"

The seven numbered poems titled "The Song Turning Back into Itself" are a spiritual autobiography of the poet, from the baby's first breath through the adult shouting joyfully: "SING/ one sweet long song to undo/ all sickness & suffering." This persona draws on many sources for inspiration, including Billie Holiday (who sings "variations on the theme/ of human love &/ its shadow/ loneliness") and Rainer Maria Rilke (whose eighteenth "Sonnet to Orpheus" may be heard in "Feel today/ vibrating/ in the throat"). Singing the blues becomes, in these poems, an exploration of the singer's identity and roots. Images from his personal memories merge with historical events to suggest recurring cycles, as in the speculation: "Consider Nazis & crackers/ on the same stage/ splitting the bill."

Who Is Angelina?

Type of work: Novel
First published: 1975

While the narrative voice of *Snakes* provides contrast and consistency—a gradual merging of the maturing young man with his adult consciousness—the narrative voice of *Who Is Angelina?* accomplishes neither. Angelina is already grown, but her adult life has entered a phase of meaningless triviality. This she blames on the shifting cultural milieu of Berkeley, California. Life in Berkeley seems different now—dangerous—and the people's sense of freedom and fun, that community spirit of festivity, is gone. She uses the burglary of her apartment as the justification, and a friend's convenient cash as the means, to skip town—an act she considers the prerequisite for introspection. She flees not only her fictional problems but also her reader as well; a character with both brains and beauty who struggles with mere communal ennui is less than sympathetic. Moreover, even the reader who can overlook her escapist behavior needs to know more about her, and most of her background is provided through recollection and reminiscence. The novel's principal events—travel in Mexico, some romantic sex, an emergency trip home to Detroit, an encounter with a street thief—facilitate reflection by the viewpoint character, and the reader must simply accept her gradual appraisals. Dramatically, little takes place. Most of this novel is exposition; what little action there is consists of Angelina's consideration of an adaptation to what goes on around her.

The unifying thematic metaphor of *Who Is Angelina?* is the act of taking away: Angelina is robbed (her reaction is passive); her lover's mysterious occupation suggests more of the same; her father is robbed and nearly killed; a friend's purse is stolen (her reaction this time is spontaneous and violent). Eventually, Angelina's searching appears to reach some sort of resolution that makes her worthy of new self-esteem. Yet the reader can only observe, not participate in this search, because—unlike *Snakes*'s composer-narrator—Angelina does not experience within the narrative a process of growth.

Plainly, Angelina is a woman experiencing a crisis of self-identity during a series of events that propel her toward introspection. What she ultimately discovers within herself is a typical American complex of contradictions, such as the one she describes to a fellow traveler early in her journey, the contradiction Americans create by equating individuality with isolation: "Angelina explained that in America it's the individual who matters most and that she and her family, such as it was, lived at separate ends of what's called reality. She too was lonely and fed up with a kind of life she'd been leading."

Whether the narrator addresses the reader directly or through the medium of a letter to a former lover, the exposition continues: "Everyone nowadays is busy digging for roots. Well, I know them well and it doesn't make a damn bit of difference when it comes to making sense of who I am and why I make the kinds of mistakes I do. In the end, I've discovered, it all comes down to being in competition with yourself." At moments, Angelina's concern waxes angry and the culturally contemplative author intrudes: "I'm not so sure that all those chitlins, hamhocks, hog maws, pigsfeet, spareribs and cooking with lard—soulfood so-called—isn't contributing more toward bringing about black genocide, as the phrasemongers would have it, than Sickle Cell Anemia." An important discovery about herself does take place, however, and this is what her wandering is all about. The exploration has been a contemporary one that many young, single Americans never complete: "The truth was that, most of all, she loved open-hearted vulnerable strangers for whom she wasn't strictly obliged to feel anything."

In the end, Angelina also learns that she has been changing at the same time that her surroundings have been changing. Because she has confused one process with another, separation followed by a reassertion of self followed by a return to her point of departure appears to be cathartic. If so, the reader hopes that she also learns that life is and continues to be a process of change, some small part of which is subject to each individual's conscious control. Angelina's recognition of this consciousness is both the special story and the ordinariness of Young's second novel.

Sitting Pretty

Type of work: Novel
First published: 1976

Sidney J. Prettymon, the narrative persona of *Sitting Pretty*, is streetwise, sardonic, and ironically self-conscious. He establishes early a mock superstitious mentality—astronauts may mess up the moon so that it can no longer be full—and verbalizes "the integral aspects of [his] personal philosophy to be cool." Prettymon is dangerously learned: "I cut this article out of the *National Inquirer* that maintain how you can succeed and develop yourself and transformate your whole personality by the buildin' up your vocabulary." His inborn sense of linguistic sound combines comically with his interest in discovering associative meanings (*radical chic* connotes to him the concubine of a politically motivated Arab husband of many wives), but the best humor to be found in *Sitting Pretty* is derived from Prettymon's command of the text. The reader is at all times close to Prettymon, and he exploits the closeness. Having pondered his plot-situation at the story's outset, he describes himself to himself as being "on the threshold of destiny, temptation, and fate." Turning aside, he speaks directly to the reader: "Now, that's bad! [good] Let me run through that one again so y'all can savor it."

The narrative opens below the closing sentence of Mark Twain's *Adventures of Huckleberry Finn* (1884); in many ways, Sidney J. Prettymon is a modern, self-possessed Jim. As Twain's narrative control allowed him to elevate linguistic puns through burlesque to high satirical levels, Young's narrative is successful here by virtue of its consistently controlled authorial distance: "All I mean by imagination," Prettymon says, "is the way stuff look when you pull back from it and give it some reflection room." Prettymon as first-person narrative persona allows the author to work most effectively; because his imagination provides Prettymon with overview, it allows him to construct connotative ironies.

The incongruous coexistence of common insight and aesthetic misinterpretation (Huck does not misinterpret aesthetic qualities; he misses them entirely) works through sarcastic understatement: "Carpe Diem, like they say in Latin. Save the day." The author's hand moves subtly, characterizing by misquotation.

Like M. C.'s unknown parents, Prettymon has given his son an inspirational name with which to command respect—Aristotle: "He is a lawyer." Professionally successful, Aristotle is a son ungrateful for his name, and working-class Prettymon must struggle to disguise his pride as resentment: "He go around callin hisself A. Winfred Prettymon. I'm the one give him his first name and that's his way of gettin back at me. I wanted him to stand out and be distinguished and be the bearer of a name that smack of dignity." Telephoning his daughter, Prettymon again creates linguistic pandemonium, quoting Ralph Waldo Emerson in order to reinforce some fatherly advice, then addressing the reader as the individualistic, pro-consumer Henry David Thoreau: "I hung up fast, then taken the receiver back off the hook again so the operator couldn't ring me back for that extra ten cent. I ain't got nothing but the vastest contempt for the Phone Company. Leeches and rascals! Need to be investigated."

Sitting Pretty is Young's best novel in three ways: consistency of viewpoint, ingenuity of the narrative-persona, and control of the language. The last must be perfect for an author to choose suggestive, convincing variations consistent with popular speech. Young's rendering of black dialect for artistic purpose is found throughout his fiction, and it works effectively here. The novel's language is an unconcealed treasure:

> What with all that racket and commotion and the drink I'd just taken, I was startin to feel randy—a term the Professor use, British word for horney—randy for my own private bottle of sweet wine. Got a job lines up and just *know* Aristotle gon spring my Plymouth loose. Celebratin time! Time to do that quiet furlough down to Adamo's again.

Surprised, uniquely joyful, Sidney J. Prettymon rediscovers his treasure again and again.

The Blues Don't Change

Type of work: Poetry
First published: 1982

Young's unique blending of whimsy and social satire appears in one of the twenty-seven new poems published in *The Blues Don't Change*. It is a poem written in memory of two men who died on the same day in 1973: "W. H. Auden and Mantan Moreland." Not only does Young violate snobbish propriety by considering a poet of high culture, W. H. Auden, in the same text with a popular comic motion-picture actor, Mantan Moreland, but he also overturns his readers' expectations about their speech patterns.

The poem consists of a dialogue between these two, in paradise, with Moreland praising Auden's *The Age of Anxiety* (1947) for "doubtless" engaging "our/ innermost emotions & informed imagination," and Auden responding, "No shit!" One can imagine the curiosity of a fellow poet as Young arranges for Moreland to ask Auden why he cut the line "We must all love one another or die" from his poem "September 1, 1939." The line was superfluous, as Auden's reply declares, "We gon die anyway no matter/ how much we love." Having justified Auden's technique, Young also defends Moreland, whose role-playing was harshly judged by militant activists. Auden praises Moreland's technique, "the way you buck them eyes/ & make out like you running sked all the time." That fear, Auden notes, is the essence of "the black/ experience where you be in charge of the scene." Moreland did stop "shufflin'," and Young's poem reclaims with pride this actor's achievements.

Several of the poems in *The Blues Don't Change* are tributes to black American musicians; most notable are "Billie," "The James Cotton Band at Keystone," "My Spanish Heart," and "Lester Leaps In." Each poem re-creates the impact of their performances on a rapt listener. Listening to Holiday while drinking, he seems to take in her song through his mouth. The sexuality that Holiday projected in her singing is expressed metaphorically in the listener's fantasy of swallowing her delightful body. The song and his drink intoxicate, "whirling/ me through her throaty world and higher." The listener recognizes the seductress that Holiday enacted in his tribute to her "Cleopatric breath." In contrast to the dreamily slow movement of lines in "Billie," "The James Cotton Band at Keystone" plays with a livelier rhythm, demonstrating "Believe me, the blues can be volatile too,/ but the blues don't bruise; they only renew."

The return to cultural roots revitalizes both the individual and society. In "The Blues Don't Change," his apostrophe to the relentless rhythm and brilliant images of the blues, Young again pays tribute to the uniquely American expression of life's pain and sadness, and to the performers whose artistry lifts the spirit. Working within American forms of speech and music, this poet soars, defining his own voice and enriching America's cultural heritage.

Seduction by Light

Type of work: Novel
First published: 1988

For his fifth novel, Young again employs a first-person narrative persona, female and clairvoyant. Mamie Franklin is a woman in her forties, rich in impressions and experience. She grew up in Mississippi an admirer of her namesake and imaginary tutor/yogi Benjamin Franklin, made those feelings real through writing, left home early to perform in the style of Dinah Washington with her husband's group, the Inklings, and married and had her son Benjie out of wedlock. She lives now in Santa Monica with Burley, the man she loves and whose love is returned until, cataclysmically, Mamie's past and future upheave into the narrative present.

As in *Snakes* and the adventures of Sidney J. Prettymon, there is a running commentary on situation and circumstance along with a steady stream of verbal ironies and satiric asides. Mamie works part-time in Beverly Hills as a domestic for Mr. Chrysler and his French wife, Danielle, who live in "a big stockbroker Tudor" graced with eucalyptus, or "Noxema trees." Mamie has the confidence of her employers, in fact their favor, as she drives her Honda Civic (nicknamed Sweepea) up the front driveway and strolls into the house. There she discovers a strange, unclothed woman with toenails and fingernails painted black who looks like "a bleached-out, fuzzy-headed raccoon," and a Monopoly board, which compromises Mr. Chrysler ("that man loves to play Monopoly . . . with real money").

This kind of fun—the world according to Mamie Franklin—enlivens the novel's complication. Regarding the 1970's, that too-short period when black consciousness merged with African American professional development and economic opportunity, Mamie says, "[I]t mighta looked to the public like anything black was gonna make money . . . but that wasn't nothin but an illusion."

More than witty, these quips come from a woman who made her living as a performer during the 1950's, when the business of entertainment reinstituted racial segregation, and who now sees further deterioration in the filmmaking business: "This old brotherhood junk, funny stuff and jive everybody use to be talkin—all that went out the minute the money started gettin shaky." With a tonal admonition for more education, she observes that the film industry is being run by young white men who "started readin *Variety* and *Billboard* when they were nine." For Mamie, age enables one to "ripen into know-how, or better yet, know-when." After all, she says, "The smarter you are, the harder you smart when you fall."

Throughout the novel, light and light imagery brighten the reader's way like the sunlit flowers of Alice Walker's *The Color Purple* (1982) or the moonlit landscapes of Nathaniel Hawthorne's tales. Mamie's vision captures both the brilliance and the business of the California landscape while nuances of Eastern philosophy energize her sensibility and evoke a mood of resolution. Such evocations occur in dreams or dreamlike experiences, such as the surreal state of shock following the reality of an earthquake or the emotional upheaval of sexual renewal. "It was all done with light," Mamie says of cinematic production and marketing. Like the girl she "use to be" watching a film at the Grand Lux Theatre, Mamie learns that "pretty much every last one of us out here [in California] gettin seduced." As girl and as mother, as woman and as lover, Mamie looks over her shoulder to see "nothin but light, not a thing but light quiverin and makin patterns on a screen."

Throughout her life, Mamie has had enlightening experiences. She recalls a vision of sunlight playing over a leaf, how the light "shimmered all around it; then the leaf sends out this invisible feeler [and] suck up the light around it, drink it up, sip on it like you would a glassa buttermilk." Similarly, when Mamie's housemate Burley returns in spirit, he describes his passage from life: "It was like this hole opened up in the middle of my forehead and the light started pourin into it."

Moreover, Mamie contemplates the textuality of her life by the light of her contemplations, suggesting that this affects the storyteller, too:

> Where do you begin when you start tellin your story and rememberin as you go along? Do you start with the source of light itself, the sun? Or do you start with what the sun touches, the moon? Or do you only deal with what the moonlight touches?

One must consider the light by which one lives one's life, Mamie suggests, as one rewrites the texts of one's life:

> It's actually possible in one lifetime to do so much and to get caught up in so many of your own illusions and lies and half lies until it can finally come down to sun versus moon versus moonlight.

Celebratory and down-to-earth, Young's novels glow with human warmth. In the mode of vernacular speech, *Seduction by Light* rings true with contemporary experience while transmuting everyday life into the light of love.

The Sound of Dreams Remembered

Type of work: Poetry
First published: 2001

Almost a decade passed between Young's 1992 collection titled *Heaven: Collected Poems, 1956-1990* and his 2001 volume *The Sound of Dreams Remembered: Poems, 1990-2000*. *Heaven* filled nearly three hundred pages, displayed an abundant affection for the ordinary world, and showcased several influences (noted in the collection's introduction) that included Amiri Baraka (LeRoi Jones), Vladimir Mayakovsky, and Federico García Lorca.

The work of Langston Hughes and Charles Bukowski makes its influential mark on *The Sound of Dreams Remembered.* Disjointed thoughts, full of mystique and sentiment, like those of Bukowski, are apparent here. The collection is a readable and topical history of the decade, providing meditations on love, travel, politics, and misbehavior. Casual blank verse gives way to fluid, rhyming iambic pentameter in poems like "The Old Country":

> What is it want,
> or need to haul or lug like Motorolas
> of the blood? Beep! The mileage we squander
> on these jumps from mayonnaise Minnesotas
> to curry Calcuttas, from Tokyos you could wander.

Suggested Readings

Coleman, Janet, and Al Young. *Mingus/Mingus: Two Memoirs.* Berkeley, Calif.: Creative Arts, 1989.

Draper, James P. *Black Literature Criticism: Excerpts from Criticism of the Most Significant Works of Black Authors over the Past Two Hundred Years.* Detroit: Gale Research, 1997.

Johnson, Charles. *Being and Race: Black Writers Since 1970.* Bloomington: Indiana University Press, 1988.

Lee, Don. "About Al Young." *Ploughshares* 19, no. 1 (Spring, 1993): 219.

Schultz, Elizabeth. "Search for 'Soul Space': A Study of Al Young's *Who Is Angelina?* and the Dimensions of Freedom." In *The Afro-American Novel Since 1960*, edited by Peter Bruck and Wolfgang Karrer. Amsterdam: Gruner, 1982.

Shockley, Ann Allen, and Sue P. Chandler. *Living Black American Authors: A Bibliographical Directory.* New York: R. R. Bowker, 1973.

Contributors: Joseph F. Battaglia, Sarah Hilbert, Judith L. Johnston, and Daryl F. Mallett

Appendixes

General Bibliography

General Studies and Reference

Armstrong, Jeanne. *Demythologizing the Romance of Conquest*. Westport, Conn.: Greenwood Press, 2000.

Bercovitch, Sacvan, and Cyrus R. K. Patell, eds. *The Cambridge History of American Literature*. 8 vols. New York: Cambridge University Press, 1994-1996.

Berken, Carol, Lisa Paddock, and Carl Rollyson. *Encyclopedia of American Literature*. Rev. ed. 4 vols. New York: Facts On File, 2008.

Birkle, Carmen. *Migration-Miscegenation-Transculturation: Writing Multicultural America into the Twentieth Century*. Heidelberg, Germany: Winter, 2004.

Birnbaum, Michele. *Race, Work, and Desire in American Literature, 1860-1930*. New York: Cambridge University Press, 2003.

Boelhower, William, ed. *The Future of American Modernism: Ethnic Writing Between the Wars*. Amsterdam: VU University Press, 1990.

Bona, Mary Jo, and Irma Maini, eds. *Multiethnic Literature and Canon Debates*. Albany: State University of New York Press, 2006.

Brown, Linda Joyce. *The Literature of Immigration and Racial Formation: Becoming White, Becoming Other, Becoming American in the Late Progressive Era*. New York: Routledge, 2004.

Brown Ruoff, A. LaVonne, and Jerry W. Ward, Jr., eds. *Redefining American Literary History*. New York: Modern Language Association of America, 1990.

Crane, Gregg D. *Race, Citizenship, and Law in American Literature*. New York: Cambridge University Press, 2002.

Cullum, Linda. *Contemporary American Ethnic Poets*. Westport, Conn.: Greenwood Press, 2004.

Cutter, Martha J. *Lost and Found in Translation: Contemporary Ethnic American Writing and the Politics of Language Diversity*. Chapel Hill: University of North Carolina Press, 2005.

Cyclopedia of World Authors. 4th rev. ed. 5 vols. Pasadena, Calif.: Salem Press, 2005.

Cyclopedia of Young Adult Authors. 3 vols. Pasadena, Calif.: Salem Press, 2005.

Deena, Seodial F. H. *Canonization, Colonization, Decolonization: A Comparative Study of Political and Critical Works by Minority Writers*. New York: Peter Lang, 2001.

DuPlessis, Rachel Blau. *Genders, Races, and Religious Cultures in Modern American Poetry, 1908-1934*. New York: Cambridge University Press, 2001.

Elam, Harry J., Jr. *Taking It to the Streets: The Social Protest Theatre of Luis Valdez and Amiri Baraka*. Ann Arbor: University of Michigan Press, 2001.

Encyclopedia of American Ethnic Literature. 5 vols. New York: Facts On File, 2008.

Erkkila, Betsy. *Mixed Bloods and Other Crosses: Rethinking American Literature from the Revolution to the Culture Wars*. Philadelphia: University of Pennsylvania Press, 2005.

Evans, Brad. *Before Cultures: The Ethnographic Imagination in American Literature, 1865-1920*. Chicago: University of Chicago Press, 2005.

Fischer-Hornung, Dorothea, and Heike Raphael-Hernandez, eds. *Holding Their Own: Perspectives on the Multi-ethnic Literatures of the United States*. Tübingen, Germany: Stauffenburg, 2000.

Franco, Dean J. *Ethnic American Literature: Comparing Chicano, Jewish, and African American Writing*. Charlottesville: University of Virginia Press, 2006.

Gelfant, Blanche H. *The Columbia Companion to the Twentieth-Century American Short Story*. New York: Columbia University Press, 2000.

Gilmore, Leigh. *The Limits of Autobiography: Trauma and Testimony*. Ithaca, N.Y.: Cornell University Press, 2001.

Gilton, Donna L. *Multicultural and Ethnic Children's Literature in the United States*. Lanham, Md.: Scarecrow Press, 2007.

Goldstein, David S., and Audrey B. Thacker, eds. *Complicating Constructions: Race, Ethnicity, and Hybridity in American Texts*. Seattle: University of Washington Press, 2007.

Grobman, Laurie. *Teaching at the Crossroads: Cultures and Critical Perspectives in Literature by Women of Color*. San Francisco, Calif.: Aunt Lute Books, 2001.

Hogue, W. Lawrence. *Race, Modernity, Postmodernity: A Look at the History and the Literatures of People of Color Since the 1960's*. Albany: State University of New York Press, 1996.

Jason, Philip K., ed. *Critical Survey of Poetry*. 2d rev. ed. 8 vols. Pasadena, Calif.: Salem Press, 2002.

Karem, Jeff. *The Romance of Authenticity: The Cultural Politics of Regional and Ethnic Literatures*. Charlottesville: University of Virginia Press, 2004.

Kellman, Steven G., ed. *Magill's Survey of American Literature*. 6 vols. Pasadena, Calif.: Salem Press, 2006.

Keresztesi, Rita. *Strangers at Home: American Ethnic Modernism Between the World Wars*. Lincoln: University of Nebraska Press, 2005.

Kerkering, John D. *The Poetics of National and Racial Identity in Nineteenth-Century American Literature*. New York: Cambridge University Press, 2003.

Knadler, Stephen P. *The Fugitive Race Minority Writers Resisting Whiteness*. Jackson: University Press of Mississippi, 2002.

Lape, Noreen Groover. *West of the Border: The Multicultural Literature of the Western American Frontiers*. Athens: Ohio University Press, 2000.

Lee, A. Robert. *Multicultural American Literature: Comparative Black, Native, Latino/a and Asian American Fictions*. Jackson, Miss.: University Press of Mississippi, 2003.

Manzanas, Ana Ma., ed. *Border Transits: Literature and Culture Across the Line*. New York: Rodopi, 2007.

May, Charles E., ed. *Critical Survey of Short Fiction*. 2d rev. ed. 8 vols. Pasadena, Calif.: Salem Press, 2001.

Michael, Magali Cornier. *New Visions of Community in Contemporary American Fiction: Tan, Kingsolver, Castillo, Morrison*. Iowa City: University of Iowa Press, 2006.

Minter, David L. *A Cultural History of the American Novel: Henry James to William Faulkner*. New York: Cambridge University Press, 1994.

Murphet, Julian. *Literature and Race in Los Angeles*. New York: Cambridge University Press, 2001.

Nelson, Emmanuel S. *The Greenwood Encyclopedia of Multiethnic American Literature*. 5 vols. Westport, Conn.: Greenwood Press, 2005.

Newton, Pauline T. *Transcultural Women of Late-Twentieth-Century U.S. American Literature: First-Generation Migrants from Islands and Peninsulas*. Burlington, Vt.: Ashgate, 2005.

Norton, Donna E. *Multicultural Children's Literature: Through the Eyes of Many Children*. 2d ed. Upper Saddle River, N.J.: Pearson/Merrill Prentice Hall, 2005.

Palumbo-Liu, David, ed. *The Ethnic Canon Histories, Institutions, and Interventions*. Minneapolis, Minn.: University of Minnesota Press, 1995.

Parini, Jay, ed. *The Oxford Encyclopedia of American Literature*. New York: Oxford University Press, 2004.

Patterson, Anita. *Race, American Literature, and Transnational Modernisms*. New York: Cambridge University Press, 2008.

Paul, Heike. *Mapping Migration: Women's Writing and the American Immigrant Experience from the 1950's to the 1990's*. Heidelberg, Germany: Universitatsverlag C. Winter, 1999.

Payant, Katherine B., and Toby Rose, eds. *The Immigrant Experience in North American Literature: Carving out a Niche*. Westport, Conn.: Greenwood Press, 1999.

Peck, David, ed. *Identities and Issues in Literature*. 3 vols. Pasadena, Calif.: Salem Press, 1997.

Perkins, George, Barbara Perkins, and Phillip Leininger. *HarperCollins Reader's Encyclopedia of American Literature*. New York: HarperResource, 2002.

Pernal, Mary. *Explorations in Contemporary Feminist Literature: The Battle Against Oppression for Writers of Color, Lesbian, and Transgender Communities*. New York: P. Lang, 2002.

Peterson, Nancy J. *Against Amnesia: Contemporary Women Writers and the Crises of Historical Memory*. Philadelphia: University of Pennsylvania Press, 2001.

Powell, Timothy B. *Ruthless Democracy: A Multicultural Interpretation of the American Renaissance*. Princeton, N.J.: Princeton University Press, 2000.

Rollyson, Carl, ed. *Critical Survey of Drama*. 2d rev. ed. 8 vols. Pasadena, Calif.: Salem Press, 2003.

_______, ed. *Critical Survey of Long Fiction*. 2d rev. ed. 8 vols. Pasadena, Calif.: Salem Press, 2000.

Salzman, Jack, et al., eds. *The Cambridge Handbook of American Literature*. New York: Cambridge University Press, 1986.

Schedler, Christopher. *Border Modernism: Intercultural Readings in American Literary Modernism*. New York: Routledge, 2002.

Sesnic, Jelena. *From Shadow to Presence: Representations of Ethnicity in Contemporary American Literature*. New York: Rodopi, 2007.
Siemerling, Winfried, and Katrin Schwenk. *Cultural Difference and the Literary Text: Pluralism and the Limits of Authenticity in North American Literatures*. Iowa City: University of Iowa Press, 1996.
Singh, Amritjit, Joseph T. Skerrett, Jr., and Robert E. Hogan, eds. *Memory and Cultural Politics: New Approaches to American Ethnic Literatures*. Boston: Northeastern University Press, 1996.
Sollors, Werner. *Beyond Ethnicity: Consent and Descent in American Culture*. New York: Oxford University Press, 1986.
_______, ed. *The Invention of Ethnicity*. New York: Oxford University Press, 1989.
Sommer, Doris. *Proceed with Caution, When Engaged by Minority Writing in the Americas*. Cambridge, Mass.: Harvard University Press, 1999.
TuSmith, Bonnie. *All My Relatives: Community in Contemporary Ethnic American Literatures*. Ann Arbor: University of Michigan Press, 1993.
Verhoeven, W. M., ed. *Rewriting the Dream: Reflections on the Changing American Literary Canon*. Atlanta, Ga.: Rodopi, 1992.
Vogel, Todd. *Rewriting White Race, Class, and Cultural Capital in Nineteenth-Century America*. New Brunswick, N.J.: Rutgers University Press, 2004.
Wilmeth, Don B., and Christopher Bigsby, eds. *The Cambridge History of American Theatre*. 3 vols. New York: Cambridge University Press, 2006.
Winter, Molly Crumpton. *American Narratives: Multiethnic Writing in the Age of Realism*. Baton Rouge: Louisiana State University Press, 2007.
Wonham, Henry B. *Playing the Races: Ethnic Caricature and American Literary Realism*. New York: Oxford University Press, 2004.

African American

Auger, Philip. *Native Sons in No Man's Land: Rewriting Afro-American Manhood in the Novels of Baldwin, Walker, Wideman, and Gaines*. New York: Garland, 2000.
Beaulieu, Elizabeth Ann, ed. *Writing African American Women: An Encyclopedia of Literature by and About Women of Color*. Westport, Conn.: Greenwood Press, 2006.
Brown, Lois. *The Encyclopedia of the Harlem Literary Renaissance*. New York: Facts On File, 2006.
Carbado, Devon W., Dwight A. McBride, and Donald Weise, eds. *Black Like Us: A Century of Lesbian, Gay, and Bisexual African American Fiction*. San Francisco: Cleis Press, 2002.
Carroll, Anne Elizabeth. *Word, Image, and the New Negro: Representation and Identity in the Harlem Renaissance*. Bloomington: Indiana University Press, 2005.
Clark, Keith. *Black Manhood in James Baldwin, Ernest J. Gaines, and August Wilson*. Urbana: University of Illinois Press, 2002.
Davis, Thadious M., and Trudier Harris, eds. *Afro-American Writers After 1955: Dramatists and Prose Writers*. Dictionary of Literary Biography 38. Detroit, Mich.: Gale Research, 1985.

Decker, Jeffrey Louis, ed. *The Black Aesthetic Movement*. Dictionary of Literary Biography 8. Detroit, Mich.: Gale Research, 1991.

Effiong, Philip Uko. *In Search of a Model for African American Drama: A Study of Selected Plays by Lorraine Hansberry, Amiri Baraka, and Ntozake Shange*. New York: University Press of America, 2000.

Fisch, Audrey, ed. *The Cambridge Companion to the African American Slave Narrative*. New York: Cambridge University Press, 2007.

Gates, Henry Louis. *The Signifying Monkey*. New York: Oxford University Press, 2008.

Gates, Henry Louis, and Evelyn Brooks Higginbotham, eds. *The African American National Biography*. 8 vols. New York: Oxford University Press, 2008.

Graham, Maryemma, ed. The *Cambridge Companion to the African American Novel*. New York: Cambridge University Press, 2004.

Harris, Trudier, and Thadious M. Davis, eds. *Afro-American Writers Before the Harlem Renaissance*. Dictionary of Literary Biography 50. Detroit, Mich.: Gale Research, 1986.

_______, eds. *Afro-American Writers from the Harlem Renaissance to 1940*. Dictionary of Literary Biography 51. Detroit, Mich.: Gale Research, 1987.

_______, eds. *Afro-American Writers, 1940-1955*. Dictionary of Literary Biography 76. Detroit, Mich.: Gale Research, 1988.

Hay, Samuel A. *African American Theatre*. New York: Cambridge University Press, 1994.

Hill, Errol G., and James V. Hatch. *A History of African American Theatre*. New York: Cambridge University Press, 2003.

Hutchinson, George, ed. *The Cambridge Companion to the Harlem Renaissance*. New York: Cambridge University Press, 2007.

Japtok, Martin. *Growing up Ethnic: Nationalism and the Bildungsroman in African American and Jewish American Fiction*. Iowa City: University of Iowa Press, 2005.

Kim, Daniel Y. *Writing Manhood in Black and Yellow: Ralph Ellison, Frank Chin, and the Literary Politics of Identity*. Stanford, Calif.: Stanford University Press, 2005.

Notable African American Writers. 3 vols. Pasadena, Calif.: Salem Press, 2006.

Ostrom, Hans, and J. David Macey, Jr., eds. *The Greenwood Encyclopedia of African American Literature*. Westport, Conn.: Greenwood Press, 2005.

Perkins, Margo V. *Autobiography as Activism: Three Black Women of the Sixties*. Jackson: University Press of Mississippi, 2000.

Riss, Arthur. *Race, Slavery, and Liberalism in Nineteenth-Century American Literature*. New York: Cambridge University Press, 2006.

Samuels, Wilfred D., ed. *Encyclopedia of African-American Literature*. New York: Facts On File, 2007.

Sanchez, Marta Ester. *"Shakin' up" Race and Gender: Intercultural Connections in Puerto Rican, African American, and Chicano Narratives and Culture, 1965-1995*. Austin: University of Texas Press, 2005.

Schwarz, A. B. Christa. *Gay Voices of the Harlem Renaissance*. Bloomington: Indiana University Press, 2003.

Williams, Tyrone, ed. *Masterplots II: African American Literature*. Rev. ed. 4 vols. Pasadena, Calif.: Salem Press, 2009.

Young, Kevin, ed. *Giant Steps: The New Generation of African-American Writers*. New York: Perennial, 2000.

Asian American

Alam, Fakrul, ed. *South Asian Writers in English*. Dictionary of Literary Biography 323. Detroit, Mich.: Gale Research, 2006.

Cheung, King-Kok, ed. *An Interethnic Companion to Asian American Literature*. New York: Cambridge University Press, 1997.

Hillstrom, Kevin, and Laurie Collier Hillstrom. *The Vietnam Experience: A Concise Encyclopedia of American Literature, Songs, and Films*. Westport, Conn.: Greenwood Press, 1998.

Kim, Daniel Y. *Writing Manhood in Black and Yellow: Ralph Ellison, Frank Chin, and the Literary Politics of Identity*. Stanford, Calif.: Stanford University Press, 2005.

Lee, Esther Kim. *A History of Asian American Theatre*. New York: Cambridge University Press, 2006.

Madsen, Deborah L., ed. *Asian American Writers*. Dictionary of Literary Biography 312. Detroit, Mich.: Gale Research, 2005.

Oh, Seiwoong. *Encyclopedia of Asian-American Literature*. New York: Facts On File, 2007.

Ty, Eleanor, and Donald C. Goellnicht, eds. *Asian North American Identities: Beyond the Hyphen*. Bloomington: Indiana University Press, 2004.

Yasmin Hussain. *Writing Diaspora: South Asian Women, Culture, and Ethnicity*. Burlington, Vt.: Ashgate, 2005.

Yin, Xiao-huang. *Chinese American Literature Since the 1850's*. Urbana: University of Illinois Press, 2000.

Caribbean and West Indian

Alexander, Simone A. James. *Mother Imagery in the Novels of Afro-Caribbean Women*. Columbia: University of Missouri Press, 2001.

Balderston, Daniel, and Mike Gonzalez, eds. *Encyclopedia of Latin American and Caribbean Literature, 1900-2003*. New York: Routledge, 2004.

Irele, F. Abiola, and Simon Gikandi. *The Cambridge History of African and Caribbean Literature*. New York: Cambridge University Press, 2004.

Lindfors, Bernth, and Reinhard Sander, eds. *Twentieth-Century Caribbean and Black African Writers*. Dictionary of Literary Biography 157. Detroit, Mich.: Gale Research, 1996.

MacDonald-Smythe, Antonia. *Making Homes in the West Indies: Constructions of Subjectivity in the Writings of Michelle Cliff and Jamaica Kincaid*. New York: Garland, 2001.

Turner, Joyce Moore. *Caribbean Crusaders and the Harlem Renaissance*. Urbana: University of Illinois Press, 2005.

Jewish

Aarons, Victoria. *A Measure of Memory: Storytelling and Identity in American Jewish Fiction*. Athens: University of Georgia Press, 1996.

Bloom, Harold, ed. *Jewish Women Fiction Writers*. Philadelphia: Chelsea House, 1998.

Brauner, David. *Post-war Jewish Fiction: Ambivalence, Self-Explanation, and Transatlantic Connections*. New York: Palgrave, 2001.

Budick, Emily Miller. *Ideology and Jewish Identity in Israeli and American Literature*. Albany: State University of New York, 2001.

Cappell, Ezra. *American Talmud: The Cultural Work of Jewish American Fiction*. Albany: State University of New York Press, 2007.

Codde, Philippe. *The Jewish American Novel*. West Lafayette, Ind.: Purdue University Press, 2007.

Furman, Andrew. *Contemporary Jewish American Writers and the Multicultural Dilemma: The Return of the Exiled*. Syracuse, N.Y.: Syracuse University Press, 2000.

Japtok, Martin. *Growing up Ethnic: Nationalism and the Bildungsroman in African American and Jewish American Fiction*. Iowa City: University of Iowa Press, 2005.

Kahn-Paycha, Danièle. *Popular Jewish Literature and Its Role in the Making of an Identity*. Lewiston, N.Y.: Edwin Mellen Press, 2000.

Miles, Barry. *The Beat Hotel: Ginsberg, Burroughs, and Corso in Paris, 1958-1963*. New York: Grove Press, 2000.

Omer-Sherman, Ranen. *Diaspora and Zionism in Jewish American Literature: Lazarus, Syrkin, Reznikoff, and Roth*. Hanover, N.H.: University Press of New England, 2002.

Sherman, Joseph, ed. *Writers in Yiddish*. Dictionary of Literary Biography 333. Detroit, Mich.: Gale Research, 2007.

Sicher, Efraim, ed. *Holocaust Novelists*. Dictionary of Literary Biography 299. Detroit, Mich.: Gale Research, 2004.

Walden, Daniel, ed. *Twentieth-Century American-Jewish Fiction Writers*. Dictionary of Literary Biography 28. Detroit, Mich.: Gale Research, 1984.

Weber, Donald. *Haunted in the New World: Jewish American Culture from Cahan to the Goldbergs*. Bloomington: Indiana University Press, 2005.

Wirth-Nesher, Hana, and Michael P. Kramer, eds. *The Cambridge Companion to Jewish American Literature*. New York: Cambridge University Press, 2003.

Latino/Hispanic

Aldama, Frederick Luis. *Brown on Brown: Chicano/a Representations of Gender, Sexuality, and Ethnicity*. Austin: University of Texas Press, 2005.

Arteaga, Alfred. *Chicano Poetics*. New York: Cambridge University Press, 1997.

Benson, Sonia G., Rob Nagel, and Sharon Rose, eds. *UXL Hispanic American Biography*. Detroit, Mich.: UXL, 2003.

Bost, Suzanne. *Mulattas and Mestizas: Representing Mixed Identities in the Americas, 1850-2000*. Athens: University of Georgia Press, 2003.

Erro-Peralta, Nora, and Caridad Silva, eds. *Beyond the Border: A New Age in Latin American Women's Fiction*. Gainesville: University of Florida Press, 2000.

Flores, Juan. *From Bomba to Hip-Hop: Puerto Rican Culture and the Latino Identity*. New York: Columbia University Press, 2000.

Guajardo, Paul. *Chicano Controversy: Oscar Acosta and Richard Rodriguez*. New York: Peter Lang, 2002.

Huerta, Jorge. *Chicano Drama: Performance, Society, and Myth*. New York: Cambridge University Press, 2004.

Laezman, Rick. *One Hundred Hispanic-Americans Who Shaped American History*. San Mateo, Calif.: Bluewood Books, 2002.

Lomelí, Francisco A., and Carl R. Shirley, eds. *Chicano Writers: First Series*. Dictionary of Literary Biography 2. Detroit, Mich.: Gale Research, 1992.

_______, eds. *Chicano Writers: Third Series*. Dictionary of Literary Biography 209. Detroit, Mich.: Gale Research, 1999.

Madsen, Deborah L. *Understanding Contemporary Chicana Poetry*. Columbia: University of South Carolina Press, 2000.

Notable Latino Writers. 3 vols. Pasadena, Calif.: Salem Press, 2005.

Pérez-Torres, Rafael. *Movements in Chicano Poetry*. New York: Cambridge University Press, 1995.

Perivolaris, John Dimitri. *Puerto Rican Cultural Identity and the Work of Luis Rafael Sánchez*. Chapel Hill: University of North Carolina Press, 2000.

Quintana, Alvina E., ed. *Reading U.S. Latina Writers: Remapping American Literature*. New York: Palgrave Macmillan, 2003.

Ramirez, Luz Elena. *Encyclopedia of Hispanic-American Literature*. New York: Facts On File, 2008.

Ruiz, Vicki L., and Virginia Sánchez Korrol. *Latina Legacies: Identity, Biography, and Community*. New York: Oxford University Press, 2005.

Sanchez, Marta Ester. *"Shakin' up" Race and Gender: Intercultural Connections in Puerto Rican, African American, and Chicano Narratives and Culture, 1965-1995*. Austin: University of Texas Press, 2005.

Sandin, Lyn Di Iorio. *Killing Spanish: Literary Essays on Ambivalent U.S. Latino/a Identity*. New York: Palgrave Macmillan, 2004.

Shirley, Carl R., and Francisco A. Lomelí, eds. *Chicano Writers: Second Series*. Dictionary of Literary Biography 122. Detroit, Mich.: Gale Research, 1992.

Native American

Bataille, Gretchen M., and Laurie Lisa, eds. *Native American Women: A Biographical Dictionary*. 2d ed. New York: Routledge, 2001.
Brown, Harry J. *Injun Joe's Ghost: The Indian Mixed-Blood in American Writing*. Columbia: University of Missouri Press, 2004.
Dearborn, Mary V. *Pocahontas's Daughters: Gender and Ethnicity in American Culture*. New York: Oxford University Press, 1986.
Fast, Robin Riley. *The Heart as a Drum: Continuance and Resistance in American Indian Poetry*. Ann Arbor: University of Michigan Press, 2000.
Lincoln, Kenneth. *Sing with the Heart of a Bear: Fusions of Native and American Poetry, 1890-1999*. Berkeley: University of California Press, 2000.
McClinton-Temple, Jennifer, and Alan Velie. *Encyclopedia of American Indian Literature*. New York: Facts On File, 2007.
Porter, Joy, and Kenneth M. Roemer, eds. *The Cambridge Companion to Native American Literature*. New York: Cambridge University Press, 2005.
Roemer, Kenneth M., ed. *Native American Writers of the United States*. Dictionary of Literary Biography 175. Detroit, Mich.: Gale Research, 1997.
Schort, Blanca. *Storied Voices in Native American Texts: Harry Robinson, Thomas King, James Welch, and Leslie Marmon Silko*. New York: Routledge, 2003.
Temple, Alan Velie. *Encyclopedia of American Indian Literature*. New York: Facts On File, 2007.

Electronic Resources

The online resources listed below offer students, librarians, and general readers some of the best resources for ethnic studies, both multicultural and focused on the five major ethnic populations of the United States: African American, Asian American, Jewish, Latino/Hispanic, and Native American. These consist of two basic types. First, electronic databases are integrated electronic sources to which public, college, and university libraries subscribe, installing links on their Web sites, where they are generally available only to library card holders or specified patrons. Readers can check library Web sites to see if these databases are installed or can ask reference librarians if these databases are available. The second type of resource is accessible through a Web site, sometimes free of charge but increasingly by subscription as well. We have provided URLs for these sites, but because addresses of Web pages frequently change or are moved, we also suggest accessing them through an Internet search engine.

General and Multiethnic Resources

Academic Search Premier

Available on the Ebscohost platform, this full-text database includes more than 4,500 periodicals, newspapers, and books, both text with graphic and PDF files, back to the beginning of the twentieth century and even earlier. Academic Search Premier has indexed and created abstracts for thousands of peer-reviewed journals, some of which, such as the *Latin American Literary Review*, will be of interest to students of both literature and American ethnic studies. An advanced search on two subjects, "literature" and "Asian American," for example, yields ninety hits.

American Family Immigration History Center

http://www.ellisislandrecords.org

Provides facts about the 22 million people who entered the United States through Ellis Island.

American Memory: Historical Collections for the National Digital Library

http://memory.loc.gov

Sponsored by the Library of Congress, this site gathers digital and print collections of ethnic scenes and groups. Examples include a photo of an Asian American baseball coach with his school team c. 1910-1920 and a recording of a Lebanese lullaby c. 1940.

Arts and Humanities Citation Index

This database allows users to search across disciplines to find bibliographic and reference material in more than 1,000 scholarly journals.

The Columbia Granger's World of Poetry

Columbia University Press compiles thousands of works by hundreds of poets in this database, which also includes a comprehensive glossary of poetry-related terms. Biographies and critical essays are available for some writers, and users can search for anthologies by title, category, and editor.

Diversity and Ethnic Studies

http://www.public.iastate.edu/~savega/divweb2.htm

Susan A. Vega García of Iowa State University founded this site in 1995 as a gateway to Internet resources related to African Americans, American Indians, Asian Americans, U.S. Latinos, and multicultural resources ("those dealing with more than one ethnic minority or cultural group").

Electronic Text Center

http://etext.virginia.edu/subjects/Native-American.html

Collects texts by and about African Americans, Native Americans, women, and other groups. Some texts are restricted to University of Virginia students and faculty.

Ethnic News Watch

This full-text database on the Proquest platform functions in both English and other languages, combing through half a million articles that have appeared in more than 240 minority and indigenous periodicals since 1990. Archived material from mid-1980's is also available. Categories include African American/Caribbean/African, Arab/Middle Eastern, Asian/Pacific Islander, European/Eastern European, Hispanic, Jewish, Multi-Ethnic, and Native People.

First Search

Commonly found in academic libraries, this system covers dozens of databases, some of which have links to full-text articles. Students of ethnic literature will find helpful information in the *Contemporary Women's Issues, Dissertation Abstracts, MLA Bibliography, Wilson Select*, and *WorldCat* databases.

History Reference Center

A product of EBSCO Information Services, the History Reference Center is a comprehensive world history database offering more than 2,000 reference books, encyclopedias, and nonfiction works, full text for more than 130 leading history periodicals, nearly 60,000 historical documents, 50,000 biographies of historical figures, well over 100,000 historical photos and maps, and more than 80 hours of historical video.

J-STOR

J-STOR has organized hundreds of journals in both single and multidisciplinary categories in order to streamline the search process. The collection includes several journals on American ethnic studies, such as *African American Review*, *Journal of Black Studies*, and *Hispanic Review*.

LexisNexis Academic

This full-text database indexes documents from more than 5,900 news, business, legal, medical, and reference publications, including more than 350 U.S. and world newspapers, broadcast transcripts from major television and radio networks, state and federal case law, corporate and industry information, and scholarly journal articles.

Literature Resource Center

Produced by Gale/Cenage Learning, this full-text database includes biographies, bibliographies, and critical analyses of more than 100,000 authors and works from a wide range of literary disciplines, countries, and eras. The database also features plot summaries, articles from literary journals, critical essays, and links to Web sites. Users can search by author's nationality, theme, literary movement, and genre.

MagillOnLiteraturePlus

Salem Press has created the industry standard for literary full-text integrated databases, updated continuously. *MagillOnLiteraturePlus* includes all the literary works, reviewed critical analyses, and brief plot summaries that are included in Salem's many title-driven and biographical reference volumes: thousands of plot summaries, analyses, biographical overviews, and literary reviews. A key feature for study of ethnic literatures is the "author's cultural identity" set of limiters, which included African American, Asian American, Asian Canadian, Chinese American, Cuban American, Filipino/Filipina American, Gay and Lesbian, Indian American, Japanese American Jewish, Korean American, Latino or Latina, Mexican American, Native American, Pakistani American, and Puerto Rican American at last count.

MasterFILE Premier

For public libraries, this multidisciplinary database, updated daily, provides full text for more than 1,750 general reference publications dating as far back as 1975. Covering virtually every subject area of general interest, MasterFILE Premier includes nearly 500 full-text reference books and more than 85,000 biographies, 105,000 primary source documents, and 285,000 photos, maps, and flags.

MLA International Bibliography

Thousands of journals and book citations dating back to the 1920's can be found in the Modern Language Association's electronic bibliography, which is a particularly valuable source of literary theory and history articles. Includes links to much of J-STOR's language and literature collection and to full text.

National Association for Ethnic Studies
http://www.ethnicstudies.org/

Founded in 1972, this nonprofit organization offers scholars and activists an interdisciplinary forum concerned with the national and international dimensions of ethnicity, including ethnic groups, intergroup relations, and the cultural life of ethnic minorities. Publishes *Ethnic Studies Review* and sponsors the Annual Conference on Ethnic Studies as well as student paper competitions.

NetLibrary

This e-content provider offers a subscription-based full-text, searchable collection of more than 7,000 electronic books (text and audio) in all subject areas, searchable by keyword, title, subject, or combinations of these.

Oxford Reference Online

A virtual reference library of more than 100 dictionaries and reference books published by Oxford University Press. *Oxford Reference Online* contains information about a broad range of subjects, including art, architecture, military history, science, religion, philosophy, political and social science, and literature. The site also features English-language and bilingual dictionaries, as well as collections of quotations and proverbs.

Project MUSE

A collaboration between libraries and publishers, Project MUSE offers full-text, user-friendly online access to about 400 humanities and social sciences journals from more than 60 scholarly publishers. Among these journals are *American Jewish History*, *Studies in American Indian Literature*, *Journal of Asian American Studies*, *Hispanic American Historical Review*, and many on American literatures.

Salem History

A fully integrated history database containing thousands of in-depth essays on commonly studied topics from Salem's Milestone Documents, Decades, Great Lives from History, and Great Events from History series. Many of these concern cornerstone issues, people, and events in ethnic and postcolonial history. Purchase of the print versions of these multivolume, cross-searchable reference works entitles libraries to free three-year access to the online database.

Voice of the Shuttle: Minority Literatures
http://vos.ucsb.edu/

The section titled "Literatures (Other than English)" contains some useful links to biographies, time lines, and excerpts from works by prominent authors.

Voices from the Gaps: Women Writers and Artists of Color

http://voices.cla.umn.edu/vg

An especially useful source for teachers, this site (maintained by the University of Minnesota's English department) contains teaching and planning tips and profiles authors and their works, provides discussion boards for viewers, and lists links to related material.

Wilson Biographies Illustrated

Produced by H. W. Wilson Co., this database offers more than 95,000 biographies and obituaries, and more than 26,000 photographs, of prominent people throughout history.

World History FullText

A joint product of EBSCO Information Services and ABC-CLIO, this database provides a global view of history with information on a wide range of topics, including anthropology, art, culture, economics, government, heritage, military history, politics, regional issues, and sociology.

World History Online

Facts On File, Inc., has created this reference database of world history, featuring biographies, time lines, maps, charts, and other information.

African American Resources

African American Biographical Database

This collection bills itself as "a resource of first resort" for images and information about more than 30,000 African Americans. Gathering material from periodicals, encyclopedias, biographical texts, and other sources, it allows researchers to search by city, state, country, religion, and occupation, among other fields. Though updated every two months, results are limited to the years between 1790 and 1950.

African American Literature Book Club

http://aalbc.com

A popular site that offers book reviews and recommendations, author biographies, and tips for aspiring writers. Those interested can post their thoughts and read others' opinions on several discussion boards. Also includes a useful source of information about upcoming literary events.

African American Literature Online

http://www.geocities.com/afam_literature

A good source for brief summaries of the state of African American literature in the twentieth century. Pages are divided by the decades they discuss, and each includes a summary of that period's more notable works.

The African American Mosaic: A Library of Congress Research Guide for the Study of Black History and Culture

http://www.loc.gov/exhibits/african/intro.html

This site accompanies an exhibit that took place between February and August, 1994. Rather than focusing on slavery, its first section summarizes the efforts of the American Colonization Society, which offered nineteenth century African Americans the chance to return to Africa rather than be emancipated in the United States. Later sections discuss the roles of abolitionists and the Works Progress Administration and African Americans' migration to Kansas, Chicago, and other western and midwestern cities.

African American Newspapers: The Nineteenth Century

For those looking for articles published between 1827 and 1902, this will prove an extremely useful tool. It presents complete articles from significant African American publications like *The Christian Recorder*, *The Colored American*, *Frederick Douglass Paper*, *Freedom's Journal*, *The National Era*, *The North Star*, and *Provincial Freeman*.

African American Review

Available only to those with access through the journals database J-STOR, this is a digital collection of this important journal's back issues from 1967 to 1996, including literary reviews, poetry, and essays.

African American Women Writers of the Nineteenth Century

http://digital.nypl.org/schomburg/writers_aa19/

Part of the New York Public Library's digital Schomburg collection of some 52 published works by 19th-century black women writers. A part of the Digital Schomburg, this collection of full texts provides access to the "thought, perspectives and creative abilities of black women as captured in books and pamphlets published prior to 1920." Keyword-searchable and browsable by title, author, or genre, this digital library is a rare and valuable Web-accessible resource.

African American Writers: Online E-texts

http://falcon.jmu.edu/~ramseyil/afroonline.htm

Forty-six African American authors are listed here, and each author's entry has several links to sites with further biographical information and samples of text (sometimes available in their entirety) in electronic format.

Africans in America

http://www.pbs.org/wgbh/aia/home.html

This site was built as a companion to the Public Broadcasting Service (PBS) television series of the same name. It is divided into four sections: The Terrible Transformation (1450-1750), Revolution (1750-1805), Brotherly Love (17901-1831), and Judgment Day (1831-1865). Each page's concise, logical format presents information unavailable anywhere else. Each section contains a Resource Bank with extraordinary images and stories and comprehensive teacher's guides.

American Slave Narratives: An Online Anthology

http://xroads.virginia.edu/~HYPER/wpa/wpahome.html

An amazing collection of audio files and texts excerpted from the Works Progress Administration's interviews with former slaves in the 1930's. Some of the interviews are difficult to understand, but all are worth the effort. Other sites of interest are also listed.

The Black Renaissance in Washington

http://www.dclibrary.org/blkren/index2.html

This project, sponsored by the District of Columbia's public library, includes biographies of dozens of important Renaissance writers, a list of the Harlem Renaissance's major works, a time line, and links to additional resources.

Black Studies on Disc

One of the most comprehensive bibliographic resources available to those studying the history and culture of people of African ancestry, this database lists sources from the eighth century A.D. to the present. It provides citations for many types of resources, culled from the catalog of the Schomburg Center for Research in Black Culture and the Index to Black Periodicals.

Born in Slavery: Slave Narratives from the Federal Writers' Project, 1936-1938

http://rs6.loc.gov/ammem/snhtml/snhome.html

Created by the Library of Congress, this collection of more than 2,300 accounts by former slaves and 500 black-and-white photographs, collected under the aegis of the Works Progress Administration, is searchable by keyword, narrator, or state; photographs can be searched by subject.

Callaloo

Available only to those with access through Project MUSE, this is a searchable digital collection of this important journal's current articles from 1995 and back issues from 1976 to 1989 and from 1990 to 2004.

Facts on the Black or African American Population

http://www.census.gov/pubinfo/www/NEWafamM11.html

The U.S. Census Bureau's page on African Americans in the United States offers statistics on a broad range of characteristics, both social and economic, as well as links to data sets and maps.

Journal of Black Studies

Available through J-STOR, this collection of digital back issues from 1970 through 2001 is key for African studies and is searchable.

The Martin Luther King, Jr., Papers Project

http://www.stanford.edu/group/King

Stanford University's Martin Luther King, Jr., Papers Project contains summaries of King's published works, his most popular speeches, sermons, and audio clips, biographies and chronologies, and lesson plans for teachers.

Our Shared History: African American Heritage

http://www.cr.nps.gov/aahistory

The National Parks Service sponsors this site, which contains a wealth of information about notable places in African American history (such as Baltimore, Detroit, and St. Louis), and major figures (such as Frederick Douglass, Mary McLeod Bethune, and Booker T. Washington). This is a particularly helpful place for those interested in the Underground Railroad.

Resources in Black Studies

http://www.library.ucsb.edu/subjects/blackstudies/black.html

The University of California, Santa Barbara, maintains a fairly comprehensive list of direct links to institutions, publications, and projects throughout the field of African American studies. Section titles include "Slavery and the Slave Trade," "Radio, TV, and Film," and "Historical Texts and Documents."

San Antonio College LitWeb: African American Literature Index

http://www.accd.edu/sac/english/bailey/aframlit.htm

Presents a detailed time line of major contributions to African American literature. Many entries include links to biographies, images, lists of works created, and bibliographies, though the site is limited to works produced between 1746 and 1999.

Schomburg Center for Black Culture

http://www.nypl.org/research/sc/sc.html

The New York Public Library's Schomburg Center regularly sponsors exhibits on important African American issues, and their Web site holds a considerable amount of information about exhibitions past and present, as well as summaries of their important collections (which include rare manuscripts, recordings, and photographs).

Asian American Resources

Asian American Drama

http://www.alexanderstreet2.com/AADRLive/

Searchable online edition of *Asian American Drama* offers 252 plays by 42 playwrights (about half not previously published), together with information on productions, theaters, selected playbills, photographs, and related ephemera. Access by subscription only.

Asian American Literature

http://falcon.jmu.edu/~ramseyil/asialit.htm

Compiled by school library media specialist Brenda Hoffman, offers text that addresses the following topics: Rationale for Multiethnic Literature in the Classroom, Characteristics of Good Multiethnic Literature, History of Asian American Literature, Booktalk: Amy Tan and Her Works, Other Asian American Young Adult Fiction Reviews, Laurence Yep; Book Reviews, ERIC /Periodical Resources, General Reference Resources, Anthologies, Traditional Literature, Fiction, Biography, Nonfiction, and Movies.

Asian American Net

http://www.asianamerican.net/

A gateway to news and other online resources covering a broad range of topics and issues, including Asian American organizations, general information on Asia, Asian studies, business in Asia, U.S. government and politics, and immigration resources—for all parts of Asia, from the Middle East to East Asia.

Asian American Poetry

http://asianamericanpoetry.blogspot.com/

An important personal blog on Asian American poetry started in 2004 by Roger Pao.

Asian American Writers' Workshop

http://www.aaww.org/

Established in 1991, the Asian American Writers' Workshop is a national not-for-profit arts organization devoted to the creating, publishing, developing and disseminating of creative writing by Asian Americans. Sponsors events such as readings, workshops, and awards. Designed primarily for budding Asian American writers.

Asian-Nation

http://www.asian-nation.org/index.shtml

Billing itself as "your one-stop information resource and overview of the historical, demographic, political, and cultural issues that make up today's diverse Asian American community," this site is run by C. N. Le, a sociologist who teaches at the University of Massachusetts, Amherst. Addresses issues in history and culture and offers a blog and links to other sites of interest.

AsianWeek.com

http://www.asianweek.com/

This Web site, "the voice of Asian America," is devoted to all things Asian American, including arts and entertainment.

Chinese American Librarians Association
http://www.cala-web.org/
Affiliated with the American Library Association, CALA disseminates information on Chinese American cultural observances and festivals.

Ethnic Heritage: Asian American
http://www.nps.gov/history/history/categrs/etnc5.htm
A National Park Service site with links to national historic sites related to Asian Americans, including World War II internment camps. Also offers Asian-Pacific lesson plans.

Facts on the Asian Population
http://www.census.gov/pubinfo/www/NEWapiM11.html
The U.S. Census Bureau's page on Asian Americans in the United States offers statistics on a broad range of characteristics, both social and economic, as well as links to data sets and maps.

University of California, Irvine: Asian American Studies
http://www.lib.uci.edu/online/subject/subpage.php?subject=asiamer
The university's Web page contains a long and well-organized list of links to sources for Asian American studies, arranged by topic and subpopulations.

Jewish Resources

Anne Frank Center USA
www.annefrank.com
The Anne Frank Center USA is a nonprofit organization that creates and distributes educational programs aimed at promoting the message of tolerance. The organization's Web site features excerpts from Frank's diary, photographs of Frank and her family, and time lines chronicling Frank's life and the rise of Nazism.

Holocaust Denial Literature: An Additional Bibliography
http://york.cuny.edu/~drobnick/holbib2.html#general
John A. Drobnicki, a professor and head of reference and electronic resources at York College of the City University of New York, has compiled this online bibliography of Holocaust denial literature. It is organized by categories, including general works denying the Holocaust; Holocaust revisionism in the United States, Canada, and other parts of the world; Web sites and videocassettes devoted to denial of the Holocaust; and reviews, critiques, and refutations of Holocaust revisionist books.

Holocaust Memoir Digest
http://www.holocaustmemoirdigest.org
The Holocaust Memoir Digest is a three-volume set containing detailed summa-

ries of published Holocaust memoirs by Elie Wiesel, Nechama Tec, Gerda Weissman Klein, and others. The project was created under the auspices of the Holocaust Resource Center of the Jewish Foundation in London, Ontario, Canada. The project's Web site provides three search engines that enable users to retrieve descriptions of the memoirs contained in the digests, information regarding twenty-six Holocaust-related topics, and information about specific places. It also features a study guide, maps of major concentration camps, and a bibliography.

Holocaust Pages

http://www-english.tamu.edu/pers/fac/myers/holocaust_pages.html

This collection of resources for the study of Holocaust literature has been compiled by D. G. Myers, associate professor of English and religious studies at Texas A&M University. It includes a chronology, a lexicon, bibliographies, Web links, primary documents, and English-language texts of Holocaust-related poetry and early Holocaust fiction.

Index to Jewish Periodicals

Mounted on the Ebsco platform, this cross-searchable database provides a listing of English-language articles, book reviews, and feature stories in more than 160 journals devoted to Jewish affairs, dating back to 1988, including *Jewish Culture and History* and *Studies in American Jewish Literature*.

The Jewish Virtual Library

http://www.jewishvirtuallibrary.org

Sponsored by the American-Israeli Cooperative Enterprise, the Jewish Virtual Library, offers brief essays on Jewish history, Israel, U.S.-Israel relations, the Holocaust, anti-Semitism, and Judaism, including some entries on literature. Includes essays on such topics as the political structure of the Third Reich, Adolf Hitler, Jewish ghettos, concentration camps, the Nazis' euthanasia program, Nazi book burnings, and Holocaust denial.

JewishEncyclopedia.com

http://www.jewishencyclopedia.com/

An invaluable resource, this site contains the complete contents of the twelve-volume Jewish Encyclopedia, which was originally published 1901-1906 and now is in the public domain. Includes more than 15,000 articles and illustrations.

Literature of the Holocaust

http://www.writing.upenn.edu/~afilreis/Holocaust/holhome.html

Al Filreis, Kelly Professor of English at the University of Pennsylvania, has compiled this collection of articles, book reviews, survivor memoirs, Web links, and other materials about the Holocaust and other instances of genocide.

MyJewishLearning.com
http://www.myjewishlearning.com/index.htm

In addition to many pages on Jewish history and culture, this site offers dozens of essays on Jewish American, Israeli, modern Hebrew, and other literatures identified with the Jewish people. The essays on Jewish American literature fall into the following categories: "Immigrant Literature," "Into the Literary Mainstream," "1970-2000," "The Twenty-First Century," "Jewish American Poetry," and "Children's Literature."

Ozuna Learning Resources Center Library: Jewish-American Literature
http://www.accd.edu/pac/lrc/lit-jewisham.htm

Sponsored by Palo Alto College, this site offers links to pages about more than 100 Jewish American authors as well as links to general essays.

Spartacus Educational: Holocaust
http://www.spartacus.schoolnet.co.uk/GERholocaust.htm

This is one of the excellent Web sites created by Spartacus Educational, a British organization that aims to provide Internet-based lessons for teachers. The site consists of five major sections, each with several pages of information that contain links to other pages within the site. The section titled "Nazi Germany and the Holocaust" features numerous articles that provide a history of the Holocaust, including articles about the Jews in Germany, anti-Semitism, the Nuremberg Laws, and Jewish ghettos. "Concentration and Extermination Camps" offers general information about the camps as well as several pages of information about specific camps. The "Guilty" section provides profiles of prominent Nazis and others who were responsible for the so-called final solution, "Victims" features profiles of ten people who were killed or survived the Holocaust, and "The Resistance" offers profiles of individuals who defied the Nazis.

United States Holocaust Memorial Museum
http://www.ushmm.org

The museum, located in Washington, D.C., maintains a Web site that provides an exceptional range of materials about the Holocaust. One of the site's most informative features is the Holocaust Encyclopedia, which can be found in the "History" section. The encyclopedia includes more than 500 articles about a wide range of Holocaust-related topics. In addition, the "Research" section provides a list of frequently asked questions, an authoritative biography, Web links, and a survivors' registry.

Yad Vashem
http://www.yadvashem.org

Yad Vashem, the memorial to Holocaust martyrs and heroes in Jerusalem, Israel, maintains one of the world's largest repositories of materials about the Holocaust and provides access to these materials on its Web site. Among the site's contents are photographs of the Auschwitz-Birkenau concentration camp, information about other camps, and resources for studying Elie Wiesel's *Night*. The site's Holocaust Resource Center enables users to retrieve photographs, diaries, letters, documents, testimonies, maps, and other material about anti-Semitism, the Nazis' rise to power, the Jews in Nazi Germany, and other aspects of the Holocaust.

Latino/Hispanic Resources

AfroCubaWeb

http://www.afrocubaweb.com/

Contains valuable links to both English-language and Spanish-language sites about the culture and heritage of the many Cuban subpopulations in various African traditions.

Association for Hispanic Classical Theater, Inc.

http://www.trinity.edu/org/comedia/index.html

This site contains texts for a number of plays, most of which were written during the Golden Age of Spanish Theater (1580-1680). Some of the plays have been translated into English, and a few critical essays are also included.

Brazilian Literature

http://www.unm.edu/~osterloh/BrazLit/BrazLit.htm

This pages contains a number of links and information on print-based sources that students of Brazilian, African Brazilian, and Luso Brazilian literatures may find helpful.

Centro de Estudios Puertorriqueños

http://www.centropr.org

Based at Hunter College, City University of New York, this is the major research institute for Puerto Rican studies on the U.S. mainland.

Chicano Database

The *Chicano Database* is produced by the University of California, Berkeley's Ethnic Studies Department. Its creators have broadened the definition of Chicano to include anyone of Mexican descent living in the United States. As a result, the information available in the database ranges from literature and women's studies to social work. It is particularly useful for information about *Teatro Campesino*, as well as for Chicano poetry and fiction.

Chicano Literature Index

http://www.accd.edu/sac/english/bailey/mexamlit.htm

A Web site that gives general references, short biographies, lists of major works, and links to other sites about major contemporary Mexican American writers.

Chicano Studies Research Center

http://www.chicano.ucla.edu/

The CSRC is based at the University of California, Los Angeles and is home to significant amounts of important material related to the Chicano movement (online access to the collection is pending). The prestigious journal *Aztlán* is also based at the CSRC, and its contents are listed on the site.

ClasePeriodica

This system enables users to find documents published in 2,600 Latin American journals. CLASE is devoted to research in the social sciences and humanities; PERIODICAS specializes in the sciences and technology. Results include conference proceedings, interviews, essays, articles, and books.

Cultures of the Andes

http://www.andes.org/

Visitors to this site will find original poetry in Quechua, a direct descendant of the language spoken by the Incas that is still common in Bolivia, Peru, and Ecuador. Poems are translated into Spanish and English. Also available are short stories (in Spanish and English) about life in this isolated region.

Dominican Studies Institute

http://www1.ccny.cuny.edu/ci/dsi/

The site of the main U.S. research institute for Dominican studies, located at the City College of New York in upper Manhattan.

El Andar

http://elandar.com

El Andar bills itself as "a national magazine for Latino discourse," a claim supported by the intelligent and accessible essays and wide array of fiction, poetry, and essays published each month. Highlights of the online edition include readings by prominent Latin American poets of their own work.

Facts on the Hispanic or Latino Population

http://www.census.gov/pubinfo/www/NEWhispM11.html

The U.S. Census Bureau's page on Latinos in the United States offers statistics on a broad range of characteristics, both social and economic, as well as links to data sets and maps.

Fuente Académica

This Spanish-language database provides full-text links to more than 150 academic journals.

Gay and Lesbian Themes in Hispanic Literatures and Cultures

http://www.columbia.edu/cu/lweb/eresources/exhibitions/sw25/case9.html

Part of the Columbia University exhibition "Stonewall and Beyond: Lesbian and Gay Culture," this page features an essay that locates homosexuality's meaning within Latin American tradition and points out some of the most important differences between North and Latin American perceptions of sexuality. A list of notable literary works is also included.

Handbook of Latin American Studies

http://lcweb2.loc.gov/hlas/

The *HLAS* is an annotated bibliography maintained and updated by the Library of Congress. It includes abstracts for entries, and is useful for locating books, articles, chapters, and papers on almost any topic related to Latin America, covering more than sixty years of scholarly research in the field. An essential starting point for serious research.

Hispanic American Periodicals Index (HAPI)

This valuable resource from the University of California, Los Angeles indexes the books, articles, essays, reviews, many other printed materials that have been produced in and about Latin America since the 1970's. Increasingly, the citations are linked to the full text. More than 400 periodicals are searched regularly for information about Latinos in the United States, the U.S.-Mexican border, Central and South America, and the Caribbean.

Hispanic Culture Review

http://www.gmu.edu/org/hcr/

The online version of this journal, published by students at George Mason University, includes the both recent and present contents (poetry, short narrative, essays, and book reviews) and has a number of useful (mostly Spanish-language) links, including George Mason's "The Spanish Page."

Las Culturas

http://www.lasculturas.com

An annotated list of links to various Web pages about specific Latino, Hispanic, and Latin American authors, sorted alphabetically. Information available varies by author, but several pages contain interviews, images, criticism, and official Web sites.

Latin American Network Information Center (LANIC)

http://www1.lanic.utexas.edu/la/region/literature/

LANIC is one of the most comprehensive resources available for information about and direct links to institutions, publications, and projects throughout Latin America. The site has devoted a section to every topic imaginable, and their literature pages—a few of which are in English—are categorized by country, theme, and author. Links to dozens of magazines, journals, and awards as well as regionwide sites are also listed.

Latin American Women Writers

Alexander Street Press has assembled a system organizing the memoirs, letters, essays, and works (most are in Spanish only) of Latin American women since the 1600's. Students can combine a number of parameters, including: subject (independence, slavery, love, etc.), word, time period, literary movement, birth and death dates, and country of origin.

Latino Literature: Poetry, Drama, and Fiction

Alexander Street Press's highly regarded database focuses on Latino literature in English (although some major works are in Spanish), and places most of its emphasis on writers in the United States after 1850. It includes several hundred novels and plays, and several thousand pages of poetry. Users can narrow their search fields according to a work's major themes, the author's gender, heritage, frequency of word use, and other criteria.

Libros en Venta

This system chronicles all Spanish-language books—both in and out of print—published since 1964. In addition to basic bibliographic information, researchers can also find contact information for publishers and sales distributors.

Literature of South America

http://gosouthamerica.about.com/od/literature1/

This site, created by About.com, consists largely of book reviews, short stories, biographies of prominent novelists, and other information, sorted by country. Only South American countries are featured.

Proyecto Sherezade

http://home.cc.umanitoba.ca/%7Efernand4/

This Spanish-language site has devoted itself to the preservation and presentation of Latin America's strong tradition of fiction. Many of its stories have been chosen as aids for Spanish-language teachers. Each piece is introduced by the Webmaster, and a number of author interviews are posted.

Puerto Rico and the American Dream

http://prdream.com/

Award-winning site about the history, culture, and politics of Puerto Rico and the Puerto Rican diaspora. Offers a film section, an online gallery, discussion boards, historical time lines, oral histories, and current events postings.

Sur Database

This is the online edition of the prominent Latin American literary magazine (1931-1992). It includes images, advertisements, and a searchable index of more than 6,000 articles.

Native American Resources

American Indian Heritage Foundation (AIHF)

http://www.indians.org/

This national foundation, dedicated to assisting underprivileged Native Americans, maintains a resource page with links to federally recognized tribes, Native American literature and art essays and links, and a broad array of other links organized topically.

American Indian History and Related Issues

http://www.csulb.edu/projects/ais/

A wide-ranging list of links to sites dealing with mostly modern American Indian history. Contains links to tribal home pages, federal departments, image banks, cultural resources, and much more.

American Indian History as Told by American Indians

http://www.manataka.org/page10.html

Links to more than 100 U.S. and Canadian Native American sites with information on American Indian history from a native perspective.

American Indian Library Association (AILA)

http://www.nativeculture.com/lisamitten/aila.html

The affiliate of the American Library Association devoted to Native American libraries, librarians, and collections, offering access to the AILA newsletter and listservs.

American Indian Resource Directory

http://www.indians.org/Resource/natlit/natlit.html

An index page from the Indians.org Web site (sponsored by the American Indian Heritage Foundation) that offers links to summaries on topics from "Abenaki Literature" to Tse-tsehese-staestse (Cheyenne) literature.

American Indian Resources

http://jupiter.lang.osaka-u.ac.jp/~krkvls/naindex.html

A collection of links for academic research in Native American studies. Includes links to oral and written tribal histories, primary source documents, maps, and bibliographies.

American Indian Tribal Directory

http://www.indians.org/tribes/tribes.html

The site of the American Indian Heritage Foundation, with a useful directory to all federally recognized tribes and resource library.

Black-Indian History Resources

http://anpa.ualr.edu/f_black_indian.htm

A fascinating site on the intermixing of African Americans and the Five Civilized Tribes.

CodeTalk

http://www.codetalk.fed.us/

Hosted by the U.S. Department of Housing and Urban Development, Office of Native American Programs, a federal Web site designed as a central electronic resource for all government offices and programs affecting Native Americans. Links to most federal government offices dealing with Indian affairs.

Doe & Moffitt Libraries, Native American Collections

http://www.lib.berkeley.edu/doemoff/gov_ntvam.html

The University of California, Berkeley maintains this site, which offers comprehensive links for researching Native American history and culture, including bibliographies and directories, guides and handbooks, law and civil rights, treaties and federal programs, congressional publications, statistical indexes and guides, basic statistics, census data, declassified federal documents and federal surveillance files, special collections, California documents, and Internet resources.

Edward S. Curtis's *The North American Indian*

http://memory.loc.gov/ammem/award98/ienhtml/curthome.html

Allows search on the text and images of this controversial yet highly influential publication, issued 1907-1930. Curtis's monumental twenty-volume work contains more than 2,000 photogravure images and narrative, representing traditional customs and lifeways of eighty Indian tribes. Organized by tribes and culture areas. The site features more than 1,500 illustrations and more than 700 plates, browsable or searchable by subject, tribe, or geographic locale.

Facts on the American Indian and Alaskan Native Population

http://www.census.gov/pubinfo/www/NEWamindM11.html

The U.S. Census Bureau's page on Native Americans in the United States offers statistics on a broad range of characteristics, both social and economic, as well as links to data sets and maps.

First Nation Information Project

http://www.johnco.com/firstnat/index.html

A thorough resource for information on all aspects of life among the Canadian First Nations.

First Nations Histories

http://www.tolatsga.org/Compacts.html

Provides short histories of all Canadian First Nations, along with bibliographies and maps.

Harvard University Pluralism Project
http://www.pluralism.org
A search page offers access to a list and links to Native American spiritual centers nationwide.

Index of Native American Resources on the Internet
http://www.hanksville.org/NAresources/
A comprehensive index to Internet resources, frequently updated.

Indian Affairs: Laws and Treaties
http://digital.library.okstate.edu/kappler/index.htm
A digitized edition of Charles J. Keppler's 1904 work on the relations between the U.S. government and Native American tribes.

Indian Peoples of the Northern Great Plains
http://libmuse.msu.montana.edu:4000/NAD/nad.home
A searchable photographic database.

Indian Trusts Assets Management
http://www.doi.gov/indiantrust/index.html
The U.S. Department of the Interior's Web site covering issues regarding Indian Trusts, with updates on the ongoing legal disputes.

Institute of American Indian Arts (IAIA)
http://www.iaiancad.org/
Established in 1962 by the United States Bureau of Indian Affairs (BIA), the IAIA is now an independent two-year college, contemporary Indian art musuem, and member of the American Indian Higher Education Consortium located in Santa Fe, New Mexico. Its site offers information about programs and exhibitions, a tour of the collection, and access to the virtual library by tribe, subject, or geographical locale.

Internet Law Library: Indian Nations and Tribes
http://www.nsulaw.nova.edu/library/ushouse/31.htm
Links to numerous sites with information on legal relations between the U.S. government and Native American tribes. Includes a number of links dealing with treaties.

Internet Public Library: Native American Authors
http://www.ipl.org/div/natam/
Provides information on Native North American authors: bibliographies of their published works; biographies; and links to interviews, texts, and tribal Web sites.

National Indian Gaming Association (NIGA)
http://www.indiangaming.org
The main advocacy group for Indian gambling enterprises, offering access to government officials, a virtual library and other resources aimed at advancing Indian gaming.

National Museum of the American Indian
http://www.nmai.si.edu/
The Web site for this, one of the Smithsonian museums, lists a calendar of events, exhibitions, and links to the New York, Maryland, and Washington, D.C., facilities.

Native American Authors
http://www.ipl.org/div/natam/
Maintained by the University of Michigan's School of Information, this is an interactive search engine by authors, book titles, and tribes, including biographical information and bibliographical information and links to news stories and other sources for hundreds of Native American authors.

Native American Authors: Teacher Resources
http://falcon.jmu.edu/~ramseyil/natauth.htm
Part of the Internet School Library Media Center Web site, this page offers biography, bibliography, lesson plans, e-texts, and critical reviews of selected authors whose works are taught at the high school and undergraduate levels. Literature includes both adult and juvenile.

Native American Documents Project
http://www.csusm.edu/nadp/
Provides primary source documentation of the allotment system, published reports of the Bureau of Indian Affairs in the 1870's, and information on the Rogue River War and the Silitz reservation.

Native American History and Studies
http://www.tntech.edu/www/acad/hist/nativam.html
A collection of historical links hosted by the history department at Tennessee Technological University.

Native American Music Awards (Nammys)
http://www.nativeamericanmusic.com/
Supports and promotes contemporary Native American artists through the Nammys (which began in 1998) as well as the Native American Music Hall of Fame.

Native American Research Page
http://maple.lemoyne.edu/~bucko/indian.html
A collection of links to resources on all aspects of Native American culture and life.

Native American Rights Fund (NARF)
http://www.narf.org/
Legal activist group dedicated to advancing and defending Native American civil rights and liberties. Maintains pages listing current cases, calls to action, and the National Indian Law Library.

NativeCulture.com
http://www.nativeculture.com
An organized set of links to indigenous culture sites by tribe, arts, and teaching tools. Arts are further categorized under arts, dance, media, music, literature, and "hand arts."

NativeWeb
http://www.nativeweb.org/
Maintained by academicians and Web technicians, NativeWeb describes itself as "an international, nonprofit, educational organization dedicated to using telecommunications including computer technology and the Internet to disseminate information from and about indigenous nations, peoples, and organizations around the world; to foster communication between native and non-native peoples; to conduct research involving indigenous peoples' usage of technology and the Internet; and to provide resources, mentoring, and services to facilitate indigenous peoples' use of this technology." Hosts sub-sites such as NativeTech, links to resources, news stories, and other resources related to Native American culture. Accepts donations.

The Newberry Library
http://www.newberry.org
Located in Chicago, the Newberry maintains one of the world's finest collections of books on American Indian culture and history, the Edward E. Ayer Collection. The site offers a searchable catalog.

Office of Tribal Justice
http://www.usdoj.gov/otj/
The Web site of the division of the U.S. Department of Justice that deals with Native American issues. Includes a statement of the Department of Justice's sovereignty policy.

On This Date in North American Indian History
http://americanindian.net/
A site dedicated to time lines of Native American historical events.

Smithsonian Institution: Native American History and Culture
http://www.si.edu/resource/faq/nmai/start.htm
Links to Native American resources at the Smithsonian, including a number of online museum exhibits. The "Native American Portraits from the National Portrait Gallery" exhibit features many historically important Native Americans.

Treaty Negotiations Office of the Attorney General of British Columbia
http://www.gov.bc.ca/tno/
Contains information about treaties between Canada and First Nations, with updates on current legislation and negotiations.

Tribal Law and Policy Institute
http://www.tribal-institute.org/lists/tlpi.htm
The site of a Native American nonprofit institute dedicated to increasing resources for tribal judicial systems and operations.

Indexes

Author Index

Authors by Ethnic Identity

Titles by Ethnic Identity

Titles by Genre

Title Index